For Business & Pleasure

STUDIES IN INDUSTRY AND SOCIETY

Philip B. Scranton, *Series Editor*

Published with the assistance of the Hagley Museum and Library

For Business & Pleasure

Red-Light Districts and the Regulation
of Vice in the United States, 1890–1933

MARA L. KEIRE

The Johns Hopkins University Press
Baltimore

© 2010 The Johns Hopkins University Press
All rights reserved. Published 2010
Printed in the United States of America on acid-free paper
2 4 6 8 9 7 5 3 1

The Johns Hopkins University Press
2715 North Charles Street
Baltimore, Maryland 21218-4363
www.press.jhu.edu

Library of Congress Cataloging-in-Publication Data
Keire, Mara L. (Mara Laura), 1967–
For business and pleasure : red-light districts and the regulation of vice in
the United States, 1890–1933 / Mara L. Keire.
p. cm. — (Studies in industry and society)
Includes bibliographical references and index.
ISBN-13: 978-0-8018-9413-8 (hbk. : alk. paper)
ISBN-10: 0-8018-9413-1 (hbk. : alk. paper)
1. Red-light districts—United States—History—20th century.
2. Prostitution—United States—History—20th century. 3. Vice control—
United States—History—20th century. I. Title.
HQ125.U6K45 2010
363.40973'09041—dc22   2009020233

A catalog record for this book is available from the British Library.

Frontispiece: "Devere's High Rollers Burlesque Co." Lithograph, 1898. As an idealized member of the sporting class, the "High Roller Girl" outdrinks and outsmokes the punter who has passed out and lost his toupee. Theatrical Poster Collection, Library of Congress Prints and Photographs Division, http://memory.loc.gov/cgi-bin/ query/r?pp/var:@field(NUMBER+@band(var+0296)).

Special discounts are available for bulk purchases of this book. For more information, please contact Special Sales at 410-516-6936 or specialsales@press.jhu.edu.

The Johns Hopkins University Press uses environmentally friendly book materials, including recycled text paper that is composed of at least 30 percent post-consumer waste, whenever possible. All of our book papers are acid-free, and our jackets and covers are printed on paper with recycled content.

To Chris
From A to Zee

Contents

Acknowledgments

On 29 April 2008, my son, Nathaniel Keire McKenna, was born. Coming five and a half weeks before his due date, Nat was, as my friend Chris Kobrak observed, the first Keire/McKenna to deliver early. Chris's statement holds particular true for this book.

This project took years to complete, and over that time, I wracked up many debts. I owe the most to my academic "parents," David Musto, Ron Walters, and Dorothy Ross.

As my senior essay advisor at Yale, David taught me the joy of following out a hunch and grounding it in a strong evidentiary base. I am forever thankful for his willingness to take on an undergraduate with strong polemical views but little methodological rigor. Over the hours we spent talking in his office, he guided me into a fascinating area of study even as he gently taught me the rudiments of academic investigation. I've since moved away from the history of drug use, but just as readers can see traces of that topic in my book, I can see David's lasting influence in the way I write and research.

From the moment Ron Walters picked me up at the airport wearing a brown leather jacket and driving an Alfa Romero convertible with a duct-taped ragtop, I knew that I'd found my ideal advisor. Every interaction since then has proved that initial impression right. Ron encouraged me to expand my interests and explore topics I would never have had the courage to investigate without his backing. I came into graduate school arguing for the benefit of studying narrow topics deeply, but Ron's arguments about the beauty of a well-written synthesis won me over. If he occasionally teases me that he didn't intend for me to embark on an archival synthesis, I can only shrug and blame it on an incomplete conversion. Sorry Ron, if dissertation boot camp didn't cure me, nothing will.

I owe more to Dorothy Ross than I can put into words. That's not surprising given the stunning breadth of her knowledge and her astonishing grasp of sources in areas outside her apparent specialty. But as much as she broadened my scholarly grounding, Dorothy taught me an intellectual rigor that I could not have learned from anyone else. Still, for all the influence she's had on my scholarship, I'm most grateful for her mentorship. Dorothy's proved an inestimable guide on how to balance the strains of career and family. And for that she has my heartfelt gratitude.

While David, Ron, and Dorothy are the ones to whom I owe the most, I would also like to thank the senior scholars who graciously gave their time to talk to someone at an earlier stage in her career. For their assistance, counsel, and support I want to thank

Lou Galambos, John Russell-Wood, Toby Ditz, Judy Walkowitz, Vernon Lidke, Geoff Jones, Tim Gilfoyle, Paul Boyer, John Burnham, Bill Rorabaugh, David Courtwright, Austin Kerr, Gary Kornblith, Carol Lasser, Michael Denning, Ann Fabian, Harry Stout, Tony Badger, Michael O'Brien, Iwan Morgan, Richard Carwardine, Mitt Regan, Ann Schofield, Maggie Walsh, and Catherine Clinton.

This book benefited immensely from the extensive financial support of many generous institutions. The History Department at the Johns Hopkins University provided graduate fellowships as well as travel allowances. When money for graduate education seemed increasingly scarce, a George Soros Dissertation Fellowship from the Drug Policy Alliance and a Charlotte Newcombe Dissertation Fellowship from the Woodrow Wilson Foundation provided invaluable assistance during my final years of graduate school. After I achieved gainful employment, the British Arts and Humanities Research Council awarded me matching sabbatical leave at a crucial time for finishing the manuscript. I would also like to thank the following institutions for fellowships and travel grants: the American Historical Association; the Center for the History of Business, Technology, and Society, Hagley Museum and Library; the Radcliffe Institute for Advanced Study, Harvard University; the Rockefeller Archive Center; the American Institute of Pharmacy History; Newcomb College, Tulane University; and the Historic New Orleans Collection.

Money is always good, but so is time and space. As a postdoctoral fellow at the Rothermere American Institute at the University of Oxford and later as a sabbatical scholar at the Georgetown Law Center, I not only gained office space and library access, I also found much needed communities for starting and finishing my book manuscript.

Just as important as money and time was the assistance of people who helped me find crucial source material. I'd like to thank the archivists and librarians from the Central Archives for the History of the Jewish People, Jerusalem, Israel; the Chicago Historical Society; the Department of Special Collections, Regenstein Library, University of Chicago; Special Collections, Columbia University; the Hagley Museum and Library, Wilmington, Delaware; the Law Library, Harvard University; the Historic New Orleans Collection; Special Collections, the University of Illinois at Chicago; the Department of Archives and Special Collections, Noel Memorial Library, Louisiana State University in Shreveport; the Social Welfare History Archives, University of Minnesota, Minneapolis; the Newberry Library, Chicago, Illinois; the New York Library for the Performing Arts at Lincoln Center; the Rare Books and Manuscripts Division, New York Public Library; the Rockefeller Archive Center, Pocantico Hills, New York; the Schlesinger Library, the Radcliffe Institute for Advanced Study, Harvard University; the Center for American History, University of Texas, Austin; the William Ransom Hogan Jazz Archive, Tulane University; the United States National Archives; and most especially the stalwarts at Johns Hopkins University's Inter-Library Loan.

All scholars need to present their work and I was fortunate to receive invitations from a number of institutions. The Center for Interdisciplinary Studies (ZiF), University of Bielefeld; Yale School of Medicine; the American Historical Association; the

College of Physicians of Philadelphia; the Business History Conference; the Center for the History of Business, Technology, and Culture, Hagley Museum and Library; the American Studies Association; the Irish Association for American Studies; the Urban History Group; the British Association for American Studies; King's College London; University of Oxford; University of Reading; the Institute for Historical Research, University of London; University of Nottingham; University of Cambridge; University of Sussex; Queen Mary, University of London; University of Limerick; the European Centre for the Study of Policing, the Open University; the School of Advanced Study, University of London; the Reading Historical Association; Duquesne University; and the Johns Hopkins University gave me the opportunity and the audience to test my ideas.

I also benefited from the insight of journal editors, notably Peter Stearns, and the anonymous reviewers who critiqued my articles. An earlier version of Chapter 4 appeared as "The Vice Trust: A Reinterpretation of the White Slavery Scare in the United States, 1907–1917" in the *Journal of Social History* 35 (Fall 2001): 5–41, while part of Chapter 1 was published previously as "The Committee of Fourteen and Saloon Reform in New York City, 1905–1920" in *Business and Economic History* 26 (Winter 1998): 573–583. The feedback I received from these articles guided me as I finished the rest of the book.

The institutional support I received was invaluable, but I also owe a debt to the friends who fed and housed me while I visited archives and attended conferences. At the time, they got little in return except naughty stories about nasty people. So, now let me properly thank Rachel Carner, Richard Rothschild, Jordy Kleiman, Katy Coyle and Shannon Maguire, Jamie and Natalie Schofield, Christine Skwiot and Larry Gross, Lilly Keire and Virginia Card, Margie Rung and Andy Virkus, Matthias Kipping, Greg Novak, and Tracy Druce. I couldn't have done this book without you.

While in Baltimore, I shared the trials and tribulations of graduate school with many good friends including Jim Mokhiber, Bill MacLehose, Ann Corbett, Russ Covey, Carolyn Eastman, Erik Ledbetter, Dalit Baranoff, Kelly Schrum, and Nadja Durbach.

In Oxford, I've been fortunate to get to know Martin Ingram, Abigail Green, Daniel Howe, Richard Carwardine, Peter Thompson, Gareth Davis, Jay Sexton, Desmond King, and the various Harmsworth professors, especially David Hollinger, Linda Kerber, and Rick Beeman. My understanding of history is all the better because of them.

At Queen Mary, University of London, I benefited from my conversations with Sam Halliday, Dan Todman, James Ellison, Jon Smele, Roger Mettam, Peter Hennessy, Mark Glancy, Miri Rubin, John Ramsden, and Colin Jones. I'm sure I also owe each of them at least a drink or two.

If during my five years at the University of London, Queen Mary provided me with an institutional base, the American History Research seminar, co-sponsored by the Institute for the Study of the Americas and the Institute for Historical Research, gave me an intellectual home. I want to thank Adam Smith, Bruce Baker, Kendrick Oliver, John Kirk, Jon Bell, John Howard, Vivien Miller, Elizabeth Clapp, Iwan Morgan, and all the other participants who made Thursday nights both fun and intellectually exciting.

From dissertation committee to the final copyeditor, numerous people helped me take a rough dissertation and turn it into a polished book. The manuscript would never have achieved half its coherence without the input of Ron Walters, Dorothy Ross, Thomas Izbicki, Bruce Hamilton, Matthew Crenson, Thomas LeBien, Phil Scranton, Robert J. Brugger, Camilla Stack, and Kathleen Capels. I'm particularly grateful to Paul Boyer and Wendy Gamber for their lengthy and insightful critiques of my work. And I'd especially like to thank Michael Henderson and Kate Doyle, who saw me through the final stages of preparing the manuscript. This book would not exist without their help.

And then there are my friends. I couldn't have made it through my life let alone this book without the love and support of people like Joanne Mancini, Graham Finlay, Elaine Parsons, Natalie Zacek, Larry Platt, Ruth Diener, Paul Tarr, Laura Reilly, Jon Rottenberg, Roger Horowitz, Sos Eltis, Eric Thun, Jennifer Good, Camilla Russell, Franziska Schulz, Meghan Spencer, Maike Bohn, and Michael Cullen.

If my friends have enriched my life, my family has given me strength. I would like to thank David Keire, Anita Keire, Marissa Leja-Valette, Lilly Keire, Dagnija Skulte, and Baibe Grube for their love and understanding. I would also like to thank my mother-in-law, Elizabeth McKenna, and my late father-in-law, John McKenna, for making me feel most welcome. I'm sorry that John and I did not have more time together, but Elizabeth inspires me with her intellectual curiosity and her acerbic wit. Most importantly, I owe a boundless debt of gratitude to my parents, Fred Keire and Anita Keire, who never wavered in their faith in me. Even when they did not understand why a nice girl from the suburbs wanted to study the seamy side of city life, they respected my intellectual endeavors and generously supported me during the seemingly neverending years of graduate school. They taught me how to question, how to reason, how to argue, and, most importantly, how to love. I often laugh that with a minister for a mother and a lawyer for a father I had no choice but to become a historian. Historical relativism is the only out when caught between the absolutes of god and the law. But the joke does my parents a disservice because from them I learned the abiding truth that morality matters.

My greatest debt belongs to my husband, Chris McKenna. He's been there from the earliest stages of dissertation planning to the final approval of page proofs. I've never had an idea that didn't get better after discussion with Chris. He's pushed me intellectually, nurtured me spiritually, and stood with me through quiet and chaos. Most of all, though, I adore him for giving me Nathaniel and sharing with me the joy of watching Nat grow.

For Business & Pleasure

It's A Wonderful Life

Red-Light Districts and Anti-Vice Reform

In 1947, when director Frank Capra first released his Christmas classic, *It's A Wonderful Life*, he impressed neither the film critics nor American audiences.[1] Hopelessly anachronistic from its cinematography to its subject, *It's A Wonderful Life* seemed more a product of the 1920s than a new film for the postwar era. Indeed, as with another nostalgic classic, *The Wizard of Oz*, released only eight years earlier, viewers immediately recognized that the movie's version of small-town America had already largely vanished. Although Capra's sentimental message appeared painfully obvious, his audiences typically missed one of the subtexts of *It's A Wonderful Life*. For just as the characters in *The Wizard of Oz* depicted an increasingly obscure allegory about bimetallism, Populism, and the 1896 presidential election, Capra wrapped his vision of all that might have gone wrong had George Bailey never been born around a visual recapitulation of Progressive-era arguments against the toleration of vice in American cities.[2] By self-consciously juxtaposing Bedford Falls and Pottersville, Capra made concrete the dire warnings of early twentieth-century anti-vice reformers as to what would happen if commercialized vice—the business of urban pleasure—went unchecked by the good people in the community. Although this context is now entirely forgotten, *It's A Wonderful Life* demonstrates the lasting cultural impact of an important Progressive-era struggle to close tolerated red-light districts.

From the late 1890s through World War I, one of the central debates in American municipalities concerned the location and regulation of urban vice. Different factions within cities—machine politicians, upper-class reformers, settlement-house workers, vice proprietors, and participants in commercial nightlife—fought over the appropriate place of sex and saloons in urban America. For Capra, the answer was clear. The charming innocence of Bedford Falls far outweighed the worldly decadence of Pottersville. For a historian, however, his contrast provides an analytical starting point.

Capra showed George Bailey's importance to Bedford Falls by contrasting small-town charm with big-city seediness. Without a Bailey to stand in his way, Henry F. Potter, the commercial banker who controlled most of the town, re-named the city after himself and turned its quiet main street into a thriving red-light district full of burlesque houses, strip clubs, disreputable bars, and pawn-shops. Where the Bijou theatre in Bedford Falls played *The Bells of St. Mary's*, in Pottersville the bright lights advertised "Girls—Girls—Girls" and "Georgia's Strip-tease Dance." A cacophony of jazz issuing from Pottersville's competing dives supplanted the Italian folk ballads of Martini's sedate watering hole in Bedford Falls. For George, and the audience, Pottersville represented a nightmare incarnate in which the powers of good have overturned the world in order to convince George of the value of his life. When the angels ultimately gave him back his life, George knew that everything was well again because the town's taxi driver recognized him, his daughter's rose petals were in his pocket, and his car was once again wound around a neighbor's tree. The audience knew all was well when the gentle glow of Bedford Falls' Christmas lights replaced the flashing neon signs of Pottersville.

Capra's heavy-handed juxtaposition of respectable Bedford Falls with disreputable Pottersville exemplifies the dualism that successive generations of cultural commentators and present-day policymakers have imposed on the regulation of vice. Pottersville and Bedford Falls capture the binary extremes of expressive/repressive; wet/dry; pro/con; just-say-yes/just-say-no. In contrast, in the late nineteenth and early twentieth centuries, influential factions within American cities saw sex, drugs, alcohol, commercial leisure, and social order as multifaceted and interconnected problems for which no single, easy answer existed. Thus, even though Capra recapitulated the fears of Progressive reformers in his portrayal of Pottersville, his clear-cut values obscured the Progressives' more nuanced approach to managing urban morality.

Anti-vice reformers at the turn of the century also wished to establish clear distinctions. They wanted to separate residence from commerce and respectable from disreputable, but they never expected to eliminate completely one side of the divide. Instead, these moral reformers sought to reduce the worst effects of urban vice. Bedford Falls could have a movie theater, a drugstore with soda fountain, and even an Italian café, but no burlesque halls or pawn shops. Although these early twentieth-century reformers abhorred the "social evils," especially prostitution and drinking, they eschewed a "Mosaic conception of law." As quintessential Progressives, they dismissed the thou-shall-not extremes of prohibitory law as unrealistic and instead sought pragmatic solutions to complicated problems.[3] Ultimately, the advocates of total suppression won—on prostitution and drugs, if not alcohol—but when present-day policymakers dismiss positions less extreme than "zero tolerance" because American morality would never allow such ethically ambiguous legislation, they misrepresent history and exclude a number of regulatory possibilities that politicians from both parties once considered viable options.

No panacea exists that solves the problems of prostitution, drinking, and drugtaking, but I chose to study the business and regulation of vice from the establishment of vice districts in the 1890s to the repeal of Prohibition in 1933, because during these years urban reformers explored a range of social-order policies, including licensing, geographic limitation, suppression, and incarceration. In particular, this book explores the consequences of "reputational segregation," the geographic confinement of commercial vice to distinct city neighborhoods. Starting in the 1890s, elite reformers, who resembled Henry Potter in terms of class background if not social attitudes, fought to establish red-light districts as a way to manage urban immorality and limit the visibility of vice. Yet, contrary to the expectations of reputational segregation's Gilded-Age advocates, these tolerated tenderloins encouraged the economic growth of disreputable leisure and the cultural efflorescence of the "sporting class," as the participants in commercial vice called themselves.

As the 1900s progressed, a new generation of social reformers, who often came from the professional class and shared both the demographics and the values of George Bailey, sought to eliminate the "commercializers" of vice. The Progressives reviled the managers of disreputable leisure for exploiting humanity's worst impulses in their endless quest for profit. During World War I, urban reformers succeeded in their quest to alter the business of vice and closed red-light districts in cities across the United States, and in so doing, they ended the era of controlled toleration. The elimination of the districts and the passage of Prohibition marked the start of a new regulatory regime.

But regulation represents only part of the story. While reformers implemented their plans to improve urban morality, the participants in disreputable leisure adapted to changing social-order policies with resilience. As a result, this book looks beyond the passage of these repressive policies and continues into the 1920s in order to evaluate the impact that the closure of the districts and the passage of Prohibition had on the consumers and providers of commercial vice. Even when excluded from the respectable confines of regulatory politics, participants in disreputable leisure still managed to challenge government policies through their everyday practices and their use of city space. They too shaped urban society.

The sporting class played an important role in the development of the new popular culture that emerged at the turn of the century. In cities as diverse as Hartford, Connecticut, Butte, Montana, Macon, Georgia, and El Paso, Texas, vice districts formed an integral part of the city center. Situated near the commercial downtown and overlapping the "white-light district" of the theater area, red-light districts gained an implicit legitimacy that blurred the line between respectable and disreputable nightlife.[4] Neither a wellspring of wickedness nor a site of complete liberatory license, the world of commercial leisure offered its own set of social codes for calculating class status. As such, the sporting class persistently challenged the moral precepts of mainstream society. But the transgressions of the sporting world should not lead us to romanticize red-light districts. The tenderloin encouraged cultural creativity—jazz originated in these disreputable turn-of-the-century venues—but it also produced grotesque brutality and unabated ugliness. Drunken bums wallowed in district gutters, pimps beat their prostitutes to death, johns waited in line for quick fifty-cent fucks, and angry whites attacked more successful blacks. However brightly the lights shone in Pottersville, even its most avid advocates recognized its ugly side.

Nevertheless, long after the closure of the districts, the manners and mores of the sporting world continued to influence the new popular culture of commercial recreation. Rejecting bourgeois restraints during their leisure hours, some urbanites participated in their city's nightlife and embraced the sporting world's expansive vision of gender, consumption, and having a good time. George Bailey and suburban audiences may have appreciated the quiet stability of Bedford Falls, but some city dwellers would always revel in the opportunities offered on Pottersville's thriving strip.

CHAPTER ONE

Segregating Vice, 1890–1909

Reformers closed the red-light districts, but first they created them. In the 1890s, elite good-government advocates proposed the establishment of vice districts as a way to isolate working-class politicians from their more unsavory constituents. By repudiating the moral extremes of prohibition, the symptomatic focus of social hygiene, and the individualized efforts of rescue work, these Gilded-Age reformers broke with previous anti-vice movements and offered reputational segregation as a pragmatic solution to the social and political ills of urban life. They thought that municipalities should tolerate brothels, saloons, and gambling dens, as long as the venues associated with vice stayed inside designated geographic confines. Reformers believed that without neighborhood saloons in which to meet the locals, or payoffs from brothels and gambling dens to finance their candidates, the city's working-class partisan political organization, popularly called the machine, would lose its stranglehold on urban government. Embracing a contingent view of public morality, these municipal reformers, also known as mugwumps, sought to change both the structure of municipal politics and the organization of urban space. At the end of the nineteenth century, the mugwumps cracked down on politically protected vice, fighting brutal battles in cities across the United States to move disreputable leisure out of residential neighborhoods and into the commercial downtown.

The mugwumps gained their reputation as anti-corruption elitists during the 1884 presidential election. Instead of supporting the candidacy of Senator James "Boodle" Blaine, known for kowtowing to the "railroad interests," they bolted from the Republican party and voted for Grover Cleveland, the New York State governor who made his name opposing New York City's Irish-run, Democratic party machine, Tammany Hall.[1] As political cartoonist Thomas Nast explained when endorsing Grover Cleveland: "We love him most for the enemies he has made."[2] The prime movers behind this campaign against political corruption came out of the urban social elite and included bankers, industrialists, career philanthropists, and upper-class clergy from liturgical Protestant denominations, mainly Episcopalians and Presbyterians. They believed that the "best men" should govern, mistrusted democracy, and despised "professional" politicians for their unabashed political corruption. If mugwumps generally advocated limited government and the enforcement of existing laws on national issues, they willingly accepted political initiative and police power at the local level when it was located in the right hands—their own hands. Announcing that they would rather vote their conscience than blindly follow party precepts, the mugwumps led the way in nonpartisan political reform.[3]

If the mugwumps represented a venerable patrician tradition that advocated elite rule, then members of the urban machine spoke for both the reputable and disreputable working class. Men like "Boss" William Tweed, "Honest" John Kelly, and "Big Tim" Sullivan grew up in the inner city and earned their livings as artisans, dock workers, newsboys, and boxers before devoting themselves to rising within the ranks of the local Democratic party organization.[4] As full-time politicians who worked even when the legislature was in recess, these men built the machine's constituency through the favors they traded. If the son of a loyal party member needed a job, ward captains asked around about open positions in the city government or businesses run by other party faithfuls. These men also prided themselves on no-questions-asked charity. If a family within their ward lost its home, machine politicians arranged new accommodations. Big Tim Sullivan burnished his reputation in New York City's Bowery by distributing thousands of shoes to the poor without once asking about the recipients' moral standing. Likewise, other party leaders made their names organizing picnics and excursions, entertaining everyone who came so long as they understood on election day that the machine provided the largesse.[5] For all their generosity, machine politicians expected to benefit financially from their participation in the party organization. While George Washington Plunkitt, "the sage of Tammany Hall," distinguished between "honest graft" (profiting from preferential contracts) and "dishonest graft" (extracting payoffs from brothels and gambling dens), not all machine politicians made these fine distinctions.[6] As a result, the mugwumps presumed that the machine received a substantial part of its financial backing from the proprietors of commercialized vice.

Unsurprisingly, given their completely incompatible cultural and political values, mugwumps and the members of the machine disagreed over the role of commercial vice in urban society. The machine wanted to maintain the status quo of unconfined leisure, while good-government advocates wanted to reconfigure the geography of American municipalities before the cities grew too big to change. In their efforts to realize this ambitious project, late nineteenth-century reformers devoted themselves to defeating the machine. But before their battles began, the mugwumps outlined their vision of urban life, an integral part of which included segregated vice districts.

DEFINING THE DISTRICT

Vice districting, a distinctly American phenomenon, arose out of the United States' creole cultural heritage and the new science of city planning. Usually located near a city's commercial downtown, red-light districts abutted the respectable theater district and were easily accessible from the train station. The most famous of these districts included New York's Tenderloin, Chicago's Levee, San Francisco's Barbary Coast, and New Orleans's Storyville, but smaller cities such as Bridgeport, Connecticut, Louisville, Kentucky, and Tacoma, Washington, also featured vice districts.[7] Sociologist Robert Park considered the clustering of drinking, gambling, and prostitution into distinct neighborhoods a spontaneous phenomenon, but the records of city councils and local reformers reveal a different story.[8] Although never entirely successful in concentrating all of a city's vice into the commercial downtown, the mugwumps made the tolerated tenderloin a part of America's urban landscape.

In Europe, reglementation, or the venereal inspection of prostitutes, served as the official norm for controlling the sex trade. Unlike American reformers, European regulators generally left city space unchanged. As a policy based on public health, not urban planning, reglementation did not require geographic concentration.[9] That is not to say that city leaders in the United States never proposed public-health measures for managing urban immorality. In 1870, St. Louis's city council enacted its notorious Social Evil Ordinance, requiring the venereal inspection of prostitutes. Four years later, after a vituperative campaign against the program, the Missouri legislature nullified the law. The outcry over the St. Louis "experiment" not only killed the ordinance within the city, but its failure discouraged other cities from implementing similar programs, despite support from most medical doctors.[10] The rejection of reglementation in the United States carried important consequences. While the public-health approach to prostitution existed as a possible policy throughout the Gilded Age and the Progressive era, reglementation never gained enough adherents to serve as a politically viable alternative to either suppression or segregation.

To American reformers, restructuring the city's moral geography mattered more than monitoring the health of already-errant sinners. The mugwumps wanted to rethink how municipalities managed the business of vice, not how they handled the detritus associated with that business. This institutional emphasis explains why urban reformers did not concern themselves solely with prostitution. The proprietors of saloons, gambling dens, and dance halls needed to pay "blackmail money" to the machine as much as brothel-keepers did. This comprehensive view of urban immorality distinguished the mugwumps from rescue workers, who hoped to save prostitutes by returning them to a righteous path. By contrast, the mugwumps, unwilling to settle for rerouting a few fallen women, used districting to reconfigure entire city streets, physically altering the organization of urban environments.

Despite their lofty goals, Gilded-Age reformers recognized with rare pragmatism that the demand for drinking, gambling, and prostitution would not disappear. They hoped that by restricting vice to the downtown—and forcing men to travel out of their neighborhoods if they wanted to engage in disreputable activities—they would decrease urban youths' accidental introduction to illicit vice and sever regular patrons' ties to the politics of a particular ward.[11] Men like good-government advocate George Frederick Elliott argued that controlled toleration in designated areas would satisfy the demand for disreputable pleasure without reinforcing the negative impact laissez-faire leisure had on urban neighborhoods.[12] During a heated campaign before the 1901 municipal elections in New York City, social hygienist Prince Morrow condemned "a vice crusade that would scatter the vicious all over the city," but William H. Baldwin, railroad magnate and anti-vice reformer, countered Morrow's criticisms by arguing for the segregation of vice: "Logic has it that the social evil must tend to particular localities. . . . I would rather see a little hell than a big hell."[13] In creating their "little hells," municipal mugwumps fought to remove commercial leisure from residential neighborhoods.[14] They intentionally homogenized workingmen's pastimes by divorcing them from the ethnic and political particularities of different city neighborhoods. The mugwumps believed that geographic separation would decrease the impact of disreputable leisure on the city as a whole.

The most notorious way to concentrate illicit vice was to adopt municipal ordinances that explicitly defined the boundaries outside of which prostitutes could not practice their trade. New Orleans's Storyville remains the best-known district created through city ordinances, but other cities, including Shreveport, Houston, and El Paso, also enacted red-light ordinances.[15] Despite the claims in the Blue Books, directories promoting New Orleans's vice, Storyville was not the only legal district; it was, however, the only red-light district vetted by the U.S. Supreme Court.[16] Shortly after Storyville's establishment in 1897, George L'Hote, Bernardo Gonzales Carbajal, and the Church Extension Society of the Methodist Episcopal Church challenged the legitimacy of Councilman Sidney Story's ordinance, arguing that the new district constituted both a public and a private nuisance. The Justices disagreed and ruled in 1900 that districting involved legitimately exercised local police powers.[17] As the U.S. Supreme Court saw it, municipalities had "one of three possibilities" when it came to the regulation of disorderly houses: "First, absolute prohibition; second, full freedom in respect to place, coupled with rules of conduct; or, third, a restriction of the location of such houses to certain defined limits."[18] In other words, cities could officially segregate vice.

L'Hote v. New Orleans declared districting constitutional, but most of the time neither the city council, the police commissioners, nor the citizen's associations found it necessary to define red-light districts quite so explicitly. Informal methods worked just as well and caused significantly less controversy. Through tacit localization, the position of a city's red-light district stayed more customary than codified.[19] Yet, even if a core of brothels and disreputable saloons already existed within a city, at the turn of the century, municipal politicians sought to sharpen the district's boundaries. They fought to limit saloons to the commercial downtown, and when they could not directly regulate dance halls, pool parlors, and shooting galleries based on their primary purpose, they concentrated these venues through their control of liquor licenses. Just as importantly, though, urban reformers ordered the police to pull prostitutes, gamblers, and other disorderly individuals out of places in respectable neighborhoods and push them into venues within the red-light district. The police accomplished this relocation through the unequal enforcement of the law, arresting those who loitered outside the district's designated confines.

In the 1890s, a decade marked by an "outburst of investigations" into police corruption, reform-minded law enforcement officials sided with the mugwumps and quietly offered reputational segregation as a solution to reduce crime, corruption, and the open, uninhibited expression of urban vice.[20] Commissioners like

New York's William McAdoo believed that restricting vice to certain neighborhoods reduced crime throughout the city.[21] Going beyond the often-cited cliché that prostitutes served society because they saved respectable women from sexually importunate men, police commissioners argued that districting reduced crime because, sooner or later, most criminals patronized prostitutes, who then provided a ready-made pool of informants.[22] From the police perspective, the centrality of the city's vice district made the surveillance and apprehension of the city's criminals easier.[23] Long after Progressive reformers stopped advocating districting as a disciplinary measure for managing urban immorality, the police continued to support segregation as a means of controlling vice.

The city courts also played their part in concentrating vice within defined limits.[24] Judges, many of whom sympathized with municipal reformers, favored localization and reinforced their city's red-light district by sentencing vice offenders more harshly if they operated outside of the district's understood limits.[25] As housing advocate Lawrence Veiller observed thirteen years after the passage of New York's 1901 Tenement House Law, the "theory . . . was to make the penalty for prostitution in tenement houses so much more severe than it was for prostitution in ordinary disorderly houses as to make it attractive for the prostitutes to leave the tenement houses and to go into regular houses of prostitution."[26] Although less systematic than districting through city ordinance, tacit localization garnered the support of key municipal officials and, at the turn of the century, it aroused little outrage from the general public.[27] Indeed, some found it quite advantageous.

Real estate speculators, in particular, strongly supported vice districting. While individual homeowners decried the presence of commercialized vice near their residences, absentee landlords endorsed the centralization of vice at the edges of the central business district.[28] Landlords who owned property near the commercial downtown often based their investment on the eventual expansion of the business district. When leasing to tenants engaged in illicit but profitable activities, absentee landlords demanded higher rents from their disreputable tenants than they could ever ask of respectable ones. Thus the owners of real estate within red-light districts raked in exorbitant sums while they awaited the further development of the downtown to increase the value of their land.[29] In Shreveport, aware of the inflated rents that they could ask within the district, landlords with property adjacent to St. Paul's Bottom successfully lobbied the city council to redraw the Bottom's boundaries to include their properties.[30] Although most landlords showed greater circumspection in their support of vice districts, few objected to a policy that made a long-term landholding strategy profitable in the short term.

Vice districts proved viable because a couple of key constituencies supported them. With allies in the excise department, police department, and the city courts, the mugwumps reordered city space with the specific intention of changing the way men and women socialized when out on the town. Yet for all their concerns about popular morality, municipal elites at the turn of the century saw vice districting as a way to attack the urban machine.

THE POLITICS OF DISTRICTING

The creation of vice districts was a high priority on the anti-machine agenda of elite reformers. Municipal mugwumps sought to concentrate drinking, gambling, and prostitution in the commercial downtown in order to separate disreputable leisure from popular politics. By restricting saloons, and their attendant vices, to a distinct district, reform politicians hoped to denature the political function of drinking establishments and limit the power of saloonkeepers within city government.[31] Similar to reformers' attempts to remove polling places from saloons, centralize the police force, and eliminate wards altogether through a commission form of government, vice districting constituted part of their larger project to detach ring politicians from their neighborhoods.[32]

Districting held particular importance to the mugwumps because of its perceived financial ramifications. Convinced that payoffs from vice proprietors constituted the financial backbone of the machine, reformers like Charles Parkhurst, minister of the elite Madison Square Presbyterian Church in midtown Manhattan, argued that his crusade between 1892 and 1894 to close brothels and gambling halls weakened Tammany Hall.[33] In the sermon that started the campaign, Parkhurst swore to rid the city of "the polluted harpies that, under the pretence of governing the city, are feeding day and night on its quivering vitals."[34] More practically, Parkhurst and his compatriots in the Society for the Prevention of Crime raided disreputable venues to show the underworld that despite the blackmail money paid to ward leaders, Tammany Hall could not protect them from arrest.[35] By exposing the extent of machine corruption to reputable voters and discrediting ward politicians' promises to disreputable voters, Parkhurst and other anti-machine agitators endeavored to influence elections, unseat ring politicians, and usher reformers into office.[36]

In New York City, reformers' attempts to concentrate vice into just a few neighborhoods were particularly public, extended, and never entirely successful.[37] Consequently, Manhattan never had a red-light district as such, but identifiable pockets of disreputable entertainment always existed. Five Points, the Tenderloin, the Lower East Side along the Bowery, "Little Coney Island" around

110th Street and Cathedral Parkway, and, later, part of Harlem, north of 125th Street on Lenox and Seventh Avenues, all gained national reputations as red-light districts.[38] The concentration of brothels, saloons, dance halls, and cheap theaters distinguished these neighborhoods from other areas of poor repute, but immorality alone did not define a vice district. The sheer commerciality of the entertainment offered there gave these areas an identity distinct from neighborhoods with more casually proffered immoral services. Over the years, these places of persistent immorality garnered the attention of entertainment entrepreneurs, graft-taking government officials, and urban reformers trying to improve the city's image. Then, as now, city leaders asked what they should do about such places. New York City at the turn of the twentieth century was no different.

In 1900 and 1901, against the backdrop of the charter battles to unify Brooklyn and Manhattan, New York's Committee of Fifteen attempted to eradicate prostitution and gambling from the tenements and consolidate these activities into a limited number of commercial districts. When Tammany Hall established an anti-vice committee, the Committee of Five, in early November, New York City's Chamber of Commerce battled back by forming the Committee of Fifteen. Despite its official-sounding name, the Committee of Fifteen was a private association founded by a self-appointed mix of Manhattan's most successful bankers, lawyers, publishers, industrialists, and clergymen.[39] Inspired by Charles Parkhurst's successful unseating of machine candidates in the 1894 election, the Fifteen swore to uncover the Tammany-tolerated vice they believed the Committee of Five would endeavor to hide.[40]

The Committee of Fifteen was composed of New York's "best men," including railroad magnate William H. Baldwin, banker Jacob Schiff, publisher George Haven Putnam, and renowned academic E. R. A. Seligman.[41] Sparing no expense, they hired a team of detectives to document the moral geography of Manhattan. From their investigators' reports, the Fifteen created a precinct-by-precinct catalog that mapped the organized toleration of prostitution and gambling in Manhattan. At the same time, they used the investigators' notarized testimony to prosecute illicit activity occurring in the tenement districts. In the latter endeavor, the Committee of Fifteen worked hand-in-hand with the newly formed Tenement House Commission to drive prostitutes out of tenement apartments and to fine landlords a thousand dollars for each documented instance of immorality.[42] As the Fifteen moved prostitution and gambling out of residential neighborhoods and into commercial centers, the New York Times endorsed their efforts at vice districting, observing that "the diffusion of vice . . . is more to be dreaded than the localization of it."[43] Playing to the press throughout their tenure, the Committee of Fifteen fronted their every move against the backdrop of Tammany corruption.[44]

Earlier in November 1900, Tammany's Executive Committee had appointed a Committee of Five to "investigate the moral conditions of the city." Following a well-publicized letter condemning Tammany's toleration of vice that Episcopal Bishop Henry C. Potter sent to Mayor Robert A. Van Wyck, Tammany Boss Richard Croker ordered the formation of the Committee of Five to demonstrate the speciousness of Potter's accusations.[45] To repair Tammany's reputation, the Committee tried to construct the rampant toleration of vice as purely a problem of police corruption, independent of any Tammany involvement. The Five argued that the police kept all the payoffs they received and that not a single cent went into Tammany coffers, despite easily exposed examples of political patronage. Many members of the force, from the lowest beat cops to the police chief himself, received their positions as a reward for their partisan support of the Democratic machine. As a result, the Committee of Five neither persuaded the press of its claims concerning the police nor of its sincerity in rooting out political corruption.[46] Even the crackdowns the Committee conducted received censure. During its tenure, the Five orchestrated a series of spectacular raids against pool rooms and brothels, but the district attorney attested that these raids produced insufficient evidence for prosecution.[47] A *Harper's Weekly* cartoon illustrated the extent to which the Progressive press discredited the Five's investigation. With a poster in the background announcing "The Greatest Show on Earth"—an overt reference to the Barnum and Bailey Circus—the foreground showed the Five riding the Tammany tiger while it chased its tail. The subtitle asked, "Just suppose we should catch up with ourselves?"[48] But they never did. The Committee of Five tried to use popular disgust with police corruption to deflect criticism of Tammany practices; however, in the end they did more to show the extent of corruption riddling city government than to burnish the reputation of Tammany politicians.[49]

The Five reached only one area of accord with the Fifteen: they both favored reputational segregation. As 1901 progressed, New York's newspapers published successive proposals from the Committee of Fifteen and the Committee of Five concerning the regulation of vice. Eventually, the Five joined the Fifteen in supporting segregation, but the two committees never reached a consensus about who should oversee districting and how those supervisors should deal with vice outside of designated district confines. This disagreement involved process more than policy, but the Committees controlled neither. As ephemeral commissions, the Five and the Fifteen could recommend solutions, but they left implementation to the politicians they endorsed. In the short run, the Chamber of Commerce

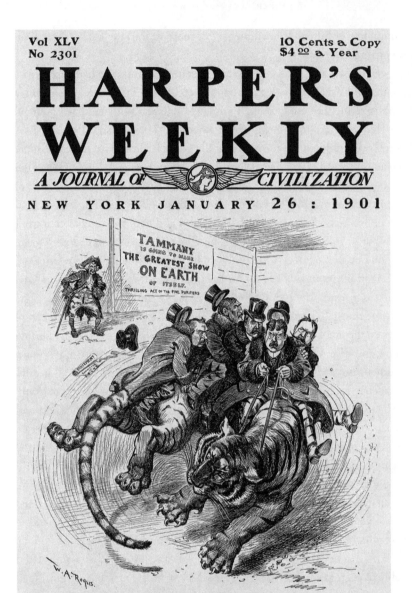

Vol XLV
No 2301

10 Cents a Copy
$4 00 a Year

HARPER'S WEEKLY

A JOURNAL OF CIVILIZATION

NEW YORK JANUARY 26 : 1901

AN AWFUL POSSIBILITY

"JUST SUPPOSE WE SHOULD CATCH UP WITH OURSELVES?".

"An Awful Possibility," cover, 1901. Mugwump cartoonist W. A. Rogers lampoons the likelihood of the Tammany-appointed Committee of Five discovering any politically tolerated vice in New York City. *Harper's Weekly* 45 (26 Jan. 1901).

and the Committee of Fifteen triumphed—Seth Low and the Fusion ticket won the 1901 elections—but after the elections, and with the dispersion of the Committee of Fifteen, the pressure to police neighborhood vice eased.[50] By 1904, the lid was off and New York City was once again wide open. Tenement prostitution had decreased, but the Raines Law hotels, which combined the worst of saloons and brothels, became the new *bête noire* of New York's anti-vice reformers.[51]

The 1901 campaign taught important lessons to both machine politicians and municipal reformers. Police corruption remained an intransigent problem, and a touchstone in election rhetoric, but in segregation ring politicians found a way to manage vice without seeming to favor a wide-open city. Moreover, Tammany politicians ably appropriated the reformers' rationale for districting and managed to present themselves as moderate, pragmatic candidates.[52] The Committee of Fifteen, on the other hand, learned the limitations of raiding. As an enforcement technique, raiding accomplished little, merely pushing prostitutes and gamblers into other parts of an unregulated city, while as a political message, repetitious raiding wearied a sophisticated electorate.[53] Nevertheless, the Committee of Fifteen showed that a private association could, with the proper leverage and a departmental ally in the city's executive branch, police urban vice and successfully suppress some of its manifestations.

Before disbanding, the Fifteen called for the end of "spasmodic" reform and the establishment of a permanent organization to apply persistent pressure on the police and vice proprietors; a call that the Committee of Fourteen answered four years later in 1905.[54] As the century turned, and mugwumps became Progressives, the component parts of larger campaigns developed into causes of their own. Like other points in the anti-machine platform, anti-vice reform gathered the momentum to turn into its own movement.[55]

WORKING THE SYSTEM

The Committee of Fourteen, which existed from 1905 to 1930, was a highly influential anti-vice association. From the start, the Committee of Fourteen's members supported vice districting. Although they later rejected segregation, their early acceptance of vice districting meant that the Fourteen's method for managing urban entertainment was both flexible and contingent.[56] Adopting a sliding scale to judge a venue's acceptability, they took into account the functional distinctions of place and purpose. Their ratings depended not only on the establishment's roughness, but also on its proximity to reputable mixed-sex entertainment like the theater district, and whether eating, drinking, gambling, dancing, or sex served as the venue's primary purpose. For the Fourteen, districting turned into an almost invisible issue. Whether they assumed, accepted, expected, or rejected segregation, they built it into their system of social regulation.[57]

Although it was the self-designated successor of the Committee of Fifteen, the Committee of Fourteen was less elite and more diverse than its predecessor.[58] The Fourteen included more women, Catholics, and Jews than the Committee of Fifteen ever even considered.[59] Still, the Committee hardly qualified as a plebeian organization. Both its membership and its approach toward anti-vice reform reflected its strong bourgeois bias. Certain of the righteousness of their efforts, the clergymen, businessmen, and settlement-house workers who comprised the Fourteen had few qualms about bypassing the legal process or sitting in judgment on saloonkeepers and their patrons. While some of its members also belonged to neighborhood vigilance associations, the Committee of Fourteen set itself a much larger task. The Fourteen sought to impose their vision of appropriate morality on patrons in entertainment venues throughout New York's five boroughs. It mattered little to them whether this standard clashed with neighborhood customs. Instead, the Fourteen saw themselves as an extra-legal solution to the problem of a negligent city government.[60] If city officials would not police New York's barrooms, then the Fourteen decided they would.

The Committee of Fourteen initially focused on the infamous Raines Law hotels, which they considered responsible for the spread of commercialized prostitution into residential neighborhoods.[61] The much-vilified Raines Law hotels resulted from a legal loophole in an 1896 excise law that decreed that hotels could serve alcohol on Sundays, a right that saloons did not share. A hotel was, however, any place that offered something resembling a restaurant and had at least ten bedrooms. Therefore enterprising proprietors throughout the city added ten rooms to their saloons and started providing lunch, serving alcohol on Sundays, and renting out those ten extra bedrooms to prostitutes. What State Senator John Raines intended as a reform measure to limit prostitution quickly turned into an unanticipated bonanza for saloonkeepers throughout the city.[62]

On first considering how to attack the Raines Law hotels, the Committee of Fourteen's members decided to fight for new legislation. Members reasoned that since a legal loophole created the Raines Law hotels, they should lobby to alter the law; however, in implementing this plan, they found only frustration. During the first half of 1905, the Fourteen's representatives in Albany, New York's state capital, endured countless delays and endless filibustering. By the end of the session the law remained unchanged.[63] Even after the state legislature compromised and amended the law in their second session, the situation did not improve in Manhattan, despite the Fourteen's best efforts. Under the amended Raines Law and with the cooperation of the Building Department, the Excise Department, and the Police Department, the Committee of Fourteen organized raids on over a hundred Raines Law hotels. Unfortunately, the Committee soon discovered that police action did not suffice. Not only did a number of judges dismiss the cases, but some judges even went so far as to grant the proprietors protection against police interference in their business.[64] At this point, the Committee of Fourteen reached the conclusion that guided its members for the next twenty-five years: laws are an inadequate instrument for social control.[65]

This conclusion differentiated the Fourteen from their predecessors. Where the Committee of Fifteen and the Committee of Five conducted their investigations as an election tactic, the Committee of Fourteen separated itself from electoral politics at both the municipal and the state levels. As an organization with an open-ended tenure, the Fourteen wanted to maintain a working relationship with commissioners in the Excise Department despite changes in the Mayor's Office.[66] The Committee of Fourteen saw laws as potentially useful supplements, but only as supplements, to more effective means of anti-vice enforcement. Distanced from electoral politics, and disillusioned with legislation, the Fourteen instead embraced an entirely different model of municipal politics: the back-room bargaining table.

New York was a "high-license" state, which meant that the economics of alcohol distribution gave brewers tremendous power over saloon proprietors. By their sheer expense, high-license fees kept the number of saloons down, the fly-by-nighters out, and, not incidentally, increased government revenue.[67] The mechanics of licensing required that each alcohol retailer pay the Excise Department $1,200 for its liquor license and then take out an additional bond of $1,800 from an insurance company to cover penalties incurred during the revocation or forfeiture of the license.[68] These costs posed an enormous problem for most saloonkeepers and made them vulnerable to corporate control. Breweries often owned the building, held a chattel mortgage on the bar fixtures, or fronted the money for the excise-tax certificate and bond. When a brewer subsidized the license, the saloonkeeper usually signed over power of attorney to the brewer.[69] The Committee of Fourteen used these complexities of the liquor trade to coerce city saloonkeepers into policing their venues according to the standards the Fourteen set.

The Committee found its strongest allies in New York's Brewers Association. Fearing increased support for prohibition, the Brewers needed the goodwill that a cleanup might incur.[70] In 1905, the Association's representatives approached the

Committee of Fourteen and offered to help them reform the Raines Law hotels.[71] Peter Doelger, chairman of New York's Lager Beer Brewers Board of Trade, argued that "the purification of the saloon is essential to the continued existence of the liquor traffic with the consent and approval of the Public."[72] Although New York remained a wet state, the Brewers feared that without positive action showing their good intentions toward home and family, the stalemate between the wets downstate and the drys upstate might collapse into an anti-saloon, if not anti-alcohol, consensus.[73] For this reason, they aided the Fourteen in the Committee's campaign to reshape sociability.

Starting in 1906, a month before the Excise Department renewed the year-long liquor licenses, two representatives of the Committee of Fourteen met with five representatives from the Brewers Association and two from the Reinsurance Association. At this meeting, the Fourteen presented its "Protest List," in which they categorized whether a place was too disreputable to continue, needed some improvement, or ran just fine.[74] This committee, sometimes referred to as the Joint Committee, then proceeded to wrangle over which places they would close and which proprietors they needed to intimidate. Over the next month, the Brewers and the Committee of Fourteen threatened saloonkeepers, while the surety companies refused to write bonds until the Committee of Fourteen gave them the go-ahead.[75] The Fourteen's Protest List, together with the cooperation that they received from the Brewers and the Reinsurance Association, provided the necessary leverage for the Fourteen's successful, extra-legal manipulation of saloon proprietors.

If the Protest List dominated the Fourteen's negotiations with the Joint Committee, then "promissory notes" symbolized the Fourteen's coercion of saloonkeepers. In order for blacklisted saloonkeepers to upgrade their standing to probationers, they needed to go to the Fourteen's offices, plead their case, and, if given a second chance, sign a letter pledging that in the future they would more strictly control the behavior of their patrons. Generally, the letters required proprietors to promise that they would observe the one o'clock closing time and prohibit unescorted women from patronizing the premises at night; but the Committee also tailored these pledges to fit specific activities that the Fourteen found offensive in a saloon. Depending on the conditions in their barrooms, some proprietors also needed to agree to forbid dancing, stop serving mixed-race parties, and keep gangsters and drug dealers from making their saloon a hangout.[76] After a saloonkeeper signed the letter, the Fourteen then sent a note to their brewer and surety agent saying that the saloonkeeper was back in good standing—this year.[77] If at any time, however, the Fourteen's investigators found that the saloonkeeper had broken his or her parole, the brewers stopped supplying beer and, if they controlled the venue's liquor license, they removed it, effectively closing down the saloon.[78] When the brewery did not control the license, the Fourteen filed violation complaints with the Excise Department. If the Excise Department did not revoke the offending venue's license by the end of the excise year, the Fourteen contacted all the surety companies that covered excise bonds to make certain no one would insure the blacklisted proprietor.[79] The thoroughness of the Committee of Fourteen's astonishingly overt blackmail left resort-keepers with little legal redress to counter the Fourteen's manipulation.

By 1912, the Committee of Fourteen's scheme for limiting sexual immorality in saloons worked, and it worked well. Over the next few years, the Joint Committee faced occasional problems, but nothing that compromise and a little financial pressure could not settle. The Fourteen liked to brag that "its policy is to clean up, not to close up the doubtful or disorderly places."[80] Frederick Whitin, the general secretary, confided to Mrs. Barclay Hazard, one of the Fourteen, that he thought that the Committee of Fourteen's anti-Raines Law efforts had succeeded in making hotel saloons as moral as feasibly possible.[81] A number of outside observers agreed. Reformers from Chicago, Boston, and Minneapolis all lauded the Fourteen's endeavors, but they could not duplicate the Committee of Fourteen's scheme, with its complicated checks and balances.[82] Early innovators in the Progressive-era fight against vice, the Fourteen remained alone in their idiosyncratic approach to managing urban morality.[83] Other Progressive reformers needed to look outside of New York City for a working model that they could apply in cities across the country. They found that model in Chicago.

CHICAGO, THE SECOND CITY

In Chicago, a city as wracked with political corruption and as rife with reformers as New York, the open toleration of vice appeared as an almost intractable problem. Reformers wondered which organization contained more corruption: the police, the city council, or the mayor's office. Frustrated by the strength of the machine, and stymied by its well-oiled electorate, municipal reformers did not even have the excise law on their side; Illinois was a local-option state. Secure in their position, or at least well ensconced in Chicago, the brewers had no incentive to cooperate with reformers to monitor saloon morality. Instead, municipal reformers relied on an investigative commission, and a well-researched report, to instigate change.[84]

As in New York City, Chicago's anti-vice investigations began with the crusade of an outraged individual. When British journalist W. T. Stead visited Chicago for the World's Fair in 1893, he blasted the city's open toleration of vice, but unlike Charles Parkhurst, who directed his anti-vice agitation against Tammany Hall, Stead aspired to loftier goals. Best known for his article "The Maiden Tribute of Modern Babylon," which rallied sentiment against the Contagious Diseases Act (the forced medical inspection of prostitutes), Stead came to the United States hoping to inspire a cross-class, civic revival that would throw out the "host of unclean spirits" corrupting the city.[85] Despite the publication of his sensational book, *If Christ Came to Chicago*, Stead failed in his mission. Many Americans frowned on prostitution; however, they shied away from Stead's evangelical fervor in fighting it. Even Stead's successes failed. He helped establish the Chicago Civic Federation, but without his insistent presence, Federation members quickly turned their efforts to campaigning against Chicago's machine. In the 1890s, municipal reformers cared more about electing a good-government slate, which they thought would solve a myriad of problems, than in directly tackling the rampant toleration of vice.[86]

Nevertheless, in Chicago, as in other cities, the 1890s marked an increased effort to address the political impact of urban vice. In 1898, at the governor's request, Illinois reformers initiated an investigation into police malfeasance in Chicago. Taking New York State's Lexow Commission as their model, state legislators crafted their report to make the partisan point that the current city administration openly and defiantly protected organized gambling. Predictably, the results of the report proved ephemeral, their significance hardly lasting beyond election day.[87] In 1904, to remedy official inaction, Chicago's City Club hired Alexander Piper, a former deputy police commissioner from New York City, to uncover police corruption. Finding numerous prostitutes openly soliciting in neighborhoods throughout the city, Piper, a compatriot of William McAdoo, suggested that, as in New York, better-defined districts would benefit Chicago.[88] He concluded that "prostitution should be hammered and kept down . . . but do not . . . hammer it to the extent of scattering it all over the city and into the residential portions."[89] City officials accepted Piper's suggestion with alacrity and concentrated prostitution and gambling into three already vice-ridden neighborhoods. Chicago politicians never codified the North, West, and South Side districts through city ordinances, but they explicitly defined the three districts' boundaries in published police instructions.[90] Up to this point, Chicago's official anti-vice endeavors imitated the efforts of other cities, but in 1910 city officials and social reformers created something new and different: the landmark Chicago Vice Commission.

Initially, the formation of the Vice Commission fit the typical template for an anti-vice crusade. Walter T. Sumner, another Episcopal divine, wrote a well-publicized letter to Chicago's mayor complaining about police toleration of prostitution. The Cathedral of Saints Peter and Paul, where Sumner served as dean, was in the heart of the West Side red-light district, and Sumner found the flagrant solicitation intolerable.[91] Whereas, in New York City, Bishop Potter's letter to Mayor Van Wyck triggered a Tammany investigation into Tammany corruption, in Chicago, Mayor Fred A. Busse, who was also a machine politician, made a much more canny move. Instead of waiting for the Chamber of Commerce or a similar organization to convene a retaliatory committee to expose machine complicity in tolerating vice, in March 1910 Busse established a nonpartisan vice commission, appointing thirty local notables and designating Sumner as its chairman.[92] Busse charged the Commission, which included department store magnate Julius Rosenwald and University of Chicago professor W. I. Thomas, to settle the question about the desirability of vice districts once and for all.[93] Although most members started out in favor of vice districting, after months of exhaustive research and regular meetings, the Commission unanimously condemned reputational segregation. In its place, they offered almost one hundred different recommendations for actions the city, the state, and the federal government to take. These suggestions had less effect, however, than the Commission's fervent declaration against segregated vice: "CONSTANT AND PERSISTENT REPRESSION OF PROSTITUTION THE IMMEDIATE METHOD: ABSOLUTE ANNIHILATION THE ULTIMATE IDEAL."[94]

Carter Henry Harrison IV, Busse's successor and an outspoken advocate of segregated vice, did not close the city's three districts, but the Chicago Vice Commission marked the end of municipal reformers' already weakened support of vice districting. During the 1900s, Progressive reformers quietly endorsed the mugwumps' efforts at localization, but after 1911 they invariably explained how, once they read the Commission's report, *The Social Evil in Chicago*, they realized the fallacy of their former position.[95] After the Chicago Vice Commission, urban Progressives could not support reputational segregation and still maintain credibility as committed anti-vice reformers.

—ↄ·ↄ—

Reconstructing the political antecedents of Progressive-era anti-vice reform demystifies reformers' repudiation of red-light districts. The strength of their early acceptance fueled the virulence of their later rejection. After the successful election of nonpartisan mayors failed to reduce commercial vice, or crush the urban machine, anti-vice reformers grew disillusioned with the efficacy of districting as a political expedient. Nevertheless, despite these disappointments, the mugwumps did achieve the dubious distinction of turning red-light districts into a well-recognized feature of early twentieth-century cities.

To the disgust of the mugwumps and their heirs, the segregation of vice also failed culturally. Reformers at the turn of the century sought to clarify the distinction between respectable and disreputable leisure and reduce the visibility of vice within a city as a whole, but the location of tolerated tenderloins near commercial downtowns made vice more conspicuous, not less. Indeed, proximity to the business and theater districts imputed an unspoken legitimacy to activities within the vice district. At the same time, geographic consolidation significantly strengthened an already-existing subculture that flouted mainstream norms concerning sex and sociability. At a time when commercial leisure played an increasingly important role in urban recreation, red-light districts allowed the sporting class to expand its cultural influence. Toleration and geographic concentration gave the advocates of urban vice the stability they needed to create a world in which they welcomed everyone who chose to enter, even as they endorsed an anti-bourgeois ethos distinctly their own.

CHAPTER TWO

The Sporting World,
1890–1917

Vice districts had a very different impact on urban life than the one the mug-wumps first imagined when they proposed reputational segregation as a solution to cities' social-order problems. After some initial protests, members of the urban machine heartily embraced districting as a method of anti-vice control. Reformers, disillusioned by the machine's co-option of vice districting, eventually found the growing diversity of commercial entertainment even more troubling than the political corruption that inspired the creation of the districts in the first place. Despite city leaders' best attempts to confine the disreputable into one neighborhood and make vice less visible in the city as a whole, the very act of restriction relied on a paradox: the business of vice required the flow of people in and out of the delimited red-light district. From the disreputable pimps, gamblers, and prostitutes who may or may not have lived where they solicited, to the respectable shopkeepers, laundry women, and messenger boys who kept the districts running, district workers moved in and out of the tenderloin freely. Customers added to the traffic, and their mobility connected red-light districts to the rest of the city.[1] Vice districts concentrated disreputable recreation next to the city center, but geographic confinement did not equal cultural containment.

Physical stability suited commercial recreation. It allowed venues to advertise, gave pleasure-seekers a starting point for their evening's diversions, and attracted a wide range of entertainers looking for jobs. Vaudeville and popular theater needed performers, but when actors, dancers, and musicians could not find respectable work, they turned to entertainment establishments in the tenderloin for employment.[2] These people, along with pimps, prostitutes, gamblers, and madams, formed the core of what contemporaries called the "sporting class."

As movies, music, and dancing became increasingly common pastimes among young men and women of the respectable working class, the red-light districts, which frequently abutted the cities' theater districts, gained an institutional legitimacy that obscured the difference between respectable and disreputable nightlife. Under "liberal" administrations, tenderloin proprietors established dance halls, pool rooms, and restaurants alongside the more traditional brothels and saloons. Seizing the opportunity to siphon off visitors' cash in as many ways as possible, proprietors took advantage of new technology and showed naughty stereopticons, or exploited the enduring appeal of "leg shows" by offering burlesque musical reviews.[3] At the turn of the century, the range of recreation offered in the tenderloins made them as integral a part of the new popular culture as the legitimate entertainment of the white-light districts.

CONSTRUCTING THE VICE DISTRICT

In a delightful historical coincidence, George Tilyou built Steeplechase on Coney Island in 1897, the same year that New Orleans's city council established Storyville.[4] This synchronicity did not herald the end of one type of commercial recreation and the rise of another, but rather the concurrent growth of both. Tilyou chose Coney Island, a place with a name for disreputable entertainment, because it already attracted people looking for amusement. While the tone of Coney Island improved with the addition of Steeplechase and the other parks, when visitors left the parks' gates they promenaded along the Bowery, which boasted beer gardens, burlesque shows, and cigar shops—the same venues offered in the entertainment district of any city center.[5] Geographically bounded spaces, Storyville and Coney Island drew customers from the outside into their environs. People came to see Mahogany Hall and the Arlington in Storyville, or Steeplechase, Luna Park, and Dreamland on Coney Island, but they stayed on at the ephemeral places, moving among the hotels, dance halls, ten-cent cinemas, musical reviews, and cafés that enterprising members of the sporting class built in hopes of profiting from the holiday cheer of people going to the big draws. Situated on a continuum of reputability, entertainment venues filled the storefronts as close to the star attractions as their proprietors' budgets allowed. These forgotten places physically linked the white-light and red-light districts of turn-of-the-century urban America, while the people wandering the connecting streets made them part of one coherent culture.

In his landmark 1925 essay "The City," sociologist Robert Park observed that in most American cities, the "unit of distance is the block. This geometrical form suggests that the city is a purely artificial construction which might conceivably be taken apart and put together again, like a house of blocks."[6] The architects of segregated vice districts certainly held this belief when they drew lines on the grid of city streets. In Bridgeport, Connecticut, the district began "at Water street and Fairfield avenue, bounded by Water street to Congress street, Congress street to Main street, to Elm street, to Harrison street, to Fairfield avenue, to Courtlandt street, to State street, to Water street, and back to Water street and Fairfield avenue."[7] In Lexington, Kentucky, "the so-called vice district . . . is generally understood to include Megowan Street and part of Wilson Street, or from 34 Wilson Street to E. Short Street Extended."[8] These artificially sharp boundaries looked impressive on a map, but disreputable leisure did not abide by the limits set. Even Storyville, the most notoriously defined district, was not separate from the city fabric. Basin Street fronted on the main train tracks leading into the city, with the French Quarter just across the way. On the lake side, above St. Louis Cemetery #2, was Claiborne Avenue, the center of bourgeois black retailing, while Canal Street, New Orleans's central business district, was just one block to the left, running perpendicular to Basin Street. The plan for institutional isolation never stood up to the vice districts' integration into city space.

If the city grid encouraged aldermen to believe that they could sequester vice by drawing boundaries around certain blocks, the electrical grid connected the red-light, white-light, and central business districts, creating a visually consistent continuum of incandescent excess. Strings of electrical lights festooned the interiors and exteriors of theaters, amusement parks, brothels, and dance halls.[9] Muckrakers could no longer use the metaphor of casting light on the shadowy world of urban vice, at least not in the post-Edison world of brilliantly lit commercial recreation. Thousands of bulbs illuminated the night sky, boldly revealing a city's after-hours entertainment. In Bridgeport, an observer noted that the most popular cabarets and saloons were "probably known to nearly all the citizens for their electric signs; their attractive exteriors are no indication . . . of the character of the patrons or the practices that make them profitable."[10] Proprietors readily invested in the latest electrical innovations. In 1912, a high-class brothel in Lancaster, Pennsylvania, not only boasted Morris chairs and Brussels rugs, but also tungsten lamps, which used bulbs the General Electric Company had released

just the year before.[11] To increase the effect, owners added mirrors inside to amplify the illumination, while outside they hung electrical signs made out of artfully arranged bulbs to draw the attention of the browsing public.[12]

Even during the day, with the lights turned off, red-light and white-light districts shared a common visual vocabulary. The aesthetics of vice districts and amusement parks exhibited this cultural connection. Once again, Storyville and Coney Island stand out as illustrative extremes for understanding the interconnected world of urban leisure at the turn of the century. The pastiche of architectural styles on Basin Street, Storyville's posh main drag, resembled the stylistic

Sheet music and theater posters targeted two very different demographics, as demonstrated by the contrasting depictions of *The Tenderfoot*'s main character for a respectable middle-class audience and for the differentially reputable urban market. *Left*, "The Tenderfoot, Lyrics by Richard Carle, Music by H. L. Heartz," cover, 1903. Lester S. Levy Sheet Music Collection, Johns Hopkins University. *Right*, "Richard Carle in The Tenderfoot, an Operatic Comedy in 3 Acts: Book by Richard Carle; Music by H. L. Heartz," lithograph, 1903. Theatrical Poster Collection, Prints and Photographs Division, Library of Congress. http://memory.loc.gov/cgi-bin/query/r?pp/var:@filreq(@field (NUMBER+@band(var+0975))+@field(COLLID+var)).

excesses of Coney Island. The fantastical structures of Luna Park, Steeplechase, and Dreamland created a setting of exotic otherness with their turrets, cupolas, and crenulations. These same architectural features also figured prominently on Basin Street. In Storyville, however, the "observation towers" showcased the sporting women who worked within the whorehouse rather than providing customers with a panoramic view of the playground below. In both settings, impresarios believed that "more was more." The cluttered objects of a brothel or dance-hall interior barely contained the plethora of cultural references that designers invoked in their quest to make sure that customers received their money's worth. Whether referencing Italy, the Orient, or the *ancien régime*, the people who

decorated entertainment venues freely mixed styles from radically different peri-
ods and places. All this over-the-top ornamentation combined to create a singular
"kitsch aesthetic" that wove the commercial entertainment of early twentieth-
century cities together.

The aesthetics of excess carried over into the iconography of urban recreation.
Illustrators depicted women in equivalent, exaggerated fashions in sporting papers
such as New Orleans's *Mascot* and on theater posters for musical reviews. Short
skirts, low necklines, beads, feathers, lace, and ruffles dominated the representation of women. Even when artists drew chorus girls and sporting women with long
skirts, they frequently left off the bustles and petticoats and raised the hems to
show ankles and calves clad in black stockings. Only their wasp waists visually
linked these women with the decorous Gibson Girl.[13] Culturally, musical theaters
shared more with the urban vice district than with respectable society, a fact that
came across clearly in different pictorial portrayals of the same show. Images on
theater posters displayed on city streets to advertise a new review had little icono-
graphic overlap with sheet music sold to the middle class for their enjoyment at
home. The sharp contrast between the poster and the sheet-music cover for "My
Alamo Love," a song featured in *The Tenderfoot*, an "operatic comedy" from 1903,
demonstrates the dramatically different markets targeted for the show's audience
and for the buyers of its musical arrangements. Both the sheet music and the
poster depicted the central character, but there the similarities ended. On the
sheet-music cover, the country rube, with his flat hat, too-short trousers, high
white collar, and out-of-date frock coat, looked forlorn. His somber dress even
suggested a religious calling. The theater poster obviated any such suggestion of
piety. The tenderfoot's trousers were still too short, but now he wore a cutaway
dinner jacket and smiled smugly as he strutted beside a high-stepping leading
lady. Two chorus lines danced behind the happy couple. In the front, the seno-
ritas bared their ankles, and the women behind them cross-dressed as cigarette-
smoking caballeros. Although the music of popular theater often skated the line
between respectable and disreputable, the iconography of its streetside advertisements shows that more than just physical proximity linked the white-light and red-
light districts.

Geography and architecture played an important role in creating the sporting
world. A map of New York's white-light district, from 36th to 47th Streets, illustrates how theaters dominated Broadway, but houses of prostitution controlled the
side streets. If the map had also included the district's saloons, hotels, cigar stores,
and pool halls, a wash of black would cover it. Yet even those additions would not
give a true picture of the entirety of entertainment offered.[14] For example, the

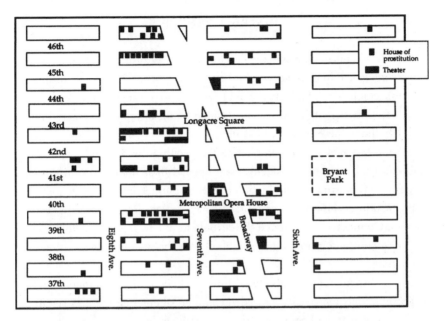

"Houses of Prostitution on Longacre Square, 1901." This map of Longacre Square, later known as Times Square, illustrates the continuum of reputability connecting the white-light districts of commercial theater and the red-light districts of commercial vice. Reproduced by permission from Timothy Gilfoyle, *City of Eros: New York City, Prostitution, and the Commercialization of Sex, 1790–1920* (New York: W. W. Norton, 1992), 208.

New York Theater, located at Broadway and 44th Street and the place where *The Tenderfoot* played in 1904, included two large auditoriums and two smaller stages, one of which became the famous Winter Garden where Florence Ziegfeld produced his first five Follies. But that was not all. Oscar Hammerstein, who opened the theater in 1895, also offered his customers an "oriental café," bowling, and billiards.[15] This multistory complex, while grander than most venues, nevertheless represented the range of entertainment available in physically limited spaces. Indeed, the verticality of big-city vice struck observers as a source of its diversity. "Houses" of prostitution regularly occupied the upper floors of saloons, pool rooms, and theaters.[16] Clinics treating "men's diseases" resided next to chop suey restaurants that, in turn, abutted vaudeville theaters and concert saloons.[17] Different entertainment venues, from the reputable to the disreputable, existed in close proximity to each other, sometimes even sharing space within the same building. This propinquity united commercial leisure and propagated a recognizable urban subculture.

DISTRICT VENUES

A diversity of venues comprised the Progressive-era vice districts. Tenderloins were usually integrated into already-established neighborhoods. Legitimate businesses and respectable inhabitants shared public space and private residences with their more notorious neighbors. Known to outsiders for the disreputable entertainment available there, these urban locales drew visitors from other parts of the city to partake in the activities the area offered. Exploiting the demand for drinking, gambling, and sex, some residents even opened their homes to provide these services, thus blurring the distinction between commercial and residential. The red-light district, however, was more than just a location awash with sex and alcohol. Commerciality sounded the keynote for the turn-of-the-century tenderloin, distinguishing it from other neighborhoods that merely suffered from poor reputations.

Just as disreputable neighborhoods preceded city leaders' attempts to district vice, community conviviality preceded commercial entertainment. A keg in the kitchen, a regular card game on the back porch, and sex offered from the front stoop obscured the distinctions between public and private recreation. In particular, kitchen barrooms, also know as blind tigers and blind pigs, served as neighborhood centers. The Committee of Fifty, a celebrated organization that researched the "liquor problem" across the country during the 1890s, reported that kitchen barrooms littered "the alleys, tenements, and tumbledown houses in the poorer sections of the city," with "the dark alleyways, crooked passageways, and general character of the houses aiding their concealment."[18] Moreover, since Irish communities considered operating kitchen barrooms a customary right of widows trying to make ends meet, blind tigers signaled mixed-sex drinking.[19] Treading the line between commercial enterprise and home entertainment, and between masculine conviviality and feminine hospitality, blind tigers provided a casual place for men and women to drink together and exchange the latest gossip.[20] This informality, which obscured the differences between residence and business venture, made kitchen barrooms ideal scapegoats to "take the punishment of the law when raids are in order." Vice districting offered male pub proprietors an opportunity to drive out their unlicensed female competitors.[21] Saloonkeepers sought to make their establishments welcoming, but they also wanted to distinguish their bars from the domestic sphere.

An anti-domestic ethos did not exclude women from turn-of-the-century saloons. The pre-Prohibition saloon conjures an image of a row of white working-class men with their bellies up to the bar, but "the saloon was not a uniquely male institution."[22] This stereotype represented an ideal, and a regulatory construction, rather than the reality of naturally occurring social patterns.[23] Women participated in the saloons' supposedly all-male domains as patrons, bartenders, proprietors, and most especially as prostitutes.[24] The back rooms of saloons, also known as wine rooms, family rooms, and ladies parlors, served as one of the most common locations for prostitutes to hang out and solicit customers.[25] As a waiter in Newark, New Jersey, admitted in 1914: "Everybody knows what goes on here; we all stand in right. . . . We let the girls sop up all night and don't charge them a nickel."[26] Men typically drank with other men at the bar in the front room, but if they sought female companionship, they went farther into the building to imbibe at the tables set up in the back room. The women there encouraged the men to drink and rack up a tab. In the same Newark saloon, prostitutes received "a rebate of fifteen cents on a dollar on their sale of beer, and twenty-five cents on liquor."[27] Saloon prostitutes also solicited customers to have sex upstairs, thus making more money for themselves and allowing saloonkeepers to profit from the full use of the building, not just the front barroom.[28]

In contrast to saloons, madams at the most notorious sporting houses deliberately blended home and business to sell a salacious simulacrum of upper-class respectability. The elegant interiors of Basin Street's brothels, and their use in advertisements, show that just as amusement-park owners sold more than vertigo, madams sold more than sex.[29] Contemporaries called the very best brothels parlor houses for a reason. The entertainment centered not just in the bedrooms, but also in the front parlor, where prostitutes, overseen by the madam, met and mingled with the customers.[30] Sometimes a piano player provided musical accompaniment, giving jazz pianists such as Jelly Roll Morton their start. Other times, madams bought Victrolas, which cost as much as $200, to play the latest phonographic release.[31] Yet the elegance of the big-name sporting houses did not provide a straightforward index of the clientele's class, as the most elite brothels protected the anonymity of their customers through quiet integration into respectable residential neighborhoods.[32] Nevertheless, the idea of exclusivity appealed powerfully, and madams made sure to sell that fantasy, even if their customers' manners did not always measure up. A theater poster from the late 1890s illustrated the contrast between customers and setting for comedic effect. Six beautiful women fawned over a drunken, cigar-smoking lout with patched trousers, pouring him champagne and toasting him with their own glasses. Although the room had upper-class accoutrements like oriental rugs and an ornate flower vase, other items—the daybed the man lay on, the reclining nude in the oil painting over the fireplace, the large bucket filled with champagne bottles in the foreground, and

"The Tiger Lilies," lithograph, n.d. A brothel's opulence did not always correspond to the class of its customers. Theatrical Poster Collection, Prints and Photographs Division, Library of Congress. http://memory.loc.gov/cgi-bin/query/r?pp/ var:@filreq(@field(NUMBER+@band(var+1842)+@field(COLLID+var)).

the women's stocking-clad ankles on display—indicate that the scene took place in a brothel's parlor.[33] "My Dear Alphonso" might have received first-class treatment, but he probably paid dearly for it. With madams charging up to twenty times more than the wholesale price for the alcohol they served, going to a sporting house and paying "sporting house prices" meant that men expected to spend extravagantly when they treated themselves to an evening in one of the city's posh brothels.[34]

The parlor houses, with their ostentatious excesses, commodified class to increase the price of admission, but the cribs around the corner confirmed that sex without frills also drew customers.[35] Residents and visitors alike categorized these establishments by the price of their prostitutes. They called posh brothels five- or ten-dollar houses (the price for basic service), dubbed more ordinary brothels dollar houses or fifty-cent places, and named the lowest of the low dime cribs.[36] Not all cities had actual cribs—buildings with a row of rooms that opened out onto the street, each just big enough for a bed and washbasin—but that did not stop proprietors from achieving the same effect by using sheets of plywood to partition larger rooms into flimsy cubicles.[37] Cheap brothels like these routinized the business of prostitution. Men waited in line, paid from fifty cents to a dollar, got off, then went on their way.[38] The attractiveness of the women usually matched the quality of their surroundings. Prostitutes in down-market places often wore "Mother Hubbards," sacklike dresses that went on and came off easily, while in midlevel houses women preferred kimonos, robes that enabled them to flash potential customers.[39] In the classiest houses, women donned street dresses or more elegant evening apparel to entice their clients.[40] Throughout the district, brothel owners and prostitutes calibrated costs and customer expectations to determine how much of an effort they needed to make in presenting a pleasing appearance.

The differential pricing shows that economics mattered when men selected among the sexual options offered, but little information remains on how johns chose where to go. Most men relied on local knowledge and word of mouth. Outsiders asked bartenders, dance-hall waiters, taxicab drivers, and messenger boys where they could find prostitutes. In some cases, prostitutes and proprietors hired these men to send johns their way.[41] As one chauffeur in Philadelphia boasted, he "receives 50 cents to $1.00 commission on drinks bought by men he brings in, and $1.00 on every $5.00 spent by the men in the houses." In 1911, he earned $1,733 in commissions from one house alone.[42] Some district entrepreneurs helped orient their potential customers by publishing directories that men could buy from newsboys selling papers in the vice district or at the train terminal.[43] Billy Struve, the editor of the New Orleans Blue Books, explained that people should buy the directory because "it puts the stranger on a proper grade or path as to where to go to be secure from holdups, brace games and other illegal practices usually worked on the unwise in Red Light Districts."[44] Blue Books provided the addresses and phone numbers of the more established venues, featured advertisements from saloons both inside and outside of the district, and offered "reviews" of the more expensive bawdy houses. Besides assuring readers that Miss Cora DeWitt "has a lot of jolly good girls, who are indeed superfine" or that Miss Lillian Irwin runs "one of the best establishments . . . where swell men can be socially entertained by swell ladies," these write-ups included sporting-world euphemisms for specialty services.[45] For example, a "house of all nations" where "everything goes" did not advertise an ethnically diverse bawdy house any more than the "Parisian Queen of America" ascribed the correct nationality to its madam, Emma Johnson.[46] A sporting man reading this entry would know that at Johnson's Basin Street brothel, he could pay for such "perversions" as oral (French), anal (Greek), or sadomasochistic (English) sex. Some prostitutes even made it a point to offer package deals for "a trip around the world."[47] In the vice district, variety came at a price.

When men did not have much money, they went to a dive. Usually located in back streets, basements, or in the middle of blocks instead of the more coveted corners of major thoroughfares, dives skirted the line between brothels and saloons. Indeed, a dive signified a place of prostitution run by a man. Where brothels had madams, dives had barkeepers. If the parlor served as the social center of parlor houses, the bar dominated dives.[48] Dives offered few atmospheric extras to make their customers more comfortable, and dive-keepers did not discriminate in their clientele, which meant that men and women from racially and ethnically diverse backgrounds came together to drink and fuck. Dives were rough places, devoted to hard alcohol and raw sex, where white men and black men could socialize with women of either race without interference from the proprietor. The only consistency among "low-down dives," whether run by Italians, Jews, or African-Americans, was the poor reputation of their regular clientele.[49] Describing one of the "toughest places" in Bridgeport, Connecticut, a sport warned that "you can't look cross-eyed or say anything in that joint; you're liable to get a punch on the nose or hit by a bottle. There's no room to duck either."[50] As the most disreputable of all the tenderloin's venues, dives lacked the clubbiness of more respectable saloons, the faux domesticity of elite brothels, or the musical entertainment of dance halls.

Men did not always go to brothels or saloons for sex; hotels also played a significant part in the vice economy. Prostitution in hotels worked in one of three ways. Men could go out and pick up one of the women who solicited on the streets, in the lobbies of theatres, or at nearby restaurants. Bellhops, desk clerks, and other hotel employees aided their guests by telling them where to go to bring a woman back to their rooms or by vouching if a girl was "sporty" and "willing to do business."[51] In other places, guests might not even need to leave the building, as some managers hired sporting women to work in the hotel. In Portland, Oregon, one "landlady" with a forty-six-room hotel kept three prostitutes on the premises, while another landlady at a different, but similarly sized hotel kept six. At the first hotel, the prostitutes paid the landlady half the "bed money" they made each time they serviced a man, while at the second establishment, the women paid weekly rent for their rooms.[52] The third way involved prostitutes soliciting elsewhere and leading men to a hotel that tolerated sexual activity. In a time when hotels had permanent residents, some sporting women lived in these quarters, paying extra to rent rooms "with privileges." Mostly, though, these independent prostitutes did not live where they worked. Instead, they took their tricks to hotels that catered to the "transient trade." Johns rented rooms directly from desk clerks and paid the prostitutes separately, a highly profitable arrangement.[53] One owner confessed that in his new hotel, he planned to "put his permanent guests on the upper floor and reserve at least 75 rooms [out of 170] for transient trade."[54] Prostitution kept many Progressive-era hotels running in the black.

Sometimes, however, sex was not enough. Too much routine and insufficient alternate entertainment discouraged repeat business. In order to combat customer boredom and gain a competitive edge in a saturated market, vice-district entrepreneurs added non-sexual services to their venues.[55] As soon as they had sufficient money, some hoteliers converted part of their building into a cabaret, restaurant, or grill to draw the sporting class to their establishment.[56] Other proprietors also adopted this strategy. Although the term saloon, then as now, served as a straightforward designation for drink-centered establishments, changing sumptuary licensing laws—and the desire to serve liquor to a large mixed-sex clientele—meant that owners renamed their places for maximum latitude under the law, turning "saloons" into "cafés" or "restaurants" and "dance halls" into "clubs" or "cabarets."[57] The more a venue differed from a conventional saloon, the wider a demographic it attracted. This generalization held particularly true for women as their status expanded from the role of worker to include that of customer. By offering food, music, and dancing in addition to alcohol and easily available sex, these commercial venues, generically called resorts in underworld parlance, blurred the boundaries of reputability in urban entertainment and made the limits of illicit activities indistinct.[58]

In ambiguously reputable resorts, the sporting class mixed and mingled with other urbanites looking for an enjoyable evening out. Compared to the unabashed crudity in dives, decorum ranged widely within resorts. A photograph from a New Year's Eve celebration in 1906 at the Restaurant Martin demonstrates this point. Located in Manhattan on Fifth Avenue and 26th Street, the restaurant menu offered more than food, as the sea of lifted champagne glasses shows. Although it is impossible to say whether any of the women in the photograph practiced prostitution, the high spirits and questionable sobriety of these women indicates that, at least for one night, they abandoned bourgeois prescriptions for the pleasures espoused by the sporting world.[59] Not all women who went to resorts solicited men for money; some went purely for their own enjoyment. At a dance in Lancaster, Pennsylvania, "the prostitutes and their pimps, the 'respectable' women and their escorts, sat enfolded in each other's arms, singing in unison, 'We won't get home 'til morning.' When the band struck up all rushed out of the rooms to go upstairs to dance."[60] The time of night affected the raucousness of a resort. After midnight, when most theaters and many saloons had closed, members of the sporting class, their jobs done for the night, joined in the revelry. Like the other partiers, district workers wanted to have a good time after a hard day.[61]

Theaters, even relatively respectable ones, emphasized life's pleasures in order to draw in urban audiences. On stage, the dialog ranged from "suggestive" to "absolutely obscene."[62] Indeed, when the *Prince of Pilsen* debuted in 1903, the theater critic for the *New York Dramatic Mirror* found it worth noting that "it is neither above nor below the average of the day. It possesses the virtue, however, of being clean and delightfully free from the slang of the Tenderloin."[63] Cabaret performers sometimes went a step further taking popular songs, adding new verses, and altering the lyrics to make the implicit explicit.[64] Costumes reinforced musical theater's sexual message. Some women wore "fleshings" (nude body stockings), but generally burlesquers preferred more froufrou. Feathers, beads, lace, ribbons, and floral decorations all featured in the costumes of chorus girls.[65] An 1898 poster for the High Roller's Burlesque Company showed a chorus girl wearing fairly typical apparel. Her clothes, the champagne, and her cigarette all situated her as a member of the sporting class, while the poster's caption, "Dining a High Roller Girl after the Show," pointed to another way in which musical theater integrated into urban entertainment (see frontispiece to the book). Men often waited at stage doors to meet performers, hoping to take them out to dinner or a dance.[66] In Newark, New Jersey, the bartender at a café below a burlesque theater boasted that "he can always get [chorus] girls for men customers."[67] In the poster, however, the high-roller girl outlasted her date. His inability to hold his

"Restaurant Martin," photographic print, 1907. At Restaurant Martin, a stylish venue on Fifth Avenue, a crowd of revelers drunkenly celebrate the start of New Year's 1907. Prints and Photographs Division, Library of Congress. http://lcweb2.loc.gov/cgi-bin/query/h?pp/PPALL:@field(NUMBER+@1(cph+3b13928)).

alcohol made him pass out and lose his toupee while she still remained fresh. This picture, like many of the cultural artifacts from the sporting class, mocked the punters even as it affirmed the vitality of good sports. High-rollers could party well into the night; after all, the woman in the poster held up the candle not to blow it out, but to light a cigarette. Within the sporting world, attending the theater signaled the start, not the end, of an evening. Visits to the district's restaurants, cafés, cabarets, and especially its dance halls still awaited.[68]

Dance halls in particular attracted a large clientele with diverse reputations. The dance craze of the 1910s merely accelerated an already-existing trend. Yet, through most of the early twentieth century, commercial dance halls remained closely associated with red-light districts in terms of patronage, proprietorship, and physical proximity.[69] Indeed, concert saloons and cafés where bands played, such as Johnny Lala's Big 25 and Fewclothes' Cabaret in Storyville, were as notorious— and, for some customers, as much of a draw—as the more infamous bordellos that presented the public face of New Orleans's district.[70] The simplest offerings in concert saloons and black-and-tans, their mixed-race corollaries, included a piano and a "professor" to play it, but managers of larger halls hired singers and multi-piece bands to attract customers.[71] Beside the ever-popular animal dances—"the turkey trot, grizzly bear, monkey glide, bunny hug, lame duck, or fox-trot"—more notorious dance halls allowed "wiggle" or "spot" dancing.[72] In these "one-step" dances, the man wrapped his arms around the woman's hips and slid his right knee between her thighs. Pressing their bodies as closely together as possible, some men bent backwards, lifting their partners off the ground in this turn-of-the-century version of the Lambada.[73] Moonlight dances also encouraged sexual exploration. In Portland, Maine, dance-hall managers turned off all the lights but one, sometimes dimming the hall further by placing that light behind a red shade.[74] When frottage no longer satisfied dance-hall patrons and the hall's dark corners proved too uncomfortable, couples left and rented rooms at nearby hotels.[75]

Not all commercial entertainment venues catered to a mixed-sex crowd. When men wanted to socialize with other men, they went to the entertainment district's pool halls and gambling dens. Pool halls, which featured billiards and, less frequently, off-track betting on horse races, figured prominently in most tenderloins. Second only to saloons as a location where pimps loitered, pool rooms thus served as meeting places for men working in the district.[76] If billiards did not appeal, gamesters went to gambling dens. A proper "gambling joint," with purpose-built craps tables and other paraphernalia, cost as much as $10,000 to fit out, so most proprietors stuck to card games.[77] For example, on New York's Lower East Side in the 1910s, "stuss houses" prevailed. The eponymous card game stuss, a variation of the popular eighteenth-century game faro, dominated, but gamblers could also play "pinochle, 21, klobiosh," and other "short games," including hearts.[78] Chinese gambling dens offered their mixed-race clientele fan-tan, a game based on guessing the correct number of beads, buttons, or brass counters that remained after a croupier reduced the random number of objects in the pile by groups of four.[79] To keep their customers' attention on the game, proprietors in some pool halls and gambling dens had nearby restaurants deliver meals to their establishments, while others supplied free drinks.[80] In these so-called hang-out joints, men passed the time playing games, gossiping, and, on occasion, looking for work either for themselves or their "meal tickets."[81]

It took more than geographic concentration and diverse venues to create a viable vice district, let alone a coherent subculture. To Minneapolis reformers, "the dance-hall, the theater or picture show, the down-town café and the street" posed a threat to wayward girls and foolish boys, not merely for the diversions available, but because of the "indiscriminate associations" made within such places.[82] The people who populated the sporting class turned these physical sites into something more than just places to work and play. They made the urban entertainment districts a world of their own.

THE SPORTING CLASS

The geographic centralization of vice crystallized the cultural identities associated with the vice district. With localization, the sporting world became an increasingly coherent subculture, one strong enough and distinct enough to inspire emulators among city youths, attract curious sightseers, and incur detractors among respectable citizens. When it came to scripting gender roles, an important distinction existed in the sporting world between those who lived and worked in the district and those who visited it. Madams, pimps, and prostitutes, along with other people employed in the district, set the tone and offered the cultural models within the tenderloin. Prostitutes provided, and madams and other resort-keepers oversaw, the sexual commerce that underpinned all the attractions offered within the district. Welcoming outsiders formed a key part of the sporting ethos, but sporting men and women constructed their identities with a self-conscious rejection of respectable norms.

Values and interests, not family or income, confirmed membership in the sporting world. The ethos of the sporting class esteemed free-spending conviviality and a wide-ranging approach to a "good time," not the more conventional bonds of family, work, or religion. As famous beauty and Broadway star Lillian Russell promised in "Queen of Bohemia," a popular song from 1890, "women are pretty, men clever and bright, / where to do as you like is the only delight. / And the music of laughter is heard day and night." Of course Russell, who contrasted herself with Queen Victoria in the chorus, sang about the ideal, but hedonism reigned supreme in the district.[83] Emphasizing today's wants over tomorrow's worries, the sporting class spouted all the typical clichés about pleasure, partying, and the joys of profligacy over frugality. Hedonism came at a price, however, and not just the wear-and-tear of hard drinking, sexually transmitted diseases, or drug addiction. The value that the sporting world placed on voluble sociability never quite obscured the fact that making money underlay all of the district's culture. A poster advertising Charles H. Hoyt's musical comedy *A Stranger in New York* reminded viewers that "a woman is always as old as she looks, but a man as old as he feels." This motto and the attendant image exemplified the inequalities of the sporting ethos. A smartly dressed and smiling older man with his arms around two identical dancing women reinforced the message of good times for those who could pay. The sporting world always welcomed high-rollers, but the interchangeable women who entertained them lost their status when they ceased being good money-getters.[84] Still, that did not mean that the good times stopped. Those barred from the best places moved down-market, or stayed down-market, still espousing the "Bohemian" ideal of manufactured pleasure, while the party in the posh places continued on without them.

A constant tension existed in the sporting world between openness and exclusivity. Business required accepting outsiders into their midst, but sports turned this necessity into a virtue by emphasizing the value of a welcoming attitude. "Jolly good fellow," a common sobriquet for prostitutes, epitomized the worth that the sporting world put on joviality and good fellowship.[85] But fellowship also carried a connotation of exclusivity. Not everyone could belong. Belonging required a conscious affiliation with the ethos espoused in the urban tenderloins. Indeed, membership, and being a member of "the club," had an important rhetorical place in sporting discourse.[86] Here, though, inside knowledge meant more than club dues. Customers received a degree of deference within the district, but the people who worked in its venues determined its manners and mores. Wise to the ways of the sporting world—its slang, its important personages, and its hip places— district insiders judged what made someone "swell." At times, members of the sporting class felt the sting of their exclusion from respectable society, but they also battled back, denigrating those who sneered at their way of life. Songs from the period, like "You Needn't Go to College If You've Been to College Inn," mocked middle-class aspirations even as they poked fun at the sporting class.[87] The district welcomed outsiders, but its denizens had no intention of assimilating the values of its visitors.

As with other subcultures, public presentation and dress set sporting men and women apart from mainstream society. They adopted distinctive clothes and body language in order to announce their participation in the world of urban leisure. Sporting men and women spent lavishly on fancy garb, indulging a love of finery that signaled a flamboyant, aggressive sexuality at odds with respectable social norms.[88] A risqué public persona served as more than just a rebellious gesture. For prostitutes, their revealing dresses, gaudy stockings, and makeup literally advertised who they were and what they sold. As an anti-vice investigator reported about a prostitute in Portland, Oregon: "Mazie is a bold, dissipated, loud, flashy brunette. She wears an enormous purple hat with a long, fluffy willow plume and purple satin dress, simply an outfit which advertises her business on the street, as

she desires." Thus the prostitute's distinctive trademarks of short skirts and cigarettes, along with a slow saunter and bold eye contact, served as "professional"
signifiers.[89] Similarly, the stylishness of a pimp's clothes or the value of a madam's
jewelry indicated the quality of their "stock."[90] When a Blue Book entry for
Mahogany Hall boasted that "aside from her beauty," madam Lulu White possessed "the largest collection of diamonds, pearls, and other rare gems in this part
of the country," it directly confirmed the house's prestige. That beholding White,
"at night, is like witnessing the late electrical display on the Cascade, at the late St.
Louis Exposition," merely added to Mahogany Hall's sightseeing appeal.[91] Ostentatious apparel simultaneously attracted customers and reassured them that the
sex for sale merited the price.

Customers, of course, played a crucial role in maintaining the vice districts,
but other than the generalization that men from all classes and backgrounds
visited prostitutes, information about johns living outside of the tenderloin is
fragmentary. In 1915, the vice commissioners from Lexington, Kentucky, reported
that the "customers in Lexington's houses of prostitution are, as a general rule,
boys, students, laborers, clerks on small salaries, and strangers in the city," but this
broad description says little more than that younger working-class men were the
district's main customers.[92] A few madams from Portland, Oregon, claimed that
they had a higher class of customers, with "prominent business men" rounding
out their clientele.[93] Whatever his class status, a man's introduction to commercial sex followed a fairly set form. Men living outside the immediate environs of
the district often went to the tenderloin for the first time in the company of an
older male relative. Couched as an initiation—the youth had turned sixteen or
eighteen—an older brother, cousin, uncle, or, in some cases, father, would take
the teenager to the local district and show him how to pick up a prostitute or how
to act in a brothel.[94] Locals who used district services, but otherwise shunned its
culture, did not qualify as sports. They might spend an afternoon, evening, or
lunch-break whoring before they returned home, but even though their money
made the districts possible, they did not embrace its ethos. Other consumers
immersed themselves in the culture without fully joining the sporting class. Never
crossing the line between partaker and provider, they abandoned their sporty
attitude and resumed their everyday identities when they left the district's confines. The historical anonymity of johns reflects the double standard that kept
customers out of the arrest records, but it also indicates the ordinariness of these
visits to vice districts.

In general, out-of-town johns made more of an impression than local customers. Travelers were important patrons in vice districts. Temporarily freed from

the restraints that work and family put on their pastimes, visitors went out on the town looking for entertainment. The white-light and red-light districts served as an easy starting point for an evening out.[95] In 1892, T. H. Young, a salesman whose territory included Illinois, Iowa, and Missouri, mentioned going to brothels in Springfield and Chicago, Illinois, in his diary. These trips, however, merited no more or less attention than watching the town band practice in Elgin, Illinois, seeing a baseball game in Washington, Iowa, or attending a religious revival in Chautauqua County, Kansas. For a drummer such as Young, "going sporting" meant just another search for amusement between sales pitches.[96] Most travelers' visits to the tenderloin happened without incident, but not all out-of-town johns escaped unscathed. New Orleans's newspapers reported the misadventures of men from such places as Franklin, Louisiana, Biloxi, Mississippi, Jacksonville, Florida, and the United Fruit Company's steamship *Mobilia* who suffered run-ins with muggers in Storyville and the French Quarter, while songs from the musical stage, such as "When Reuben Comes to Town," made fun of the mishaps endured "when a chump's as green as grass."[97] Some unfortunates included convention-goers, a group well known for its visits to vice districts. Certainly the Shriners took time out to go Storyville during their 1910 annual meeting in New Orleans. Events such as the 1893 World's Columbian Exposition in Chicago, the 1915 Panama–Pacific Exposition in San Francisco, and other less-famous fairs increased demand to such a degree that some prostitutes temporarily relocated to these cities to fill understaffed brothels to full capacity.[98] Arguing that keeping a city wide open had economic benefits, defenders of vice districts contended that their city's tenderloin attracted conventions, encouraged visitors to spend money, and outweighed the cultural dangers the sporting world posed.[99]

In the differentially reputable resorts of the red- and white-light districts, women customers occupied a more ambiguous position than the men who visited these entertainment venues. When a woman went to one of these establishments, the question always arose as to whether she prostituted herself or not. Sporting women went to dance halls, cafés, and cabarets. They even attended the theater, making eye contact with other members of the audience and using intermission to their advantage.[100] Then again, "charity girls" also went to these places and behaved in a similar manner. "Charity" was the derisive name given by those "in the life" to these girls in their late teens who had sex with men for no other reason than to have a good time.[101] As one seventeen-year-old from New Jersey explained when asked about her "unladylike manner," she was "a hot baby" who was "just tuned up tonight."[102] Charity girls asked their dates to take them to a show, buy them expensive drinks at a "palm garden," or go dancing at a café. In other words,

they wanted to participate as consumers in the new popular culture.[103] Despite
the sporting world's disdain, little distinguished these young women from part-
time "clandestine prostitutes," as anti-vice reformers called the shop girls, domes-
tics, and factory workers who supplemented their wages by sporting a couple
of nights a week.[104] Indeed, streetwalkers, who generally charged parlor-house
prices, sometimes cajoled their tricks into taking them to cabarets or the theater
before continuing the evening in their lodgings or a local hotel.[105] Yet by charging
for sex, clandestine prostitutes garnered greater respect from the sporting class
than charity girls. Like other sporting women, part-timers combined business and
pleasure, embracing the district's first principles. Only saps refused to make
money when they had a chance.[106]

If outsiders found the nuances that differentiated charity girls and part-time
prostitutes from other women in the sporting class perplexing, insiders also suffered confusion in categorizing female customers. Since men almost always paid
for services, members of the sporting class viewed consumption as a masculine
activity. For women to pay their own way meant taking on masculine characteris-
tics, an economic cross-dressing that, at least in the iconography, translated into
actual cross-dressing.[107] A poster of "The Ladies Alimony Club" from the May
Howard Extravaganza of 1898 illustrated the unease, and pictorial overdetermina-
tion, surrounding independent female consumers. The setting recapitulated the
familiar stereotypes about men's clubs: dark wood paneling, statues and oil paintings of women, palm trees, and gas lighting. Two women customers in the foreground sat at their ease in masculine poses, smoking cigarettes and drinking
champagne. They wore form-fitting trousers, dark jackets, and ties, as comfortable
in their masculine dress as they were with the accoutrements of male privilege.
With the exception of a single African-American waiter, white women staffed the
club. Other than the hat-check girl, they too wore modified male garb—dinner
jacket, white tie, and voluminous knee-length skirts—but their clothes, a uniform
shared with the male waiter, indicated the club's high status, while the women's
short skirts added a lesbian subtext. In the background two men, barred from
entering, stood shocked by what they witnessed within the venue. In the center of
it all, a woman, presumably a new divorcée, ignored the entreaties of a stereotypi-
cally Jewish man, perhaps her attorney, as she listened to the well-to-do Irish sport
who showed her the club around them. But for all that May Howard's character
stood between two men, she appeared to have already made her decision. Despite
the apron around her waist, the style of hat she wore signaled her affinity with the
smoking, cross-dressed women who clearly belonged to the sporting world. Membership in the Ladies' Alimony Club meant economic freedom, the social and

"May Howard Extravaganza," lithograph, 1898. The sporting world portrayed consumption as a masculine prerogative. In this 1898 theater poster, economic transgression translates into actual cross-dressing. Theatrical Poster Collection, Prints and Photographs Division, Library of Congress. http://memory.loc.gov/cgi-bin/query/r?pp/var:@field(NUMBER+@band(cph+3g08224)).

possibly sexual company of masculine and feminine women, and the prerogatives of the independent man-around-town. The sporting world had room for such images of female power, as indeed it had room for lesbians.[108] But like the racist cartoon from the Reconstruction era that depicted an upside-down world with African-American dandies attending a ball while white men waited at their feet, the image of the Ladies' Alimony Club pushed the limits of acceptable gender transgression.[109]

Of all the women who solicited within the vice district, saloon prostitutes violated respectable Victorian gender roles to the greatest degree. Often drunk, frequently profane, and almost always disreputable, they played a highly visible and extremely vocal role in urban nightlife.[110] Instead of staying home or logging in hours on the factory floor, they smoked, drank, and had sex. A waiter from Bridgeport, Connecticut, confessed that he quit his job because "I was getting drunk every night and had fights and quarrels over those old whores that come up there . . . that's an awful bunch."[111] Vulgar even by sporting-world standards, saloon prostitutes tossed around terms like "cocksucker," "son-of-a-bitch," and "goddamn bitches" with casual disregard.[112] Men suffered derision just as frequently as women. Saloon prostitutes even ridiculed their customers' penises, giving running commentaries about their size and hardness for the amusement of the room. This commentary could sometimes turn into a sales pitch. In a hotel barroom on Myrtle Street in Brooklyn in 1912, when a man hesitated to accept a prostitute's terms, the woman groped him, saying, "I don't believe you have a prick." The man, perhaps feeling the need to prove his masculinity, then acquiesced to her sexual advances.[113] Saloon prostitutes commodified their sex, and quite frequently had pimps of their own, but they did not defer quietly to men's whims.

For all that the men and women in the sporting world rejected the mainstream version of separate spheres, they substituted in its place their own iteration of gender differentiation. Brothel prostitution in particular underscored the difference between men's and women's roles in the sporting world. When a woman joined a house, she acknowledged her full-time entry into the vice economy.[114] Working in a house provided women with greater security than soliciting on the street. Brothel prostitutes did not worry about inclement weather, nor did they work as hard to drum up trade. Madams, doormen, and other go-betweens built up business for them.[115] Brothel prostitutes did, however, sacrifice their independence and approximately half their earnings.[116] If they lived in the house where they worked, women paid room, board, and bed money for every trick turned.[117] Moreover, brothel prostitutes did not set their own hours. Some prostitutes negotiated the terms of their employment with their madams, but usually their pimps bargained for them. Men arranged for their women to "sit" in a house, while they acted as "runners," bringing in clients.[118] Having an outside representative affected earnings to such a degree that if a prostitute did not have a pimp, or thought her current one did not work hard enough, she arranged to get another.[119] Messenger boys provided a ready pool of recruits. Already well-versed on important district personages and places by the time they reached their late teens, messenger boys moved smoothly from delivering messages to brothels to delivering clients there.[120] Male mobility complemented female stability.

Due to persistent underemployment among poor men, including district men, women had a greater likelihood of securing steady work.[121] Respectable jobs did not, however, provide the only employment for poor families. The "brothels, gambling houses, and saloons" of Seattle's black demimonde "employed numerous musicians, bouncers, maids, cooks, and janitors and provided more jobs than the barbershops, restaurants, and other 'respectable' establishments."[122] Whether black, Hispanic, Asian, Irish, Italian, or some other impoverished ethnic group, the people who decided to work within the sporting world relied on women to provide a steady income through prostitution, while men sought ancillary jobs within the district economy. To contextualize the possibilities for male employment, in one Wisconsin town where the district consisted of twenty-one parlor houses, all the brothels but one included rooms for dancing and employed "one or two musicians who sing and play for the dancers. This means about forty men who make a living by entertaining, on the line."[123] In Chicago, an official police list from 1910 enumerated over five hundred parlor houses, assignation apartments, hotels, and saloons where prostitution occurred, expanding exponentially the number of jobs available to men looking for work.[124] District venues might need entertainers, but they also needed bartenders, waiters, doormen, and desk clerks.

When they could not find work, chronically underemployed inner-city men hung out in saloons, a Progressive-era version of employment agencies, hoping to hear of opportunities. Besides finding odd jobs and occasional work as strikebreakers or the like, saloon idlers learned lessons from their peers on how to support themselves in the underground economy of the sporting world.[125] On the Lower East Side during the 1910s, people such as Abie "The Chink" Treibtz, Bernard Barth, and Louis "Bridgie" Webber worked as "fixers," bribing policemen to settle cases favorably; "steerers," hiring lawyers for pimps, prostitutes, and gamblers in jail; bail bondsmen; and fences.[126] Others made money as drug sellers, stuss dealers, and "guns" (Yiddish street argot for pickpockets).[127] And then there were the pimps. Pimps spent hours in cafés, restaurants, and saloons. Sometimes they sought a good time, but they also lingered in these places for specific purposes.[128] In lunchrooms with dancing, like the cafeteria at New York's Strand Theater, pimps looked for hungry young factory girls to recruit into prostitution. Across from courthouses such as the Essex Market Court on the Lower East Side, sporting men hung out in saloons listening to the gossip of lunching lawyers and treating lawyers and bondsmen to drinks and cigars in order to accumulate good will for the times when they might need a favor. At night, pimps acted as escorts in establishments that would not let women enter without men; however, they kept track of their prostitutes' earnings, even as they sat drinking and gambling with their companions.[129] Saloon idlers made it difficult to ascertain the difference between participating in disreputable consumption and perpetuating it. Many outsiders viewed these men as parasites living off the proceeds of commercialized prostitution, but they played a high-profile part in sporting society.

The same dependence on women that made pimps appear effeminate to outsiders gave these men high status within the district and imbued them with a heightened masculinity. The pimp inverted middle-class conventions, but he was not an "invert" in the emerging medical sense of the term: he was a heterosexual male.[130] Retaining his masculinity because he retained power over women, the pimp attracted admiration within the urban vice district. The more money his prostitutes earned, the better he could dress, the more drinks he could buy for his fellows, and the higher the stakes at which he could gamble. The flamboyance of a pimp's life directly correlated with the value of his prostitutes.[131] As such, the pimp's relationship to prostitutes resembled an inversion of the bourgeois gender relations that Thorstein Veblen described in his 1899 classic, *Theory of the Leisure Class*.[132] The pimp threatened conventional gender roles because he offered a masculine model that linked male domination to supposedly feminine patterns of consumption and idleness. An 1898 poster for Charles H. Hoyt's play, *A Parlor Match (Enough Said!)*, illustrated this dynamic. The faces of all four figures showed the gaiety so valued within the district. But the man sitting at his ease, drinking champagne, and resting his feet on a footstool did not command the women's attention. They high-kicked and sent their come-hither looks to an unseen audience. Unlike "My Dear Alphonso," this sporting man oversaw the entertainment and participated as a provider, not a consumer, of the women's services. Just as his dark clothes counterbalanced the women's white petticoats, his passive oversight complemented their active flirtation with potential customers.[133] The alliance between pimps and prostitutes shaped both the structure of business within the vice district and the gender ideals of the sporting world.

"Evans and Hoey's Evergreen Success. A Parlor Match. Enough Said!," lithograph, 1898. A well-to-do pimp watches as his prostitutes flirt with an unseen audience of potential customers. Theatrical Poster Collection, Prints and Photographs Division, Library of Congress, http://memory.loc.gov/cgi-bin/query/r?pp/var:@field (NUMBER+@band (var+0964)).

Popular representations, both neutral and negative, of pimps and their relationship to prostitutes obscured the ways sporting men and women cooperated to improve their lives. Rarely noticed amid all the uncontestable accounts of pimps physically abusing their prostitutes are stories of sporting men and women working together amicably, as part of an agreed-upon family strategy, to acquire enough capital to improve their status.[134] Whether in a purely economic partnership or as half of a committed couple, many sports aspired to manage or, better yet, own a hotel, parlor house, saloon, or other type of resort. Quite a few sports, either individually or with their spouse, achieved this goal.[135] Together some couples climbed the ranks within the sporting world. Josie Arlington and Tom Anderson in New Orleans, Rosie and Jacob Hertz in New York, and Julia and Maurice Van Bever in Chicago ascended to the acme of the sporting world, achieving national notoriety as white slavers for their role in building up the business of vice in their cities.[136] Outsiders condemned them in the most hyperbolic terms, but, according to their subculture's social scripts, these people succeeded. They put on the finery, played the "jolly good fellow," and embraced the ideals of the sporting world. Their ethos challenged the values of mainstream society, but the ultimate goal of many sports—to own a small business—represented just another variant of the American dream.

City leaders could define red-light districts by law and police practices, but they could not contain the people or the values associated with the demimonde. The flow of people in and out of the district meant a perpetual blurring of social boundaries, while its proximity to more respectable entertainment made its geographic boundaries just as indistinct. That the sporting class welcomed customers into their world further obliterated any geographic limits associated with district culture. The mobility of the sporting class appalled moral reformers, but they also found the stability of the sporting world just as galling. Outsiders watched as prostitutes and pimps moved up the ranks, taking jobs as proprietors, even as charity girls and messenger boys moved in to fill the vacancies they left behind. The sporting world did not wither away when sequestered into its own part of the city; instead it developed a vibrant culture that thrived financially and perpetuated itself socially.

—୦� ୦—

When moral reformers and municipal politicians initially envisioned segregated vice districts, they drew sharp lines on the city grid to delimit the district's boundaries, but these boundaries defined an ideal rather than an enforced, or enforceable, reality. The tenderloin resisted the easy control imagined by urban leaders.

The geographic centrality of red-light districts, the institutional permeability of district venues, the commercial requisites of cultural interaction, and the architectural and electrical integration of the tenderloin with the white-light districts of respectable entertainment meant that early twentieth-century vice districts were more open, and the sporting world more accessible, than the Progressives, in their "search for order," could tolerate. By 1910, vice reformers would have serious reservations about the public space that they helped to create.

The notion of segregation promoted by anti-vice reformers had further unforeseen consequences, thanks in part to the localization of vice into the poorest of poor neighborhoods. African-Americans, Asians, Hispanics, and recent southern European immigrants inhabited these neighborhoods. The johns coming into the tenderloin, and the sporting class asserting its right to a good time, impinged on the lives of the respectable people unable to find housing elsewhere. Social tensions resulted from white outsiders' horror at the district's mixed-race sociability, while respectable insiders despised the disreputable interlopers. When the realities of urban racism collided with the artificiality of politically constructed vice districts, the results devastated more than one African-American community.

CHAPTER THREE

Race, Riots, and Red-Light Districts, 1906–1910

The modern definition of segregation, meaning racial division in society, only emerged in the twentieth century. During the late nineteenth century and into the early twentieth century, Americans called red-light districts "segregated districts" and described the process of localizing vice into delimited neighborhoods as "segregation."[1] Segregation's association with vice districts was so ubiquitous that in 1917, when an anti-vice investigator in New Jersey reported on a "segregated district," following the new usage of the word, he felt compelled to explain to his supervisor that "what he meant by a 'segregated' district was the district set aside for colored people, and not a red light district."[2] Even leading race reformers linked segregation with vice. As late as 1914, four years after the Baltimore city council passed the first racial residential segregation ordinance, Margaret Murray Washington, the wife of Booker T. Washington, called on fellow African-Americans to "resist the very common practice of establishing the district of segregated vice near residency districts of colored citizens."[3]

Both racial and reputational segregation involved an attempt to restrict a despised population to a geographically distinct neighborhood through city ordinances and more subtle social coercion. Whether trying to keep African-Americans in the "badlands" or limit prostitutes and gamblers to the tenderloin, urban leaders sought to prevent the integration of a defined group into larger society.[4] Yet racial and reputational segregation could not coexist. Separation by reputation encouraged the development of a mixed-race sporting culture that clashed with the black/white divide of Jim Crow. When urban leaders tried to combine the two distinct forms of segregation, they exacerbated existing frictions in urban society. Throughout the Progressive era, the conflicting mandates of racial separation and reputational segregation created significant conflict, including the tenderloin-based race riots that devastated Atlanta, Georgia, in 1906 and Springfield, Illinois, in 1908.

Notwithstanding these virulent demonstrations of white rage at black success, most social-order policing, even that concerning race and reputation, remained a local issue, enmeshed in local politics. Throughout this chapter, New Orleans serves as a touchstone, even as examples from other municipalities highlight paths not taken in New Orleans. The politics of vice control and racial repression differed from city to city, but despite the parochialism of policing, urban leaders knew what was happening in the rest of the nation. In this way, New Orleans and other cities shared common urban geographies, police practices, and methods of social control. Integral to the trench warfare of municipal politics, the "spasms" of moral reform and racial repression emerged as part of an ongoing argument among different factions in the city. Whether a city was "wide open" or "tight shut," when urban leaders sought to maintain social order, they regularly evaluated the relative merits of preventing race mixing versus reducing the visibility of vice.

THE POLITICS OF RACIAL POLICING

When anti-vice reformers started their campaign against segregated districts in the 1910s, they asked on which neighborhoods the city should impose the vice district, a rhetorical question for which they presumed there was no answer. In the years preceding the abolition of the districts, however, municipal officials unequivocally responded by situating districts in the poorest neighborhoods, inhabited by ghettoized and racialized populations.[5] Sociologist Sophonisba P. Breckinridge lamented in 1913 that "the segregation of the Negro quarter is only a segregation from respectable white people. The disreputable white element is forced upon him."[6] Racial conservatives exhorted people of color to stay in their place, but nowhere was it clearer than in the ghettoized vice district that white men easily invaded the others' space.[7] Although more racially open than mainstream society, the sporting world still imposed its own restrictions on racial and sexual interaction. The color line proved difficult enough to navigate in daily interactions, but its ambiguity and inherent double standard made race relations within red-light districts particularly volatile. The stark dichotomies of white supremacy regularly clashed with the more nuanced social scripts of the vice district.[8] In the 1910s, commentators concluded that the districts' diverse social mix was a tinderbox awaiting a racial conflagration, but in the 1890s, city officials deliberately privileged segregation by reputability over separation by race, thereby perpetuating a heterogeneous urban underworld.

When officials created vice districts, they initially cared little about the racial make-up among prostitutes, pimps, and dive proprietors. In 1900, at the acme of vice districting, distinct ghettos were in their infancy in most cities. In contrast, concentrated red-light districts figured as increasingly obvious urban landmarks.[9] The denizens of the vice districts usually reflected the demographic composition of a city's poorer populations. Blacks and whites lived next to Asians; immigrants worked side-by-side with native-born prostitutes.[10] This diversity did not indicate either equality or integration. Segregation by reputability was color blind, but color was integral to calculating district hierarchies. Both the customers going to the districts and the people working there recognized the status differentials among district establishments and, with the exception of a few elite houses with light-skinned prostitutes, the more racially mixed a venue, the lower its prestige. Most elite brothels catered to white men only; however, in the backstreet saloons, dance halls, and cribs, racial proscriptions meant less than a person's status within the sporting world.[11] Prostitutes had greater leeway in choosing their clients in dives than in brothels, where madams monitored their sexual interactions and doormen determined who entered the establishment. Part of what made "low dives" low was that white customers vied for service with black customers and sometimes lost those contests.[12] Despite the nuances in calculating status in the district, from the perspective of white visitors, people of color were there to serve them, whether they worked as proprietors, musicians, waiters, or prostitutes. White men resented the intermittent insistence by male residents of color that not only did they belong, as customers, in the saloons, whorehouses, and pool halls of the district, but that their rights, as residents, superseded those of the white visitors.[13]

Interracial violence occurred in vice districts, but, as in the rest of society, most fights happened between people of the same color. While covering Storyville, New Orleans journalists reported stories about jealous lovers murdering suspected rivals or gamblers killing cheating opponents, but they did so with little fanfare.[14] In contrast, the much more infrequent interracial violence made very good copy. In August 1908, shortly after the Springfield race riot, the *New Orleans Item* reported that Alfred ("Buddie") Phillips, after spending the night carousing with two friends in Storyville, shot the black proprietor of a district restaurant. Phillips, whom the police called one of the "worst characters who frequent the district," gunned down Manuel Antoine, the restaurant proprietor, saying that "its been a long time since I shot a nigger, and I guess I might just as well."[15] The most commonly reported interracial crimes were assaults on white women by black men and the lynching of black men by white men, but these generally happened outside of vice districts, in the parishes and counties beyond the city limits.[16] Reformers such as Philip Werlain, the president of the New Orleans Progressive Union, excoriated mixed-race sex in Storyville, but he never suggested that such sex entailed rape.[17] Although pimps often beat prostitutes, most of the violence in the district, both intra- and interracial, occurred between men.[18]

District violence, like district demographics, reflected that of the larger city, yet even routine law enforcement exhibited racist aspects. Policing the tenderloin typically involved rousting loiterers, arresting drunks, cleaning up after bar fights, and following through on johns' accusations that prostitutes stole from them.[19] African-Americans were, however, overrepresented in the arrest statistics. Even though they comprised a little over a quarter of New Orleans's population in 1910, persons of color made up 40 percent of those arrested that year.[20] The New Orleans Item's editors acknowledged that the police arrested African-Americans in disproportionate numbers, yet the editors argued that this imbalance resulted not from any inherent criminality among African-Americans, "but because they happen to be the least taught and therefore the most ignorant element in our society, crowded thickly into sordid localities, developing even worse conditions from the thriftlessness and idleness which result from their lack of schooling and training."[21] Despite the Item's relatively enlightened environmental explanation, crime statistics still raised questions about police prejudice. After the police swept South Rampart Street, a black commercial district, for loiterers, an African-American minister wrote to the Item that "careful investigation shows that only a small per cent are professional or habitual loafers. The majority are laborers who have been faithful at their jobs every day of the week and who are seeking a little pleasure in the only public way open to them."[22] Nevertheless, to the police, social order meant reducing the number of African-Americans, particularly African-American men, participating in public leisure.

State legislators and city councilmen in both the North and the South enacted laws that the police used to keep black men off the streets and out of the districts. Vagrancy laws and "dangerous-and-suspicious ordinances" were particularly important to racial intimidation and the maintenance of public order.[23] Less studied than the vagrancy laws, "D-and-S" charges circumvented the need for proof. If the police suspected someone of a crime, but had no evidence, they could arrest the individual on suspicion.[24] In New Orleans, black pimps joked that they needed to have jobs as musicians; otherwise the police could arrest them.[25] African-American sports based these jibes on experience. In September 1908, the police picked up Charles Navarro, a so-called dangerous-and-suspicious character, "in the restricted district . . . last night on general principles." A year later, Navarro, also known as "Mexican Slim," protested to the press that "the police are persecuting me: they lock me up repeatedly, but have never convicted me of anything. I don't know how true it is, but I understand the word has been passed around to grab me whenever I am out of the house after nine or ten o'clock." Since dangerous-and-suspicious arrests did not require the police to prove wrongdoing, they used the law with relative impunity.[26]

Vagrancy laws were almost as flexible. Notoriously broad in defining vagrants, they applied not only to transients and the homeless, but also to prostitutes and other people with residences who could not prove respectable employment on demand. As such, vagrancy laws were ideal for policing red-light districts.[27] In the weeks leading up to the Atlanta riot of 1906, the Atlanta police hauled in many African-Americans as vagrants as part of their campaign to "clean up" Decatur Street, part of an important black neighborhood in the Old Fourth Ward and a well-known center for vice.[28] Analyzed on a case-by-case basis, arrests the police made under dangerous-and-suspicious ordinances and vagrancy laws were inequitable; when viewed together, a pattern of strategic racism emerges.

For city administrations, the basics of social-order policing—disorderly conduct arrests, vagrancy sweeps, and raids on venues dedicated to vice—formed an essential vocabulary in the dialog among different factions within urban politics. The accusations by reformers and the response by the city's administration followed a fairly set form. Political opponents to the party in power accused the current administration of lax enforcement of a particular type of law, and the maligned officials responded by ordering the police to crack down on loitering, blind tigers, open gambling, or whatever other offense to which city officials supposedly showed leniency. Unfortunately, this pattern of accusation and action came with a basic problem. If the administration corrected the enforcement oversight directly, they acknowledged their negligence. A crackdown could only occur if the police were as lax as their opponents contended. So municipal officials developed an alternate strategy of diversionary policing. If reformers accused the police of overlooking closing-hour violations by saloonkeepers, then the police responded by conducting sweeps removing beggars from the commercial district. Or, if the progressive press decried the city's indiscriminate issuing of saloon permits, then the police arrested saloonkeepers for selling liquor to minors and the courts revoked their licenses. In other words, the police and public officials attempted to discredit claims concerning their negligence by assiduously maintaining other, ostensibly more important aspects of social order.

The racial and ethnic background of the people the police arrested during these diversionary campaigns figured into the municipal government's attempt to assert diligence. The more serious the assault on an administration's credibility, the more racist the responding crackdown. In late 1902 and early 1903, in the course of a self-assigned crusade against the disorderly houses outside of Story-ville's limits, the editors of the *New Orleans Item* reported on the police's refusal to take action against these brothels.[29] During December and January, the police sought to redirect attention first by rounding up the homeless around the race track and, when that diversion failed, by then bringing in approximately 150 people for begging and public drunkenness in the vicinity of Canal Street, the city's major commercial thoroughfare. Unimpressed, the *Item*'s editors opined that "the patience of the public is exhausted and that the plea of 'urgent business elsewhere' would no longer be accepted or even entertained."[30]

In the final stages of the *Item*'s successful campaign, the police changed targets and conducted a series of raids against Chinese-run opium dens. The third raid even made front-page news. These opium dens hardly resembled the glamorous orientalist depictions by novelists and fin-de-siècle artists. Instead, they often oc-cupied the basements of tenements or the apartments of addicts. Like dives, they served a mixed-race clientele. This salient fact underscored the implicit message of these diversionary raids: mixed-race drug taking, and the presumed sexual intercourse that took place, trumped plain old prostitution as a problem.[31] Indeed, Progressive-era sociologist Mary Roberts Coolidge described a similar pattern in San Francisco when she observed that "the police raid the Chinese houses in order to divert attention from the wide-open white houses."[32] During the 1902 anti-vice campaign in New Orleans, however, the police's palliatives appeased neither the public nor the press. When the outcry continued against extra-district houses, despite the police's best efforts to redirect public outrage, the police slowly began to make a more earnest effort at cracking down on them.[33] In contrast to the district attorney's later crusade against the "cocaine-crazed Negro" in 1910, the police's racist diversionary tactics in 1902 failed to shift public scrutiny away from questions about official negligence. That the police raids against opium dens proved ineffective in diverting attention shows that at the turn of the century, reputational segregation still garnered more support among the city elite than policing the color line in the sporting world.

RACE RIOTS AND THE AFRICAN-AMERICAN RESPONSE

The question of racial separation in red-light districts and urban residences grew increasingly fraught after the Atlanta race riot of 1906 and the Springfield race riot of 1908. These riots accelerated elite disillusionment with separation by reputation and reinforced the increasing cultural dominance of Jim Crow segregation. Both riots started in red-light districts, were triggered by rumors of a black man assaulting a white woman, and led, not only to the death of black citizens at the hands of rampaging whites, but also to the destruction of black businesses throughout the tenderloin.[34] The 1906 and 1908 riots differed from the 1898 race riot in Wilmington, North Carolina, which originated out of electoral politics, and from the 1900 Robert Charles Riot in New Orleans, which essentially consisted of a manhunt of one besieged African-American who, in self-defense, shot twenty-seven white men. All four of these riots expressed virulent racial hatred, but the 1906 and 1908 riots stand out among the Progressive-era race riots both because of their origins in vice districts and because they changed the way that urban leaders thought about the use of city space.[35]

The Atlanta race riot started on Saturday, 22 September 1906, among the mixed-race dives on Decatur Street in the heart of Atlanta's red-light district. Running along Peachtree, Marietta, and Decatur streets, Atlanta's tenderloin, like most Southern vice districts, was located in a predominantly black neighborhood. The race riot occurred just a few days after the fall primary, during a rabidly racist gubernatorial campaign, and amid a perceived epidemic of black men raping white women. The hyperbole of the campaign combined with the hysteria of the rape scare to exacerbate white fears that blacks were gaining too much power and losing their respect for white rule. In an already-tense town, Decatur Street visibly reminded racists that black entrepreneurs based their success on flouting the color line.

The riot began on a hot Saturday evening. After drinking all day, and upon hearing the evening news "extras" of a third and then a fourth black assault on a white woman, white men idling outside the saloons along Peachtree and Decatur streets started attacking African-American pedestrians. Dissatisfied with the impact of their initial abuse, a group of men decided to send a message and "clean up Decatur street dives." Looting saloons for alcohol, and pawn shops for guns, the rioters began the "systematic destruction of restaurants, clubs, saloons and pool rooms" that African-Americans owned and frequented. After smashing the windows and ransacking the interiors of businesses throughout the black commercial district, the rioters rampaged through the rest of Atlanta's downtown, killing and looting along the way, but they always circled back to Decatur Street, the symbol of disrupted racial hierarchies. During this time, the police did little to quell the riot, while the governor hesitated to call the state militia. When the militia finally arrived just before dawn, they merely stood and watched the rioters. Over the next few days, white gangs roamed black residential areas, meeting occasional re-sistance, but the riot never regained the momentum of Saturday night. By Thurs-day, 27 September, the official death toll reached twenty-five black deaths and one white, but the impact of the Atlanta race riot went far beyond what figures such as these could communicate. Within the African-American community, Atlanta had stood as a monument to the New South, and a place of hope for the New Negro. The race riot shattered the faith the black bourgeoisie had in Booker T. Wash-ington's prescription of hard work, nonintervention, and white conciliation as the key to racial advancement.[36]

In the immediate aftermath of the riot, conservative black and white leaders joined together to express their horror at the events. Influential black leaders, like Reverend H. Proctor of Atlanta's prestigious First Congregational Church, ap-plauded the unification of " 'better elements' in both races for the purpose of restraining lower elements—black and white."[37] Proposing a Civic League with a conjoining "Coloured Cooperative Civic League," Atlanta's conservatives tried to mend the rifts that put a lie to Washington's Atlanta Compromise of 1895.[38] Washington himself traveled to the city six days after the riot. Reiterating reputa-tional explanations, which blamed the riots on the Decatur Street dives, he praised the city's black and white leaders for working together, even as he con-demned W. E. B. Du Bois and other members of the militant Niagara Movement for stirring up ill will between the races.[39] Du Bois, in contrast, remained inactive and uncharacteristically quiet in the days immediately following the riot.[40] In time, Du Bois and his associates argued that all of white Atlanta, not just lower-class disreputables, supported the racist rampage. They thus adopted a causal explanation that emphasized race over reputation, once again countering Wash-ington's conciliatory stance. Yet Du Bois's initial silence discredited the dying Niagara Movement and its call for political action.[41]

Of all the associations established after the riot, only the Neighborhood Union, a community organization founded by influential black women in 1908, survived the political and social upheavals. Offering a broad spectrum of services, the women of the Union espoused an approach in line with Washington's views that the "Negro loafer, gambler, and drunkard" deserved "the severest condemna-tion."[42] Unlike Washington, however, the founders of the Neighborhood Union, in true Progressive fashion, went to the poorest neighborhoods and, through a variety of programs, sought to improve city life. Attempting to ameliorate racial tension, but staying within a reputational framework, the Neighborhood Union embarked on a plan "to rid their blocks of prostitution and gambling dens," even going so far as to help respectable residents evict their disreputable neighbors.[43] The Neighborhood Union, a dynamic presence in Atlanta well into the 1930s, stood in sharp contrast to the interracial associations established in the immediate aftermath of the riot. The latter organizations, representing the last successful alliance between Atlanta's conservatives of both races, soon foundered. Hoke Smith and other radical racists took power in 1907, and Georgia disenfranchised black voters in 1908.[44] Neither white nor black leaders could prevent these events, demonstrating as clearly as the riot itself that the moribund rhetoric of compromise and conciliation carried little weight in the Jim Crow South.

The Springfield riot also started on a hot day after inflammatory reports about a black man "outraging" a white woman. On Friday, 14 August 1908, a crowd of angry men gathered in front of the city's jail at the eastern end of the Levee, Springfield's vice district, and demanded to see two alleged rapists—one held for a recent assault and one from an alleged rape five weeks previously. To keep the prisoners safe and divert the growing mob, the sheriff arranged for Harry Loper, a restaurateur and car owner, to transfer the prisoners, both of whom juries later found innocent of the crimes, to a jail in nearby Bloomington, Illinois. On finding out that the prisoners had escaped their wrath, the increasingly drunk and angry crowd stormed Loper's restaurant. By ten p.m., the rioters had trashed Loper's place, drunk all his alcohol, and torched the infamous escape vehicle. Still angry and not yet ready to disperse, the mob moved on to the black business district of Washington Street that, like Decatur Street in Atlanta, was the heart of Springfield's vice district. Breaking windows, looting everything of value, and chopping up all furniture and fixtures to kindling, the rioters set the street aflame, then physically prevented firemen from dousing the blaze. By one a.m., the rioters had destroyed at least twenty-one black businesses, but they remained unappeased. Moving from the commercial district to the residential area, they burned houses that African-Americans inhabited in the "badlands," but saved those places displaying white handerchiefs, which indicated where European-Americans lived. During this time, the local militia did little, the sheriff did less, and the mayor hid. The mob did not disperse until almost three a.m., when militias from nearby cities arrived. On Saturday the city smouldered. The mayor ordered all saloons closed and the militia tried to keep crowds from forming, but the rioters, still looking for targets, moved against African-Americans living in predominantly white neighborhoods. By Monday the city was once again quiet, the saloons stayed closed, more militia moved in, and the survivors began to tally the damage. Two black men had been lynched, four white men died from shots fired by the militia, and property damage totaled over $120,000. At the end of the week, most of black Springfield lay in ashes.[45]

The 1908 Springfield riot shocked concerned observers throughout the United States.[46] Where Northerners could dismiss the Atlanta riot because it occurred in the South, they could not do the same for a riot in Illinois. William English Walling, a noted white socialist, declared: "Either . . . we must come to treat the Negro on a plane of absolute political and social equality, or Vardaman and Tillman will soon have transferred the race war to the North."[47] That the events of the Springfield and Atlanta race riots so closely paralleled one another gave substance to fears about spreading racial hatred. By naming James Vardaman and Benjamin Tillman, the quintessential race-baiting Southern politicians of the period, Walling evoked a specter of bigotry that he hoped the Northern heirs of abolition would repudiate. Walling's plea, and the symbolic horror that such racial violence occurred in the "home of Abraham Lincoln," catalyzed reformers concerned about race relations.[48] Over the next three years, leaders in race reform sought to establish national organizations to foster better relations between whites and blacks and coordinate efforts to improve conditions within African-American communities in cities throughout the United States.

Ministers within the African Methodist Episcopal Church offered the first organizational response to the Springfield riot. Almost immediately following the riot, H. E. Stewart, the pastor of the Institutional AME Church in Chicago, called on black leaders to establish a national law-and-order association to combat vice in black neighborhoods. Addressing the stimulus behind the race riots, Stewart and his fellow organizers of the Lincoln Law and Order League "observed that dives and low dens of vice have been the cause . . . in almost every case where the mob spirit has taken possession of low and vicious white men." To ameliorate this situation, Stewart proposed that through the League, black leaders could help black communities rid themselves of white vice.[49]

Although Stewart did not explicitly state that racial separation aided social order, seventeen months later, at an AME regional conference in New Orleans, Bishop Edward W. Lampton did just that. In an impassioned plea, Lampton exhorted his listeners "to keep inviolate those lines of separation between the races, in public and in private, so that the mobs will have no excuse to wreak its vengeance upon my race."[50] In proposing the most conservative, yet sympathetic, institutional response to the riots, the AME ministers offered racial solutions to what they interpreted as a racial problem. The AME leaders acknowledged that black criminals needed reforming, but they attributed the race riots to the white lowlifes invading black neighborhoods. Indeed, Stewart, Lampton, and their peers sought to eliminate reputational segregation and encourage voluntary racial segregation in its place. The AME ministers never succeeded in establishing a lasting law-and-order league; however, the Atlanta and Springfield riots provided the context for the formation of two enduring organizations: the National Association for the Advancement of Colored People and the National Urban League.[51]

The NAACP and the National Urban League endorsed similar goals but followed distinctly different paths. Adhering to Du Boisian versus Washingtonian philosophies in their institutional missions, they exemplified the differences between racial and reputational perspectives. The NAACP's racial reformers offered juridical and integrationist solutions, while the Urban League's reputational reformers espoused a community-centered approach.[52] Founded in direct response to the Springfield riot, the NAACP looked outward from the African-American community and developed a mission to protect the black race through the enforcement of civil rights. While the NAACP's founders saw equality through integration as the solution, they also construed the relationship between the races as adversarial. They believed integration could only occur through the enforcement of federal law and the edicts of the U.S. Supreme Court.[53] The Urban League, on the other hand, embraced a reputational mission. Its founders asserted that the key to aiding African-Americans lay in social-service work and cooperation with local white elites.[54] The League did not contest tacitly segregated neighborhoods. Instead it looked inward to the care of the black community, attempting to acculturate the new migrants from the South and exclude those disreputables who refused to reform. As such, the Urban League exemplified middle-class uplift—a profoundly reputational endeavor. Race provided the reason for the organization, but neither civil rights nor integration into white society received anywhere near the attention devoted to urban vice and other internal community problems.[55] Through their different explanations and efforts after the riots, the NAACP and the National Urban League demonstrated the evolving reform implications of racial versus reputational interpretations of social order.

During the twentieth century, total equality between the races became the goal of many race reformers, and in that endeavor the NAACP led the way. In the 1910s, however, African-American leaders, especially within the African Methodist Episcopal Church and the National Urban League, concluded that tacit separation and the nurturing of a bourgeois black community offered greater benefits than competing with whites or changing the terms of that competition. Elite African-American reformers, like their white peers, sought to impose respectability through institutional reform, but they also challenged the right of white leaders to dictate the moral geography of black neighborhoods.

THE RACIST REGULATION OF VICE

After the Atlanta and Springfield riots, white city leaders took institutional steps to reduce the likelihood of further race riots. Police officials continued to prefer red-light districts as a way to limit and oversee vice, but influential social reformers and city councilmen sought to reinforce racial divisions within the less-reputable ranks of society.[56] Although many white leaders in Atlanta and elsewhere blamed the riots on the dregs of both races, they grew increasingly disenchanted with reputational segregation as an effective measure for social control. Indeed, they may have further reinforced racial separation because of their reputational inter-pretation of the riots. If racial friction among society's lowlifes created violent rampages, then city officials not only needed to separate respectable from disrepu-table, but also whites from blacks.[57] During the 1910s, an increasing number of white leaders renounced mixed-race red-light districts and started to think about a new type of segregation, residential separation by race, as a way to limit social disorder.

The passage of residential segregation ordinances aimed at African-Americans postdated the segregation of vice by at least ten years, but after the Atlanta and Springfield riots, Negrophobes used the close geographic association of vice and racialized others as a rationale to promote segregation by race. Especially in the South's "border states," white politicians sought to extend racial separation be-yond the use of public space and dictate the organization of private life. Baltimore passed the first residential segregation ordinance in 1910 and, over the next three years, cities such as Richmond, Virginia, Greenville, South Carolina, Louisville, Kentucky, and Atlanta, Georgia, followed suit, enacting their own versions of the Baltimore ordinance.[58] Although the ordinances were fundamentally more coer-cive than the AME's call for voluntary social separation, apologists nonetheless argued that city councils enacted these ordinances to reduce social tension. As in Baltimore, the city councilmen of Atlanta wrote this rationale into their ordi-nance, entitling it an "ordinance for preserving peace, preventing conflict and ill feeling between the white and colored races, and promoting the general welfare of the city, by providing for the use of separate blocks by white and colored people for residences and for other purposes." Despite their stated intention, the segrega-tion ordinances reinforced a crazy-quilt of residential patterns that further polar-ized neighborhoods along racial lines without ever achieving the goal of racial homogeneity.[59] More moderate racial conservatives advocated other, less-extreme measures to keep blacks and whites apart, but they too sought to separate the races socially when they introduced measures to regulate commercial recreation.

The drying up of the South was by far the most striking change in social control in the immediate aftermath of the Atlanta race riot. Prohibition served a dual purpose that straddled the two forms of segregation: it kept society's lowlifes out of saloons and prevented the races from mixing within them. In 1906, only three states in the United States were completely dry, but within two years, six Southern states, starting with Georgia in January 1907, enacted statewide prohibition. Two other states, Florida and Texas, missed passing prohibition by only a handful of votes.[60] "Clerical and civic leaders in 1907 freely granted that the recent triumph of prohibition would have been impossible without the devastating race riot and the 'epidemic of rape' which allegedly preceded it."[61] Even the states that did not adopt statewide prohibition often dried up on the county level through local option.[62] Drinking changed in wet areas, too. Legislators passed laws that prohibited mixed-race saloons and required the revocation of the license of any saloon proprietor who allowed blacks and whites to drink together.[63] Without such measures, a New Orleans Baptist warned, "all classes of both white and colored hoodlums will congregate . . . and will cause disturbance and death."[64] Northerners also urged the adoption of more stringent anti-saloon measures. Eugene W. Chafin, the prohibition candidate for president and an eyewitness to the Springfield riot, saw the widespread adoption of prohibition in the South as one of the main causes for black migration to the North. Giving a speech in Chicago a few days after the Springfield riot, Chafin argued that "it is the open town that is bringing the bad negroes up from the south. . . . They have been flocking here ever since the south struck so hard at the saloons."[65] This kind of sentiment encouraged the move away from the centralized districting of saloons, dives, and disreputable dance halls and increased support throughout the country for racially segregated recreation.

Social reformers and city councilmen continued to use already-existing ordinances for social-order policing, but they increasingly supplemented their earlier efforts to control individuals by enacting laws that altered urban sociability more generally. In particular, they sought tighter regulations for saloons and other drinking venues. After the riots, most of the Southern states unable to pass prohibition forced high license on the cities that fought to remain wet.[66] Requiring a yearly fee of up to $1,000 as well as a bond to insure good behavior, the intent and general effect of these laws was to drive the more socially and fiscally marginal establishments out of legitimate business.[67] In Louisiana, the state legislature enacted a fairly typical high-license law, the Gay-Shattuck law, in 1908. Gay-Shattuck explicitly prohibited women and blacks from holding liquor licenses and required owners of mixed-race venues to have separate bars for white customers and black customers.[68] In other words, although legislators intended high license to clean up the saloon trade and reduce the number of transgressive resorts, city officials, alcohol sellers, and social reformers defined disorder through racial and sexual stereotypes. If proprietors were women, people of color, or members of a racialized ethnic group such as Italians, Slavic Europeans, or French-Canadians, they suffered police raids and investigations by social reformers with great frequency.[69] High license also encouraged discrimination based on the proprietor's social background and political ties. Through codified restrictions and with implicit chauvinism, city officials and social reformers reduced the proportion of drinking establishments to the overall population, but they also consolidated liquor retailing into the hands of white men with political and economic pull.[70] During the intermittent morality campaigns and their accompanying diversionary raids, racism and sexism provided both the guidelines for saloon reduction under high license and the rewards for the city administration's white male supporters.

Even when municipal officials and moral reformers allowed African-Americans to keep their venues open, black proprietors endured disproportionate scrutiny. In New York City, African-American leaders actively defended the rights of black proprietors and the reputation of their community.[71] The Committee of Fourteen was particularly intolerant of mixed-race leisure and, starting in 1910, began a concerted campaign to segregate drinking venues such as black-and-tans, the forerunners to cabarets. When Walter G. Hooke and Frederick Whitin, the secretaries in charge of the Fourteen's operations, pulled in black proprietors on their Protest List to sign promissory notes, they made the proprietors swear that they would not serve "colored men accompanied by white women nor colored women accompanied by white men." First segregating parties, and then segregating venues, the Fourteen made black proprietors promise that they would serve whites in one room and blacks in another or refuse service to whites altogether.[72] Chelsea publisher and Brown University graduate David E. Tobias found the Fourteen's coercive discrimination appalling. Furious at the Fourteen's well-documented double standard and comparing their efforts to Jim Crow measures in the South, Tobias wondered "what right have private white citizens to undertake to regulate any business colored men may be engaged in"?[73] While both white and black proprietors underwent the humiliating process of going to the Fourteen's office to sign the Committee's promissory notes, only black proprietors had to swear that adhering to the Fourteen's demands benefited their race.[74]

Anger escalated within New York's African-American community when the Fourteen tried to close Marshall's, a high-class hotel that catered to an elite black clientele. James Marshall, a founding member of the Clef Club, an association of black musicians in New York, ran one of the few reputable downtown venues where African-Americans who worked in the theaters or hotels could have a meal or a drink.[75] When the Fourteen threatened to pull Marshall's license in 1911, James Reese Europe, "one of the best-known black bandleaders in the nation," wrote that taking away the hotel's license would strike a "body blow" to the Clef Club and black performers.[76] Taking a different tack, W. E. B. Du Bois demanded to know why the Fourteen blacklisted Marshall's place. Frederick Whitin replied to Du Bois that "in addition to being on the borderline of entertainment places, it has the unfortunate mixing of the races which when the individuals are of the ordinary class, always means danger." A flurry of letters ensued in which Du Bois declared the illegality of "discrimination between races . . . in places of public entertainment" and Whitin tried to defend the Fourteen's policy.[77] The conflict over Marshall's ended in a stalemate, with Fred R. Moore, editor of the *New York Age* and noted Booker T. Washington supporter, weighing in on the side of the Fourteen. Nevertheless, the Fourteen's discrimination against black proprietors, their active efforts to enforce racial segregation, and the official support that the Fourteen received remained a source of friction within the African-American community in New York City.[78]

In New Orleans, reformers tried to use high license in an equally coercive manner, but they emphasized Sunday-closing violations and the political protection given to high-profile saloon proprietors. In contrast to the situation in New York, the local district attorney successfully disrupted the anti-saloon campaign by starting a cocaine scare. After the riots, race became an integral, rather than a supplementary part of the dialog concerning urban order. The "cocaine-crazed Negro" emerged as one of the most striking symbols in this debate. A recurring figure in both national and local discourse about dangerous individuals, the invocation of the oversexed, black dope fiend crescendoed in New Orleans in the autumn of 1910.[79]

The cocaine scare began simply enough as an attempt to quell public dissent over the lax policing and licensing of saloons.[80] Starting in late July 1910, the Reverend J. Benjamin Lawrence, a Baptist minister, made a concerted effort to attack the city's nonenforcement of Sunday-closing laws.[81] Lawrence and his compatriots, who established the Gay-Shattuck League to enforce the high-license law of the same name, documented a string of blue-law violations and even went so far as to bring evidence into court against Tom Anderson: saloon kingpin, state representative, oil speculator, and self-proclaimed "Mayor of Story-ville."[82] When Judge A. M. Aucoin let Anderson off on a technicality, city elites proclaimed their outrage and Lawrence's crusade gained momentum. Even the *New Orleans Item*'s editors, who favored Sunday opening, believed that Aucoin's dismissal and the not-so-credible ineptitude of the District Attorney's Office stank of political favoritism too blatant to let pass.[83] In a series of speeches and editorials, Lawrence's Gay-Shattuck League and the *Item*'s editors ridiculed the city's justice system and reviled the city council for indiscriminately issuing saloon permits.[84]

After weeks of bad press, and the failure of two previously successful diversion-ary gambits—the arrest of Italian saloonkeepers for serving women and minors and the rounding up of "loiterers" in a black shopping district—New Orleans's machine finally took innovative action. With the help of the police, city council, and, to a lesser extent, the courts, District Attorney St. Clair Adams started a campaign against cocaine use. In particular, Adams focused on the dangers of cocaine use among people of color.[85] As a focus of racial fears, the cocaine-crazed Negro resonated with other depictions of animalistic and sexually insatiable black men.

Little evidence existed of widespread cocaine use anywhere in the United States, let alone that it was rising among blacks in New Orleans. But lack of data did not stop St. Clair Adams from alleging that "almost 80 per cent" of the Negro criminals were addicted to cocaine.[86] Like other Progressive-era commentators, he argued that cocaine catalyzed violent crimes among blacks, including the rape of white women.[87] For example, physician Edward Huntington Williams claimed that after taking cocaine, "sexual desires are increased and perverted, peaceful negroes become quarrelsome, and timid negroes develop a degree of 'Dutch courage' that is sometimes almost incredible." Moreover, "a large proportion of the wholesale killing in the South during recent years have been the result of cocaine."[88] Unlike more diffuse explanations for black violence, blaming cocaine offered a solution to the "Negro problem" that eschewed the lawlessness of the lynch mob: anti-drug legislation and increased policing of the vice district.[89] Like white addicts, black addicts bought and used their drugs in the most disreputable section of the city, the red-light district. By parsing the problem both reputa-tionally and racially, St. Clair Adams and other commentators once again con-structed underemployed district idlers as the source of black crime: not all black men posed a danger to society, just those who lived where cocaine was common.

Pro-district politicians argued that increased policing of the district, with special attention to black cocaine users, would keep the city safe.[90] The cultural currency of the cocaine-crazed Negro made the scare an easy sell, while its causal simplicity made regulating cocaine an obvious solution.

The scare itself followed a simple arc: the district attorney identified the threat and the police arrested a series of users, street-level dealers, and two "higher ups," a corrupt pharmacist and a notorious tenderloin proprietor, George "Fewclothes" Fourcault.[91] When the dealers only received light sentences from Judge Aucoin, who once again showed his typical leniency, Adams used the resulting anger to argue that current anti-drug regulation was insufficient. The D.A. successfully lobbied for city- and state-level legislation and promptly showed the efficacy of the new laws through a few high-profile arrests and harsh sentences.[92] In a report Adams helped prepare, the Orleans Parish Grand Jury assured the public that tighter controls on the cocaine trade would reduce the number of rapes and that violent crimes would dwindle.[93] The Gay-Shattuck League, on the other hand, drifted out of the public eye. In November, Lawrence squandered most of his support among the already-dubious moderate wets when he declared the futility of saloon regulation and offered statewide prohibition as the only solution. In December, he weakened what little remaining momentum his crusade maintained when he broadened the League's mission to monitor drinking violations across Louisiana.[94] After the district attorney trumped him with the cocaine scare, Lawrence made one further, fatal attempt at vice reform, striking out at mixed-sex drinking at the Mardi Gras balls. Just as New Orleanians resisted total prohibition, so too did they resent restrictions on Carnival.[95] St. Clair Adams's anti-cocaine crusade easily overshadowed Lawrence's closing-law campaign. The public found the figure of the cocaine-crazed Negro far more frightening than the thought of working men drinking on Sunday.

The cocaine crusade ran its course by early January 1911, but its effect devastated vice reform in New Orleans. Adams's efforts boosted city pride without threatening cultural change. During his campaign for new anti-drug regulation, he joined a national network of anti-narcotics reformers. Trumpeted in the local press, Adams's contact with national figures, especially Hamilton Wright, the U.S. delegate to the first international anti-drug conference, showed New Orleans at the forefront of this kind of reform.[96] Having successfully poached on the moral authority of local reformers, Adams managed to recalibrate the balance of power in New Orleans's vice regulation. The "efficiency" and "earnestness" with which he pursued his anti-drug agenda and his unrelenting repression of district drug dealers demonstrated that not all of the city administration was in league with

Tom Anderson and other red-light district bigwigs.[97] The cocaine scare ended with New Orleanians reassured that the city's law-enforcement officers would adequately protect them from rampaging black dope fiends.

The cocaine-crazed Negro was an effective symbol in the post-race-riot regime of moral regulation through racist policing. In the aftermath of the Atlanta and Springfield riots, as racial fears increased, municipal officials across the nation gave the police greater leeway in patrolling the districts. This leeway translated into the discriminatory enforcement of the law. Whether the police used vagrancy laws against individuals, conducted dragnets to pick up groups of district idlers, or used licensing laws to dictate behavior, cracking down on disreputable leisure meant ratcheting up racist policing. Few politicians and even fewer anti-vice reformers protested that cleaning up the districts meant cleaning out black men.[98] The race riots pushed city leaders to reevaluate their own strategies for social control and to reimagine the relation of commercial vice to urban life.

Throughout much of the Progressive era, urban leaders in the South, but also in the North and West, addressed racial order and vice control as intertwined problems. City officials and social reformers used the transgression of social norms and the possibility of interracial violence as a rationale for regulating urban vice. The reverse also held true. City leaders used the control of urban vice as a way to strengthen racial and sexual hierarchies. Even "liberal" municipal administrations that advocated wide-open red-light districts practiced strategic racial discrimination to shore up the credibility of their administrations. Thus, while many municipal leaders saw racial segregation as a civic reform, they also saw it as a unifying policy that both anti-vice crusaders and the machine could support.[99]

Racism provided practical guidelines for social-order policing, but it did not provoke a national movement to close tolerated tenderloins. The economic exploitation of prostitutes at the hands of villainous commercializers of vice caused more controversy, and created greater support for the closure of the districts, than the mixed-race sociability practiced in the urban red-light districts. Despite the radical and rising racism of the period, white men, including some very powerful white leaders, refused to relinquish their privileged access to black women's bodies. Focusing on the venality of district managers rather than the sexual sins of their customers avoided awkward questions about who went to the district and why. In the early 1910s, the white slavery scare, with its innocent victims and perfidious panderers, shifted attention away from racial tensions within red-light districts and gave the public much easier targets for their moral outrage.

CHAPTER FOUR

The Vice Trust

A Reinterpretation of the White Slavery Scare, 1907–1917

In the narratives of the white slavery scare, which peaked in the United States between 1910 and 1913, urban reformers intertwined the story of the sexually coerced maiden with a heated condemnation of the business of vice. Although the white slavery scare was an international panic, local reformers gave white slavery narratives local relevance by retelling the standard story in a language particular to their period and place.[1] In some countries, activists emphasized the whiteness of the debauched women and the darkness of the men defiling them, but in the United States race remained an implicit issue underlying anti-vice enforcement. It never emerged as a unifying discourse around which reformers across the nation could unite. Instead, American Progressives turned to the language of economics, particularly the corrupting power of trusts and their control of society, to frame their attack on urban vice.

Anti-monopolism was an overriding imperative in the late nineteenth and early twentieth centuries. Turn-of-the-century Americans perceived an alarming spread of organizational conspiracies—"the Trust and Wall Street, the Political Machine and the System of Influence"—that dominated ordinary citizens, but eluded their control.[2] Broad definitions of monopoly, trust, and dangerous "bigness" drove their fears. From the Progressive perspective, the informal but extensive cooperation among service corporations such as insurance companies and banks was as worrisome as the "tight combinations" of industrial trusts like Standard Oil and U.S. Steel.[3] This climate, in which Americans feared the impact of corporate centralization and saw a cooperative complicity among economic interests, provided the context for urban reformers' concern that ruthless profit-mongers had extended their control to yet another business: commercialized vice.

By situating the tale of the captive maiden within a broader condemnation of monopoly capitalism, anti-vice reformers adopted a language, and a legislative agenda, that resonated with other Progressive-era reforms. Economic allusions permeated anti-vice rhetoric, but three metaphors in particular anchored reformers' representation of social relations in urban red-light districts. The first depicted the business of vice as a trust composed of allied interests. The second likened red-light districts to marketplaces where the Vice Trust—those who profited from and controlled the vice districts—bought and sold prostitutes to fill district brothels. In the third metaphor, contemporary writers correlated white slavery with the involuntary servitude of debt peonage.[4] By shifting the rhetorical terrain away from moral arguments about sin and individual salvation and toward an economic analysis of social structures, Progressive-era anti-vice reformers appropriated the laws governing commerce and used them as a new set of legal referents to further their goals. They strategically employed these three interlocking metaphors as juridical analogies for constructing legislation and interpreting the laws that regulated vice.[5] Although this critique, with its commercial vocabulary, was not the only language that American reformers used to describe urban vice, during the Progressive era, the economic interpretation served as the unifying discourse from which anti-vice reformers constructed a powerful legislative agenda.

WHITE SLAVERY'S GENEALOGIES

The term white slavery originated from the labor movement. In the 1830s, both English and American workers used white slavery as a way to describe their low wages and intolerable working conditions. The workers' condemnation of the power relations within the capitalist system was explicit in the comparison, and the correlation between "white" slavery and "black" slavery carried particular weight in the United States.[6] Indeed, the metaphor of white slavery provided white workers with a way to condemn industrial inequities, evoke an artisanal ideal of labor republicanism, and yet differentiate themselves from black chattel slaves in the South.[7] Around the turn of the twentieth century, polemicists from the middle class appropriated the image of white slavery to describe their concerns about the political and economic disempowerment of ordinary citizens.

Railing against trusts and their perceived control of the federal government, these writers drew parallels to the Southern planters' dominance of the government prior to the Civil War. Anti-monopolists argued that just as corrupt planters derived their power from the exploitation of black slaves, trusts gained their power through the impoverishment of the working class, whose situation was little better than slavery.[8] Fearing the further decline of American democracy, middle-class social critics argued for greater economic equality, something that they hoped to achieve through the elimination of trusts.

White slavery was not the only image that Progressive-era authors used to describe the power of trusts and their exploitation of ordinary citizens. These authors consistently drew on a range of images, from villenage to serfdom and feudalism, that represented economic systems of dependence.[9] By focusing on systems of dependence, anti-trust authors extended the metaphorical cast of characters beyond serfs and slaves to include "industrial princes" and "robber barons." By shifting their discursive emphasis from the oppressed to the oppressor, anti-monopolists indicated their intention to alter society's structure, not just offer a palliative to its oppressed.[10] Anti-trust advocates hoped that inheritance taxes and the curtailment of large corporate combines would eradicate the industrial aristocracy and enable the United States to realize the ideals of republican democracy.[11]

White slavery acquired its sexual connotations unevenly over time. Abolitionists had presented chattel slavery in sexual terms, so it is not surprising that anti-vice reformers, one of the many groups that incorporated abolitionist language, kept its sexual overtones.[12] In 1870, French novelist Victor Hugo, an active advocate for social justice, wrote to British reformer Josephine Butler that "the slavery of black women is abolished in America, but the slavery of white women continues in Europe and laws are still made by men in order to tyrannize over women." In this context, Hugo used white slavery to represent state-regulated prostitution, particularly the medical examination of prostitutes required by Britain's Contagious Diseases Acts.[13] Ten years later, however, Alfred Dyer, an ally of Butler's, shifted the meaning of white slavery away from the systemic metaphor representing unequal power in the capitalist state to the meaning with which we are most familiar: involuntary brothel prostitution.[14] By emphasizing brothel prostitution over state regulation, Dyer separated the sexualized metaphor from the particularities of European prostitution and turned white slavery into a term that anti-prostitution reformers could readily employ in Asia and the Americas.

Once anti-vice reformers shifted responsibility for white slavery from the state to private enterprise, American authors began to evoke anti-Semitic stereotypes of evil capitalists. In 1907, Judge John R. Newcomer from Chicago observed, in one of the earliest Progressive-era white slavery polemics, that "the procurers are chiefly, so far as we have learned, American young men," but white slavery writers quickly shifted the ratio of blame to Russian Jews and, to a lesser extent, French *maquereaux* (pimps).[15] In his 1909 *McClure's Magazine* article, "Daughters of the Poor," muckraking journalist George Kibbe Turner lambasted the Jewish *kaftan* for selling his sisters and daughters into sin. The ambiguous appellation *kaftan*, which denotes a dresslike robe, simultaneously emasculated Jewish pimps and reminded readers of their "oriental" origins. As with the figures of Chinese opium-den proprietors and dandified French "macks," white slavery authors effeminized Jewish pimps in order to suggest to readers that these decadent facilitators of urban vice were debauching the upright virility of American youths.[16] Significantly, white slavery writers did not invoke African-American men as a slave-trading other. The image of the black man as sexual predator recurred repeatedly in Progressive-era tracts, but anti-vice authors portrayed African-American men as rapists, not traffickers of white women.[17]

Although white slavers became increasingly "oriental," white slaves did not become increasingly "occidental."[18] While white slavery polemicists found it horrifying that a racialized other might seduce and then sell white women, they also found the idea that the "other" might sell his own women just as abhorrent.[19] In order to whip up public outrage, George Kibbe Turner accentuated the pitiless-ness of the "Jewish" white slave trade when he declared that Jewish immigrants sacrificed their daughters in order to educate their sons.[20] Alternatively, Jane Addams chose to emphasize the pathos of the white slave trade by reversing the expected formulation. Addams asserted that white men working as employment agents brought African-American women up from the South to place them in Northern brothels. As Addams observed, although the women had hoped for jobs in domestic service, the procurers knew that they could send these women to houses of prostitution without repercussion, because "so universally are colored girls . . . suspected of blackmail that the average court is slow to credit their testimony when it is given against white men."[21] Even so, gender, not race, was the most pronounced dichotomy in the Progressive-era narratives. White slavery writers invariably contrasted the helpless, tricked woman with the heartless, greedy man.

Despite their sensationalism, white slavery writers never moved far from their systemic critique. White slavery narratives were overblown exaggerations, but polemicists employed this hyperbole to further their own political ends. George Kibbe Turner did not write "Daughters of the Poor" just to expose prostitution in Manhattan's Lower East Side; he also wrote it to discredit Tammany Hall. *Mc-*

Clure's Magazine carefully timed the publication of Turner's article to coincide with Manhattan's hotly contested 1909 elections.[22] Like the mugwumps before them, Progressive reformers throughout the country used white slavery narratives to challenge ring politicians.[23] Urban elites often asked sympathetic newspaper editors to publish articles denouncing the horrors found in municipally sanctioned vice districts.[24] Electioneering during the 1910s regularly featured reformers' cries against white slavery and the machine's temporary crackdown on tolerated prostitution.[25]

That urban Progressives should have adopted anti-monopolism, a critical discourse with populist appeal, as a political strategy appears at odds with their class status, but not with their stated goals. The association of the urban machine with red-light districts and "natural monopolies" such as utility companies meant that elite political reformers could employ a hybrid discourse that condemned both tolerated vice and protected corporations.[26] When Progressive reformers used the phrase white slavery, they not only described the sexual coercion of unwilling young women, they also played on its long-standing evocation of a corrupt economic system perpetuated by an illegitimate ruling class. Confident of the righteousness of their efforts, these urban reformers believed that they were the legitimate arbiters of municipal morality. White slavery activists, like anti-monopolists, believed that if they could convince people of the government's complicity in economic misdeeds, the public, in moral outrage, would give reformers a mandate to change the system.

REFORMERS AND RHETORIC

Urban reformers in the United States had attacked municipally tolerated vice since the early 1890s, but not until 1909, with the escalating white slavery scare, did they gather sufficient ideological and organizational momentum to turn local anti-vice reform into a national initiative. Participating in state inquiries and municipal vice commissions, Progressive reformers also created extra-governmental associations such as the New York Committee of Fourteen, the Chicago Committee of Fifteen, and the national umbrella group, the American Social Hygiene Association.[27] In contrast to the more cautious mugwumps, Progressive muckrakers readily used sensational exposés to make their case against urban vice.[28] Melodramatic morality tales of once-innocent men and women sacrificed to the greed of the "vice combine" had greater popular appeal than the mugwumps' carefully reasoned bulletins calling for more effective law enforcement.[29] By incorporating white slavery narratives into their attack against the machine, elite

Progressives tapped into a popular audience deeply concerned about urban immorality.

Middle-class white slavery writers and established anti-vice reformers shared an economic interpretation of urban vice, but they diverged in the tone and tenor of their rhetorical tactics.[30] Neither Clifford G. Roe nor John D. Rockefeller Jr. disagreed over the basic definition of white slavery, but the way in which they presented the evils of commercialized prostitution differed greatly.[31] Rockefeller, the quintessential New York reformer, disliked the "hysteria" of the white slavery scare and actively shunned publicity; however, Roe, an Illinois state prosecutor from Chicago, used melodramatic exaggeration to court a popular audience.[32] Differences in presentation were not just a matter of personal preference. Progressive reformers took their readers into account when they chose between a more theatrical and a more sociological mode. For example, Wirt Hallam, a Chicago white slavery activist, and Frederick Whitin, the general secretary of the New York Committee of Fourteen, were both passionately committed to closing vice districts, but in their correspondence they argued about the value of white slavery narratives in the campaign against commercialized vice. Hallam advocated telling lurid tales of wasted youth, while Whitin touted the power of a tempered legalism. Both Hallam and Whitin believed that sensational stories would "arouse human sympathy," yet Whitin feared that these stories would discredit anti-vice reformers.[33] In part, Hallam and Whitin disagreed about white slavery narratives because they had different goals. Like the melodramatic Roe, Hallam wanted to create a thoroughgoing change in the way ordinary people perceived prostitution, while Whitin sought the support of New York's political and philanthropic elite.[34] Neither the white slavery activists nor the anti-vice reformers were entirely comfortable with the other faction's approach, but despite the range of rhetorical modes that reformers employed, from histrionic hyperbole to social-scientific rationalism, the disparate factions within the anti-vice movement shared a common economic discourse for interpreting urban prostitution that superseded their more superficial, stylistic differences. During the early years of the white slavery scare, reformers accommodated their rhetorical and strategic differences in order to build the anti-vice movement.[35]

Significantly, institutional divisions within the anti-vice movement reinforced rather than ameliorated the tensions between white slavery writers and anti-vice reformers. Unlike journalists, independent social critics, or members of the short-lived municipal vice commissions, reformers within established organizations downplayed the more hyperbolic expressions of anti-trust rhetoric because they could not afford to alienate either the business interests that worked with them or the wealthy philanthropists, like Julius Rosenwald, Andrew Carnegie, and Jacob Schiff, who supported their efforts.[36] From the mid-1910s onward, as Chicago white slavery activists lost their rhetorical hegemony and New York anti-vice reformers gained institutional strength, Rockefeller's distaste for publicity increasingly dictated that the urban reformers who worked with Rockefeller-subsidized organizations needed to temper their rhetoric, avoid the newspapers, and fight tolerated vice with as little fanfare as possible.[37] Institution-based reformers sustained the Progressive-era anti-vice movement, but the independent white slavery activists, with their economic images and melodramatic message, provided the catalyst and the critique that moved anti-vice reform beyond the particularities of local city politics and made municipally tolerated prostitution a national concern. The sensational narratives of the white slavery scare were the first effective salvo in this campaign against commercialized vice.

WHITE SLAVERY AND DEBT PEONAGE

There were two parts to the Progressive-era white slavery stories, corresponding to two different but related representations of white slavery. Most white slavery narratives began with a stereotypical abduction melodrama. In this section, writers described the abduction, sale, and imprisonment of innocent women unwilling to prostitute themselves. Thus the first part of the white slavery narrative is a genesis story, a story of becoming that explained how women entered prostitution. The most melodramatic and racially loaded part of the tale, it is the one on which most modern scholars have focused.[38] The second, just-as-important section of the white slavery narrative, the story of being, addressed the key question of why women remained prostitutes.

In the often-overlooked subjugation story, white slavery turned into a form of debt peonage.[39] Here reformers explained why prostitutes—apparently free from physical restraint and notoriously resistant to "rescue"—were innocent victims without agency.[40] In this section, white slavery writers answered their critics by pointing to the economic inequities of prostitution. In particular, anti-vice reformers argued that the white slave's financial plight kept her "in the life" during the critical transition from innocent dupe to unresisting prostitute.[41] Beginning with the "seasoning," or breaking-in period, the subjugation story started where the genesis story left off, with the white slave's sexual initiation.[42] For example, Clifford G. Roe, in his novelistic exposé *Panders and Their White Slaves*, related how Harry Balding, "a well-known agent of houses of ill repute," and an anonymous madam forced Mona M. into prostitution. Balding first wined and dined and then drugged and raped Mona. The following day he sold her to the madam for $50. This transaction marked Mona's official incorporation into the vice district. Mona's madam, anticipating her new recruit's resistance, forestalled Mona's escape by informing her that she owed the madam $100 for her new "parlor clothes" and $50 for Balding's finder's fee. Ignorant of the law, Mona, Stella, Adelaide, and countless other honorable young women fearing prosecution because of the money they supposedly owed futilely sought to repay their madams through prostitution.[43] Unfortunately, as a federal immigration commission reported in 1909, by the time the novice prostitute had "learned, through suffering, to become resourceful," the once-innocent victim had "become so nervously weakened, so morally degraded, that she can not look to any better life, and apparently even loses desire for any change."[44] In the Progressive-era white slavery narratives, money, not manacles, chained women to prostitution.

To reinforce the peonage analogy, white slavery writers correlated prostitutes' perpetual indebtedness to the madam with contract workers' indebtedness to the company store.[45] Both anti-vice reformers and labor activists consistently emphasized three egregious aspects of worker indebtedness that madams and managers institutionalized through their control of employees' accounts and consumer goods.[46] First, in the red-light district and in the company town, workers bought necessities directly from their employer or an allied subsidiary. In the red-light district, that meant purchasing goods from the madam or buying them from a district salesman making house calls, both of whom belonged to what Chicago native Robert Harland called the "Kimono Trust."[47] Secondly, critics of both the district and the company town emphasized the significant overpricing of goods: between 10 and 20 percent in company towns and, with typical exaggeration, between 100 and 200 percent in red-light districts.[48] Finally, reformers contended that because the madam rarely paid prostitutes in cash, she forced them into debt. In the company towns, workers sometimes had the intermediary of scrip, but prostitutes never even saw this money substitute. Instead, they saw, and then only infrequently, the madam's account book, listing debits and credits, with the larger totals in the debit column.[49] Both the industrial relations writers and the white slavery activists believed that continual underpayment relative to profits earned, deliberate encouragement of debt, and persistent overcharging for necessities made workers—whether miners, lumberjacks, or prostitutes—vulnerable to corporate control.

By emphasizing economic relationships over individual agency, Progressives exonerated prostitutes by shifting the blame for urban vice from prostitutes to the profiteers who exploited them.[50] Using economic practices within the brothel to epitomize the problems that the red-light districts nurtured, white slavery writers offered a critique, delivered in commercial terms, that underscored the systemic corruption supporting urban prostitution.[51] By making social change a higher priority than individual redemption, Progressive-era reformers largely repudiated what New York reformer Frederick Whitin called "old fashioned emotional rescue work."[52] Neither anti-vice reformers nor white slavery activists particularly wanted to save the white slave. Rather, they wanted to smash the white slave traffic; or, in its less melodramatic formulation, they wanted to decommercialize vice by closing tolerated red-light districts.

RED-LIGHT DISTRICTS AS MARKETPLACES

For reformers all along the rhetorical spectrum, red-light districts represented the strongholds of organized vice. Also known as restricted or segregated districts, these areas of municipally tolerated prostitution epitomized the commercialization of sex at its worst.[53] The Progressives' economic indictment of urban vice was not, however, an indictment of consumption. When white slavery writers depicted red-light districts as marketplaces, they described the economic apparatus that district proprietors constructed to exploit prostitutes; but beyond the requisite call for a single sexual standard, these writers quickly exonerated the customer, accusing instead the unscrupulous businessmen who systematized women's degradation for profit.[54] By emphasizing commercialization over commodification, and focusing on profiteers instead of patrons, white slavery writers dismissed the consumer's crucial place in the districts' economy. Condemning district businessmen maintained the conceptual continuity of the writers' commercial critique, but it also permitted a political sleight-of-hand. Anti-vice reformers used the economic interpretation of urban vice to legitimate their anti-machine agenda, implicate their political opponents, and obscure the role that the mugwumps had played in the creation of red-light districts. After the onset of the white slavery scare, Progressive-era anti-vice reformers would repudiate their predecessors' efforts to segregate vice into specially designated districts, but creating sanctioned tenderloins had been a high priority on anti-machine agendas in the 1890s.

By the 1910s, consolidated prostitution had clearly helped, not hindered, the urban machine. Despite the best intentions of Gilded-Age localizers, "segregation did not segregate."[55] Venal politicians and corrupt policemen quickly embraced the municipal toleration of vice. Continuing to demand a percentage from madams within the new districts, grafting officials also increased the protection fees for brothels operating outside of the districts' limits.[56] In addition to bankroll-

ing ring politicians, the districts also strengthened the machine's core constituency. Wards with vice districts consistently elected important tenderloin businessmen, usually leading saloonkeepers, guaranteeing the machine at least one
seat on the city council.[57] In return, ring politicians rewarded district flunkies
with patronage positions, even as district proprietors listed ward heelers on their
employment roles.[58] This mutuality extended further. As Progressive historian
Charles Beard explained, machine-run municipal monopolies, especially street-
car franchises and gas-and-electric companies, favored wide-open cities, because
district denizens and patrons used these services late into the night.[59] Segregation
clearly failed as an anti-machine endeavor, but the unexpected alliance between
the red-light districts and the utilities meant that localization also failed to lessen
the visibility of urban vice.[60]

Following the logic of Progressive-era anti-monopolism, segregated districts
were the marketplaces of commercialized vice; however, the focus on the production of prostitution, not its consumption, gave this metaphor a twist particular to
the period.[61] Working from the premise that the red-light districts across the
country needed 60,000 new prostitutes a year, white slavery writers argued that
"commercializers" had turned the districts into "clearinghouses" where they
bought and sold women in order to fill the brothels and keep the districts func-
tioning.[62] Pushing the marketplace metaphor further, Progressive-era polemicists
compared the trade in women to the sale of cattle, the red-light districts to stock-
yards, and commercialized prostitution to modern disassembly lines where "not
one shred of flesh is wasted."[63] The markets that anti-vice reformers described
were, therefore, what economists would later call intermediate-product markets,
not final-product markets.[64] This comparison made the closure of the red-light
districts seem particularly urgent. Extrapolating from the economic models implicit in their anti-trust imagery, anti-vice reformers used the evolution of other
industries to forecast a dire increase in urban immorality unless they could inter-
vene and halt the development of commercialized vice.[65] Fortunately, the marketplace metaphor also came with a solution: if reformers could close the district
markets, they could eliminate a crucial step in prostitution's production and
wreck the commercial infrastructure of tolerated vice.[66] Strategic vulnerability
did not, however, provide the only economic argument for eliminating red-light
districts.

When rallying sentiment against the vice districts, Progressive reformers invariably portrayed the districts as harming the urban economy.[67] Applying anti-
monopolism's distinctly pre-Keynesian economic models to prostitution, anti-vice
reformers saw the districts' economy as mirroring the linear structure of corporate

HAVE YOU A GIRL TO SPARE?
Sixty Thousand White Slaves die every year. The Vice Resorts
cannot run without this number is replaced annually. Are you willing to give your daughter to keep up this terrible business?

"Have You a Girl to Spare?" Reformers often compared the vice district to a factory that consumes women. Clifford G. Roe, *The Great War on White Slavery: Or, Fighting for the Protection of Our Girls* (n.p., 1911), plate following p. 48.

combines. Here the reformers' focus on intermediate-product markets instead of final-product markets is particularly important. Where a final-product market implies a circular cash flow between consumers and producers that has a positive impact on the economy—the Keynesian multiplier effect—the Progressive-era emphasis on vertical integration meant that white slavery writers envisioned money traveling up the corporate hierarchy and out of the community.[68] As Charles Beard observed in 1912, "monopoly profits [go] to private pockets."[69] By privileging production over consumption, urban reformers saw the cash that con- sumers spent in the districts as money the Vice Trust took out of circulation.[70] District supporters tried to answer this criticism by arguing that red-light districts attracted tourists, provided a significant number of jobs, and strengthened the city's economy, but these arguments held little appeal for elite Progressives.[71] Urban reformers knew the economic strength of the vice districts, but they did not see either the money spent or the jobs filled as contributing to society.[72] Anti-vice reformers embraced a program in which they intentionally strove to dismantle prostitution's commercial infrastructure and put as many "leeches and blood suckers" out of work as possible.[73] To do that, anti-vice reformers not only needed to shut down the red-light districts, they also needed to unmask and eliminate the commercializers profiting from urban vice: the Vice Trust.

THE VICE TRUST

The concept of the Vice Trust developed out of the Progressives' condemnation of the red-light district's productive infrastructure. Anti-vice reformers argued that just as corporate executives were reorganizing the structure of their companies, so to were the magnates of the vice district rationalizing the district's economy and integrating the district's diverse denizens into an increasingly streamlined, and corporate, hierarchy.[74] As Ellen Henrotin, a member of the Chicago Vice Com- mission, observed, "the modern tendency towards centralization has not passed by so promising a field for exploitation."[75] White slavery writers attributed the changing economic structure of urban vice to the enterprising men who had reputedly taken over the business of vice after politicians created segregated red- light districts in the 1890s.[76] In an unusual distortion of the tenets of social house- keeping, anti-vice reformers lamented women's loss of control in the vice business as a moral and economic disaster because men, in their efforts to maximize profit, callously applied the lessons of corporate capitalism to urban prostitution.[77] As white slavery writers frequently concluded, prostitution was a business run by men for men.[78]

The members of the Vice Trust included anyone who enabled prostitution's commercial production, from the pimp in the corner saloon complaining about the size of his cut to the shadowy "higher-ups," of whom only the most notorious, such as Max Hochstim, were known to the public.[79] The relative anonymity of the higher-ups made the Vice Trust metaphor particularly menacing because, like corporate stockholders, these higher-ups maintained a veneer of respectability even as they profited from the corrupt practices of the Trust.[80] Urban reformers confronted "the vested interests of the [disorderly house] keepers, the real-estate owners, the liquor interests, and their lawyers and doctors," but among all these antagonists, anti-vice reformers found the duplicity of seemingly respectable land-owners and real estate agents particularly reprehensible.[81] To the Progressives, the "quiet combines of greed" represented the extent to which tolerated vice had corrupted society.[82]

Reformers were not alone in their corporate characterization of urban vice or in their disgust for the hypocritical rich. In silent movies such as *Traffic in Souls*, *Inside the White Slave Traffic*, and *Smashing the Vice Trust*, filmmakers empha-sized the menace and the melodrama of the era's commercial critique.[83] In 1913, director George Loane Tucker devoted most of the first act of *Traffic in Souls* to following the flow of cash up the corporate ladder of the white slave trade. The money trail started with a morning accounting in a brothel. After receiving a percentage of the night's take, the brothel's representative, a cadet, went to the offices of "A. E. Jones Investments." "Mr. Jones" acted as a "go-between," a man who collected money from the city's pimps and madams and directed the procure-ment of women. For all his managerial responsibilities, however, the go-between was only an intermediary. In a visual reinforcement of Mr. Jones's subordination and the Vice Trust's vertical integration, the go-between's offices were directly below those of the higher-up: William Trubus, the hypocritical head of the "Inter-national Purity and Reform League," an organization dedicated to the eradication of the white slave traffic.[84] Tucker's representation of the Vice Trust reinforced the economic critique of the period, even as the character of Trubus challenged the authority of elite reformers.[85]

As the use of business metaphors in the film *Traffic in Souls* suggests, the Vice Trust was a difficult image for reformers to deploy because they could not contain the subversive populism inherent in the anti-trust rhetoric's systemic critique. Indeed, at the urging of the Committee of Fourteen, the National Board of Censors tried to have Trubus's association with reformers cut from *Traffic in Souls*, but Universal released the movie intact.[86] Concurrently, madams and saloon proprietors used the comparison between corrupt corporations and anti-vice asso-

The "allied interests" of the Vice Trust, clipping, 1917. The captions reads, "A Few of Those Who Are Getting Uneasy. The announcement that a committee of twenty is to investigate vice conditions in Utica has created something of a furore in the nether world. Let us hope that the probe goes deep enough to reach the profiteers rather that the mere tools and victims." *Utica Sunday Globe*, 15 Dec. 1917, Committee of Fourteen Collection, New York Public Library.

ciations to condemn the unpopular and seemingly arbitrary enforcement of anti-vice laws. When the Committee of Fourteen cooperated with the New York Brewers Association in an attempt to eradicate prostitution from saloons, saloon-keepers accused the Committee of Fourteen of complicity with the business interests.[87] That Rockefeller money backed the Committee of Fourteen only further reinforced the saloonkeepers' antipathy, their perception of persecution, and their certitude of the Committee's corruption.[88] Vice-district denizens effectively reinscribed the white slavery scare's anti-monopolism back onto the "industrial princes" who tried to engineer working-class lives through moral reform. Thus, even though the corporate comparison was integral to Progressive reformers' economic interpretation of urban prostitution, anti-vice reform's elite supporters were never as comfortable with the more overt anti-trust analogies as they were with the less-volatile constructions of debt peonage and vice districting.

The Vice Trust metaphor was more unstable, both conceptually and politically, than either the analogy between prostitution and debt peonage or the comparison of red-light districts to marketplaces. "Vice Trust" was an epithet that a wide variety of people could use to condemn multiple, diverse, and even mutually opposing individuals and organizations. Nevertheless, the way that reformers, muckrakers, filmmakers, and even district denizens employed this metaphor provides insight into how people evaluated economic interaction during the Progressive era. Despite insurmountable differences between independent owners and anti-vice reformers, both groups shared a common antipathy toward "organized vice." Small-time saloonkeepers and madams wanted to compete in a market where bigness did not grant special privileges to prominent proprietors.[89] Anti-vice reformers also wished to disband the Vice Trust, but they wanted to hinder growth, not facilitate competition. What the independent proprietors saw as an opportunity, white slavery writers perceived as disorganized, ineffective, and unprofitable.[90] Yet the fact that small proprietors and elite reformers could, for very different reasons, agree that bigness was bad shows the flexibility of the commercial critique, even as it highlights its analytical bluntness. Nevertheless, the adaptability of the interconnected Vice Trust metaphors worked to the anti-vice movement's advantage. The breadth of the underlying commercial critique meant that a range of reformers could employ a variety of rhetorical styles and yet stay within the parameters of their shared economic discourse. By having a series of broadly construed metaphors to portray urban vice, different factions within the anti-vice movement could choose which aspects of the critique they would emphasize, and with what rhetorical mode, but in making those choices, these reformers did not necessarily alienate other anti-vice reformers. For as long as the red-light districts ran wide open, and the Vice Trust metaphors approximately described commercialized prostitution, Progressive reformers with stylistic and strategic differences could share a conceptual framework, build alliances, and establish a common legislative agenda.

TRUST BUSTING

The Vice Trust metaphors were more than just a brief discursive curiosity that marked the white slavery scare as particularly Progressive. Unlike the mugwumps, Progressives did not limit their legal strategies to the more strenuous enforcement of existing laws. They also campaigned actively for new laws that, in turn, carried the distinctive imprimatur of their economic understanding of urban vice. Politicians, lawyers, and judges integrated the commercial critique into the American legal system when they created juridical analogies that recast anti-vice regulation to fit their anti-trust interpretation of urban vice.[91] Progressive reformers took the forms and forums of corporate law—notably the commerce clause, labor laws, and the courts of equity—and used them to rewrite older anti-prostitution statutes in innovative ways. Through legislation and case precedent, these hybrid statutes became the legal basis for anti-vice enforcement in the twentieth century.[92]

During the Progressive era, anti-vice reformers lobbied for two types of laws: white slave traffic acts and, later, red-light abatement laws. From 1907 into 1913, in the early years of the white slavery scare when it was at the height of its melodramatic hyperbole, three Chicago lawyers, Edwin W. Sims, Clifford G. Roe, and James R. Mann, led the fight for a series of white slave traffic acts, also known as pandering laws, on the federal and local levels.[93] Reformers intended for these white slave traffic acts, of which the 1910 Mann Act was the exemplar, to disrupt the movement of women into red-light districts, thus halting prostitution's production. When, contrary to expectations, the Mann Act did not cripple commercialized prostitution, and local state's attorneys only ended up prosecuting low-level pimps and madams, anti-vice reformers shifted their emphasis from people to places.[94] Starting in 1912, the members of the American Vigilance Association and its successor, the American Social Hygiene Association, oversaw a national campaign for the state-by-state enactment of red-light abatement laws.[95] Through injunction and abatement, anti-vice reformers hoped to harm the higher-ups that eluded them under the pandering laws: the owners of property in the red-light districts. Reformers reasoned that if they could not stop the flow of women into the vice districts with the Mann Act, then perhaps they could close down the district marketplaces with red-light abatement laws.[96] To that end, Bascom Johnson, George Kneeland, and other members of the American Social Hygiene Association's staff helped local reformers establish municipal vice commissions to rally state support for the acts.[97] Although the vice commission reports did not have the flash of the white slavery narratives, and injunction and abatement acts turned on arcane points of law, Progressive reformers successfully shifted their legislative strategy from pandering laws to red-light abatement acts without losing momentum or abandoning the commercial language of their critique.

Congress passed the Mann Act at the point when the white slavery scare approached its emotional acme. Although the Mann Act may now seem ludicrous and convoluted, members of Congress supported the White Slave Traffic Act because they shared with their contemporaries an economic interpretation of urban vice—the contextual key to understanding the statute's construction.[98] The purpose of the 1910 Mann Act was "to further regulate interstate and foreign commerce by prohibiting the transportation therein for immoral purposes of women and girls." As such, the Mann Act embodied the widespread belief that an organized interstate traffic in women existed. Even more specifically, legislators assumed that the business practices of this traffic resembled those of a multistate trust.[99] Chicago Congressman James R. Mann, who also wrote the Pure Food and Drug Act and the Mann-Elkins Act that significantly broadened the powers of the Interstate Commerce Commission, purposely chose to frame the White Slave Traffic Act using the commerce clause. He reasoned that commercialized vice, like other corporate combinations, was an organized and interconnected business that was national in scope and exceeded the jurisdiction of local police powers.[100] Some anti-vice reformers, caught up by the sensational sweep of the more simplistic narratives, thought that the Mann Act, reinforced by local law enforcement, would prove a panacea for curtailing urban prostitution, but they were soon disappointed.[101] By 1917, the small size of the Justice Department's enforcement apparatus, and the Supreme Court's reorientation of the statute toward noncommercial sex, convinced anti-vice reformers that the Mann Act was an important statute, but not the regulatory revolution for which its proponents had hoped.[102]

Ironically, the local white slave traffic acts, which were only supposed to supplement the Mann Act, proved more effective tools for fighting commercialized vice.[103] Unlike Congress's construction of the Mann Act, which rested on the commerce clause, state legislators modeled local white slave traffic acts on contract labor laws.[104] In part a way around the conflict between state and federal jurisdictions, this emulation of contract labor laws allowed politicians and policemen to target prostitution's profiteers more effectively than either the Mann Act or the older disorderly house laws.[105] Where the Mann Act was limited to the procurers who transported prostitutes, and disorderly house laws generally only applied to the "keepers," by defining pandering as profiting from the earnings of a prostitute, state legislators expanded the number of potential offenders to include not only procurers and madams, but the pimps in collusion with them.[106] In keeping with reformers' antipathy toward profiteers, both the pandering laws and the contract labor laws implicated the agents arranging and enforcing illegal employment, even as they exonerated the prostitutes and immigrants enticed into service.[107] Still, despite the juridical strength of the comparison between pimps and *padrones*, pandering laws did not eliminate commercialized prostitution. Just as contract labor laws did not alter the productive structure of big business, white slave traffic acts never challenged the economic base of the vice districts.[108] To achieve that end, anti-vice reformers turned to the red-light abatement acts with increasing frequency after 1912.[109]

Legislators designed the red-light abatement acts to crush the vested interests of the Vice Trust.[110] Like pandering laws, red-light abatement laws were a new,

economic iteration of older criminal laws. With them, anti-vice reformers sought
to recast the keeping of disorderly houses as a civil offense.[111] During the early
1910s, white slavery writers argued that the fines judges imposed on brothel-
keepers served as a virtual licensing system.[112] Since police raids did not perma-
nently close the houses, and madams apparently budgeted for fines in much the
same way that legal businesses anticipated quarterly tax payments, urban Progressives contended that criminal law alone could not eradicate the business of vice.
Moreover, anti-vice reformers maintained that because the revenue from police
raids formed an integral part of municipal budgets, criminal proceedings perpetuated the system of tolerated vice.[113] To redress the limitations of criminal law, anti-
vice reformers argued that the civil courts of equity were the appropriate arena
for squashing commercialized vice.[114] Under equity, anti-vice reformers could
make the partnerships behind brothels—landlords, management companies, sub-
lessors, and furniture owners—more culpable for the persistent illicit use of their
property than the madams who merely managed the houses.[115] Reformers' economic analogies worked. In case after case, anti-vice reformers successfully shifted
disorderly house litigation from the criminal courts to the civil courts of equity.[116]

Red-light abatement laws included several procedural advantages. The primary advantage of equity adjudication was that lawyers started civil proceedings to
stop the misuse of property in the future, not just punish criminal acts in the
past.[117] In practice, this distinction meant that prosecutors did not need to prove to
the judge whether property owners knew how their tenants had used their property.[118] Indeed, landlords needed to show their good faith to the court by immediately evicting their tenants and filing a substantial monetary bond to guarantee
their good behavior.[119] If the owners and their agents did not respond quickly
enough to the initial injunction, the state would oust the current tenants, auction
off the furniture and fixtures, padlock the property for up to a year, and perma-
nently prohibit its use as a brothel or saloon.[120] To prevent corrupt politicians from
obviating the red-light abatement laws, state legislators empowered private citizens, as well as public servants, to start injunction and abatement proceedings.[121]
These legal threats were potent. Since they were civil proceedings, judges, not
juries, heard red-light abatement cases, thus circumventing the "whims" of popular opinion.[122] As an action in equity, injunction and abatement required that the
"vested interests" change their practices or forfeit their property.[123] The beauty of
these laws, as Bascom Johnson, the head of the American Social Hygiene Association's legal department, observed, was that they turned former enemies into formi-
dable allies.[124]

Even more importantly, the red-light abatement acts united anti-vice re-

formers across the country. Progressive reformers believed that through the injunction and abatement laws they could fulfill two of their most important goals:
to destroy the segregation of vice and prevent its "scatteration" into the rest of the
city.[125] Unlike the Mann Act, red-light abatement worked extremely well. By
making landlords, real estate agents, furniture companies, and breweries responsible for the use of their property, anti-vice reformers cut into the profits of prostitution and pushed old-fashioned parlor houses into near extinction.[126] By 1917,
urban reformers had closed the segregated districts in over eighty cities, including
the entrenched tenderloins in Buffalo, New York, Omaha, Nebraska, Duluth,
Minnesota, and Portland, Oregon.[127] With vigilance, urban reformers believed
that they could solve scatteration. When madams tried to dodge a district's closure
and relocate to other sections of the city, anti-vice reformers pursued the landlords
in those parts of town.[128] The empowerment of ordinary citizens, combined with
the absence of a jury trial, meant that through the red-light abatement laws,
Progressives sidestepped government officials, overrode popular toleration of prostitution, and effectively challenged the tacit localization of red-light districts.

The white slavery scare changed the way Americans prosecuted urban vice.
When the Progressives shifted responsibility for commercialized prostitution from
the prostitute to the profiteers who exploited her, the Progressives not only reas-
signed culpability rhetorically, they also redefined responsibility juridically. To
punish pimps and the "partners" profiting from prostitution, anti-vice reformers
used their economic interpretation of urban vice to rewrite the law in innovative
ways. Through the commerce clause, labor laws, and the courts of equity, Progressive reformers implicated the previously unindicted and effectively extended the
range of anti-vice enforcement. Both the Mann Act and the red-light abatement
laws established important case precedents that allowed legislators to redefine the
acceptable limits of government intervention. With red-light abatement laws,
Progressive reformers introduced the legislative precursor to the property forfeitures of today's war on drugs, while the enforcement apparatus that the Justice
Department created following the passage of the Mann Act established the institutional base for the Federal Bureau of Investigation.[129] The Vice Trust metaphors
were overdetermined, and the white slavery narratives were often hyperbolic, but
the legal legacy of the Progressives' economic critique of commercialized vice
changed criminal justice in the United States.

_ↄ ↄ_

In retrospect, the images of the Vice Trust, the red-light district as company town,
and white slavery are overblown. Even during the Progressive era, many observers

debated the merit of the analogies drawn. White slavery activists, however, used these interlinking metaphors for a particular purpose: the decommercialization of vice. Progressive-era reformers sought to curtail the business of vice for precisely the same reason that they sought to regulate other businesses; they believed that the search for profit drove businesses to incite people's inherent tendency to excess. Understanding that the purpose of the anti-vice movement was to destroy the business of vice explains an apparent contradiction between reformers' words and their actions. The Progressives pursued a program that, despite their rhetorical concern for victimized women, materially worsened the lives of prostitutes.[130] By this measure, the anti-vice reformers' efforts indisputably failed. If reformers intended to destroy the economy of the red-light districts, and not improve prostitutes' circumstances, then a different conclusion emerges. The Progressive-era movement was often coercive, and its legislative agenda constitutionally questionable, but by 1918, urban prostitution was less commercial, more furtive, and less lucrative than it had been at the beginning of the century. Anti-vice reformers did not eradicate prostitution, and they did not emancipate women, but by closing the tolerated vice districts, Progressive reformers thoroughly restructured urban sociability and successfully reduced the volume and visibility of organized prostitution.

CHAPTER FIVE

The War on Vice,
1910–1919

The economic critique of commercialized vice gave the Progressive era movement its intellectual coherence. It also set its programmatic agenda: closing
down the segregated red-light districts found in most cities across the country. To
achieve this goal, reformers worked nationally to build an anti-district consensus,
but in the seven years before the United States entered the First World War, the
most difficult battles for anti-vice reformers occurred in the city-by-city fight to
close and keep closed the once-tolerated tenderloins. Through municipal vice
commissions, Progressive reformers exposed the unalloyed greed of those who
lived off of the ill-gotten proceeds of commercialized vice. At the same time,
reformers used the commissions' reports to debunk the argument that urban order
required red-light districts. A powerful weapon on the local level, vice commissions also served a purpose nationally. The findings of each commission received
press coverage across the country. Through this publicity, what happened in one
locality affected the reform movement in other places. Urban leaders in successive cities closed their districts to show their solidarity with the national quest for
morally clean municipalities, but they also embraced anti-vice reform as an integral element in the competition between municipalities to prove their city's civic
superiority.

The sporting world resisted the clamp-down on disreputable leisure, but as public opinion turned against vice districts, the sporting class adapted to the increasingly stringent regulations governing urban entertainment. By first targeting brothels, anti-vice reformers effectively used red-light abatement laws to eliminate the tenderloin's main draw. A concurrent crackdown on open solicitation in other district venues created further difficulties for a city's sports. Closing the districts fundamentally altered the market structure of urban vice, making it both less profitable for insiders and less accessible to outsiders seeking a good time.

On the eve of the United States' entry into World War I, anti-vice reformers could point to significant gains. Over eighty cities had abolished their tenderloins, but local initiatives had reached their limit. Persuasion only went so far, and without federal authority, anti-vice reformers struggled to convince those municipalities supporting the sporting world that red-light districts hurt their cities rather than helped them. Martial rhetoric sounded superb when mobilizing a movement, but it took an actual war to eradicate tolerated vice districts from America's cities.

MOBILIZING A MOVEMENT

Since the 1890s, urban reformers across the nation kept apprised of the happenings in other cities through private correspondence, memberships in organizations such as the National Municipal League, and subscriptions to *Charities and Commons*, renamed the *Survey* in 1909. After the formation of the American Vigilance Association in 1911, anti-vice reformers used their own national organization to track the fight against red-light districts and advise other Progressives on how to join in the battle. Despite this development, anti-vice reform remained a local issue. When reformers wished to show their commitment to the fight against red-light districts, they organized municipal vice commissions to investigate their city's immoral entertainment. Although urban Progressives participated actively in the national movement to eliminate commercial vice, they did so through local campaigns.

The Chicago Vice Commission galvanized the national movement for anti-vice reform. Mayor Fred Busse's creation of the commission in 1910 was a canny move. When accused of tolerating vice, the mayor neither denied the charges nor ordered diversionary raids; instead, he forced the reformers themselves to investigate the problem. Led by Walter T. Sumner, dean of the Episcopal Cathedral of Saints Peter and Paul, thirty prominent Chicago citizens proceeded to examine the situation in the full view, not just of the city, but of the whole country. Graham Taylor, a sociology professor at the University of Chicago, organizer of the Chi-

cago Commons Settlement House, member of the vice commission, and contributing editor to the *Survey*, used his ties to the journal to publicize the commission's findings and the political response to them.[1] Thus primed, the national
reform community awaited the publication of the Chicago Vice Commission's
report with great anticipation.

Upon its release, the report, *The Social Evil in Chicago*, garnered immediate
coverage in newspapers across the country, and its initial print run of 25,000
copies soon sold out.[2] J. Frank Chase, the secretary of the New England Watch
and Ward Society, proclaimed it a "national monument," while Walter Lippmann
condemned *The Social Evil in Chicago* as "well meaning but unmeaning."[3] In
contrast, Maude Miner, the guiding force behind the New York Probation Association, commented most presciently. She predicted that "one of the greatest
results that can follow from the study into conditions in Chicago will be that this
investigation and report will point the way to other similar investigations."[4] The
report itself presented the facts baldly, using excerpts from the investigators' accounts. With code numbers assigned to the names of people and places, the report
achieved a gloss of academic legitimacy that the more passionate white slavery
exposés lacked. As with other Progressive initiatives, the social sciences benefited
the anti-vice movement, a fact that did not escape reformers in other cities.[5] In
both its style and content, the Chicago Vice Commission report marked a turning
point in the war on vice. For years to come, anti-vice reformers would confess that
they once supported reputational segregation, but after they read *The Social Evil
in Chicago* they converted to the belief that only the annihilation of red-light
districts and the persistent repression of vice's commercial manifestations would
suffice.[6]

The resulting fervor drove the members of scattered anti-vice committees and
sex hygiene associations to create a single, national organization. In 1911, the
National Vigilance Committee joined forces with the American Purity Alliance to
create the American Vigilance Association. Based in Chicago, the Association
included veterans of the Chicago Vice Commission, notably Walter Sumner, and
stalwarts in the crusade against white slavery, such as Clifford Roe and physician
O. Edward Janney of Baltimore.[7] The AVA pledged to coordinate the national
effort to eliminate red-light districts, encourage the passage of uniform state laws
to fight the problem, and publish propaganda in support of a single sexual standard.[8] Even after the American Vigilance Association merged with the American
Federation of Sex Hygiene in 1914 and moved its headquarters from Chicago to
New York, the new American Social Hygiene Association continued to give anti-
vice investigations, legislation, and law enforcement higher priority than medical

issues like venereal diseases.[9] Although ASHA subsequently shifted its attention to ensuring the country's venereal health, at its inception, ASHA fought for the suppression of commercial vice.

The American Social Hygiene Association created a sense of community and shared purpose for its members. ASHA kept its readers current on the news from cities across the country in a monthly bulletin that came free with membership, while its quarterly journal, *Social Hygiene*, provided more in-depth articles. These publications distributed information about best practices, a service that the Association supplemented with pamphlets that members could buy to distribute locally.[10] ASHA also provided more direct and tangible aid. For example, Bascom Johnson, head of the legal department, tracked the most effective dance-hall regulations, nameplate ordinances, and red-light abatement acts. Before lobbying their respective state legislatures, local reformers consulted Johnson's legal department for advice on how to write the law in order to withstand the legal challenges sure to follow.[11] ASHA's officers ensured that the lessons learned in one locality benefited anti-vice reformers everywhere, thus building a foundation for the rising national consensus against tolerated vice.

Despite ASHA's significance, the municipal vice commission always stood as the symbolic centerpiece of the prewar movement. Convening a commission signaled a city's commitment to anti-vice reform. Between 1910 and 1917, twenty-eight cities and four states conducted investigations into vice in their localities.[12] "As soon as a town or city desires to join the campaign against commercialized vice, the American Vigilance Association will be prepared to assist it," Clifford Roe announced shortly after the AVA's formation. "The association recommends first, a careful survey and study of vice conditions similar to that made by the Vice Commission of Chicago; then, based upon a convincing and reliable report, a campaign to arouse the public conscience to its moral and civic duty."[13] In city after city, anti-vice reformers followed this template for action. They formed a commission, sponsored an investigation, wrote up a report, and proposed a set of key laws to the city council and state legislature.[14] Predictably, the reports shared a similar style and drew comparable conclusions.

This isomorphism did not, however, result merely from reformers embracing an idea whose time had come, but also because of ASHA's active role in supporting municipal vice commissions.[15] For a fee, city leaders could hire ASHA's investigative team. Led by George Kneeland, the man who spearheaded the investigations in Chicago and New York, ASHA detectives provided both credibility and competency to the commissions for which they worked.[16] Before the First World War, Lancaster, Pennsylvania, Syracuse, New York, and eleven other cities took advantage of ASHA's investigative department to further their local movement to suppress commercialized vice.[17] Indeed, the Association provided a $500 subsidy to the Lexington, Kentucky, Vice Commission to help cover the cost of its investigation.[18] Thus, even though ASHA provided an invaluable service in coordinating the assault against red-light districts and ensuring consistency in the recommendations of different vice commissions, anti-vice reform continued to operate as a locally driven, city-centered movement.

The anti-district consensus did not occur without some coercion. Over the summer of 1912, while the Atlanta Vice Commission conducted its inquiry, the *Atlanta Constitution* published anti-vice bulletins by the Men and Religion Forward Movement in order to influence the Commission's conclusions.[19] Reformers' agitation grew urgent in September, when word reached the Atlanta newspapers that the vice commissioners intended to endorse strict reputational segregation when they submitted their report to the mayor in early October.[20] Two weeks before the report's submission, after consultation with the city's ministers and the leaders of the Men and Religion Forward Movement, Chief of Police James Beavers made a preemptive strike. On 24 September 1912, he ordered all "houses of ill-repute" to close within five days.[21] The next few weeks produced a frenzy of activity as the police raided open resorts, reformers tried to rescue the women within them, and the city officials who supported segregation protested the police chief's unilateral action.[22] The vice commissioners, however, succumbed to community pressure. On the last two pages of their report, they recommended "a policy of repression" and commended Beavers. "Whatever differences of opinion might have previously existed as to the best method of handling this most difficult of all municipal problems, it is the duty of all good citizens . . . to sustain the police authorities to break up vice and crime in this city."[23] Atlanta's anti-vice reformers, with the police chief's backing, won the battle against the district's supporters. Just as importantly, Beavers's actions enabled anti-vice activists in cities across the nation to claim that all the country's vice commissions unanimously condemned red-light districts.[24]

For all its symbolic importance, a vice commission, and the publication of its report, rarely signaled the end of a city's fight against commercialized vice. Not every municipal government acted on the recommendations set forth. Nor did the problems cease when a city closed its vice district. Indeed, the vice commissions in Minneapolis, Minnesota and Hartford, Connecticut, convened after their respective cities had already eliminated their vice districts.[25] Following up on a tenderloin's closure required the cooperation of the police and the municipal courts, an uncertain prospect at best during the Progressive era.[26] In Atlanta,

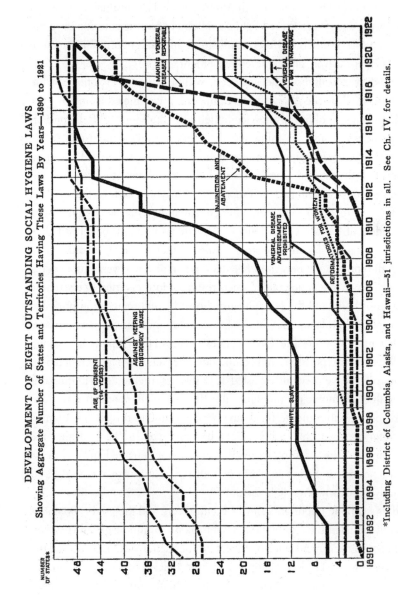

DEVELOPMENT OF EIGHT OUTSTANDING SOCIAL HYGIENE LAWS

Showing Aggregate Number of States and Territories Having These Laws By Years—1890 to 1921

*Including District of Columbia, Alaska, and Hawaii—51 jurisdictions in all. See Ch. IV. for details.

"Development of Eight Outstanding Social Hygiene Laws." The chart shows the growth of the anti-vice movement as measured by the passage of legislation. Joseph Mayer, *The Regulation of Commercialized Vice: An Analysis of the Transition from Segregation to Repression in the United States* (New York: Klebold Press, 1922), 8.

Chief Beavers lost his job as a result of his anti-vice enforcement, having alienated too many members of the city's machine.[27] Even when a municipality succeeded in closing its district, no guarantees existed that the next administration would honor the policies of its predecessor. Moreover, maintaining gains required following through on the tedious work of overseeing the new status quo. In 1915, a year after the publication of the Syracuse Moral Survey Commission's report and the closure of the city's district, Frederick Betts, the commission's chairman, observed that "the end is not yet. There will be no more spectacular events. It is a state of siege. Our aim is unchanged."[28] Nevertheless, anti-vice reformers believed that with persistence and the implementation of a few key laws, they could suppress the old-time red-light district with its wide-open brothels. Of all these laws, they considered the red-light abatement act the most important. Between 1910 and 1920, thirty-five states followed Iowa's lead and passed injunction and abatement laws that empowered private citizens to proceed against parlor houses and other places of ill repute.[29]

The passage of California's red-light abatement act involved a particularly dramatic battle. As usual, the referendum posed the greatest hurdle to its enactment, and, as usual, Northern Californians rebelled against restrictions on their personal liberties. In 1913, Los Angeles did not have a tolerated red-light district, while San Francisco boasted not just one, but three tenderloins, including the infamous Barbary Coast, which specialized in dance-hall prostitution.[30] The people of San Francisco believed so strongly in the benefits of segregated vice that they went a step further than any other municipality during these years and founded a venereal clinic in 1911 to monitor the physical health of the city's prostitutes. Although the clinic closed in 1913, after only two years in operation, its mere presence showed the depth of San Francisco's commitment to the controlled toleration of prostitution.[31]

The vote on the red-light abatement law reflected Northern Californians' opposition to anti-vice control. The bill went through the California Legislature with majority support in 1913, but the vote fell along strict regional lines. Out of the eighty-seat Assembly, seventeen voted against the bill, with twelve of those seventeen coming from San Francisco. Similarly, in the forty-seat Senate, five of the eleven who voted against the bill represented that city's constituents.[32] Despite their defeat, the bill's opponents rallied almost immediately and petitioned for a referendum.[33] California's Progressives found the situation insupportable and pledged themselves to obtaining the red-light abatement act. Nonetheless, muckraker Franklin Hichborn and other seasoned campaigners knew that such strong support from San Francisco meant yet another battle for the state's reformers.

Even as a statewide initiative, the fight for the injunction and abatement act still centered on local politics and the issue of municipal control.

After forming the California Committee for the Red-Light Abatement Law to battle the "tenderloin interests," its leaders immediately divided it into a Northern Committee and a Southern Committee, with the Tehachapi Pass as the territorial dividing line. The Southern Committee focused on making certain that supporters of the bill actually voted in the referendum, while the Northern Committee devoted its members' efforts to debunking the "astonishing misrepresentations" touted in "practically every saloon of the state, most cigar stores and barber shops, and many club centers."[34] A massive propaganda campaign followed. Over the next eleven months, the Northern Committee sent out 1,250,000 copies of four pamphlets to rally support for the injunction and abatement act.[35] Nor did matters rest there. Members of the organization combed through California's newspaper for articles that supported segregation and derided the red-light abatement bill. "Upon the notification of the publication of such an article, if it contained misstatements, the committee at once took the matter up with the editor of the paper, giving him the facts, well-backed by examples." If the newspaper persisted in its opposition to the law, the Committee contacted its supporters within the community and gave them the "data for effective refutation . . . and to show the publisher where he was in error."[36] This barrage of information produced results, and in 1914, with a margin of almost 50,000 votes, the injunction and abatement bill won the referendum and became law.[37]

Hichborn and other anti-vice reformers across the country fought so hard for the red-light abatement statute because they not only saw its effective use by public officials, they also witnessed its devastating application by private citizens. Chicago's Committee of Fifteen, in particular, wielded the red-light abatement law with extraordinary virtuosity in the ongoing fight against protected vice. Incorporated in 1911 in the immediate aftermath of the Chicago Vice Commission, by 1914 the Committee of Fifteen "directed its efforts chiefly to the work of destroying market places for traffic in women."[38] More ready to call on the press than New York's Committee of Fourteen, the Chicago Committee of Fifteen used a combination of publicity and law to put pressure on Chicago's landlords. With the injunction and abatement act as their main weapon, the Fifteen conducted title searches on properties used for "immoral purposes." Notifying both the owners and then, shortly thereafter, the city's newspapers of their findings, they found the threat of exposure almost as effective as the injunction proceedings themselves in eliminating vice.[39] As Samuel Thrasher, the Committee's general secretary, reported, within the first ten months after Illinois passed the act in 1915, the Committee contacted the owners of 205 properties, warning them to change their property's use. The threat of injunction and abatement was so effective that they only took four owners to court for noncompliance.[40] The Progressives knew that reform through self-policing and self-interest had a greater chance of changing urban vice than the self-serving theatrics of pre-election crusades.

In 1917, after seven years of persistent effort, anti-vice reform reached a plateau. With the use of red-light abatement laws and the old standby of reporting liquor-license violations, Progressive anti-vice reformers focused on managing their city's morality and keeping its district closed. A problem remained, however. While ASHA could effectively advise anti-vice reformers seeking to alter their city's social policing, unless a municipality had strong community support, neither local nor national reformers had sufficient authority to break the stalemates between those who opposed and those who supported segregated vice. Over eighty-five cities embraced the new anti-district paradigm, but recalcitrant municipalities such as New Orleans, San Antonio, and San Francisco continued to run their towns wide open, blatantly disregarding national disapproval and overriding the efforts of local anti-vice advocates.[41]

THE RETRENCHMENT OF THE SPORTING WORLD

When anti-vice reformers boasted that "the old, wide-open district is closed bang tight," they meant that they had shut down their town's brothels.[42] Eliminating a city's vice district involved closing everything from the cheapest cribs to the poshest parlor houses. Every subsequent action, from forbidding mixed-sex drinking in the back rooms of saloons to requiring that all women who entered dance halls had escorts, supplemented the initial strike against brothels. Without open houses, customers did not know where to go for prostitution. As reformers intended, closing a vice district fundamentally altered the market structure of a city's commercial vice. The sporting class adapted to the changes, sometimes evading regulatory restrictions with innovative creativity, but many of its members suffered great financial losses.

The clamp-down devastated business within the vice district. Nellie Busbee, an Atlanta madam, committed suicide, damning Chief Beavers "to hell" rather than face her losses, while another madam asked the bitter rhetorical question, "Did you ever stop to think what an order to move in less than a week's time means to a woman who has $40,000 tied up down here?"[43] Two years after Syracuse's district closed, the chairman of the Moral Survey Committee boasted that an excise official "reports that on an evening not long ago he counted only three women in a group of cafés, at 11 p.m. where, one year ago, Clement Discoll, of the Bureau of Municipal Research of New York, said he could count seventy-five girls almost any evening, at the same hour."[44] Saloonkeepers who rigorously implemented a policy of men-only suffered a similar loss of business.[45] When asked, members of the sporting world agreed that they had not received "a square deal."[46]

Prostitution did not disappear just because madams posted "for rent" signs on their brothels' front doors. Pro-district supporters often prophesied that ending segregation would result in scatteration, the spread of the sporting class into the rest of the city. Anti-vice reformers, however, argued the opposite, asserting that under segregation more prostitution existed outside the district than within it. In other words, scatteration already existed, but closing the district would shut down a city's most easily accessed source of vice.[47] Prostitutes did relocate to new venues when a district closed, but instead of deluging respectable residential districts, as segregation's advocates predicted, they moved into the cheap hotels and lodging houses of the central business district, or the dance halls, cafés, and cabarets of the adjacent white-light district.[48] Even such minor moves made life more difficult for men-about-town. Without an obvious destination, customers struggled to fulfill their quest for pleasure. Madams, saloonkeepers, and other venue owners did what business they could, running things "on the q.t." and restricting their dealings to people they knew. Even when locals vouched for an outsider, strangers frequently got the brush-off and were told "nothing doing."[49] If they made an effort, seasoned sports usually discovered where their peers relocated, but outsiders and out-of-towners lacked the necessary connections.[50] When an investigator in Bridgeport, Connecticut, met some "fellows" after the closure of the city's district, he observed that "no one knew where to go. We walked for awhile, then went to (—G—) cabaret, from there to the (—E—) cabaret. Then the party broke without having been able to 'pick up' any girls."[51] The "new popular culture" benefited from the business the tenderloin lost. The fellows in Bridgeport might not have stayed at either cabaret, but as men acclimated to life without vice districts, they spent more time in such places. As a sport complained in early 1917 about Little Rock and Argenta, Arkansas, "the only choice a man has in these towns during the week is to go to the movies or else to bed—On Sundays the movies are closed."[52] When the sporting class scattered to other parts of a city, reformers succeeded in making vice both less visible and less viable. Eliminating the districts did not stop people from going out on the town, but it shifted their patronage to more respectable venues. Anti-vice activists knew that red-light abatement and license revocation would work as effectively in closing venues outside the district as they did within it. Reformers soon realized, however, that a lack of customers would drive many sports out of business before they even needed to proceed against them.[53]

In the new post-district sexual economy, both supply and demand decreased. Many prostitutes left town rather than face the insecurity of working outside a brothel. Besides the problems of inclement weather, streetwalkers lacked protection from violent johns and needed pimps to coordinate their "dates" to a greater degree than when they worked in a house. Streetwalkers and café prostitutes could charge more per trick, but they serviced fewer customers and experienced far harsher conditions while earning less money to compensate for the difficulties.[54] Since reformers usually followed the initial closure of the brothels with subsequent restrictions to clean up the venues of disreputable leisure, independent prostitutes never knew if dance-hall managers or café proprietors would cease tolerating their presence. Similarly, hotel owners offered no guarantees that they would continue to rent their rooms to sporting women.[55] Even when prostitutes worked through a call house, they earned less money than they would in an open parlor house. Running their business quietly, with no women residing in the apartments, call-house madams coordinated far fewer transactions. Men needed insiders to vet them, and then they usually waited either a couple of hours or maybe even until the next day to meet a woman.[56] Many men decided that the difficulties in finding prostitutes outweighed the pleasure of having sex with them. As a rule, these complications made vice more expensive for customers, less profitable for prostitutes and resort owners, and generally required a degree of discretion at odds with the sporting ethos.

When they could, sports resisted the changes. Some used their connections to the machine and tried to influence municipal administrations. Others decided to wait out this clamp-down as they had all previous crusades. Buoyed by past experience which showed that "the lid" always "tilted" back in their favor, many sports believed that they just needed to hold fast until support for the campaign waned.[57] "Wait till [sic] things get settled after this coming election. . . . My friend says they are going to oust the judge and the prosecuting attorney. Things will hum again," an out-of-work madam in Hartford, Connecticut, assured herself and her listeners. "Everybody is anxious to have the sports back again. They didn't bother anyone but gave money to the town."[58] In many cities, however, the sporting world waited with misplaced faith. The Progressive reform of urban government decreased the power of city councils and increased the importance of nonpartisan appointments to executive-branch positions, depriving the tenderloin interests of the influence they once possessed. Moreover, anti-vice reformers were themselves veteran participants in pre-election crusades. They swore that this campaign would differ from the rest, and that the gains made would outlast any particular municipal administration.

In Chicago, the city's sports deviated from a purely political approach and formed a professional association, the Chicago Hotel Keepers' Protective Association, to fight reformers. Its members attracted national attention in December 1915 after they plastered fifteen thousand posters across the city condemning the menace of paid reformers. The Association's members, for the most part owners and managers of "assignation hotels," claimed that reformers hurt Chicago's reputation and drove away conventioneers and "the travelling public" from the city.[59] Interestingly, instead of turning people against the Committee of Fifteen, the unnamed target of the broadsides, the Protective Association weakened the already-precarious reputation of smaller hotels. The Hotel Association of Chicago, which represented the city's larger hotels, repudiated the Protective Association's claims. They asserted that they had just had the "most profitable year in their history" and endorsed the Committee of Fifteen's efforts. Concurrently, the American Hotel Men's Association, which was in Chicago for its national convention, "took a strong stand against the illicit use of their buildings" and sought to prohibit smaller places, many of which tolerated prostitution on their premises, from calling their businesses hotels.[60] A year earlier, the Cook County Real Estate Board, the Chicago Real Estate Board, and the Apartment Buildings Association bolstered their own positions by declaring their solidarity with anti-vice reformers and pledging not to rent or sell to any disreputable clients.[61] Like the Brewers' cooperation with New York's Committee of Fourteen to eliminate saloon prostitution, the hoteliers hoped that their advocacy of Progressive values would increase their standing within the business world. Even if they lost a percentage of their profits, repudiating the sporting class improved their status and forestalled external regulation.[62] Once again, self-policing, a professional prerequisite, worked to the advantage of anti-vice reformers seeking to make the urban environment inhospitable to the sporting world.

Perhaps the most profound economic effect the new prohibitory ethos had on commercialized vice was the disaggregation of services previously provided under one roof.[63] No longer could a sporting man go to a brothel, have a couple of drinks, share a dance or two with a prostitute, then adjourn to her room, bottle of champagne in hand, and only pay the madam once for the services provided. Now, both prostitutes and customers negotiated multiple, separate transactions. When possible, streetwalkers reached accords with the police on their beat, while prostitutes who wished to work indoors sought out café and cabaret owners who would allow them to solicit in their venues for at least part of the evening.[64] But under the new post-district regulatory regime, proprietors required deniability. Prostitutes needed to act with greater decorum, make their solicitations more subtle, and generally appear more like customers than employees. Some cities demanded that women in commercial amusement resorts have male escorts, while others forbade women from moving between tables or making overtures to strangers.[65] These rules increased the importance of pimps and other male go-betweens, adding yet another layer to the independent prostitutes' daily negotiations. To succeeded in such a difficult market, sporting women sought to ensure that waiters, bartenders, and cabaret managers would send tricks to them rather than to other sporting women.[66] Even after a prostitute hooked a john, she still needed to establish her price and find a place for them to have sex. Sporting women usually worked a circuit of hotels where they knew the management tolerated transient trade.[67] Once at the hotel, the customer paid the desk clerk directly and the prostitute separately. If the man wanted a drink, he needed to buy it from a nearby saloon or from an enterprising hotel employee.[68] These separate transactions complicated the previously streamlined process of going to a brothel and getting laid. Reformers hoped that the hassles of the new regulations would drive sporting women out of the business, even as they reduced the number of customers to those truly dedicated to commercial sex.[69]

Life also changed for pimps. Besides complaining that their "humps" did not bring in the money that they once did, pimps themselves needed to work harder to ensure that their prostitutes got what little business they did.[70] In some cases, that meant finding employment as a waiter or bartender, both to supplement the family income and to act as a go-between for a prostitute and her potential customers.[71] In other cases, pimps acted as escorts in resorts that only admitted women with male partners. Once inside the venue, pimps drummed up business for their "girls," since many entertainment venues forbade women from approaching men they did not know.[72] Similarly, when former brothel prostitutes worked as singers and dancers in a cabaret, they relied on their male partners in the audience to make dates for them after the show.[73] But pimps did not remain within the confines of the sex trade. In 1912, a messenger boy from Philadelphia complained bitterly that "the pimps are taking to selling opium and cocaine, too." Before the police started closing down the parlor houses, "the night messengers used to do that business. . . . But now that the women didn't make much, the pimps are making something on the side."[74] This trend accelerated after the Harrison Narcotic Act of 1914 made it more difficult for pharmacists to sell opiates and cocaine to "recreational" users without a doctor's prescription.[75] Pimps took over this newly illicit trade, profiting from the higher prices they could charge tenderloin addicts. In a few years' time, after the passage of National Prohibition, these same men would move into bootlegging. For the moment, they scrambled to replace the income they once received from district prostitutes.

Rather than fight the ever-increasing restrictions, many prostitutes, pimps, gamblers, and other people with little local investment relocated when a city closed its district.[76] A significant portion of the sporting class usually came from the immediate region, but more often than not, a good percentage came from elsewhere. For example, in Newark, New Jersey, although less than 10 percent of the prostitutes interviewed by the vice commission were immigrants, over three-quarters of the 102 women questioned came from outside of the city. Even in cities with less-mobile populations, approximately one-half to two-thirds of the sporting women had already moved at least once in their search for better opportunities.[77] If a town grew too dead and their profits too meager, sporting men and women went to places with better prospects. As a Hartford waiter observed, "the girls will have to hunt new hunting grounds or starve."[78] One woman's quest for financial success took her from Louisville, Kentucky, to Portland, Oregon, via the Hawaiian Islands.[79] Most sports, however, took less circuitous routes. Other Portland madams came from Chicago, San Francisco, Spokane, and Lincoln, Nebraska.[80] Nevertheless, with the closure of the districts, an already-mobile population started traveling with even greater frequency.

Inevitably, when one city cracked down on vice, other cities gained the sports who left. After Atlanta closed its district, a journalist reported that most sporting women "are going to other cities. Birmingham, Macon, Memphis, New Orleans, Louisville and Richmond are the points to which a majority have emigrated."[81] Neither the resident sports nor the local reformers appreciated the in-migration. "We do not need any of these women here," a Macon madam warned Atlanta women. "There are already about 150 recognized prostitutes in Macon and that is a few too many for a city of 40,000 people."[82] Meanwhile, Macon's ministers called for a vice commission and the chief of police in Dawson, Georgia, at the urging of the mayor and city council, ordered its tenderloin's residents to leave town.[83] In more than a few cities, the sporting world's mobility caused reformers to reassess their position on segregated vice and pursue their own campaigns against red-light districts rather than harbor the influx of sports from other places.[84]

Unlike their more mobile employees, district proprietors who owned their venues stood to lose the most, but they also had the capital to fight reformers. Used to the pro forma raids by the police and the occasional arrest for keeping a disorderly house or for liquor-law violations, sporting men and women knew how to negotiate the city's criminal justice system. Red-light abatement laws, however, went through the courts of equity, which had a different set of judges and no juries ready to sympathize with the plight of small-business owners. Yet these disadvantages did not prevent brothel owners from contesting the validity of the laws.[85] Despite these challenges, reformers won both in the courts and in the red-light districts. The differences between equity and criminal law confounded most tenderloin attorneys, while the threat of padlocking a place for a year, and selling off its furnishings and fixtures, deterred even the most profligate district proprietors.

Rather than give up, some venue owners shifted the apparent purpose of their resorts. Already well-versed in exploiting the loopholes in liquor-licensing laws for maximum hours and the widest possible clientele, proprietors embarked on reconfiguring their venues yet again. Brothel owners faced the most difficulties. They could try to turn their place into a hotel or lodging house, but anti-vice reformers looked askance at such a marginal recasting of a brothel's intended purpose.[86] As a result, many madams abandoned their parlor houses. Landlords found it extremely hard to rent out the buildings, although they occasionally found "respectable colored families" willing to take up residence.[87] In contrast to sporting-house owners, saloonkeepers had more options. Turning their upstairs into separate hotels, boarding houses, or apartments, and renaming their back rooms cafés, cabarets, or grill rooms, they added exterior entrances to each of these subdivisions and closed off the interior doors that once connected the upstairs, the barroom, and the back room.[88] Owners of venues with sufficient square footage took advantage of the dance craze, hiring singers, dancers, and multipiece bands. These changes represented more than just structural renovations; they also indicated a cultural shift. As anti-vice reformers hoped, when faced with the choice between closure or toning down behavior in their resorts, many owners opted for respectability over bankruptcy.[89] Frederick Betts, chairman of the Syracuse Moral Survey Committee, reported that "the manager of the worst offender among the cafés, where once we found a pimp at the piano and from twenty-five to thirty-five girls plying their trade, is trying to run his place decently and is succeeding fairly well."[90] Although Betts's definition of success differed from that of the sporting world's, some proprietors did make a successful transition from the red-light to the white-light district.

To make this shift from disreputable to respectable, proprietors sidelined sex as the primary purpose of their venues. Vice districts had always offered a range of entertainment to draw in customers, but more often than not, these amusements provided the backdrop for the sexual flirtations that everyone knew would end in an economic exchange. In the post-district world of urban entertainment, however, no such guarantee existed that the customer would get laid or that the woman would get paid. Cabarets provide a particularly striking example of the changing social relationships. Although some prostitutes had previously worked within cabarets, they now formed part of the audience. They could still arrange business on the side, but they needed to act with greater discretion so as not to attract the attention of either the police or possible anti-vice investigators.[91] Once a mainstay of vice-district conviviality, sporting women's outrageous antics only had a place in the new post-district world when confined to the stage. Between acts, female performers still emulated the saloon prostitutes of old and encouraged drinking, but they downplayed the concomitant sexual solicitation. With rules about apparel and limits on performers interacting with patrons, managers needed to police their employees for fear of losing not just their liquor licenses, but also their dance-hall or cabaret licenses, as Progressive reformers added layers of regulation in their quest to limit transgressive recreation.[92]

The sharpening distinction between patron and performer fractured the sporting class. Although the sporting world accorded a higher status to those who worked in the district over those who played in it, the ethos they espoused emphasized the ideal of equality through pleasure. Everybody should have a good time together. Seasoned prostitutes, youths just off the farm, shop girls sporting on their night out, gamblers dealing stuss, fat-cat politicians glad-handing their constituents—all of them belonged to the sporting world if they so chose. But when proprietors and performers could no longer mix with their patrons, and women could not enter venues without a male escort, the easy intermingling that the sporting ethos prized became as much of an anachronism as the open parlor house.

On the eve of World War I, urban entertainment stood in the balance. In the cities where reformers had successful clamped down on commercialized vice, the newly configured entertainment districts showcased the possibilities of more respectable recreation. The sporting world adapted to the new regulatory circumstances with resilience, but the creativity with which its members eluded reformers' restrictions did not hide a fundamental restructuring of the sex trade. Disaggregating services previously offered as part of a package made prostitution more difficult for both sporting women and their customers. In order to stay in business, resort owners shunted sexual solicitation to the sidelines and emphasized other types of entertainment. This shift in focus disrupted the old continuum linking respectable and disreputable leisure. Thrilled with the successes of their economic and cultural manipulations, anti-vice reformers pledged themselves to changing urban entertainment across the country. World War I provided the ideal opportunity to realize their vision. With the authority of the War Department behind them, anti-vice reformers crushed their political opposition and overrode local compromises concerning the acceptable parameters of commercial leisure.

GOING TO WAR

The United States mobilized for World War I with lightning speed. Even while ostensibly still a neutral nation, government officials and private citizens readied themselves for war. In their preparations, America's anti-vice reformers looked to the 1916 border conflict with Mexico to predict the moral readiness of the army. Newton Baker, the newly appointed Secretary of War, sent Raymond Fosdick, one-time Commissioner of Accounts of New York City, author of *European Police Systems*, and future president of the Rockefeller Association, to determine the truth of rumors about drunken revelry among the troops.[93] What Fosdick and subsequent investigators saw disgusted them. Border towns already had a reputation for raucous red-light districts, but the tenderloins of southwestern cities such as Douglas, Arizona, El Paso, Texas, and Columbus, New Mexico, exceeded even the most dire expectations of debauchery. Barely able to keep up with demand, enterprising members of the sporting world, many of whom gravitated to the region in hopes of a quick profit from the troops, erected cheap, shoddily built cribs and saloons to service the soldiers.[94] Later, Fosdick recalled that the "red-light districts . . . were crowded with hundreds of troops and drunken riots which were not infrequent had to be suppressed by the Provost Guard. Meanwhile the venereal disease rates were soaring."[95] Swearing that such scenes would not replay during a mass mobilization of troops, the United States' top anti-vice reformers plotted how to safeguard the moral and physical health of new recruits.[96] To that end, Newton Baker devised the idea of a Commission on Training Camp Activities (CTCA) that would provide "wholesome" amusement to the troops even as it suppressed less-acceptable recreation.

When Congress issued the Selective Service Act on 18 May 1917, it included the infamous Sections 12 and 13, which empowered the War Department to effect the coercive side of Baker's plan. Section 12 prohibited the sale of alcohol to soldiers and allowed for the establishment of dry zones around the camps. Similarly, Section 13 authorized the secretary of war "to do everything by him deemed necessary to suppress and prevent the keeping or setting up of houses of ill fame, brothels, or bawdy houses within such distance as he deem needful of any military camp."[97] Baker set five miles as the radius for the dry zone and ten miles as the radius within which no prostitution could exist; however, as he warned the mayors in cities near cantonments, the War Department would not tolerate "any restricted district" or "places of bad repute" outside the zones yet "within easy reach of the camp."[98] Quite a few resort-keepers protested the War Department's authority to interfere with local vice control, but the federal courts, to which the members of the sporting class appealed, saw the matter differently. In successive cases, judges decided that "war powers" superseded the states' "police power."[99] Once formed, the Commission on Training Camp Activities had the right to dictate moral standards to both soldiers and civilians for the duration of the war.

Ordered to expunge all disreputable entertainment within reach of the training camps and to replace it with more socially acceptable alternatives, the CTCA embodied both the constructive and destructive sides of Progressive reform. Raymond Fosdick, now in charge of the CTCA, relied heavily on already-existing organizations when he implemented the Commission's programs. Joseph Lee, president of the Playground and Recreation Association of America, John R. Mott, the general secretary of the International Committee of Young Men's Christian Associations, and Lee F. Hanmer of the Russell Sage Foundation served as three of the eight commissioners under Fosdick.[100] In addition to working with the CTCA, these men brought with them the people and resources of their organizations. Similarly, many of ASHA's employees moved into the army, continuing the type of work they did before the war.[101] For example, Bascom Johnson, the influential head of ASHA's legal department, ran the law-enforcement division of the new Commission. To do his job, he regularly worked with ASHA's investigative team and frequently tapped into the resources of the local reform associations that had previously turned to ASHA's legal department for advice on fighting commercialized vice.[102] Even some of the CTCA's funds originated from the same sources that supported the prewar movement. The Rockefeller Foundation donated $200,000 to the Playground and Recreation Association of America for its programs at the cantonments and $100,000 to the CTCA for educating the troops about venereal disease and for stamping out vice near the camps. Out of that $100,000, the Foundation specified that $20,000 cover the salaries of ASHA personnel working for the CTCA.[103] In the CTCA, some of the Progressive era's most influential anti-vice reformers came together to fight for their long-held dream of destroying tolerated vice districts. Programs, people, networks, and funding recapitulated the old private associations, but now anti-vice reformers had the power of the federal government to back their agenda.

With a ready-made organizational infrastructure, the CTCA wasted little time implementing its plans. As the Playground Association and the American Library Association supplied the camps with sports equipment and books, ASHA's investigators did what they knew best: finding out whether a municipality tolerated a vice district, determining the accessibility of a city's disreputable venues, and evaluating the likelihood of "keeping the lid on" after an initial cleanup.[104] Some cities anticipated the War Department's objections and made preemptory strikes against the sporting world. Indeed, Shreveport closed its district in the hopes of attracting a training camp to the area.[105] But other municipal leaders protested the CTCA's demands. Southern officials, in particular, resisted abandoning reputational segregation. As one ASHA investigator observed about Macon, Georgia, "from the patrolman in Tybee (the old district) to the mayor and the state's solicitor general, every official thought the government was making a great mistake to close the district."[106] The CTCA had powerful leverage, however. If a city refused to eliminate its red-light district, the government would remove the camp from the vicinity.[107] With camps averaging over nine thousand soldiers when operating at their minimum capacity and almost thirty-nine thousand soldiers when working at their maximum, even the most ardent supporters of segregated vice renounced their principles in favor of the business the armed forces brought to town.[108] "We are under no illusions as to some of the motives back of this," four of San Diego's leading reformers wrote to Newton Baker, "but we are very glad to have it so."[109] In the end, all of the major cities complied with the War Department's order to close their districts, even New Orleans. From July 1917 to September 1918, over a hundred cities eliminated their tenderloins, resolving longstanding stalemates between reformers and the political machines that had kept the red-light districts open.[110]

The two main aims of anti-vice reform—keeping the districts closed and cleaning up urban amusement—did not change during the war, but the movement's rhetoric altered radically. When prostitution did not disappear, despite the closure of the districts, and soldiers continued to have sex, the training camp commissioners stopped blaming the commercializers of prostitution and started blaming the women themselves.[111] By ordering men to "keep away from prostitutes priced and private," the CTCA made money irrelevant to a woman's reputation as a whore.[112] Indeed, the disgust reformers leveled against charity girls and "patriotic prostitutes" exceeded their antipathy for professional prostitutes. At least the monetary motive of the professionals made sense, but the " 'khaki mad' girl" who gave away sex for a night on the town could not even plead poverty as an excuse for her actions.[113] H. L. Mencken parodied the shift in discourse when he lampooned the dangers posed by "predatory country girls," but neither Frederick Whitin nor Raymond Fosdick saw the humor. Indeed, Fosdick dismissed Mencken as "a superficial writer with no ideas" whose attack on the CTCA did not deserve a reply. Unfortunately, even though Mencken honed in on the contradictions of the Commission's propaganda with his characteristic insight, Fosdick correctly judged the idiosyncrasy of Mencken's opinion.[114] During the war, anti-vice reformers stopped describing prostitution as an institutional problem based on the economic exploitation of innocent women and started blaming women for men's sexual adventuring.

Focusing on the health of the recruits medicalized the anti-vice movement. Reformers abandoned the interlocking economic arguments against the Vice Trust and began defining prostitution as a medical problem of diseased individuals, specifically disease-spreading women.[115] From the CTCA's perspective, all women who had sex with soldiers, for whatever reason, deserved the severest censure. After all, as one wartime pamphlet explained, if a woman was "willing to 'give you a good time,'" she must "have either [the] clap or syphilis or both."[116] Thus, even though statistics showed that more women named soldiers as the source of their infection than the reverse, the CTCA insisted on classifying women as the "carriers of venereal disease" and soldiers as their target for contagion.[117] Reducing women to disease vectors discounted the structural causes of commercialized vice, but even more importantly, it legitimated a virulent misogyny that allowed government authorities to treat women with a callous disregard for their civil liberties.

The new contempt toward sexually active women not only permeated War Department propaganda, it also affected the CTCA's administrative structure. In September 1917, Raymond Fosdick ordered the creation of a Committee on the Protective Work for Girls to address the issue of "young girls" in the neighborhood of the military camps. He envisioned the Committee addressing "reformative problems" as a means of preventing "an increase in delinquency."[118] Headed by Maude Miner, nationally renowned advocate of probation and parole, the CPWG aimed to protect impressionable young women from the "lure of the uniform" and the soldiers who would take advantage them.[119] With protective workers posted to the vicinity of the camps, the CPWG policed places of amusement for "dangerous intimacies," and when they found girls succumbing to soldiers' charms, the Committee proposed "to study the personal problems of the girl, to awaken her to the foolhardiness of her course, and when possible to give her new, wholesome interests."[120] As initially planned, protective workers hoped to reform the girls' self-destructive tendencies, but within six months of the Committee's formation, the CTCA forced the CPWG to abandon such idealism. Dismantling the Committee, the CTCA eschewed protective work for girls and focused on the protection of boys: the troops.[121]

In April 1918, the CTCA established the Section of Women and Girls in the commission's Law Enforcement Division.[122] The new section treated "promiscuous" women with draconian severity. Where once the CTCA did not care where sexually active women went, as long as they left the vicinity of the camps, now they insisted upon their imprisonment, when practicable.[123] In the pamphlet *Next Steps*, written to advise communities on what to do after the closure of their vice districts, Bascom Johnson asked and answered the following questions: "How can we protect young girls? . . . By providing detention houses. . . . How can we make prostitutes hard to find? By internment in State reformatories, etc."[124] The money for the detention facilities came from President Wilson's War Emergency Fund. He allotted $250,000 to the CTCA either to renovate existing buildings or construct new ones.[125] In an irony that went unrecognized at the time, when section workers sought buildings suitable for detaining the diseased women, they sometimes found that abandoned parlor houses provided the best accommodations. With large reception rooms, many bedrooms, and a disproportionately high number of bathrooms, brothels made ideal detention houses. Government contractors usually only needed to fit the brothel with an infirmary and add a high wall topped with barbed wire to complete the conversion.[126] In the prewar white slavery narratives, reformers elaborated on the economic imprisonment of innocent women, pleading forgiveness for society's prodigal daughters, but during the war they made the metaphor real by confining women in sporting houses as punishment for their sexual transgressions.

According to the new strictures, both the military and civilian police could apprehend anyone they suspected of suffering from venereal disease. Moreover, any woman arrested for a sexually related offense underwent a mandatory medical examination. If a woman's tests came back negative, her case proceeded through the normal channels of criminal justice. But if she suffered from venereal disease, the authorities sent her to a reformatory or to a detention house, depending on the presumed malleability of her character. Jettisoning *habeas corpus*, the CTCA held women on indeterminate-length sentences, until doctors pronounced them cured. In many states, the disease-free women then returned to court to face the original charges leveled against them.[127] Women's constitutional rights mattered little in the quest to protect soldiers from venereal infection.

Over the course of the war, the CTCA interned 15,520 women in federally funded reformatories and detention houses. The length of stay averaged a year in reformatories and ten weeks in detention houses.[128] But these figures only hinted at the impact of the CTCA's new policies. Federal officials did not count women incarcerated in local jails or quarantined in local hospitals when they tallied the number of women interned during the war. For example, in Puerto Rico, authorities arrested over a thousand women on vice-related charges from the beginning of July 1918 to the beginning of January 1919. Of these, they convicted and confined 809 women. In addition, the U.S. District Court found 58 women guilty of sex offenses and ordered them imprisoned in Puerto Rican jails. These arrests and convictions resulted directly from War Department policy. In contrast, between 1917 and 1918, the Puerto Rican jails housed an average of 790 prisoners at any given time, of which only 25 to 30 were women.[129] The internment of diseased women altered the lives of thousands, but their punishment represented only the most extreme consequence of the new antipathy toward women.

Official misogyny and the demonization of sexually active women, whether prostitutes or "uniform-crazed" girls, sanctioned a street-level disregard for women's self-determination. In the entertainment venues of the prewar vice district, women initiated sexual solicitations more often then men. Outside of brothels, both men and women could approach each other with impunity, but women usually determined both the price and place of the sexual exchange. The closure of the districts, and the wartime crackdown on female promiscuity, created a new social distance between men and women, with men now brokering sexual meetings. During the war, men started talking about women differently. In the commercial dance halls and cabarets where they gathered in search of sex, men reduced women in their conversations to objects of exchange incapable of agency. The change in market negotiations, combined with female deference toward enlisted men, precipitated a sharp decline in women's status.

The Commission on Training Camp Activities' reforms disrupted long-term gender dynamics in urban recreation. Men and women participating in urban nightlife adopted new social scripts, scripts that shifted the power to initiate sexual negotiations from women to men. Wartime repression and the closure of the districts caused many prostitutes to mute their professional signifiers, making it more difficult for men to judge whether someone was, in their words, "out for the sugar" or just wanted a "good time."[130] As a result, soldiers, sailors, investigators, and ordinary customers turned to male insiders to decipher the sexual codes of a particular dance hall or cabaret and categorize the women around them. Since regulations frequently forbade men from approaching women they did not know, men relied on waiters, bartenders, and managers to inform them which women were "charity girls" and which ones were "money girls." Then, if a man seemed like a "good fellow" and a heavy tipper, a waiter would "stake" him to a woman.[131] To reassure their customers that a charity girl was a "regular fellow" who would "go the limit," the waiter would tell the interested party that he, or someone else he knew, "had made her."[132] Besides telling their customers which women offered sex willingly, bartenders also coached customers on how quickly they could push a woman for sex. An evening with a charity girl cost less, especially since managers made sure to warn their customers if the women who interested them were "bleeders," a term that denoted women's economic exploitation of men, even as it connoted their sexual unavailability because of menstruation.[133] Although not pimps per se, waiters, bartenders, doormen, and managers facilitated other men's search for sex by labeling the women around them.

During the war, men's sexual objectification of women manifested itself most clearly in their profanity. In a noticeable discursive shift, men started referring to women by their sex organs. For example, in March 1917, one New York City waiter in an Eighth Avenue venue observed that "there aint one girl that remains here at this hour that aint 'C——t' . . . they are all hall way rubs."[134] Another declared that "there is so much gash around that he is sick of it."[135] Indeed, by 1919, waiters and their male patrons had reduced these exchanges to a kind of shorthand, with "gash" or "cunt" as an umbrella term to describe all sexually willing women. Only then would they go on to qualify which women were prostitutes ("hustlers," "whores," or "gold diggers") and which women were only out for a "good time" ("charity," "charity bums," or "charity gash").[136] More women could participate in the cleaned-up cabarets and dance halls without irrevocably damaging their individual reputations, but the virulence of the wartime campaigns against sexually active women encouraged a marked misogyny.[137]

When men in the dance halls lumped all the women around them under the category of cunt, they followed the lead of the Commission on Training Camp Activities, which set the tone by describing all sexually willing women as "dirty sluts."[138] Like male waiters and their customers, the CTCA elided social distinctions for venereal distinctions. The men in the dance halls reduced women to "gash," but training camp officials reduced women to a "dirty dose."[139] The CTCA reinforced this symbolic diminishment of women through metaphors that compared sexually willing, *ergo* venereally diseased, women to any other object or animal that spread death and disease: German bullets, malarial mosquitoes, venomous vipers, and, in the most extreme version of women as a disposable object, other men's toothbrushes.[140] The vilification of women in wartime propaganda gave official sanction to men's objectification of the women they met in dance halls and other heterosocial arenas. Although the misogynistic propaganda from World War I was ephemeral, what would remain from the War Department's campaign against women was men's ready reduction of all women to their sex organs.

With the closure of the districts during World War I, the anti-vice movement lost both its programmatic and its conceptual cohesion. With an increasing focus on social hygiene, in particular the venereal health of newly drafted soldiers, anti-vice reformers stopped seeing prostitutes as innocent white slaves and started viewing them as diseased predators.[141] These wartime portrayals repudiated the Progressive-era characterizations of prostitutes, a discursive reversal made possible because Progressive-era anti-vice reformers had never fully redeemed the white slave. When they incorporated anti-trust metaphors into their rhetoric, the white slavery writers adopted anti-monopolism's systemic critique, but they never embraced its republicanism. Without virtue, prostitutes could never be citizens. By denying prostitutes their rights, social-hygiene reformers turned prostitutes from blameless victims into self-conscious sexual psychopaths.

--- C̃ C̃ ---

At the end of World War I, reformers congratulated themselves on a job well done. The American troops maintained the lowest venereal infection rates of all the combatants, and, at home, the CTCA succeed in closing, and keeping closed, the red-light districts in all of America's major cities, and more than a few of its minor ones as well. These successes came at a cost, however. Federal intervention ignored local politics and local compromises. The CTCA forced a single sexual morality on communities across the country, despite a diversity of opinion regarding the management of urban entertainment. Ironically, this emphasis on the venereal health of the troops encouraged a resurgence of the double standard for men and women. No longer seen as innocent victims of male exploiters, women now bore the responsibility for corrupting men morally and physically. The War Department chided soldiers for their sexual peccadilloes and forced them to undergo painful prophylactic treatment, but, when possible, the CTCA arrested and imprisoned the women with whom soldiers had intercourse.

Not all Progressives endorsed this change in policy. Maude Miner resigned rather than remain associated with the CTCA's punitive programs.[142] Some women, such as Ethel Sturges Dummer and Jessie Binford, stayed on, but they did so in the hopes that they could ameliorate the impact of the new policies.[143] They found themselves in a small minority. Most male reformers and many female reformers, especially those with medical experience, supported the quarantining of infectious women and the prophylactic treatment of sexually active soldiers. To them, the American Plan made infinite sense.[144] Yet to anyone who knew the history of international anti-vice reform, the plan rankled. That ASHA, a successor to the American Purity Association—an organization founded in solidarity with Josephine Butler's crusade against the British Contagious Diseases

Acts—supported the venereal inspection and incarceration of diseased women in order to protect the health of soldiers and sailors proved a bitter irony. After all, Butler and her allies fought for over fifteen years for the repeal of just such a policy. When challenged, the CTCA and its defenders protested that the American Plan and the Contagious Diseases Acts in no way resembled each other because the CTCA did not issue women with medical certificates, but opponents to the plan found the argument specious.[145] Nevertheless, public health and the arrest of errant individuals dominated the efforts against prostitution in the postwar period.

The anti-vice movement stagnated after demobilization. The League of Women Voters joined forces with male Progressives after the passage of the Nineteenth Amendment, guaranteeing women's suffrage, to ensure that the red-light districts did not reopen.[146] As old-time tenderloins appeared increasingly anachronistic, and relatively reputable entertainment absorbed the former patrons of the districts' tawdry amusements, anti-vice reformers believed that they had achieved the movement's aims. The sporting class lost its cultural coherence, parlor houses no longer dominated notorious thoroughfares, and streetwalkers and café prostitutes eked out a precarious existence at the criminal margins of society. The Eighteenth Amendment—National Prohibition—not only closed saloons, it also closed their back rooms, the standby for prostitutes going through tough times. But National Prohibition brought with it a myriad of new problems. Organized crime replaced commercialized vice as the greatest obstacle to urban order.

CHAPTER SIX

The Syndicate

Prohibition and the Rise of Organized Crime, 1919–1933

Neither the sporting class nor anti-vice reform survived World War I intact. Anti-vice reform, which started as a city-based movement to fight urban political corruption, had turned into a national initiative to eliminate brothels and close down red-light districts. With the power of the federal government behind it, the Commission on Training Camp Activities overrode local sentiment and ended a twenty-year attempt by municipalities to control urban vice through geographic segregation. Many reformers, having finally achieved their goals, either retired from the fight or shifted their focus elsewhere, only renewing their interest when they feared a city might reinstitute the practice of segregating vice.

Just as the anti-vice movement fragmented, so too did the sporting world. Prostitution, gambling, and drinking continued in cities across the United States, but when the federal government closed the districts, the sporting world lost the geographic concentration that gave it its cultural cohesion. Sports valued visibility, even as they relied on their electrically lit excesses to draw customers into the district. Yet, as sociologist Henry Zorbaugh observed retrospectively in 1929, wartime policies drove vice behind "closed doors and drawn blinds."[1] Displaced from open brothels, prostitutes moved into saloons, dance halls, hotels, and caba-rets, but even these minor relocations made it more difficult for prostitutes to meet customers. Soon, with the passage of National Prohibition, the sporting class could no longer even linger in saloons, the second cornerstone of its culture. Jazz-Age revelers embraced the subterfuge of speakeasies, closed clubs, and rent parties; however, old-time sports defined themselves through their overt, everyday rejection of respectable norms. Without brothels and saloons—the essential commercial institutions of their society—the members of the sporting class lost both their audience and the stage on which they had proudly flaunted their disreputable way of life. Secrecy strengthens some cultures, but it destroyed the sporting world.

Prohibition also shattered the precarious control the remaining anti-vice reformers maintained on urban social order. Even before its passage, some reformers predicted the devastating effect that a bone-dry policy would have on fighting commercial vice. Yet, despite the fact that many anti-district reformers did not support Prohibition, Prohibition stands as the quintessence of early-twentieth-century moral reform. Certainly, the anti-vice movement influenced both the passage of the Eighteenth Amendment and the enforcement of National Prohibition. The 1919 Volstead Act, which defined the parameters of Prohibition, drew on the regulatory rationale informing both the Mann Act of 1910 and the Harrison Narcotic Act of 1914.[2] Moreover, the experiences of the Federal Bureau of Investigation and the Treasury Department, which administered the Harrison Act, combined with the example set by the Commission on Training Camp Activities, appeared to prove not only that the federal government could successfully mandate moral standards, but that it could also enforce something as momentous as National Prohibition. Finally, the Draft Act of May 18, 1917, enabled the Commission on Training Camp Activities both to close tolerated tenderloins (Section 13) and enact wartime prohibition (Section 12).[3] The intersection of these influences means that the history of the red-light districts' closure remains forever tied to the impact of the Eighteenth Amendment on urban vice.

The closure of the vice districts fundamentally altered America's cityscape at the same time that Prohibition irrevocably changed the economics of vice. Law-enforcement officials, however, continued to work within the conceptual framework of anti-vice reform in their pursuit of liquor-law violators. Anti-vice policies were uniform and national, as Progressive reformers had wished, but their enforcement, whether competent or incompetent, exceeded the influence of private reform associations. The cities' political machines continued to cooperate with crime bosses, yet urban reformers, having turned to the federal government to crush local stalemates, could no longer broker compromises with municipal officials to counterbalance the corrupt alliances between ring politicians and the purveyors of vice. Thus, the anti-trust rhetoric that enabled the federal government to close the red-light districts, and the regulatory armature that reform politicians created with the help of that rhetoric, nationalized policing and organized crime.[4]

MAKING A KILLING

The Vice Trust served as a powerful metaphor in anti-district propaganda, but in one of the great ironies of urban reform, the enforcement infrastructure that anti-vice reformers developed to fight this fictive construction resulted in the development of true crime cartels. The passage of the Eighteenth Amendment opened up monopoly opportunities within urban vice inconceivable in the loosely organized markets of the prewar vice districts. In the 1920s, a few prescient individuals from the sporting class took control of the illicit liquor trade. By controlling the alcohol supply to disreputable entertainment venues, canny district operators such as Johnny Torrio in Chicago, Arnold Rothstein in New York, and Max Hoff in Philadelphia created highly lucrative crime cartels. These syndicates kept the price of alcohol up and competition among different bootlegging gangs down. They subordinated the once-powerful district proprietors, creating whole new hierarchies of underworld prestige, as they dictated from whom venue owners would buy their alcohol and at what price. Prohibition changed the organization and economics of illicit enterprise.[5]

Prior to the ratification of the Eighteenth Amendment in 1919, the business of vice was profitable, but not disproportionately so, when compared to reputable commercial recreation. Most vice-district proprietors, both male and female, ran their businesses with varying degrees of success, yet no one, even if he or she owned a string of brothels, dance halls, and popular cafés, made the kind of fortunes that middle-level gangsters amassed during Prohibition.[6] Ada and Minna Everleigh, who owned the Chicago Levee's poshest brothel before Prohibition, reportedly earned $100,000 annually, while Johnny Torrio, who became one of the city's most powerful gangsters in the 1920s, managed a dollar house with seven women for "Big Jim" Colosimo in Chicago's Levee. In one week in 1912, he netted approximately $300, including the sale of beer, a comfortable but not spectacular sum.[7] As independent entrepreneurs, district proprietors achieved high status through political connections and their reputations as "good fellows," not through the economic control of the district.

In the 1920s, however, as power shifted from venue proprietors to alcohol suppliers, urban vice turned incredibly lucrative. The sale of drinks at inflated prices had always kept district establishments in the black, but controlling the distribution of alcohol to disreputable venues brought in even more money than selling drinks to customers at sporting house prices.[8] In 1921, a relatively anonymous New York gangster called Steinberg, first name and underworld sobriquet unknown, netted a little over three-quarters of a million dollars. In 1925, the Genna gang, which controlled Chicago's Near West Side, supposedly grossed $350,000 per month from liquor sales, of which $150,000 was profit. Meanwhile, Edwin Olson, the U.S. district attorney in Chicago, estimated that the Torrio-Capone operation ran a $70 million-a-year enterprise and that Torrio and Capone each netted about $100,000 per week, quite a difference from the $300 per week Torrio earned only a decade earlier.[9] The cartelization of the illicit alcohol trade distinguished the earnings of the commercialized vice proprietors from the fortunes of organized crime bosses.

During Prohibition, cartelizing vice meant controlling the wholesale alcohol trade. Cartels are brokered agreements among businesses that keep prices up and profit-cutting competition down. Through cartels, different producers selling the same product collude to set prices, control market distribution, and prevent competitors from entering the market. In other words, cartels allow the many to act like a monopoly. This market control makes cartels extremely profitable.[10] For example, in Rockford, Illinois, in the early 1930s, Sam Capriola, Louis Dodaro, and William D'Agostin controlled the wholesale liquor supply, and whisky sold for "$6 per gallon for quantities over 100 gallons and $6.25 for lesser amounts." In Portland, Oregon, where no such cooperation among wholesalers existed, whisky sold for $3 per gallon.[11] By comparison, in 1909, mediocre whisky sold for $1.40 per gallon.[12] Cartelization came at a price, however. When the gangs succeeded in working together, they made millions, but when they fought, the winners made millions and the losing gang leaders died bloody deaths.[13]

The career of Chicago gangster Johnny Torrio illustrates the changes in commercial vice during the early twentieth century. Torrio, a Neapolitan immigrant whose involvement in the Chicago underworld spanned Clifford Roe's white slavery crusades in the early 1910s through to the bloody Beer Wars of the mid-1920s, exemplifies the possibilities for power and profit that Prohibition opened up for district men. Both gangsters and government officials believed that Torrio, the man who mentored Al Capone, changed commercial vice from a localized and entrepreneurial endeavor into an organized and wildly profitable regional cartel.

Torrio, whose parents immigrated to the United States in 1884 when he was two, started out as a numbers runner and brothel manager in Brooklyn. In 1909, already well respected and known as a peacemaker, Torrio went to Chicago when "Big Jim" Colosimo asked for his help to run off some blackmailers. Impressing

Colosimo with his tact, his intelligence, and ultimately his ruthlessness, Torrio stayed on in Chicago and began to manage Colosimo's accounts and the Saratoga, the latter's Levee resort on 22nd Street.[14] Over the next few years, Torrio saw white slavery crusader Clifford Roe take down Maurice and Julia Van Bever, owners of a brothel one block up from Colosimo's whorehouse on Armour Avenue, and witnessed Mayor Carter Harrison oust the Everleigh sisters from the district in 1911 in a fit of pique. Watching the waves of reform, including State's Attorney John Wayman's implementation of the Chicago Vice Commission's recommendation to close the Levee in 1912, Torrio decided that geographic centralization made poor business sense and that specializing in prostitution left Colosimo's ventures economically vulnerable. Colosimo was only partially convinced. Like other district proprietors, he had seen moral reform campaigns come and go. His businesses made good money, and geographic stability meant that customers knew where to find his brothels and café.[15] So Colosimo coasted, but he gave Torrio the autonomy to investigate the political climate in Chicago's suburbs. Finding corrupt, or corruptible, administrations in Burnham, Stickney, and Cicero, Torrio gambled that geographic dispersion would spread the political risk of simultaneous crackdowns, while automobiles would overcome the distance between his new venues and the Chicago residences of his customers. When World War I came, the Commission on Training Camp Activities caught other Levee proprietors flat-footed, but Torrio was more than ready.[16]

After the Armistice, when wartime prohibition went from an emergency measure to a federal amendment, Torrio approached Colosimo about buying the region's illegal breweries and establishing networks to distribute alcohol. Once again Colosimo did not see the point, and once again Torrio disagreed. This time, however, Torrio needed true authority to implement his plan, so with Colosimo unwilling to innovate, Torrio arranged his death. After Colosimo's assassination on 11 May 1920, Torrio took over the sale of illicit alcohol in the Greater Chicago area. As part of his plan, Torrio, now the uncontested boss of commercial vice, brokered a peace among the different gangs who, before the war, had idled in the saloons and pool halls of the tolerated tenderloins.[17] Where once they worked as strongarm men and strikebreakers, or relied on prostitutes to support them, district men came into their own with Prohibition. Under the watchful eye of Torrio in Chicago, Frankie Yale in Brooklyn, Charles Solomon in Boston, and Joseph Roman in Denver, these gangsters distributed alcohol to the soda shops, speakeasies, and nightclubs in their areas. They forced the proprietors of these places to buy the syndicate's liquor, and collected a percentage of the venues' take.[18] In return, the syndicate offered protection from police raids and from rivals trying to muscle in on the business. By controlling the alcohol trade in Chicago, Torrio brought the once loosely connected proprietors of gambling dens, houses of prostitution, dance halls, and pool rooms under his economic auspices. In this context of hostile takeovers and economic expansion, Torrio, needing men he could trust, invited Al Capone to come to Chicago from Brooklyn in 1920. Capone, the quintessential crime boss, came to epitomize the new underworld.[19]

If the emblematic male figure of the turn-of-the-century tenderloins was the pimp, then the gangster represented Prohibition-era vice. Like other soon-to-be-famous racketeers, including "Legs" Diamond, "Dutch" Schultz, "Greasy Thumb" Guzik, "Waxey" Gordon, and "Lucky" Luciano, "Scarface Al" Capone had worked in, yet remained economically peripheral to, the disreputable vice venues of the prewar period. Managing pool halls, pimping in dance halls, dealing stuss in gambling dens, and selling drugs in saloons, men like these participated in district society but, until Prohibition, they lacked status.[20] As they gained prestige, they embraced new gender roles at odds with the masculinity espoused by the sporting world. Where the conspicuously indolent pimp waited for his prostitutes to bring him money, the new gangster went out and made his own. Moreover, young men now made it clear to anyone who inquired that they repudiated the pimp and his way of life. When asked about available women, waiters and speakeasy managers protested that they were not "a F—ing pimp," a "cuntseller," or a "whoremaster."[21] A gangster may have had a lover, or more than one, but he supported her. The "gun moll" was now a gangster's girlfriend, not a thief in her own right.[22] Unlike the prewar pimps, these men prided themselves on being go-getters.

Journalists occasionally emphasized the background of bootleggers; however, in the 1920s, gangsters cared more about organizational viability than ethnic homogeneity.[23] Even the Torrio-Capone operation, considered the prototype of the American Mafia, included men from a wide variety of backgrounds. Indeed, Torrio and Capone both came from Naples, the home of the Camorra, not Sicily, the home of the Mafia.[24] Moreover, while Torrio and Capone collaborated with the Sicilian Genna brothers, they also crafted alliances with the WASP Joseph Stenson and the Irishmen Frankie Lake and Terry Druggan.[25] Torrio's main competitor, Dion O'Bannion, ran a mostly Irish gang, but when the latter died, first Hymie Weiss and then George "Bugs" Moran succeeded him. Weiss, despite his apparent Jewish ethnicity, was Polish, having been born Earl Wajciechowski. Moran's alias was similarly misleading. Baptized Adelard Cunin, Moran had a French-Canadian mother and a father from Alsace-Lorraine.[26] Thus even when a gang showed an apparent ethnic coherence, closer examination of its personnel revealed diverse social, if not economic, origins. This generalization also held true outside of Chicago. Bootleggers came from a wide variety of backgrounds and readily overlooked their allies' ethnic antecedents in their pursuit of profit.[27] Commentators similarly viewed the way immigrants and the children of immigrants exploited the economic opportunities opened up by Prohibition as a sign of how well these men had assimilated into American society. Their can-do attitude and ruthless efficiency meant that they had embraced American economic models, a far more terrifying prospect than inner-city ethnic cabals.[28] Cooperation, not ethnicity, made gang members a threat.

With a new way of doing business, racketeers developed a recognizable style that Hollywood moviemakers soon exploited. As with sporting men, gangsters embraced conspicuous consumption. Pinstripe suits, plush overcoats, boutonnieres, diamond tie-pins, and spats are now clichéd gangster garb, but in the 1920s, they carried important meanings. More than just a sign of success, a gangster's clothes told nightclub proprietors, gambling-hall managers, and speakeasy owners what he did, while the extravagance of his dress showed where he stood in the syndicate's hierarchy.[29] Lavish accoutrements reinforced the message of monopoly power, but another signifier from the period enforced it: the Thompson submachine gun.[30]

After the passage of Prohibition, urban vice turned deadly. Economists argue that cartelization encourages violence in illicit enterprise. Unlike legal businesses that can turn to the courts, crime syndicates use force and foul play to protect their markets, discourage competitors, and settle disputes.[31] A few tenderloin notables died bloody deaths during the Progressive era, but their murders were unusual occurrences that the press covered in great detail.[32] During Prohibition, however, killings became routine.[33] In Gary, Indiana, Gaspar Monte, the so-called King of Little Italy, died in March 1923 because he agreed to testify for the federal government about Mayor Roswell Johnson's and Judge William Dunn's complicity in the city's liquor traffic. The day before the trial started, assassins gunned Monte down an hour after the funeral of Tony Cucinella, himself a victim of gang warfare.[34] Six years later, when Irving Wexler, alias Waxey Gordon, wanted to consolidate his control of the beer business in northern New Jersey, he murdered two of the four owners of the Eureka Brewery.[35] These examples are unexceptional. The same story of duplicitous dealings and murder as a first resort played out in cities across the country. Only when a nationally renowned crime boss such as Arnold Rothstein was assassinated, or when a syndicate took out a rival gang, as in the St. Valentine's Day Massacre, did newspapers give these events the same coverage they previously accorded the murders of relative minor district figures during the Progressive era.[36]

This escalation in violence indicated that the business of vice was no longer a loose market run by a range of sporting men and women, but a monopoly under the control of a few individuals. The Chicago Beer Wars of the mid-1920s bear out this contention. Johnny Torrio, despite a fracas with the O'Donnell gang in 1923, held Chicago's disparate gangs together for four years with only a few killings to keep them in line.[37] This détente ended in 1924 when Dion O'Bannion, who belonged to the Torrio organization, decided that he wanted more. Increasingly insubordinate, O'Bannion refused to give Torrio a cut of his Cicero enterprises or "make nice" with the Genna gang. Arranging a raid on a brewery he sold to Torrio as a supposed gesture of reconciliation, O'Bannion set Torrio up for a fall. On 19 May 1924, O'Bannion met Torrio at the brewery to oversee one last shipment of beer, but O'Bannion had tipped off the federal authorities about the delivery. After the police raid, Torrio found himself in the hands of the U.S. District Attorney, not the local officials whom he "owned." Six months later, O'Bannion died, gunned down in his flower shop, a casualty of the gang war that erupted in Torrio's absence.[38]

And so began the Beer Wars that gave Chicago its reputation as the bloodiest of all Prohibition-era cities. Cartels are unstable, even under the best of circumstances. That Torrio kept his multimillion-dollar enterprise intact for four years testifies to his business acumen and his canny mix of diplomacy and brutality. In 1925, having survived an assassination attempt by the O'Bannionites because his killer ran out of bullets before the *coup de grace*, Torrio lost his willingness to wage the kind of war necessary to bring his shattered cartel back into order. While serving a nine-month prison sentence resulting from the ill-fated brewery raid, Torrio deeded his empire over to Al Capone, a man ready to use violent means to rebuild Torrio's trust. Four years later, after the St. Valentine's Day Massacre eliminated the last of the O'Bannion gang, Capone stood as the uncontested leader of organized crime in Chicago.[39]

Both contemporary commentators and subsequent historians have emphasized the increased verticality of crime during Prohibition, but they missed the fact that horizontal integration—specifically, monopoly control of the wholesale liquor market—mattered more for the pioneers of organized crime than vertical integration. After a gang cornered the wholesale market, branching out into distribution, transportation, and retail sales logically followed, but without horizontal control, competing syndicates battled for dominance. Until a syndicate achieved horizontal control, either through cartelization or the elimination of competitors, vertical integration meant little to a gang's long-term survival. In an open market, even the most tightly organized, hierarchical crew suffered from diminished income and cutthroat competition.

PADLOCKS, PROPRIETORS, AND PARTIES

In this context of enormous profits and extreme violence, the once-innovative methods law-enforcement officers inherited from Progressive reformers proved ineffective. Sometimes federal agents succeeded where local officials could not, but jurisdictional ambiguity created incredible enforcement woes. After the ratification of the Eighteenth Amendment, the executive branch was loath to encroach on states' rights, although most states thought that the federal government should shoulder the economic and administrative burden of enforcing National Prohibition.[40] Despite local expectations, treasury department officials believed that they should only pursue the large-scale enterprises, leaving the household stills, basement speakeasies, and low-level dealers to state and municipal authorities. But fighting scattation, the inevitable result of breaking up big operations, required the support of both the police force and the local populace, something that Prohibition lacked in the areas federal agents thought needed cleaning up the most.[41]

With both a new market structure and a new regulatory regime, vice proprietors suffered a loss of prestige as they struggled to keep their venues open and their customers satisfied. In general, if speakeasy proprietors ran their joints quietly and sorted matters out with the cops on the beat and the precinct captain, they could keep their establishments going without too much official interference. "New York could support a handful of luxurious speakeasies and a great number of dirtier, darker, unadorned places," observed Stanley Walker, city editor of the *New York Herald Tribune*; however, "the big place, with its Babylonian gardens and costly mirrors, might make money for a time, but unless protection was sure, it was a safe bet that sooner or later it would be wrecked."[42] As a result, proprietors needed to budget bribes for government officials and lower their expectations about their venue's ambience.

Sometimes this tribute took the form of a unit tax. In Thermopolis, Wyoming, retailers paid $1 for each gallon of whisky and each case of beer.[43] Elsewhere, proprietors paid a weekly or monthly fee. In Earlsboro, Oklahoma, that meant handing over $5 or $10 per week to the triumvirate consisting of Marion Fuller, the chief of police; Homer Knappenberger, the mayor; and Frank Fox, the county sheriff. Unfortunately, the triumvirate's collectors grew overzealous, shaking down bootleggers and proprietors two or three times a week. Fearing that the bootleggers would kick up a fuss, Fuller turned to a unit scheme where wholesalers paid $2 for every case of beer and every gallon of whisky, half of which went to the city police and half to the county authorities.[44] In Wallace, Idaho, however, city officials started to pursue a policy in 1927 that was "not in vogue within the past few years." They charged brothels $20 per month and gambling dens $40 per month for the privilege of selling liquor, but instead of pocketing the cash, Wallace's officials siphoned it into the city budget.[45] Still, even after bribing local authorities, proprietors risked federal officials shutting down their venues as public nuisances. And most proprietors agreed that prohibition agents demanded the greatest payoffs with the least amount of courtesy.[46]

Cities had always faced difficulties in punishing liquor-law violators. Policemen saw their jobs as keeping order, not imposing moral standards at odds with urban norms. This attitude explained their support for vice districts before the war and their toleration of low-profile speakeasies during Prohibition.[47] The police tried to close up the places serving poisonous alcohol and sought to eliminate the "clip joints" that exploited suckers to the limit. Soaking their patrons with bills that far exceeded the cost of the actual amount of alcohol imbibed, clip-joint managers gladly accepted checks in lieu of cash, but then they declared the first few signatures indistinct and promised to tear up the "worthless" checks. The next day, however, marks found themselves out of the cumulative value of the checks they wrote and any IOUs that they had guaranteed.[48] Unlike speakeasies, these places gave cities a bad name and the police happily put them out of business. A little illegality, as long as it did not create too public a nuisance, kept people happy and padded the police's pockets, but larcenous intimidation and poisoning the populace agitated both wets and drys.

Juries rarely had a problem with people who sold alcohol after closing hours or on Sunday, especially if they did it quietly and behind closed doors. To ordinary men-on-the-street, saloonkeepers were good fellows who provided an appreciated service.[49] After the passage of Prohibition, juries accorded the same leniency to speakeasy proprietors and low-level bootleggers selling a couple of cases of beer or a few gallons of gin.[50] Selling a few drinks reflected positively on a man's reputation. And without having to worry about arrests endangering their liquor licenses, retailers readily took the risk. In 1926, with a five-month backlog for Prohibition cases in New York City and juries reluctant to convict, journalist Morris Markey reported with sly derision that Emory Buckner, the district attorney, and Lincoln C. Andrews, the treasury department official in charge of prohibition enforcement, "advocated drastic changes in criminal procedure, asking that the Constitution be amended if necessary so that a man may be sent to jail for Prohibition violation without the right of jury trial."[51] Prosecutors did not have to take such extreme measures, they just needed to change their tactics.

The unwillingness of juries to convict, and the marginal impact that the few convictions had on the retail market forced law-enforcement officials to follow the lead of Progressive-era anti-vice reformers and turn to the courts of equity. Now called "padlocking" rather than the more cumbersome "injunction and abatement proceedings," these actions closed public nuisances in order to prevent future misuse of the property.[52] The civil court judges, in contrast to the criminal court's juries, shared the government's disgust for liquor sellers. When granting an injunction, which the judges did more often than not, they ordered a place locked for a year—premises to remain vacant—and all the alcohol, furniture, and fixtures either destroyed or sold off at auction.[53] Padlocking proved disastrous for proprietors with any investment in their venues. "Prohibition's toll has fattened largely on those places the town could spare least: the colourful, traditional eating and drinking establishments," the wits at the New Yorker lamented. "The padlock is no great threat for the newcomer, who can move east or west as the enforcement needs of the moment dictate. But against the places which depend for success on traditional association with a particular locality, it has been a real weapon."[54] Without liquor licensing to control the number of venues, anyone who rented a room and bought a batch of liquor from a bootlegger could call himself a speakeasy proprietor.[55]

Closing the saloon, like closing the brothel, disaggregated services. If people wanted to drink when they went to a nightclub or roadhouse, they brought their own hip flasks and bought mixers from the proprietors. These "set-ups" usually consisted of a bottle of ginger ale, cracked ice, and a glass. Proprietors compensated for their loss of income from selling alcohol by charging exorbitant prices for set-ups.[56] In 1925, just outside of Denver, the owners of the Boulevard Café sold bottles of ginger ale or mineral water at $2 apiece, approximately fifteen times the price in legitimate soda shops.[57] That same year, in New York City at least, the worst nonbranded alcohol retailed at $1 a pint or more.[58] With the average unskilled worker earning only $3.64 per day, going out drinking during Prohibition meant spending more money than most Americans could afford, even in the prosperous 1920s.[59]

Some managers allowed their patrons to keep the alcohol they brought with them in full view, while others tried for greater subtlety. One savvy Miami proprietor posted cards warning "The Prohibition Law is strictly enforced here. Please help us obey the law." Nevertheless, the management provided shelves under the tabletops so that customers could hide the bottles they brought with them.[60] Unfortunately, even when venue owners did not actually sell alcohol, they remained vulnerable to padlocking.[61] After all, despite the separation of services, such proprietors "furnished the facilities for tippling with the intent and expectation that the guests would be attracted thereby," a Colorado district judge observed. "In fact large numbers of patrons came to the [roadhouse] and remained until the small hours of the morning for the purpose of consuming their intoxicating liquor in fancied security."[62] By allowing patrons to drink on their premises, and by providing them with overpriced mixers to make the moonshine more palatable, proprietors profited from violating liquor laws, thus turning their places into a public nuisance.

Always more reliant on transient trade than they liked to admit, hotel owners also went through difficult times during Prohibition. Although hoteliers sometimes tried to keep their grills, restaurants, and cafés open, losing the right to sell alcohol seriously affected even the most prosperous hotel's profitability. The Knickerbocker Hotel in New York City went bankrupt because of the Eighteenth Amendment. " 'The bar in the Knickerbocker used to take in four thousand dollars a day,' observed Mr. Regan, [a former employee], 'and when you remove four thousand dollars of profitable daily revenue from a hotel's receipts, you have to do some tall thinking to make them up.' "[63] In Washington State, the Butler Hotel played the same game as the roadhouses, allowing patrons to bring liquor into the exclusive Rose Room, a restaurant and entertainment venue. The high-class status of their clientele did not, however, protect the hotel from padlocking. When the owners appealed to the district court for leniency, citing the restaurant's necessity in the running of the hotel, the judges allowed the owners to keep it open through the dinner hour. Managers needed to close the restaurant at nine p.m., however, because after that the government agents observed a precipitous drop in both the adherence to liquor laws and the quality of the customers served.[64] Rather than take such risks, some hotel owners closed their cafés and turned their ground floors into storefronts, renting the space out to bazaars—retail outlets for anything other than food and drink.[65]

Prohibition affected the distribution of alcohol and the economics of running a joint, but it also led to the decline in proprietors' prestige. Where district proprietors once sat at the top of the sporting world's social hierarchy, now bootleggers defined the acme of underworld status. In the heyday of the red-light districts, owners of disreputable venues risked the loss of their liquor licenses and the closure of their premises during periodic campaigns to clean up the city, but they never worried about threats from the alcohol dealers who supplied their venues. During Prohibition, however, proprietors still chanced incurring official wrath, but they also feared getting caught in the turf wars of bootleggers. Buying alcohol from the wrong wholesaler could result in the bombing of their venue.[66] Even under less-hostile circumstances, gangsters demanded deference and strongly recommended that proprietors buy their products and accept their "protection"; otherwise, they would put the owners out of business.[67] No matter the relationship of owner to supplier, once proprietors went bankrupt from repeated raids, they required the help of gangsters to reestablish themselves. If drinking venues lost their "draperies, panelings, mirrors, carpets, bars, paintings, the finest kitchen equipment" through official action, that loss affected the owner more than his bootlegger. Selling liquor mattered more to gangsters than the atmosphere created by proprietors for their customers.[68]

Proprietors also lost status because, frankly, with the disaggregation of services, neither bootleggers nor customers needed them. Prohibition laws penalized the seller, not the buyer, a loophole that those with enough money to buy directly from bootleggers exploited to their advantage.[69] Drinking at home or at the home of friends, meant never worrying about getting raided. As long as the hosts refused payment for the alcohol they served, they stayed on the licit side of the legal distinctions between public and private, commercial and recreational. Private residences did not qualify as public nuisances.[70] This dodge encouraged the wild parties that gave the Roaring Twenties their notoriety as a decade devoted to good times, a stereotype enshrined in the movies and literature of the period.[71] In *The Great Gatsby*, F. Scott Fitzgerald described one such bash. "By midnight the hilarity had increased. A celebrated tenor had sung in Italian, and a notorious contralto had sung in jazz, and between the numbers people were doing 'stunts' all over the garden, while happy, vacuous bursts of laughter rose toward the summer sky. A pair of stage twins . . . did a baby act in costume, and champagne was served in glasses bigger than finger-bowls."[72] Ironically, Gatsby's virtual absence as a host reflected the insignificance of a strong managerial presence, even at private parties. Whether going to a speakeasy or to a splendid mansion, people did not care who owned the joint as long as they could get together and drink.[73]

Wealthy men and women embraced the ethos of having a good time, but that did not mean that they admired the sporting class. The sporting world played at exclusivity, but Jazz-Age revelers practiced it. Nightclubs necessitated membership, speakeasies only unlocked their doors to those who knew the passwords, and roadhouses required cars to reach them, encouraging visits from self-contained cliques.[74] Ellin Mackay, a self-proclaimed postdebutante and future wife of Irving Berlin, explained in 1925 that her generation chose to go to cabarets not "as our Elders would have it, because 'we enjoy rubbing elbows with all sorts and kinds of people,'" but rather because "we are fastidious." Mackay and her peers would rather go to a cabaret with a small, exclusive party and ignore the rest of the patrons than attend a society function and mix with the "extremely unalluring specimens" of the stag line.[75] Members of the sporting class rarely disguised their mercenary motives, welcoming anyone with cash-in-hand; yet for all their pecuniary disregard, participants in slumming parties perpetuated a class snobbery that reinforced social divisions rather than superseded them.

Sporting women suffered the most in the transition from controlled toleration to prohibition. In Western boomtowns, which local officials ran as wide open as federal officials allowed, madams retained a level of control proportionate to the old-time tenderloins. But generally the elimination of the districts and the closure of the brothels meant an increasing number of male proprietors of clandestine venues and a corresponding decrease in power for women.[76] Now when women owned a venue, they almost invariably did so with their husbands.[77] Prostitutes also had a harder time making their way in the post-district sexual economy. In big cities, the market split into a small elite class of women who attended the cabarets and nightclubs, spent the night with a single man, and charged up to $30 a trick. Sometimes working as chorus girls in the popular reviews of the period, these women blurred the line between mistress and independent prostitute.[78] In New Orleans, madam Willie Piazza joked that country-club girls destroyed her business; while not technically true, sporting women lost both economic and cultural status in the 1920s.[79]

Less-attractive women could not enter the rarefied world of upper-class clubbing, let alone survive within it. These women relied on pimps, worked as hostesses in speakeasies, or tried to make a go of it in gangster-run roadhouses. Roadhouses catered primarily to a clientele of mixed-sex parties that came in by the carload, but on occasion, roadhouse proprietors also staffed women to entertain all-male stag parties. They danced with the customers, encouraged them to drink, and solicited them to go upstairs for sex.[80] In the prewar districts, madams usually received half of a prostitute's earnings; however, in syndicate places in Chicago, the male proprietors demanded half of what the women earned and then took another 10 percent, which the syndicate "pooled together . . . to pay fines and for legal advice." Still exploited, low-status prostitutes now needed to cover their own protection costs, even though they sacrificed their independence by working in a venue rather than on the street.[81] Once central to district society, after Prohibition prostitutes became liminal figures eking out a desperate existence on the edges of the criminal underworld.

With the Eighteenth Amendment, the Anti-Saloon League banned all legal drinking venues, from the perfectly respectable working-class barroom to the most decadent sporting resort. By this criterion, they succeeded in their mission. Saloons no longer featured as an integral part of the urban landscape, and alcohol-peddling proprietors no longer presided as the jolliest of jolly good fellows in the sporting world. During Prohibition, venue owners lost power as gangsters dictated what booze they would buy and which resorts they would run. Proprietors also lost their cultural authority as the class status of their clientele increased. With only the wealthy able to afford the exorbitant prices for alcohol, nightclub and road-house managers drifted into the background, subsumed into the category of servants catering to their customers' needs. For the postwar generation, partying mattered more than the places to which they went.

INCOME TAX AND CRIMINAL CONSPIRACIES

Unable to eliminate all the outlets for alcohol, state and federal authorities turned their attention to drying up the sources of supply and imprisoning the higher-ups. Mythology about Prohibition makes much of the fact that the Internal Revenue Service brought down Al Capone when no one else could, but the Treasury Department intended from the very beginning to use unpaid taxes as a way to incarcerate bootleggers. The idea of employing the federal income tax merely came a few years later, yet it followed logically from both the legislative intent of Congress and from the administrative structure of the Treasury Department. The legal offices of the Internal Revenue Service specialized in looking for innovative ways to collect taxes and prosecute those who would evade paying the money they owed the government. With lawyers trained in both civil and criminal law, the Treasury Department aggressively sought to expand the range of actions that its agents could take while pursuing their intended targets. The law offices insured that the lessons learned by one branch of the Internal Revenue Service benefited every agent working for the Treasury Department.[82]

The federal government used their right to tax as their justification for policing the sale of alcohol. The United States did not have a national police force, and no one in Washington, DC, or in the state capitols wanted the federal government to build one. The policing that did exist was specialized work through a hodge-podge of departments. With the Mann Act, the government succeeded in twisting the Interstate Commerce Clause to regulate what most people perceived as a moral issue, but the alcohol trade needed a rationale that allowed federal authorities to supervise the traffic within the states, not just between them. Since the Treasury Department taxed alcohol, tobacco, and oleomargarine, it already had a claim for Prohibition enforcement.[83] In 1917, with only 507 distilleries operating, a decrease of almost a hundred from 1916, the government still collected over $187 million from the already-existing taxes on distilled spirits, fruit brandy, and wine. This figure represented 23 percent of all the revenue collected that year.[84] People believed that the Treasury Department's knowledge of the legitimate market would aid its agents immeasurably when it came time to enforce Prohibition.

Even before the ratification of the Eighteenth Amendment, the Treasury Department succeeded in using taxation as a way to regulate illicit products. The Harrison Narcotic Act, passed in 1914, forbid the sale of opiates and coca derivatives except through registered professionals. Doctors could write prescriptions for patients under their care, and pharmacists could fill the prescriptions issued, but the days of over-the-counter sales and bike messengers delivering standing orders to addicts had passed.[85] Between 1915 and 1919, the Treasury Department managed to win a few key court cases upholding the Harrison Act that would eventually strengthen their power to enforce Prohibition. In 1915, for example, in *United States v. Jin Fuey Moy*, the Supreme Court affirmed that the moral intent behind a revenue measure did not negate its legitimacy as a tax.[86] In 1919, the Justices decided in *Webb v. United States* that in certain instances the government had the power to determine the parameters of appropriate practice for physicians.[87] These wins legitimized the Treasury Department's police powers and closed some key potential loopholes for evading the ban on liquor.

The *Webb* case carried important ramifications. Most significantly, it discredited doctors and their right to medicalize the discourse of drug enforcement in particular and moral enforcement more generally. Doctors had long debated the merits of prescribing opiates to addicts to stave off their withdrawals, but when *Webb* reached the Supreme Court, the Court affirmed the anti-maintenance orthodoxy and decreed that physicians who pursued any course of treatment that did not involve weaning their patients off of opiates violated the law.[88] With private practitioners banned from prescribing opiates to addicts, a number of municipalities stepped in to address the problem of their addict populations. As many as sixty municipalities—including Atlanta, Georgia, New Haven, Connecticut, and Youngstown, Ohio—established maintenance clinics to ease the suffering of their city's addicts. The Treasury Department, however, concluded that *Webb* also made these clinics illegal and harassed city officials into closing them.[89] In

Shreveport, Louisiana, Willis Butler, who operated the longest-running clinic, had both the police and the city council strongly behind him. When federal agents came to town, everyone from the chief of police and parish sheriff to the district court judge protested that the clinic eliminated the city's illicit traffic in narcotics and significantly reduced street crime.[90] The Treasury Department closed the Shreveport clinic anyway in February 1923, thus ending "legal access to organized maintenance treatment" until 1965, when Marie Nyswander and Vincent Dole opened an experimental methadone clinic in New York City.[91]

Besides disastrously affecting the quality of life for addicts, the Treasury Department's anti-maintenance policy also effectively prevented municipalities from countermanding federal policy with local health initiatives. In contrast to morphine maintenance, which continued to have a few reputable adherents, physicians who insisted that drinkers needed access to alcohol remained entirely suspect; however, from the perspective of social-order policing, the Treasury Department's closure of the clinics mattered most as a preemptory strike against local public health officials asserting their authority over issues the federal government deemed within their regulatory purview. After *Webb*, city public health departments could not establish alcohol dispensaries where doctors could register users, record consumption, and regulate the alcohol trade. In the United States, moral absolutism trumped medicalization. The Treasury Department successfully turned the power to tax into the power to set social policy.

In 1921, Congress passed the Willis-Campbell Act, which strengthened the earlier Volstead Act. On the same day, in the Revenue Act of 1921, Congress dropped "lawful" as a modifier describing taxable businesses, the first tax revision since 1913.[92] The Treasury Department took this legislative synchronicity to mean that they could prosecute bootleggers for unpaid income taxes. In 1922, federal agents arrested Manley Sullivan of South Carolina for failing to file a tax return on the $10,000 he made the previous year. Outraged, Sullivan sued, contending that paying taxes on illegally acquired income meant confessing to the crimes he committed while making that money. In other words, by expecting him to pay income taxes, the Treasury Department required Sullivan to incriminate himself, a violation of his Fifth Amendment rights. In 1926, the Circuit Court of Appeals agreed with Sullivan's contention, but the Supreme Court overturned the decision a year later.[93] Government counsel successfully argued that the Internal Revenue Service's 1040 form only asked for general information about the taxpayer's business, "none of which in itself constitutes proof of unlawful dealings." The Supreme Court Justices declared taxing illicit income constitutionally valid, although Oliver Wendell Holmes Jr. noted in his opinion that the Court would consider the question of whether bribery counted as a deductible expense "when a taxpayer has the temerity to raise it."[94] According to Congress, the Supreme Court, and the executive branch, Americans needed to pay taxes on both legally and illegally obtained income.

With their test case a success, the Treasury Department immediately announced its intention to pursue tax-delinquent bootleggers. The *New Yorker* howled with laughter, wondering how the government would do it.[95] But prosecuting income-tax evasion did not require the Treasury Department to determine how much a gangster made selling liquor, just that he lived beyond his declared means.[96] For example, when the government took Jake "Greasy Thumb" Guzik, a crony of Al Capone's, to court, they merely showed through bank deposits, cashier's checks, and stock dividends in his doctor's name that Guzik had made at least $640,000 in 1927, $338,000 in 1928, and $54,000 in 1929. For defrauding the government of the income tax that he owed, Guzik received the maximum penalty: a two-year prison sentence and a $10,000 fine.[97] In other cases, federal authorities pointed to the price of cars driven, the cost of apartments rented, the size of checks written, and, in the case of Ralph Capone, Al's older brother, the value of racehorses owned.[98] The courts generally found in the government's favor. Yet for all the publicity accorded income-tax cases, the Treasury Department used tax evasion as a strategy of last resort.

Income tax took down the bigwigs, and padlocking chased speakeasy proprietors around the town or out of business, but neither approach sufficiently disrupted the business of bootlegging. For that, law-enforcement officials turned their attention to the operational details of the traffic itself. Busting up distilleries, padlocking breweries, and seizing the trucks, cars, and boats used in transportation, Prohibition agents went after all the physical accoutrements for manufacturing and distributing alcohol.[99] Historians frequently cite the budgetary constraints on the Prohibition Unit, pointing out that during the 1920s, Congress only allocated an average of $8.8 million a year to enforce Prohibition.[100] But the Prohibition Unit also brought in money, and not just in the form of bribes.[101] For instance, the Treasury Department took in approximately $3.1 million a year from the vehicles seized and sold between 1926 and 1929.[102] Add to this figure the fines and forfeitures levied on liquor-law violators, which averaged almost $5.4 million a year between 1924 and 1926, and this branch of the Internal Revenue Service did quite well for itself financially.[103] The impact of these actions, however, drove small players out of business and encouraged gangland mergers that consolidated the trade under the auspices of a few regional crime bosses.[104]

To take on these syndicates, the Treasury Department adopted a holistic approach and used the conspiracy statute to apprehend everyone who profited from a bootlegging operation, from the manufacturers of the moonshine to the truck drivers who transported it. In 1923, the Prohibition Unit began to use the "conspiracy provisions of the Criminal Code . . . to break up organized dens of bootleggers."[105] By 1927, conspiracy cases proved so successful that the renamed and reorganized Bureau of Prohibition established "special conspiracy squads to work on major conspiracy cases" in each of the regional administrative districts.[106] On both a conceptual level and in terms of actual enforcement, alleging that criminal conspiracies violated prohibition law was the most important innovation that the Treasury Department made in prosecuting vice.

Conspiracy cases offered three advantages over other types of enforcement strategies. First, as a violation of a criminal statute, conspiracy cases were tried by juries, which gave conspiracy convictions greater credibility than padlocking, forfeitures, and property seizures in the battle against illegal alcohol sales. Second, they applied to a greater number of people than income-tax cases. With a conspiracy charge, prohibition agents could arrest all the suspected members of a bootlegging operation, not just those who earned the big money. Indeed, some cases included over seventy defendants.[107] Finally, conspiracy cases required less evidentiary specificity and provided for harsher sentencing than straightforward liquor-law violations.[108]

Americans love a good conspiracy theory and, during Prohibition, the underworld networks of illegal alcohol wholesalers not only made good copy, they also played well in court. If juries admired a good fellow for selling the occasional drink, they abhorred the idea of secret societies plotting to subvert the law. Whether lambasting the king's ministers, Masonic Lodge members, or the Money Trust, conspiracy theorists played to culturally ingrained fears about organized assaults on American freedoms. Wets did not mind ordinary people having access to alcohol, but criminal gangs who operated outside the law, embraced their own exclusive culture, and swore allegiance to some tyrannical boss did not deserve to survive. The bootlegging operations that developed during Prohibition fit the conspiracy formula without much distortion on the part of either government prosecutors or sensation-seeking journalists.[109]

To make a successful conspiracy case, government lawyers needed to present circumstantial evidence that the conspirators worked together to break the law and to show at least one "overt act" that a conspirator committed in pursuit of the group's larger goal.[110] In a 1922 indictment of a group of bootleggers from Jacksonville, Florida, the U.S. attorneys claimed that the arrested men "unlawfully, willingly, knowingly, feloniously, and maliciously did combine, conspire, confederate, and agree together . . . to commit an offence against the United States."[111] This language resonated with that of the Sherman Anti-Trust Act, because trusts are a type of conspiracy. Monopolists collaborated to obstruct free trade. Bootleggers, on the other hand, also combined to break the law, but in their case they violated the Eighteenth Amendment, not statutes concerning interstate commerce.[112] Interestingly, conspirators did not need to succeed in their quest, or know all the members of the conspiracy, for the jury to find them guilty, as long as the prosecutor could show that the group intended to break the law.[113] The one point the prosecutors absolutely and conclusively needed to prove, however, was that an organized and preferably vertically integrated cabal existed.

This requirement elided a crucial economic fact. Verticality without horizontal integration resulted in brutal gang warfare. Bootleggers only achieved market stability through cartelization, or monopoly control, of the wholesale market. Despite Oliver Wendell Holmes defining conspiracy as a "partnership in criminal purposes," a phrase which implies horizontal cooperation, prosecutors imposed verticality on conspirators in order to make successful cases.[114] Early on, in 1922, a Pennsylvania district court judge opined that "the success of the conspiracy was dependent upon an unbroken chain of cooperating links." And wholesaling constituted just one link.[115] Without other links, prosecutors did not convince judges and juries. As a Florida district court judge observed that same year, "possession is lawful, unless it be coupled with the illegal 'manufacture' or 'sale' or 'transportation' or 'importation' or 'exportation.'"[116] Since the Volstead Act made it illegal to "manufacture, sell, barter, transport, import, export, deliver, furnish or possess any intoxicating liquor except as authorized," government counsel created the strongest conspiracy cases when they linked bootlegging operations to at least three of the nine banned acts.[117] For all its economic importance, under the law, horizontal control mattered little.

When crafting a conspiracy case, prosecutors needed to demonstrate vertical integration. For example, in the 1926 case *Weinstein v. United States*, U.S. attorneys showed how a group of distillers from Chelsea, Massachusetts, sold all the alcohol they manufactured to a single agent, Ernest "Dutch" Henry. Operating as the sole wholesaler to the city's retailers, Henry directed the transportation and delivery of the alcohol to the local speakeasies.[118] This emphasis on functional specialization and a coherent chain of command created the image of organized crime that persists in America today: rigidly hierarchical, strictly run, secretive societies. In other words, the Mafia, as represented in movies, novels, and government reports.[119]

Through the conspiracy statute, the fight against commercialized vice turned into a vendetta against organized crime. Commercialization, once the bugbear of

A Typical Syndicate Layout

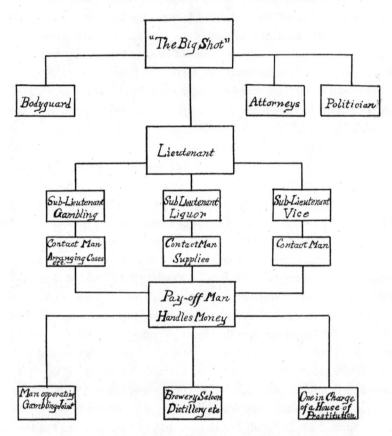

"A Typical Syndicate Layout." In order to make successful conspiracy cases, the government portrayed organized crime as a vertically integrated business. National Commission on Law Observance and Enforcement, *Enforcement of the Prohibition Laws,* 71st Cong., 3d sess., S. Doc. 307 (Washington, DC: Government Printing Office, 1931), vol. 4, 311.

anti-vice reform, no longer mattered. Bootleggers commercialized their trade, of course. But their sin was that they combined, confederated, and acted in concert. For all the easily spouted clichés about unintended consequences and self-fulfilling prophecies, Progressive reformers managed to create exactly what they hated.

American manners and morals changed during the roaring storm of the 1920s, but they did so dragged free from their geographical moorings in the urban vice district. The sporting class no longer survived as a coherent urban culture, yet some of their ideals persisted in the media and among affluent urbanites. The search for good times, the appreciation of a big spender, and the celebration of mixed-sex conviviality turned into acceptable mainstream pursuits. Moreover, while anti-saloon activists argued that they wanted to close saloons to protect the American family from their harmful influence, Prohibition succeeded not only in bringing alcohol into the home, it also made it chic for women to drink.[120] Just as closing the vice district created the very market structure reformers dreaded, so too did the destruction of the sporting world spread a culture moralists despised.

Even before Repeal, social commentators asked whether Prohibition, the "noble experiment," was a failure. Parsing the question in a number of ways, both contemporaries and historians have argued that the dichotomous question of failure or success obscured multifaceted answers.[121] Despite appearances to the contrary, Prohibition did decrease aggregate demand. Martha Bensley Bruère reported the relative adherence to Prohibition among the urban working class in *Does Prohibition Work?*, her thorough 1927 survey of social workers across the country. The often-repeated refrain was that men no longer drank their paychecks away in saloons, husbands beat their wives with significantly less frequency, and living conditions improved as workers bought consumer goods for their families with the money they would otherwise have spent on alcohol.[122] In 1932, economist Clark Warburton estimated that Prohibition reduced alcohol consumption by one-third to one-half of its prewar rates.[123] Still, people continued to drink. And some drank quite flamboyantly. Many moralists worried that such blatant disregard of the law created a general disrespect for all regulation, especially among the nation's youth. Critics of Prohibition pointed to the increase in gun violence to argue that the lawlessness engendered by the Eighteenth Amendment went far beyond the damage done by the occasional drink.[124] By the early 1930s, in a country devastated by the Great Depression, politicians on the federal, state, and local levels decided that the demoralization created through a rampant disregard for the law, and the benefits derived from revenue-producing excise taxes, far outweighed the social benefits of a strict moral stance. On 5 December 1933, Utah became the thirty-sixth state to ratify the Twenty-Sixth Amendment, which repealed National Prohibition.[125]

Progressivism, Prohibition, and Policy Options

During the 1920s, the Lost Generation ridiculed the "Puritanism" of their parents' generation, in part for its support of Prohibition. Their characterization, like historian Richard Hofstadter's influential dismissal of temperance as outside of the mainstream of Progressive reform, unfairly discredited the Progressives and their initiatives.[1] The people they ridiculed for endorsing moral reform during the first quarter of the twentieth century had tried an array of options to regulate vice. These urban reformers, whom later generations would portray as narrow prohibitionists, showed admirable openness in evaluating a range of possible ways to manage vice. Even after their goals hardened, they pursued innovative legal strategies based on a complex analysis of economic relationships within red-light districts. These structural reformers were both pragmatic and visionary.

Yet H. L. Mencken and his cohort were also right. By the 1920s, positions on vice had become more puritanical, if puritanical meant less flexible. Although urban Progressives had frequently assessed the results of their endeavors, after World War I, both anti-vice policies and enforcement techniques stultified as federal officials assumed control. Without needing to answer directly for the local consequences of their national policies, federal authorities took a more Mosaic approach to the law. And that is how the Puritanism that Mencken found so abhorrent became embedded in anti-vice reform. The Progressives who tried to limit commercial vice frequently spoke in moral absolutes, but in their pragmatic recognition of an irreducible minimum in urban immorality and through the deals they brokered with municipal politicians, Progressive reformers endorsed programs tainted with an ethical ambiguity that federal officials could not, or perhaps more accurately, would not tolerate. This methodological inflexibility, combined with the moral precepts they advocated, produced the hypocrisy that social critics of the 1920s so fervently condemned.

No system lacks its faults, as vice reform's swing from tolerated dispersion to geographic concentration and finally to institutional prohibition demonstrates. Neither the mugwumps nor the Progressives had all the answers, but they explored a range of regulatory possibilities, despite the moral ambiguities of those systems. The policies the Progressives tried showed demonstrable weaknesses. Yet reformers examined the consequences of their programs and attempted to minimize their negative effects. Unfortunately, federal intervention hardened earlier analytical elasticity into intolerance. By turning to the federal government, local moral reformers effectively broke local stalemates, but in so doing they created regulatory precedents and helped establish a law-enforcement armature that prevented them from resuming control once federal intercession enabled them to achieve their goals. Moreover, once in place, federal officials rarely considered the particularities of local circumstances or honored existing compromises when they imposed their "solution" to long-standing social-order problems. In their attempt to create uniformity, national officials embraced a prescriptive inflexibility that the loosely connected private associations of urban Progressives had wanted but were unable to implement.

The legacy of the Progressives persists. Reformers' anti-vice initiatives made the growth of federal police powers possible, yet in the process, private anti-vice associations lost their influence and local leaders soon found their authority undercut. Congress repealed the Eighteenth Amendment, but kept its jurisdictional gains over moral issues. Government officials soon forgot the innovative compromises that anti-vice reformers negotiated among the police, business leaders, and district proprietors, even as they continued to limit the power of local law enforcement to set policy for regulating urban vice.

The national policing of moral problems helped lay the groundwork for the New Deal safety net of the modern welfare state, but through the self-conscious separation of the capable from the criminal, and the deserving from the disreputable, it also turned the old-time underworld into the modern underclass. When local anti-vice associations, with the backing of the federal government, criminalized brothels, opium dens, and saloons and cleaned up dance halls, movie theaters, and amusement parks, they succeeded in altering the moral geography of American cities. This structural success, however, had a lethal legacy for de-legitimized individuals. For those condemned by the new moral regulations, the concurrent prohibitions of drugs, alcohol, and prostitution preordained their banishment into a criminal urban underclass cut off from respectable society. Today, in a system unsympathetic to those prostitutes, addicts, and "three-time losers" caught between crime bosses and law-enforcement officials, harm-reduction measures such as needle-exchange programs, methadone maintenance clinics, and treatment-on-demand remain unpopular, underfunded, and, in some cities, nonexistent. Dependent on federal money and required to follow policies set down by federal authorities, welfare workers cannot broker more pragmatic approaches with municipal officials. The people most hurt by these policies—prostitute, addicts, and petty criminals—have little recourse to official relief, and their communities suffer accordingly.

This absolutist enforcement of urban vice not only affects crime, but also culture. When present-day policymakers talk about morality and drug enforcement, they immediately discount some positions as untenable because Americans cannot send the message that they are "soft on drugs." Their argument, however, is flawed. Prohibition, not toleration, favored the spread of the sporting ethos. The ambiance of the tolerated tenderloin was too open, too tawdry, and too déclassé to have a wide appeal among the middle class. Glamorization resulted from restriction. The celebrity status of 1920s gangsters far outweighed the esteem accorded to pool-room idlers in the pre-Prohibition period. Both mobsters and pimps came from the same background, served as intermediaries between producers and sellers, and embraced a masculinity at odds with the precepts of respectable society. Yet the gangster held a swaggering appeal that went far beyond the underworld circles of the sporting class. Speakeasies were alluring because of their illegality, low-down dives were only distasteful. The excesses of the Jazz Age required the restrictions of Prohibition.

One of the most problematic legacies of Progressive reform's prohibitory move involves the racism of its policing policies. Toleration and integration were not necessarily synonymous, but prohibition and segregation evolved as intertwined phenomenon. During the Progressive era, the police and municipal politicians tried to maintain an uneasy balance between racial and reputational segregation by juggling the exigencies of Jim Crow with the race-mixing inherent in reputational separation. But whatever equilibrium they achieved collapsed during World War I. In 1917, at the same time that the U.S. Supreme Court outlawed racial residential segregation, one of the worst race riots of the period occurred in

East St. Louis.[2] The East St. Louis riot replayed many of the same tensions as the earlier Atlanta and Springfield riots—it followed weeks of hysteria about black violence, most of the rioting centered in the tenderloin, and white rioters destroyed vast swathes of black-owned saloons and residences—but municipal leaders drew very different conclusions about the steps needed to restore social order than their peers had a decade earlier. Where city councilmen and law-enforcement officials once supplemented reputational segregation with racial policing, by 1917, anti-vice reformers had not only discredited vice districting, they had established a national regulatory infrastructure backed by the federal government to enforce it. Even more importantly, because of the cultural impact of the Great Migration, racial explanations for the East St. Louis riot overwhelmed the remnants of a reputational discourse. The East St. Louis riot convinced the few remaining doubters that reputational segregation did not work and that racial segregation offered a far better solution. The Chicago Race Riot of 1919, in which much of the fighting took place in the old "22nd Street" district, further reinforced this conclusion.[3] Thus, after demobilization, at the moment when local officials could have challenged the federal closure of red-light districts and reinstated the policy of reputational segregation, the volatility of black/white relations in public leisure spaces convinced city leaders to support Jim Crow and jettison segregated vice. After the bloody summer of 1919, racial separation triumphed over reputational segregation.

If criminalization gave cachet to middle-class rebels, it affected people in the inner city very differently. Maintaining illicit monopolies has had far-reaching consequences. High mortality coincides with large potential profits. Deaths from gang-related gun violence ravage the urban underclass, but the economic opportunities of current prohibitions also mean that gangsters can gain a level of wealth impossible in more loosely organized and less-stringently outlawed markets. During the Progressive era, whoring and pimping sometimes improved a person's standard of living, but the money an individual made almost never provided a route out of the tenderloin. Under prohibitory regulation, gains from distributing drugs offer a potential path out of the ghetto, if not for gang members, then perhaps for their families. The allure of monopoly profits helps organized crime perpetuate itself by bringing in new generations to keep the business going, despite the fact that most gangsters wind up dead or in prison instead of in that hoped-for penthouse apartment. A disproportionate number of poor men end up in jail on drug-related charges, while a disproportionate number of women head single-parent households in the poorest sections of the inner city.

The same economic analysis of the white slavery scare continues in the war on drugs, with its incessant search for the man higher up and its disregard for individual prostitutes or addicts. Now, as then, treatment remains an ancillary concern. The ongoing emphasis on drug lords and distribution networks precludes not only a public health discourse on harm reduction, but other practical approaches to law enforcement as well. Laissez-faire is not the only alternative to prohibition. Licensing, as the Committee of Fourteen so effectively showed, can work as an important lever for social control. In contrast, the defensive binaries of the present-day drug czars harkens back to the melodramatic modes of the white slavery scare, not to its more nuanced interpretations of city life and civil law. In pursuing crime bosses, federal officials make little effort to alter the environment that perpetuates the problems they supposedly seek to solve. Then again, incarcerating higher-ups and making big drug busts, like the earlier closures of the districts, garners greater accolades than the tedious, never-ending work of improving economic and educational opportunities for those living in the city center. As the safety net that the Progressives and later liberals worked so hard to create unravels from willful neglect, policymakers high up in the federal government congratulate themselves on their uncompromising moral positions.

Since World War I, the innovations that government agents have pursued, such as income-tax evasion and RICO (the Racketeer Influenced and Corrupt Organizations Act), merely extend the earlier Progressive-era economic analysis, just as technological advances like wiretapping simply elaborate on old investigative approaches. The irony is that enforcement based on the corporate model of the business of vice perpetuates the very cartelization of organized crime that it initially condemned. This fact remains unrecognized, just as the metaphors made to describe urban vice remain unquestioned. For advances to occur, federal officials must rethink their rote commitment to goals justified by century-old analogies. If historical precedent must bind us, then Americans need to move away from an intolerant instrumentalist discourse and reconsider the programmatic flexibility that the Progressives advocated in the twenty years preceding Prohibition. The proscriptions, analytical inflexibility, and moral absolutism of the current war on drugs is not the only solution to the ongoing conundrum of vice in American cities. We must once again privilege long-term improvement over short-term symbolic victories.

Notes

ASHA   American Social Health Association Papers, Social Welfare History Archives, University of Minnesota, Twin Cities Campus, Minneapolis

C14   Committee of Fourteen, Rare Books and Manuscripts, New York Public Library

CTCA   Commission on Training Camp Activities, entry 395, record group 165, National Archives

ESDP   Ethel Sturges Dummer Papers, Schlesinger Library, Radcliffe Institute for Advanced Study, Harvard University

GTP   Graham Taylor Papers, Newberry Library, Chicago

HLP   Harriet Burton Laidlaw Papers, Schlesinger Library, Radcliffe Institute for Advanced Study, Harvard University

JPA   Juvenile Protective Association Records, Special Collections, University of Illinois at Chicago

Kehillah   Judah L. Magnes Archives, Central Archives for the History of the Jewish People, Jerusalem, Israel

LSLC   Lester S. Levy Collection of Sheet Music, Special Collections, Sheridan Libraries, The Johns Hopkins University

NYC15   Committee of Fifteen Records, Rare Books and Manuscripts, New York Public Library

PPLC   Prints and Photographs Division, Library of Congress

RFA   Rockefeller Family Archives, Rockefeller Archive Center, Pocantico Hills, NY

TPC   Theatrical Poster Collection, Prints and Photographs Division, Library of Congress

INTRODUCTION. *IT'S A WONDERFUL LIFE*

1. *It's A Wonderful Life*, dir. Frank Capra (1947).

2. *The Wizard of Oz*, dir. Victor Fleming (1939); Hugh Rockoff, "*The Wizard of Oz* as a Monetary Allegory," *Journal of Political Economy* 98 (1990): 739–761.

3. [Vice Commission of Minneapolis], *Report of the Vice Commission of Minneapolis to His Honor, James C. Haynes, Mayor* (Minneapolis, 1911), reprinted in *The Prostitute and the Social Reformer: Commercial Vice in the Progressive Era*, ed. Charles Rosenberg and Carroll Smith-Rosenberg (New York, 1974), 109; Samuel P. Hays, "The Politics of Reform in Municipal Government in the Progressive Era," *Pacific Northwest Quarterly* 55 (Oct. 1964): 157–169; Melvin G. Holli, *Reform in Detroit* (New York, 1969), 161–180; Martin J. Schiesl, "A New Conception of Politics," in *The Politics of Efficiency: Municipal Administration and Reform in America, 1880–1920* (Berkeley, CA, 1977), 131–132, 156–157. Richard Hamm brilliantly analyzes the idea of a "Mosaic" approach to the law in his *Shaping the Eighteenth Amendment: Temperance Reform, Legal Culture, and the Polity, 1880–1920* (Chapel Hill, NC, 1995).

4. Mark Haller, "Urban Vice and Civic Reform: Chicago in the Early Twentieth Century," in *Cities in American History*, ed. Kenneth T. Jackson and Stanley K. Schultz (New York, 1972), 292; Mark Thomas Connelly, *The Response to Prostitution in the Progressive Era* (Chapel Hill, NC, 1980), 3–4; David C. Humphrey, "Prostitution and Public Policy," *Southwestern Historical Quarterly* 86 (April 1983): 484; Ruth Rosen, *The Lost Sisterhood: Prostitution in America, 1900–1918* (Baltimore, 1982), 78–79; Neil Larry Shumsky, "Tacit Acceptance: Respectable Americans and Segregated Prostitution, 1870–1910," *Journal of Social History* 19 (Summer 1986): 665–679.

CHAPTER 1. SEGREGATING VICE, 1890–1909

1. Richard Hofstadter, *The American Political Tradition and the Men Who Made It*, with a foreword by Christopher Lasch (1948; New York, 1973), 225–27, 230, 233; Samuel P. Hays, *The Response to Industrialism, 1885–1914* (Chicago, 1957), 27; Robert H. Wiebe, *The Search for Order, 1877–1920* (New York, 1967), 27; John A. Garraty, *The New Commonwealth, 1877–1890* (New York, 1968), 283–288. The mugwump name derives either from the name of a Native American leader or, more likely, from the aspersion that as nonpartisans they were indecisive "fence sitters" with their "mugs" on one side of the party divide and their "wumps" on the other.

2. Thomas Nast, "An Independent Victory," *Harper's Weekly* (19 July 1884), 465. The quotation Nast repeated was a Cleveland campaign slogan, but it originally came from General Edward Bragg of Wisconsin. See M. R. Werner, *Tammany Hall* (1928; Garden City, NY, 1932), 301.

3. On mugwumpery and the "best men" philosophy, see Martin J. Schiesl, "A New Conception of Politics," in *The Politics of Efficiency: Municipal Administration and Reform in America, 1880–1920* (Berkeley, CA, 1977), 6–24; Richard Hofstadter, *The Age of Reform: From Bryan to F.D.R.* (New York, 1955), 139–143; Lorin Peterson, *The Day of the Mugwump* (New York, 1961); Wiebe, *Search for Order*, 60–62; Gerald W. McFarland, *Mugwumps, Morals and Politics, 1884–1920* (Amherst, MA, 1975), 107–123; David M. Tucker, *Mugwumps: Public Moralists of the Gilded Age* (Columbia, MO, 1998). See also James Bryce, "The War Against Bossdom," in *The American Commonwealth*, new ed. (New York, 1911), vol. 2, 168–175.

4. Gustavus Myers, *The History of Tammany Hall*, 2nd ed., rev. and enlarged (1917;

with a new introduction, New York, 1971), 212–213, 251, 267, 299–300; Werner, *Tammany Hall*, 104–108, 277–278, 303–311, 438–440, 483–485; Thomas C. Cochran and William Miller, *The Age of Enterprise: A Social History of Industrial America* (1942; rev. ed. New York, 1961), 157; Daniel Czitrom, "Underworld and Underdogs: Big Tim Sullivan and Metropolitan Politics in New York, 1889–1913," *Journal of American History* 78 (Sept. 1991): 539–542; Kenneth D. Ackerman, *Boss Tweed: The Rise and Fall of the Corrupt Pol Who Conceived the Soul of Modern New York* (New York, 2005), 18–21, 334; *Encyclopedia of New York*, s.v. "Tweed, William M(agear) 'Boss,'" "Kelly, John," and "Sullivan, Big Tim"; see also "Murphy, Charles F(rancis)" and "Croker, Richard." The urban machines were usually Democratic, but occasionally they were also Republican. See Cochran and Miller, *Age of Enterprise*, 157; Shelton Stromquist, "The Crucible of Class: Cleveland Politics and the Origins of Municipal Reform in the Progressive Era," in *Who Were the Progressives?* ed. Glenda Elizabeth Gilmore (Boston, 2002), 149–150.

5. William L. Riordan, *Plunkitt of Tammany Hall: A Series of Very Plain Talks on Very Practical Politics* (1905; New York, 1963), 25–26, 90–93, 97–98; Charles F. Murphy, "A Tribute to Plunkitt by the Leader of Tammany Hall," in *Plunkitt of Tammany Hall*, xxvi; Myers, *History of Tammany Hall*, 230; Werner, *Tammany Hall*, 294–297, 497–506; Hays, *Response to Industrialism*, 98–99; Czitrom, "Underworld and Underdogs," 536, 542–545; Ackerman, *Boss Tweed*, 21, 358–359.

6. George Washington Plunkitt, "Honest Graft and Dishonest Graft," in *Plunkitt of Tammany Hall*, 3–6. See also [Lincoln Steffens], *The Autobiography of Lincoln Steffens* (Chautauqua, NY, 1931); Werner, *Tammany Hall*, 328, 371–420; *Encyclopedia of New York*, s.v. "Plunkitt, George Washington" and "Tammany Hall."

7. Royal L. Melendy, "The Saloon in Chicago," *American Journal of Sociology* 6 (Nov. 1900): 303; Neil Larry Shumsky, "Tacit Acceptance: Respectable Americans and Segregated Prostitution, 1870–1910," *Journal of Social History* 19 (Summer 1986): 665; Bridgeport Vice Commission, *The Report and Recommendations of the Bridgeport Vice Commission* (Bridgeport, CT, 1916); [Vice Commission of Louisville], *Report of the Vice Commission, Louisville, Kentucky: Survey of Existing Conditions with Recommendations to the Hon. John H. Buschemeyer, Mayor* (Louisville, 1915); Lawrence M. Friedman, *Crime and Punishment in American History* (New York, 1993), 329.

8. Robert E. Park, "The City: Suggestions for the Investigation of Human Behavior in the Urban Environment" in *The City*, ed. Robert E. Park, Ernest W. Burgess, and Roderick McKenzie (Chicago, 1925), 43.

9. Edwin R. A. Seligman, ed. *The Social Evil: With Special Reference to Conditions Existing in the City of New York*, 2nd rev. ed. (New York, 1912), 21, 45–49; Howard B. Woolston, *Prostitution in the United States*, vol. 1, *Prior to the Entrance of the United States into the World War* (New York, 1921), 192–194; Mark Thomas Connelly, *The Response to Prostitution in the Progressive Era* (Chapel Hill, NC, 1980), 12–13; Ruth Rosen, *The Lost Sisterhood: Prostitution in America, 1900–1917* (Baltimore, 1982), 9–11. Geographic concentration did occur with or without official encouragement, but the consistent emphasis was on registering prostitutes, not concentrating prostitution. See Alain Corbin, *Women for Hire: Prostitution and Sexuality in France*

after 1850, trans. Alan Sheridan (Paris, 1978; English trans. Cambridge, MA, 1990), 9–
10, 30–37, 53–60, 174–180; Judith R. Walkowitz, *Prostitution and Victorian Society:
Women, Class, and the State* (Cambridge, 1980), 76–78, 155–156.

10. John C. Burnham, "Medical Inspection of Prostitutes in America in the Nine-
teenth Century: The St. Louis Experiment and Its Sequel," *Bulletin of the History of
Medicine* 45 (1971): 203–218; David Pivar, *Purity Crusade: Sexual Morality and Social
Control, 1868–1900* (Westport, CT, 1973), 52–54.

11. D. F. Simpson, "Municipal Government of Minneapolis," *Proceedings of the
Second National Conference for Good City Government Held at Minneapolis, December 8 and 10, 1894* (Philadelphia, 1895), 102–103; Rev. Donald D. MacLaurin, "Municipal Condition of Detroit," *Proceedings of the . . . Third National Conference for Good
City Government Held at Cleveland, May 29, 30, and 31, 1895* (Philadelphia, 1896), 385–
386; "Disorderly Tenement Houses," *New York Times*, 26 Mar. 1901, card no. 535,
clipping vol. 9, box 33, NYC15; Rev. John P. Peters, "Suppression of the 'Raines Law
Hotels,'" *Annals of the American Academy of Political and Social Science* 32 (Nov. 1908):
88; Thomas C. Devlin, *Municipal Reform in the United States* (New York, 1896), 145.

12. George Frederick Elliott, "Law Enforcement Societies," *Proceedings of the . . .
Third National Conference . . . 1895*, 485; Isadore Dyer, "The Municipal Control of
Prostitution in the United States," *New Orleans Medical and Surgical Journal* (Dec.
1899): 10; "The New York Tenderloin," *Commercial Advertiser*, 21 Apr. 1901, card no.
678, vol. 12, box 33, NYC15; Willoughby Cyrus Waterman, *Prostitution and Its Repression in New York City, 1900–1931* (New York, 1932), 14.

13. "Chairman Baldwin Would Localize Vice," *New York World*, 26 Feb. 1901, card
no. 306, vol. 6, box 33, NYC15.

14. Simpson, "Municipal Government of Minneapolis," 102; Christopher G. Tiede-
man, "Suppression of Vice: How Far a Proper and Efficient Function of Popular
Government," *Brief* 3 (1900): 17–28; "Disorderly Tenement Houses," NYC15; John R.
Dos Passos, "Gambling and Cognate Vices," *Yale Law Journal* 14 (Nov. 1904): 11, 16;
Alexander R. Piper, *Report of an Investigation of the Discipline and Administration of
the Police Department of the City of Chicago* (Chicago, 1904), 15, reprinted in *Chicago
Police Investigations: Three Reports* (New York, 1971).

15. Al Rose, *Storyville, New Orleans: Being an Authentic, Illustrated Account of the
Notorious Red-Light District* (Tuscaloosa, AL, 1974), 1; Shreveport City Council Min-
utes, 1902, Noel Memorial Library, Louisiana State University at Shreveport; Thomas C.
Mackey, *Red Lights Out: A Legal History of Prostitution, Disorderly Houses and Vice
Districts, 1870–1917* (New York, 1987), 290–352; "Mistake Corrected," *American Social
Hygiene Association Bulletin* 1 (Sept. 1914): 4–5. Ordinance-created districts also ex-
isted in Arizona, Kentucky, Nevada, and New Mexico. See American Social Hygiene
Association, *State Laws Concerning White Slave Traffic, Keeping Disorderly Houses,
and Age of Consent*, Publication No. 74 (Oct. 1916), file 4, box 170, ASHA.

16. Blue Book Collection, Historic New Orleans Collection, New Orleans; Rose,
Storyville, 138; "Laws and Their Enforcement," *American Social Hygiene Association
Bulletin* 1 (July 1914): 3–4; "Mistake Corrected," 4–5; Frederick H. Whitin to W. Stan-
ley Bender, 25 Mar. 1908, box 1, C14.

17. *L'Hote v. New Orleans* 177 U.S. 588 (1900). See also Rose, *Storyville*, 2, 39.

18. *L'Hote* 177 U.S. 588.

19. Frederick H. Whitin to Max Senior, 25 Jan. 1912, box 1, C14; Timothy J. Gil-foyle, *City of Eros: New York City, Prostitution, and the Commercialization of Sex, 1790–1920* (New York, 1992), 268.

20. [Steffens], *Autobiography*, 387; Frederick H. Whitin to Judge Lane, Birming-ham, Alabama, 26 Sept. 1911, box 1, C14; Witte to Gaynor, 11 Sept. 1912, GWJ-87, Mayors' Papers, New York City Municipal Archives and Records Center, cited in Gilfoyle, *City of Eros*, 410n49; Woolston, *Prostitution in the United States*, 103. The quotation is from Robert M. Fogelson, *Big-City Police* (Cambridge, MA, 1977), 10.

21. William McAdoo, *Guarding a Great City* (New York, 1906), 72–74; Piper, *Report of an Investigation*, 15; Theodore A. Bingham to Frederick H. Whitin, 11 Sept. 1911, box 1, C14.

22. McAdoo, *Guarding A Great City*, 72; Woolston, *Prostitution in the United States*, 109; Eugene J. Watts, "The Police in Atlanta, 1890–1905," *Journal of Southern History* 39 (May 1973): 173; Shumsky, "Tacit Acceptance," 668. W. E. H. Lecky is the source of the cliché. See William Edward Hartpole Lecky, *History of European Morals from Augustus to Charlemagne* (1869; with an introduction by C. Wright Mills, New York, 1955), 282–283.

23. Woolston, *Prostitution in the United States*, 109; Waterman, *Prostitution and Its Repression*, 14; Shumsky, "Tacit Acceptance," 668.

24. Piper, *Report of an Investigation*, 15; [Steffens], *Autobiography*, 387; McAdoo, *Guarding a Great City*, 73; Watts, "Police in Atlanta," 173; Neil Larry Shumsky and Larry M. Springer, "San Francisco's Zone of Prostitution, 1880–1934," *Journal of Historical Geography* 7 (Jan. 1981): 78.

25. Frederick H. Whitin to Harry Wright, 24 Aug. 1908, box 1, C14; Jane Addams, *A New Conscience and an Ancient Evil* (New York, 1912), 36–37; "First Step toward Segregating Vice," 5 Mar. 1901, card 375, vol. 7, box 33, NYC15.

26. Lawrence Veiller to Hon. John J. Murphy, 14 Feb. 1914, file: "Tenement House Committee—Prostitution," box 168, Community Service Society Papers, Rare Book and Manuscript Library, Columbia University. On Veiller, see Roy Lubove, *The Progressives and the Slums: Tenement House Reform in New York City, 1890–1917* (Pittsburgh, 1962), 117–184.

27. Waterman, *Prostitution and Its Repression*, 12–13; Rosen, *Lost Sisterhood*, 5; Robert E. Riegel, "Changing American Attitudes toward Prostitution," *Journal of the History of Ideas* 29 (July–Sept. 1968): 448; Shumsky, "Tacit Acceptance," 669; Gilfoyle, *City of Eros*, 251–253.

28. "Mr. Story Talks on Immoral Houses," 22 Dec. 1902, 1–2; "Would Screen District from Terminal Station," 20 Dec. 1909, 1; both *New Orleans Item*; Lincoln Steffens, *The Shame of the Cities* (1904; New York, 1948).

29. "Fifteen's Evidence," *New York Mail and Express*, 23 Jan. 1901, card no. 110, vol. 3, box 32, NYC15; "Mr. Story Talks," 1–2; Woolston, *Prostitution in the United States*, 103, 118–119; George M. Reynolds, *Machine Politics in New Orleans, 1897–1926* (New York, 1936), 158; Connelly, *Response to Prostitution*, 105; Perry R. Duis, *The Saloon:*

Public Drinking in Chicago and Boston, 1880–1920 (Urbana, IL, 1983), 237; Gilfoyle, *City of Eros*, 265–267.

30. W. Bemis et al. to the Mayor and City Council, 13 Dec. 1902, Shreveport City Council Minutes; Goodloe Stuck, *Annie McCune: Shreveport Madam* (Baton Rouge, LA, 1981).

31. Simpson, "Municipal Government of Minneapolis," 102; Carl V. Harris, "Reforms in Government Control of Negroes in Birmingham, Alabama, 1890–1920," *Journal of Southern History* 38 (Nov. 1972): 572–574.

32. Duis, *Saloon*, 131–132; Alfred R. Conkling, *City Government in the United States* (New York, 1894), 209–211; Thomas J. Noel, *The City and the Saloon: Denver, 1858–1916* (Lincoln, NE, 1982; with a new introduction, Niwot, CO, 1996), 109; Fogelson, *Big-City Police*, 59; Samuel P. Hays, "The Politics of Reform in Municipal Government in the Progressive Era," *Pacific Northwest Quarterly* 55 (Oct. 1964): 161–162.

33. "Tammany's Police Department," *Harper's Weekly* 38 (10 Jan. 1894): 39–40; Charles H. Parkhurst, *Our Fight with Tammany* (New York, 1895), 53, 82–83, 154–155; James F. Richardson, *The New York Police: Colonial Times to 1901* (New York, 1970), 236; Richard L. McCormick, *From Realignment to Reform: Political Change in New York State, 1893–1910* (Ithaca, NY, 1981), 46–47; David C. Hammack, *Power and Society: Greater New York at the Turn of the Century* (New York, 1982), 147, 166.

34. Parkhurst, *Our Fight With Tammany*, 10.

35. Parkhurst, *Our Fight With Tammany*, 115, 214–216; *Report and Proceedings of the Senate Committee Appointed to Investigate the Police Department of the City of New York* (Albany, NY, 1895), vol. 1, 20–23.

36. "The New High-License Bill," *Harper's Weekly* 38 (17 Mar. 1894): 243; Charles W. Eliot, Seth Low, and James C. Carter, "Introduction," in *The Liquor Problem in its Legislative Aspects*, Frederic H. Wines and John Koren (Boston, 1897), 8; John Marshall Barker, *The Saloon Problem and Social Reform* (1905; New York, 1970), 135; John Koren, *Alcohol and Society* (New York, 1916), 212–213.

37. For this reason, the Committee of Fourteen, which existed from 1905 to 1932, could make the claim in 1918 that New York had never had a segregated vice district. See Frederick H. Whitin to Joseph Mayer, 7 Aug. 1918; Joseph Mayer to Frederick H. Whitin, 13 Aug. 1918; Frederick H. Whitin to Joseph Meyer [*sic*], 21 Aug. 1918; all box 4, C14. See also Frederick H. Whitin to L. C. Buckley, 16 Oct. 1917, box 4, C14; Joseph Mayer, *The Regulation of Commercialized Vice: An Analysis of the Transition from Segregation to Repression in the United States* (New York, 1922), 11; Waterman, *Prostitution and Its Repression*, 14; Gilfoyle, *City of Eros*, 199, 222–223.

38. Christine Stansell, *City of Women: Sex and Class in New York, 1789–1860* (1982; Urbana, IL, 1987), 42, 69, 89–101; Marilynn Wood Hill, *Their Sisters' Keepers: Prostitution in New York City, 1830–1870* (Berkeley, CA, 1993), 186–193; Neil Harris, "Urban Tourism and the Commercial City," in *Inventing Times Square: Commerce and Culture at the Crossroads of the World*, ed. William R. Taylor (1991; Baltimore, 1996), 79–82; Rev. John P. Peters, "The Story of the Committee of Fourteen of New York," *Social Hygiene* 4 (July 1918): 353; Kevin J. Mumford, *Interzones: Black/White Sex Districts in Chicago and New York in the Early Twentieth Century* (New York,

1997). See also chapters two and ten in Gilfoyle, *City of Eros*, which "tour" New York's sex districts.

39. "Thursday, November 22nd, 1900" and "Sunday, December 2nd, 1900," vol.: "Typed Abstracts of Daily Events" (hereafter "Typed Abstracts"), file 3, box 3; "Debauching Police," *New York Times*, 28 Sept. 1901, card no. 1343, vol. 22, box 35; "Chairman Baldwin Would Localize Vice," *New York World*, 26 Feb. 1901, card no. 306, vol. 6, box 32; all NYC15. See also Barry J. Kaplan, "Metropolitics, Administrative Reform, and Political Theory: The Greater New York City Charter of 1897," *Journal of Urban History* 9 (Feb. 1983): 165–194; McFarland, *Mugwumps, Morals and Politics*, 135–136; Hammack, *Power and Society*, 147–8, 154, 185–229.

40. "Sunday, November 25th, 1900" and "Wednesday, November 28th, 1900," vol.: "Typed Abstracts," file 3, box 3, NYC15; Jeremy P. Felt, "Vice Reform as a Political Technique: The Committee of Fifteen in New York, 1900–1901," *New York History* 54 (1973): 30–33. On Parkhurst's campaign, see Parkhurst, *Our Fight with Tammany*; James F. Gardner Jr., "Microbes and Morality: The Social Hygiene Crusade in New York City, 1892–1917," PhD diss., Indiana University, 1974, 52–66.

41. The initial Chamber of Commerce appointees were Felix Adler, William H. Baldwin, Robert W. de Forest, Joel B. Erhardt, Austen G. Fox, John S. Kennedy, Alexander E. Orr, George Foster Peabody, George Haven Putnam, John H. Rhodes, Jacob H. Schiff, E. R. A. Seligman, Charles Sprague Smith, Charles Steward Smith, and Alfred T. White, but de Forest and White resigned almost immediately to join the Tenement House Commission and were replaced by William J. O'Brien and Andrew J. Smith. See Roland Richard Wagner, "Virtue Against Vice: A Study of Moral Reformers and Prostitution in the Progressive Era," PhD diss., University of Wisconsin, 1971, 86–89; Gilfoyle, *City of Eros*, 418.

42. "Prostitution and Gambling in Manhattan," file 2, box 3; "To Seek Vice by a System," *New York Tribune*, 1 Feb. 1901, card no. 151, vol. 4, box 32; Minutes, 13 Feb. 1901, 1, file 1, box 3; "Evil in Tenements," *Mail and Express*, 16 Feb. 1901, card no. 203, vol. 4, box 32; "Fifteen After the Social Evil," *Commercial Advertiser*, 4 Mar. 1901, card no. 361, vol. 7, box 33; "First Step toward Segregating Vice"; all NYC15. See also Research Committee of the Committee of Fourteen, *The Social Evil in New York City: A Study of Law Enforcement* (New York, 1910), 2–3; Gilfoyle, *City of Eros*, 302–303; Lubove, *Progressives and the Slums*, 138–139.

43. "Disorderly Tenement Houses," NYC15. Throughout the year, the Committee of Fifteen sent investigators back to the tenements to check that prostitutes had not returned.

44. "To Rouse the Public Is Fifteen's Aim," *Brooklyn Eagle*, 11 Jan. 1901, card no. 43; "City Is Cursed by 'Devils on Top,'" *New York Herald*, 14 Jan. 1901, card no. 65; both vol. 2, box 32, NYC15. Even when the Committee of Fifteen announced that it was not political, both friends and foes found this claim specious. See "Fifteen Committee Not Anti-Tammany," *New York Press*, 12 Feb. 1901, card no. 189, vol. 4, box 32; "Vice Crusade Drags," *Mail and Express*, 14 Feb. 1901, card no. 195, vol. 4, box 32; "The Vice System," *Commercial Advertiser*, 26 Apr. 1901, card no. 695, vol. 12, box 33; all NYC15. The typed abstracts of daily events, as well as the clipping vols., show the

extent to which Tammany actions and the anti-Tammany campaigns were integral to the Committee of Fifteen's mission.

45. "Friday, November 16th, 1900"; "Saturday, November 17th, 1900"; both vol.: "Typed Abstracts," file 3, box 3, NYC15; Myers, *History of Tammany Hall*, 289; Peters, "Story of the Committee of Fourteen," 356–357; Richardson, *New York Police*, 277–278.

46. "The Five Defend Croker," 8 Jan. 1901, card no. 21, vol. 2, box 32; "Tammany Five After Police," *New York Telegraph*, 9 Jan. 1901, card no. 30, vol. 2, box 32; "The Blame For Abuse," *Post*, 10 Jan. 1901, card no. 36, vol. 2, box 32; "Another Link in Chain Forged," 21 Feb. 1901, card no. 254, vol. 5, box 32; "To Segregate Vice," *Mail and Express*, 21 Mar. 1901, card no. 475, vol. 9, box 33; "Report of Five," *Commercial Advertiser*, 21 Mar. 1901, card no. 493, vol. 9, box 33; all NYC15. See also Myers, *History of Tammany Hall*, 292–293; Gardner, "Microbes and Morality," 72–74.

47. "Vice Is Driven from Its Haunts by Tammany's Arm," *Journal*, 4 Dec. 1900, card no. 19a, vol. 1, box 32; "Gamblers Close in Fear of Philbin," 24 Dec. 1900, card no. 34a, vol. 1, box 32; "Philbin's Great Swoop," *Brooklyn Standard Union*, 19 Feb. 1901, card no. 218, vol. 5, box 32; "Nixon, Philbin and Jerome Raid Gamblers—Hold Court in Pool Room—Com. Holahan Caught," *Journal*, 19 Feb. 1901, card no. 219, vol. 5, box 32; all NYC15.

48. W. A. Rogers, "An Awful Possibility," *Harper's Weekly* 45 (26 Jan. 1901): cover.

49. "Thursday, January 10th, 1901"; "Monday, August 12th, 1901"; both vol.: "Typed Abstracts," file 3, box 3, NYC15; Gardner, "Microbes and Morality," 72–73.

50. "After Liquor Dealers," *Commercial Advertiser*, 22 Mar. 1901, card no. 500, vol. 9; " 'Five' and 'Fifteen' Believe Alike," *Journal*, 21 Apr. 1901, card no. 680, vol. 12; both box 33, NYC15; Myers, *History of Tammany Hall*, 294–295, 303–304; Richardson, *New York Police*, 240, 282–283; Wagner, "Virtue Against Vice," 94, 104, 106.

51. Lawrence Veiller to Hon. John J. Murphy, 14 Feb. 1914, file: "Tenement House Committee—Prostitution," box 168, Community Service Society Papers; John P. Peters to the editor of the *Evening Post*, 3 Jan. 1913, file: "1912, Proposed Morals Commission," box 83, C14; Peters, "Story of the Committee of Fourteen," 360; Gilfoyle, *City of Eros*, 301; *Encyclopedia of New York*, s.v. "Raines Law."

52. Myers, *History of Tammany Hall*, 304. See also Reynolds, *Machine Politics in New Orleans*, 129, 158–159; Noel, *City and the Saloon*, 104, 107.

53. "The Vice System," *Commercial Advertiser*, 26 Apr. 1901, card no. 695, vol. 12, box 33, NYC15; Felt, "Vice Reform," 43; Gardner, "Microbes and Morality," 84.

54. "Fifteen Committee Will Be Permanent," *New York World*, 7 Apr. 1901, card no. 584, vol. 10, box 33, NYC15; Peters, "Suppression of the 'Raines Law Hotels,' " 88; Felt, "Vice Reform," 43; Wagner, "Virtue Against Vice," 104.

55. Richard Skolnick, "Civic Group Progressivism in New York City," *New York History* 51 (1970): 415–418; Hammack, *Power and Society*, 312.

56. Frederick H. Whitin to John P. Peters, 17 Nov. 1906; Frederick H. Whitin to Judge Lane, 26 Sept. 1911; both box 1, C14; Peters, "Story of the Committee of Fourteen," 378–379; Wagner, "Virtue Against Vice," 138, 148n39. See also Whitin's condemnation of the Chicago Vice Commission's recommendations because of their impracticality in *Survey* 26 (6 May 1911): 218.

57. Waterman, *Prostitution and Its Repression*, 102–104; Mara L. Keire, "The Committee of Fourteen and Saloon Reforms in New York City, 1905–1920," *Business and Economic History* 26 (Winter 1998): 573–583.

58. The Committee of Fifteen drew its membership from the Chamber of Commerce, while the Committee of Fourteen was an offshoot of the more bourgeois City Club. "The Committee of Fourteen," 1921, 1, file: "Fesler, Mayo 1921," box 83, C14; Waterman, *Prostitution and Its Repression*, 95–96; Wagner, "Virtue Against Vice," 113–114, 116; *Encyclopedia of New York City*, s.v. "New York Chamber of Commerce and Industry."

59. The following were members of the Committee of Fourteen at its founding: Rev. Lee W. Beattie, Hon. William S. Bennet, Mr. Samuel W. Bowen, Prof. Francis M. Burdick, Rev. Father William J. B. Daly, Rabbi Bernard Drachman, Rabbi Pereira Mendes, Rev. John P. Peters, Mr. George Haven Putnam, Mr. Thomas H. Reed, Mr. Noah C. Rogers, Rev. Howard H. Russell, Mrs. V. G. Simkhovitch, and Mr. Lawrence Veiller. See "The Abolition of the Raines Law Hotels and the Work of the Committee of Fourteen," *Lincoln Magazine* (June 1905), vol. 1, box 86, C14. At its incorporation almost two years later, the constituency of the Committee had changed. The directors were Ruth Baldwin, Lee Beattie, William Bennet, Francis Burdick, Frances Kellor, William McAdoo, Pereira Mendes, John P. Peters, George Haven Putnam, Howard Russell, William Jay Schieffelin, Isaac Seligman, Mary Simkhovitch, and Francis Louis Slade. See "Certificate of Incorporation," [Jan. 1907], vol. 1, box 86, C14. See also Peters, "Story of the Committee of Fourteen," 361; Wagner, "Virtue Against Vice," 114–115.

60. Peters, "Suppression of the 'Raines Law Hotels,'" 96; "Committee of Fourteen," 1921, file: "Fesler, Mayo 1921," box 83, C14; Wagner, "Virtue Against Vice," 118–119.

61. Frederick H. Whitin to Ethel V. Fraser, 17 Dec. 1909, box 1; "Cooperation between the Committee of Fourteen and the Surety Companies," [1916], file: "Surety Companies," box 20; both C14; Peters, "Story of the Committee of Fourteen," 353–354.

62. Gilfoyle, *City of Eros*, 245; John P. Peters to the editor of the *Evening Post*, C14; Waterman, *Prostitution and Its Repression*, 31–33; Richardson, *New York Police*, 253; Gilfoyle, *City of Eros*, 245, 303; *Encyclopedia of New York City*, s.v. "Raines Law."

63. "Statement," 1 May 1905, vol. 1, box 86, C14; Peters, "Story of the Committee of Fourteen," 361; Waterman, *Prostitution and Its Repression*, 96–97.

64. "Statement of Work," Mar. 1906, vol. 1, box 86, C14. See also Peters, "Suppression of the 'Raines Law Hotels,'" 90–92.

65. Committee of Fourteen, *Annual Report for 1919*, 14, vol.: "Committee Minutes," Oct. 1916–June 1920, box 86, C14.

66. Committee of Fourteen, *Annual Report for 1912*, 2, vol.: "Committee Minutes," Mar. 1905–1913, box 86, C14; Peters, "Story of the Committee of Fourteen," 366, 373; Waterman, *Prostitution and Its Repression*, 100; Wagner, "Virtue Against Vice," 118.

67. Koren, *Alcohol and Society*, 226; Duis, *Saloon*, 26–28; Roy Rosenzweig, *Eight Hours for What We Will: Workers and Leisure in an Industrial City, 1870–1920* (Cambridge, 1983), 185; Richard Hamm, *Shaping the Eighteenth Amendment: Temperance*

Reform, Legal Culture, and the Polity, 1880–1920 (Chapel Hill, NC, 1995), 27. For example, in Chicago, where liquor licenses were $500, saloonkeepers added approximately $3.3 million to the city coffers in 1894. See John E. George, "The Saloon Question in Chicago," *Economic Studies* 2 (Apr. 1897): 78.

68. "Statement of the Committee of Fourteen for the Abolishment of Raines Law Hotels," 1 May 1905, vol. 1, box 86; "Efforts with the Bankers Surety Company," [1909], file: "Surety Companies," box 20; both C14.

69. George, "Saloon Question in Chicago," 74–76; Peters, "Suppression of the 'Raines Law Hotels,'" 93; "Cooperation between the Committee of Fourteen and the Surety Companies," C14; Thomas C. Cochran, *The Pabst Brewing Company: The History of an American Business* (New York, 1948), 143–145, 196–199; K. Austin Kerr, *Organized for Prohibition: A New History of the Anti-Saloon League* (New Haven, CT, 1985), 22–24; Duis, *Saloon*, 25–26, 40–42.

70. "Statement," Feb. 1906, vol. 1, box 86, C14. See also Peters, "Suppression of the 'Raines Law Hotels,'" 93–94; Wagner, "Virtue Against Vice," 120.

71. "Statement," Feb. 1906, C14. See also Peters, "Suppression of the 'Raines Law Hotels,'" 93–94; Wagner, "Virtue Against Vice," 120.

72. Peter Doelger to John P. Peters, 16 June 1916, vol. 2, box 86, C14.

73. "Statement for Publicity by the Chairman," [1907], vol. 1, box 86, C14; Wagner, "Virtue Against Vice," 121–122. See also George, "Saloon Question in Chicago," 67. For an example of the alcohol trade's self-regulation in a smaller city, see Rosenzweig, *Eight Hours*, 183–190.

74. The Committee of Fourteen started an informal protest list in 1905, and by 1906 the list was a formal fixture in their scheme. "Statement," Feb. 1906; Bulletin #21, 5 Oct. 1908, vol. 1, box 86; "1918 Protest List," 12 Nov. 1918, Bulletin #1196, Bulletin Book #9, box 88; all C14; Wagner, "Virtue Against Vice," 119–120. It is unclear if the number of representatives from each group varied, so I have used the one case where the makeup of the Joint Committee was mentioned, "In the Spring of 1906," n.d., file: "Surety Companies," box 20, C14.

75. Bulletin #30, vol. 1, box 86; Bulletin #21, 5 Oct. 1908, vol. 1, box 86; "Cooperation between the Committee of Fourteen and the Surety Companies," [1916], file: "Surety Companies," box 20; all C14. The Committee of Fourteen turned to the surety companies rather than the Excise Department because the latter had no discretionary power. Its commissioners could revoked licenses, but they could not refuse to issue a license. See Committee of Fourteen to Albert J. Hopkins, 6 July 1910, box 1, C14.

76. Fritz Laelzer to the Committee of Fourteen, 28 Sept. 1916, file: "Lenox Ave.–Lexington Ave.," box 17; John Rafferty to the Committee of Fourteen, 13 Sept. 1911, box 1; Proprietor of 27 East 22nd Street to the Committee of Fourteen, 30 Sept. 1913, file: "Abington Sq.–Bradhurst Ave.," box 17; Bobby Moore to the Committee of Fourteen, 26 Sept. 1916, file: "West 4th–40th Sts.," box 17; William Banks to the Committee of Fourteen, 25 Sept. 1914, file: "West 4th–40th Sts.," box 17; Proprietor of 520 Eighth Avenue to the Committee of Fourteen, 2 Sept. 1914, file: "Eighth Ave. #22–989," box 17; all C14.

77. See the various "Excise" files that comprise most of box 20 in the C14 records.

78. Contrary to the popular stereotype, there were a number of women saloon proprietors. For example, between Oct. 1906 and Nov. 1907, 19 percent of the proprietors arrested for liquor-law violations were women (111 men, 28 women, 11 indeterminate). See "Special Sessions," Oct. 1907; "Special Sessions Cases Disposed Of October 1906 to September 1907, charged with violation of Sec. 322 of the Penal Code and the Liquor Tax Law," [1907]; both file: "Court of Special Sessions," box 65, C14.

79. Bulletin #19, 14 May 1908, vol. 1, box 86; Bulletin #7, 18 May 1907, vol. 1, box 86; Bulletin #3, 22 Mar. 1907, vol. 1, box 86; Bulletin #29, Aug. 1909, vol. 1, box 86; "Cooperation between the Committee of Fourteen and the Surety Companies," [1916], file: "Surety Companies," box 20; all C14. The Committee of Fourteen needed the surety companies because the courts often decided in the favor of proprietors charged with liquor-law violations. For example, between Oct. 1906 and Nov. 1907, the Excise Department brought 142 cases of liquor-law violations to the Special Sessions Court. In 64 percent of these cases, the proprietors were able to keep their liquor licenses and, equally importantly, retain the right to acquire one the following year. See "Special Sessions"; "Special Sessions Cases Disposed Of October 1906 to September 1907"; both C14.

80. Committee of Fourteen, *Annual Report for 1916*, 70, vol. 1: "Committee Minutes," Oct. 1916–June 1920, box 86, C14. See also Keire, "Committee of Fourteen and Saloon Reform," 573–583.

81. Frederick H. Whitin to Mrs. Barclay Hazard, 9 Sept. 1911, box 1; "The Committee of Fourteen," 1921, file: "Fesler, Mayo 1921," box 83; both C14.

82. George Kneeland to Frederick H. Whitin, 5 June 1911, box 1; J. Frank Chase to Frederick H. Whitin, 14 Sept. 1917, box 4; Frederick H. Whitin to Robbins Gilman, 31 Dec. 1917, box 4; "Surety Companies," 26 Oct. 1912, file: "Surety Companies," box 20; all C14; Waterman, *Prostitution and Its Repression*, 104–107. See also Duis, *Saloon*, for a comparison of saloon reform in Boston and Chicago.

83. Wagner, "Virtue Against Vice," 187; Connelly, *Response to Prostitution*, 13–14.

84. George J. Kneeland to Frederick H. Whitin, 5 June 1911, box 1, C14. Although part of a local-option state, Chicago was sometimes under high license. See Sidney L. Harring, *Policing a Class Society: The Experience of American Cities, 1865–1915* (New Brunswick, NJ, 1983), 161–163; Duis, *Saloon*, 259, 267, 270.

85. William T. Stead, *If Christ Came to Chicago* (1894; Evanston, IL, [1990]), 331–332; Joseph O. Baylen, "A Victorian 'Crusade' in Chicago, 1893–1894," *Journal of American History* 51 (Dec. 1964): 418–419; Wagner, "Virtue Against Vice," 64–66; Duis, *Saloon*, 246. Paul S. Boyer also compares Stead to Parkhurst in his *Urban Masses and Moral Order in America, 1820–1920* (Cambridge, MA, 1978), 164.

86. Herbert Asbury, *Gem of the Prairie: An Informal History of the Chicago Underworld* (1940; with an introduction by Perry R. Duis, DeKalb, IL, 1986), 157; Baylen, "A Victorian 'Crusade,'" 426; Wagner, "Virtue Against Vice," 66; Gardner, "Microbes and Morality," 65; Boyer, *Urban Masses*, 164, 184; Duis, *Saloon*, 253.

87. *State Report on the Chicago Police System as Made by the Committee of Inves-*

tigation Appointed by the 40th General Assembly, Special Session, 1897–1898 (Spring-field, IL, 1898), 3, 10, reprinted in *Chicago Police Investigations*, 3; Lloyd Wendt and Herman Kogan, *Lords of the Levee: The Story of Bathhouse John and Hinky Dink* (Indianapolis, 1943), 115–116; Fogelson, *Big-City Police*, 5, 8–9.

88. Carl Hovey, "The Police Question: Chicago Struggling to Solve It; Phila-delphia Blinded and Bound," *Metropolitan Magazine* ([1910]): 38–40, file: "Chicago. Police. Pamphlets Concerning," GTP; McAdoo, *Guarding a Great City*, 242; Piper, *Report of an Investigation*, 15; Harring, *Policing a Class Society*, 194–195.

89. Piper, *Report of an Investigation*, 15.

90. "Chicago as Seen by Herself," *McClure's Magazine* [1906]: 67–73; Vice Com-mission of Chicago, *The Social Evil in Chicago: A Study of Existing Conditions, with Recommendations* (Chicago, 1911), 329; Asbury, *Gem of the Prairie*, 243–244; Mark H. Haller, "Urban Crime and Criminal Justice: The Chicago Case," *Journal of American History* 57 (Dec. 1970): 631.

91. Graham Taylor, "The Story of the Chicago Vice Commission," *Survey* 26 (6 May 1911): 239; Walter C. Reckless, *Vice in Chicago* (Chicago, 1933), 4; Asbury, *Gem of the Prairie*, 284; Connelly, *Response to Prostitution*, 94–95.

92. Hovey, "Police Question," 45; Graham Taylor to George R. Wallace, 18 Apr. 1912, file: "Letters. 1912," box: "Outgoing to 1919," GTP; Clifford W. Barnes, "The Story of the Committee of Fifteen of Chicago," *Social Hygiene* 4 (Apr. 1918): 145–156; Wendt and Kogan, *Lords of the Levee*, 290; Eric Anderson, "Prostitution and Social Justice: Chicago, 1910–1915," *Social Service Review* 48 (June 1974): 203–208; Connelly, *Re-sponse to Prostitution*, 99.

93. Vice Commission of Chicago, *Social Evil*, 3–4; "Vice Commission to Clean Chicago," *Survey* 23 (26 Mar. 1910): 961–962; Barnes, "Story of the Committee of Fifteen of Chicago," 146–147. The following were members of the Chicago Vice Commission: Dr. W. L. Baum, Mr. David Blaustein, Father James F. Callaghen, Dr. Anna Dwyer, Dr. W. A. Evans, Father Albert Everst, Rev. Dr. Frank W. Gunsaulus, Mr. W. W. Hallam, Dr. Abram W. Harris, Dr. William Healy, Prof. James M. Hyde, Mrs. Ellen M. Henrotin, Rabbi Abram Hirschberg, Father E. A. Kelly, Rev. John G. Kircher, Mr. Louis O. Kohtz, Mr. P. J. O'Keefe, Judge Harry Olson, Judge Merritt W. Pinckney, Mr. Alexander Robertson, Mr. Julius Rosenwald, Dr. Louis E. Schmidt, Bishop C. T. Shaffer, Hon. Edwin W. Sims, Edward M. Skinner, Dean Walter T. Sumner, Prof. Graham Taylor, Prof. W. I. Thomas, Prof. Herbert L. Willett, and Hon. John L. Whitman. When Prof. Hyde died, Prof. Charles R. Henderson replaced him. See Vice Commission of Chicago, *Social Evil*, 2, 7–8.

94. Vice Commission of Chicago, *Social Evil*, 25; Taylor, "Story of the Chicago Vice Commission," 240; Wagner, "Virtue Against Vice," 164.

95. Mayer, *Regulation of Commercialized Vice*, 10–12; Woolston, *Prostitution in the United States*, 121–122; Riegel, "Changing American Attitudes," 452; Anderson, "Prostitution and Social Justice," 203–204, 218–220; Connelly, *Response to Prostitu-tion*, 92; Rosen, *Lost Sisterhood*, 14.

CHAPTER 2. THE SPORTING WORLD, 1890–1917

1. Ernest W. Burgess, "The Growth of the City: An Introduction to a Research Project," in *The City*, ed. Robert E. Park, Ernest W. Burgess, and Roderick McKenzie (Chicago, 1925), 58–59.

2. [Hartford Vice Commission], *Report of the Hartford Vice Commission: Hartford, Connecticut* (Hartford, [1913]), 47; Vice Commission of Chicago, *The Social Evil in Chicago: A Study of Existing Conditions, with Recommendations* (Chicago, 1911), 127; [Newark Citizens' Committee], *Report on the Social Evil Conditions of Newark, New Jersey to the People of Newark* ([Newark], [1914]), 65; [Moral Survey Committee], *The Social Evil in Syracuse: Being the Report of an Investigation of the Moral Condition of the City Conducted by a Committee of Eighteen Citizens* (Syracuse, NY, 1913), 75, reprinted in *Prostitution in America: Three Investigations, 1902–1914* (New York, 1976); Martin Paulsson, *The Social Anxieties of Progressive Reform: Atlantic City, 1854–1920* (New York, 1994), 101.

3. "J. H. Brown's Inspection," 5 June 1901, NYC15; Story #485, "Harry Greene's Pool Parlor—66 E. 4th St.," 30 Mar. 1913; unnumbered story, "Saloon Hangout— Simmie Tischler—159 Rivington St.," 5 May 1913; both Kehillah; Junius Boyd Wood, *The Negro in Chicago: How He and His Race Kindred Came to Dwell in Great Numbers in a Northern City; How He Lives and Works; His Successes and Failures; His Political Outlook* (Chicago, 1916), 27; [Newark Citizens' Committee], *Report*, 76; Herbert Asbury, *The Barbary Coast: An Informal History of the San Francisco Underworld* (New York, 1933), 270–271; Kenneth L. Kusmer, *A Ghetto Takes Shape: Black Cleveland, 1870–1930* (Urbana, IL, 1976), 48; Robert F. Selcer, "Fort Worth and the Fraternity of Strange Women," *Southwestern Historical Society* 96 (July 1992): 63; James R. McGovern, "'Sporting Life on the Line': Prostitution in Progressive Era Pensacola," *Florida Historical Quarterly* 54 (Oct. 1975): 134; Mark Thomas Connelly, *The Response to Prostitution in the Progressive Era* (Chapel Hill, NC, 1980), 93; Perry R. Duis, *The Saloon: Public Drinking in Chicago and Boston, 1880–1920* (Urbana, IL, 1983), 237–238; Timothy J. Gilfoyle, *City of Eros: New York City, Prostitution, and the Commercialization of Sex, 1790–1920* (New York, 1992), 204–208; Howard P. Chudacoff, *The Age of the Bachelor: Creating an American Subculture* (Princeton, NJ, 1999), 132.

4. John F. Kasson, *Amusing the Million: Coney Island at the Turn of the Century* (New York, 1978), 5; Al Rose, *Storyville, New Orleans: Being an Authentic, Illustrated Account of the Notorious Red-Light District* (Tuscaloosa, AL, 1974), 38–39.

5. Kasson, *Amusing the Million*, 51; Sarah Nadler promissory note, 30 Mar. 1912, box 1, C14; Story #237, "Bowery," 31 Dec. 1912; Story #280, "Miners Peoples Theater— 207 Bowery," 14 Jan. 1913; Story #607, "Penny Arcade—21 Bowery," 14 May 1913; Story #644, "Joe Tough's Rest. Hangout for Macks, Thieves, Prostitutes. Surf Ave. & Henderson Walk—Coney Island," 30 May 1913; Story #744, "Chick Tricker's Saloon—241 Bowery," 28 Oct. 1913, all Kehillah; Committee of Fourteen, *Annual Report*, 1914, 16– 17, vol.: "March 1913–September 1916," box 86, C14; Gilfoyle, *City of Eros*, 215–222;

Daniel Czitrom, "Underworld and Underdogs: Big Tim Sullivan and Metropolitan Politics in New York, 1889–1913," *Journal of American History* 78 (Sept. 1991): 542.

6. Robert E. Park, "The City: Suggestions for the Investigation of Human Behavior in the Urban Environment," in *The City*, 4.

7. Bridgeport Vice Commission, *The Report and Recommendations of the Bridgeport Vice Commission* (Bridgeport, CT, 1916), 23.

8. [Lexington Vice Commission], *Report of the Vice Commission of Lexington, Kentucky*, 2nd ed. (Lexington, 1915), 13.

9. Vice Commission of Chicago, *Social Evil*, 78; Howard B. Woolston, *Prostitution in the United States*, vol. 1, *Prior to the Entrance of the United States into the World War* (New York, 1921), 107; Rose, *Storyville*, 75; Czitrom, "Underworlds and Underdogs," 542; Robert W. Snyder, *The Voice of the City: Vaudeville and Popular Culture in New York, with a New Preface by the Author* (Chicago, 2000), 87.

10. Bridgeport Vice Commission, *Report*, 23.

11. [Lancaster Citizens' Committee], *A Report on Vice Conditions in the City of Lancaster, Pa.* ([Lancaster], 1913), 25; Frank Andrews, *The Incandescent Lamp, 1900–1920*, online essay, (accessed 3 Mar. 2006).

12. Graham Taylor, "The Police and Vice in Chicago," *Survey* 23 (6 Nov. 1910): 164; "Vice Commission Will Make Report Oct. 7," *Atlanta Constitution* (19 Sept. 1912), 3; Walter Clarke, "Report for Jacksonville, Fla.," file: "Florida Jacksonville," box 6, CTCA; Rose, *Storyville*, 80, 139; Madelon Powers, *Faces along the Bar: Lore and Order in the Workingman's Saloon, 1870–1920* (Chicago, 1998), 153.

13. [Woman wearing low-cut green, blue, and yellow costume with feathers and roses in her hair] (Buffalo, NY, 1899), poster, card #var1993000341/PP, TPC; [woman wearing short-skirted dress with hands on hips and feathers in her hair] (Cincinnati, 1900), poster, card #var1994001538/PP, TPC; "Gay New York: 'Welcome to Our City'" (Cincinnati, 1907), poster, card #var1993000069/PP, TPC; Rose, *Storyville*, 22–26, 31–33; Valerie Steele, "The Corset: Fashion and Eroticism," *Fashion Theory* 3 (Dec. 1999): 456–459.

14. Gilfoyle, *City of Eros*, 208; Snyder, *Voice of the City*, 85–86. For a list of cabarets, rathskellers, and restaurants in the area ten years later, see Lewis A. Erenberg, *Steppin' Out: New York Nightlife and the Transformation of American Culture, 1890–1930* (Westport, CT, 1981), 120–121.

15. Internet Broadway Database, s.v. "Loew's New York," www.ibdb.com/venue.asp?ID=1401 (accessed 21 Feb. 2007). For a description of a more disreputable entertainment complex, see Bridgeport Vice Commission, *Report*, 46.

16. Wisconsin Vice Committee, *Report and Recommendations of the Wisconsin Legislative Committee to Investigate the White Slave Traffic and Kindred Subjects* ([Madison], 1914), 33; Vice Commission of Chicago, *Social Evil*, 34–35, 122–124; H. Gordon Frost, *The Gentlemen's Club: The Story of Prostitution in El Paso* (El Paso, TX, 1983), 161–162.

17. Committee of Fourteen, *Annual Report*, 1914, 44, C14. Gilfoyle identifies the photograph on this page of the report as "Tom Sharkey's and the Rialto." See Gilfoyle, *City of Eros*, 212. For similar photographs, see Committee of Fourteen, *Annual*

Report, 1914 and *Annual Report,* 1915, vol.: "March 1913–September 1916," box 86, C14.

18. Frederic H. Wines and John Koren, *The Liquor Problem in Its Legislative Aspects: An Investigation Made under the Direction of Charles W. Eliot, Seth Low and James C. Carter, Sub-Committee of the Committee of Fifty to Investigate the Liquor Problem* (Boston, 1897), 42.

19. Roy Rosenzweig, *Eight Hours for What We Will: Workers and Leisure in an Industrial City, 1870–1920* (Cambridge, MA, 1983), 40–45, 60. In New England, kitchen barrooms were often common within the French-Canadian community. See Wines and Koren, *Liquor Problem,* 73, 83, 208.

20. Wines and Koren, *Liquor Problem,* 79–81, 111–113; Duis, *Saloon,* 61–65.

21. Wines and Koren, *Liquor Problem,* 49, 115; Asbury, *Barbary Coast,* 283; Tera W. Hunter, *To 'Joy My Freedom: Southern Black Women's Lives and Labors after the Civil War* (Cambridge, MA, 1997), 165; Duis, *Saloon,* 106–107, 266.

22. Duis, *Saloon,* 2. For arguments that saloons were thoroughly male domains, see Jon M. Kingsdale, "The 'Poor Man's Club': Social Functions of the Urban Working-Class Saloon," *American Quarterly* 25 (Oct. 1973): 472–489; Kathy Peiss, *Cheap Amusements: Working Women and Leisure in Turn-of-the-Century New York* (Philadelphia, 1986), 16–21; Rosenzweig, *Eight Hours,* 56–64.

23. Wines and Koren, *Liquor Problem,* 12, 317, 330; [Newark Citizens' Committee], *Report,* 21–22; Duis, *Saloon,* 2–3; Mara L. Keire, "The Committee of Fourteen and Saloon Reform in New York City, 1905–1920," *Business and Economic History* 26 (Winter 1998): 573–583.

24. "Statement of Arthur E. Wilson," 9 Feb. 1901; "Report of H. S. Conklin," 16 Mar. 1901; both NYC15; Story #255, "George Koenig's Saloon—92 Ave. A.," 31 Dec. 1912, Kehillah; "Investigation Report," 128th Street and 2nd Avenue, 21 Jan. 1912, file: "1912," box 1; "Investigative Report," 300 Seventh Avenue, 21 Jan. 1912, file: "1912," box 1; "Deposition of Lawrence J. Beine," [July] 1912, *People of the State of New York v. Jim Proprietor,* box 29; "Palace," 4 Dec. 1915, box 30; "Bushwick Café," 31 Apr. 1916, box 30; all C14; [Hartford Vice Commission], *Report,* 27–31; [Newark Citizens' Committee], *Report,* 11, 70–71; [Vice Commission of Louisville], *Report of the Vice Commission, Louisville, Kentucky: Survey of Existing Conditions with Recommendations to the Hon. John H. Buschemeyer, Mayor* (Louisville, 1915), 24; Roy Lubove, "The Progressives and the Prostitute," *Historian* 24 (May 1962): 322; Connelly, *Response to Prostitution,* 95–96; George Chauncey, *Gay New York: Gender, Urban Culture, and the Makings of the Gay Male World, 1890–1940* (New York, 1994), 81–83; Brooks McNamara, *The New York Concert Saloon: The Devil's Own Nights* (New York, 2002), xvii.

25. [Vice Commission of Minneapolis], *Report of the Vice Commission of Minneapolis to His Honor, James C. Haynes, Mayor* (Minneapolis, 1911), 75, in *The Prostitute and the Social Reformer: Commercial Vice in the Progressive Era,* ed. Charles Rosenberg and Carroll Smith-Rosenberg (New York, 1974); [Hartford Vice Commission], *Report,* 33; [Vice Commission of Louisville], *Report,* 68; Norman H. Clark, *Deliver Us from Evil: An Interpretation of American Prohibition* (New York, 1976), 57; Duis, *Saloon,* 2–3, 254.

26. [Newark Citizens' Committee], *Report*, 62–63.

27. [Newark Citizens' Committee], *Report*, 64.

28. Wisconsin Vice Committee, *Report*, 60–63; Vice Commission of Chicago, *Social Evil*, 108–111; Moral Survey Committee, *Social Evil in Syracuse*, 38–40; Selcer, "Fort Worth," 57–58.

29. *The Sporting and Club House Directory: Containing a Full and Complete List of Strictly First-Class Club and Sporting Houses* (Chicago, 1889), 15, 32–35, Schlesinger Library, Radcliffe Institute for Advanced Study, Harvard University; Blue Book Collection, Historic New Orleans Collection, New Orleans; [Portland, OR Vice Commission], *Report of the Portland Vice Commission to the Mayor and City Council of the City of Portland, Oregon* (Portland, 1913), 44–45; "Scarlet Sisters Everleigh: How Vice Grew Up in Chicago," *Chicago Sunday Tribune*, 26 Jan. 1936, part 7, 7 and 2 Feb. 1936, part 7, 7; Elizabeth C. MacPhail, "When the Red Lights Went Out in San Diego," *Journal of San Diego History* 20 (Spring 1974): 11; Pamela D. Arceneaux, "Guidebooks to Sin: The Blue Books of Storyville," *Louisiana History* 28 (Fall 1987): 402.

30. For a definition of "parlor house," see Vice Commission of Philadelphia, *A Report on Existing Conditions with Recommendations to the Honorable Rudolph Blankenburg, Mayor of Philadelphia* ([Philadelphia], 1913), 6–7; [Newark Citizens' Committee], *Report*, 35.

31. [Portland, OR Vice Commission], *Report*, 43; Wisconsin Vice Committee, *Report*, 55; Vice Commission of Chicago, *Social Evil*, 75; Herbert Asbury, *Gem of the Prairie: An Informal History of the Chicago Underworld* (1940; with an introduction by Perry R. Duis, DeKalb, IL, 1986), 266; Kathy Ogren, *The Jazz Revolution: Twenties America and the Meaning of Jazz* (New York, 1989), 33.

32. Vice Commission of Chicago, *Social Evil*, 81; [Social Survey Commission of Toronto], *Report of the Social Survey Commission, Toronto: Presented to the City Council, October 4th, 1915* (Toronto, 1915), 9.

33. For descriptions of brothel parlors, see [Lancaster Citizens' Committee], *Report*, 25; [Little Rock Vice Commission], *Report of the Little Rock Vice Commission, May 20, 1918; And the Order of Mayor Chas. E. Taylor to Close All Resorts in Little Rock by August 25, 1913* ([Little Rock, AR], 1913), 9; Frost, *Gentlemen's Club*, 52–53, 60, 85, 108–111.

34. Madams could buy beer wholesale at $0.05 a pint, but they sold it as high as $1.00 a pint. See [Portland, OR Vice Commission], *Report*, 24, 28, 40. See also Vice Commission of Chicago, *Social Evil*, 111.

35. Rose, *Storyville*, 75–82; [Vice Commission of Minneapolis], *Report*, 23; [Vice Commission of Louisville], *Report*, 18; "Scarlet Sisters Everleigh," *Chicago Sunday Tribune*, 19 Jan. 1936, part 7, 1; McGovern, "'Sporting Life on the Line,'" 136–138.

36. *Sporting and Club House Directory*; Story #771, "Disorderly Dollar House—Florence—226 E. 52nd St.," 17 Oct. 1913, Kehillah; [Newark Citizens' Committee], *Report*, 31, 37; Asbury, *Barbary Coast*, 162–165, 241–245; Abe Shoenfeld, interview by Arthur Goren, 6 Feb. 1965, typescript, 23–24, 207–208, William E. Wiener Oral History Library of the American Jewish Committee, Jewish Division, New York Public

Library; George Foster, *Pops Foster: The Autobiography of a New Orleans Jazzman*, as told to Tom Stoddard (Berkeley, CA, 1971), 32; McGovern, "'Sporting Life on the Line,'" 136–138; Selcer, "Fort Worth," 69; Rose, *Storyville*, 74.

37. [Lewis W. Hine], "Sixteen year old messenger boy entering 'crib' in Red Light district. Location: San Antonio, Texas," photograph, Oct. 1913, card #ncl2004000332/PP, album: "Street Trades," photographs from the records of the National Child Labor Committee (U.S.), PPLC; [Vice Commission of Louisville], *Report*, 23; Alan Lomax, *Mister Jelly Roll: The Fortunes of Jelly Roll Morton, New Orleans Creole and "Inventor of Jazz"* (New York, 1950), 23–24.

38. [Lewis W. Hine], *America and Lewis Hine: Photographs 1904–1940* (New York, 1977), 36. See also Bridgeport Vice Commission, *Report*, 18; Ruth Rosen, *The Lost Sisterhood: Prostitution in America, 1900–1918* (Baltimore, 1982), 95–96.

39. Vice Commission of Philadelphia, *Report*, 6; Wisconsin Vice Committee, *Report*, 40, 81; Herbert Asbury, *The French Quarter: An Informal History of the New Orleans Underworld* (New York, 1936), 359; James B. Jones, "Municipal Vice: The Management of Prostitution in Tennessee's Urban Experience, Part II: The Examples of Chattanooga and Knoxville, 1838–1917," *Tennessee Historical Quarterly* 50 (Summer 1991), 117.

40. Vice Commission of Philadelphia, *Report*, 53; [Moral Survey Committee], *Social Evil in Syracuse*, 21; Rosen, *Lost Sisterhood*, 106.

41. Report of A. E. Wilson and W. C. Steele Jr., "254 W. 34th St. nr. 8th Ave., 'Maryland Kitchen,'" 22 May 1901, NYC15; Frederick H. Whitin to Paul Poponoe, 3 Feb. 1920, file: "ASHA, 1920," box 9, C14; Vice Commission of Philadelphia, *Report*, 10–12; [Newark Citizens' Committee], *Report*, 47; [Portland, OR Vice Commission], *Report*, 6; Wisconsin Vice Committee, *Report*, 70; [Massachusetts Commission for the Investigation of White Slave Traffic], *Report of the Commission for the Investigation of the White Slave Traffic, So Called* (reprinted from [Massachusetts] House [Document] No. 2881, Feb., 1914), 23, reprinted in *Prostitution in America: Three Investigations, 1902–1914* (New York, 1976); John D'Emilio and Estelle B. Freedman, *Intimate Matters: A History of Sexuality in America* (New York, 1988), 181–182.

42. Vice Commission of Philadelphia, *Report*, 70.

43. *Sporting and Club House Directory*; Blue Book Collection; George J. Kneeland, *Commercialized Prostitution in New York City*, rev. ed. (New York, 1917), 110–111; Asbury, *Barbary Coast*, 237–238; Arceneaux, "Guidebooks to Sin," 397–405; Frost, *Gentlemen's Club*, 105, 109–110.

44. "Preface," Blue Book facsimile page, reprinted in Rose, *Storyville*, 138.

45. "Miss Cora DeWitt," Blue Book facsimile page, 140; "Miss Lillian Irwin," Blue Book facsimile page, 138; both reprinted in Rose, *Storyville*.

46. Rose, *Storyville*, 84, 145. See also "The French Studio," *Sunday Sun*, 25 Feb. 1906, 4, Manuscripts Department, Tulane University Library, New Orleans.

47. Story #6 cont., 9 Dec. 1912, 8, Kehillah; "Report of Investigator (J.A.S.)," 5 Feb. 1917, box 31, C14; Vice Commission of Philadelphia, *Report*, 79. See also Asbury, *Gem of the Prairie*, 265.

48. Judge Ben B. Lindsay and Harvey J. O'Higgins, *The Beast* (New York, 1910), 88;

Booker T. Washington, "Prohibition and the Negro," *Outlook* (Mar. 1908), cited in George M. Hammell, *The Passing of the Saloon: An Authentic and Official Presentation of the Anti-Liquor Crusade in America* (Cincinnati, 1908): 344–345; Royal L. Melendy, "The Saloon in Chicago," *American Journal of Sociology* 6 (Nov. 1900): 300, 303; "Philadelphia Liquor Men After the Dives Themselves," *New Orleans Item*, 12 Oct. 1909, 5; Chicago Civil Service Reform, *Final Report: Civil Service Commission, City of Chicago, Police Investigation, 1911–1912* ([Chicago], [1912]), 16, reprinted in *Chicago Police Investigations: Three Reports* (New York, 1971); Duis, *Saloon*, 163–164.

49. Jacob A. Riis, *How the Other Half Lives: Studies among the Tenements of New York* (1890; with a new preface by Charles A. Madison, New York, 1971), 119, 166–169; [Law and Order League of Charleston], *Special Report of the Law and Order League of Charleston, S.C.* ([Charleston], 1913), 13–14; [Newark Citizens' Committee], *Report*, 69–71, 106–107; William McAdoo, *Guarding a Great City* (New York, 1906), 95–97; Story #633, "Disorderly Saloon Hangout—631 2nd Ave.," 23 May 1913, Kehillah; Harris, "Government Control of Negroes," 572, 574; Arthur A. Goren, *New York Jews and the Quest for Community: The Kehillah Experiment, 1908–1922* (New York, 1970), 138; Glenda Elizabeth Gilmore, *Gender and Jim Crow: Women and the Politics of White Supremacy in North Carolina, 1896–1920* (Chapel Hill, NC, 1996), 75–76; Roberta Senechal, *The Sociogenesis of a Race Riot: Springfield, Illinois, in 1908* (Urbana, IL, 1990), 21–22.

50. Bridgeport Vice Commission, *Report*, 32.

51. Wisconsin Vice Committee, *Report*, 47. See also [Lexington Vice Commission], *Report*, 14; [Hartford Vice Commission], *Report*, 33; [Citizens' Committee of Portland. ME], *First Report of the Citizens' Committee of Portland: February 1, 1914* (Portland, ME, 1914), 12; Bridgeport Vice Commission, *Report*, 30; [Executive Committee, Women's League for Good Government], *Vice Conditions in Elmira: Being a Report of an Investigation of the Moral Condition of the City, Conducted by the Executive Committee of the Women's League for Good Government* (Elmira, NY, 1913), 24.

52. [Portland, OR Vice Commission], *Report*, 62.

53. [Newark Citizens' Committee], *Report*, 48–49, 57–59; Wisconsin Vice Committee, *Report*, 43; [Executive Committee], *Vice Conditions in Elmira*, 26; [Hartford Vice Commission], *Report*, 32–33; Bridgeport Vice Commission, *Report*, 19–22.

54. [Portland, OR Vice Commission], *Report*, 22.

55. Wines and Koren, *Liquor Problem*, 249–250; Story #273, "D. Wasser's Saloon—242 E. 3rd Street," 14 Jan. 1913, Kehillah; [Vice Commission of Minneapolis], *Report*, 75; Vice Commission of Chicago, *Social Evil*, 125; [Vice Commission of Minneapolis], *Report*, 63; Kneeland, *Commercialized Prostitution*, 53–59; Duis, *Saloon*, 293–294; William Howland Kenney, *Chicago Jazz: A Cultural History, 1904–1930* (New York, 1993), 62–63.

56. [Hartford Vice Commission], *Report*, 33; Vice Commission of Philadelphia, *Report*, 56–57.

57. Wisconsin Vice Committee, *Report*, 59; [Hartford Vice Commission], *Report*,

27; Vice Commission of Chicago, *Social Evil*, 83; Frost, *Gentlemen's Club*, 148, 154–155.

58. [Law and Order League of Charleston, SC], *Special Report*, 23; Vice Commission of Chicago, *Social Evil*, 35; Paulsson, *Social Anxieties*, 136.

59. See also William H. Rau, "Dining room of the Café Martin 'Old' Delmonico, New York City," 1904, photograph, card #95518644; "Café Martin, New York, N.Y.," 1908, photograph, card #det1994020615/PP, Detroit Publishing Company Photograph Collection; both PPLC. On Delmonico's, see Erenberg, *Steppin' Out*, 9–12.

60. [Lancaster Citizens' Committee], *Report*, 50.

61. Vice Commission of Philadelphia, *Report*, 75; Bridgeport Vice Commission, *Report*, 30, 43; [Newark Citizens' Committee], *Report*, 105–106.

62. [Newark Citizens' Committee], *Report*, 110; Wisconsin Vice Committee, *Report*, 76; Bridgeport Vice Commission, *Report*, 25, 42.

63. *"I Wants to Be a Actor Lady" and Other Hits from Early Musical Comedies* (New World Records, 1978), liner notes, 8, www.newworldrecords.org/liner_notes/80221.pdf (accessed 23 Feb. 2007).

64. Wisconsin Vice Committee, *Report*, 55; Vice Commission of Chicago, *Social Evil*, 134; Paulsson, *Social Anxieties*, 104–105.

65. [Three women in tights and feathers] (Buffalo, NY, 1899), poster, card #var1993000339/PP, TPC; "Rice and Barton's Big Gaiety Spectacular Extravaganza Co.: Hotel Jolly or Satan's Inn" (Buffalo, NY, 1899), poster, card #var1993000326/PP, TPC; Vice Commission of Philadelphia, *Report*, 76; [Social Survey Commission of Toronto], *Report*, 52; [Ernest J. Bellocq], *Bellocq: Photographs from Storyville, the Red-Light District of New Orleans*, prints by Lee Friedlander, introduction by Susan Sontag, interviews ed. by John Szarkowski (New York, [1996]), 56–57.

66. Vice Commission of Philadelphia, *Report*, 78, 80; Woolston, *Prostitution in the United States*, 290–291.

67. [Newark Citizens' Committee], *Report*, 111. See also Vice Commission of Philadelphia, *Report*, 57–58

68. [Newark Citizens' Committee], *Report*, 80, 105–106; [Cleveland Baptist Brotherhood], *Report of the Vice Commission of the Cleveland Baptist Brotherhood* (Cleveland, OH, 1911), 14–15; Vice Commission of Philadelphia, *Report*, 75–78; Erenberg, *Steppin' Out*, 71.

69. Vice Commission of Philadelphia, *Report*, 21; Louise de Koven Bowen, *The Public Dance Halls of Chicago* (Chicago, 1917), 3–4; Peiss, *Cheap Amusements*, 96; David Nasaw, *Going Out: The Rise and Fall of Public Amusements* (New York, 1993), 104–114; Kenney, *Chicago Jazz*, 62–64.

70. Foster, *Pops Foster*, 18; Rose, *Storyville*, 74, 87; Englebert Wengel, "Music Spots in the Downtown New Orleans Red Light District," *New Orleans Music* 4 (Mar. 1994): 16–26; Burton W. Peretti, *The Creation of Jazz: Music, Race, and Culture in Urban America* (Urbana, IL, 1994), 22–38; Ogren, *Jazz Revolution*, 57–59.

71. Story #937, "206 West 37th Street. Bank's Café," 2 Feb. 1914, Kehillah; Louise de Koven Bowen, "Dance Halls," *Survey* 26 (3 June 1911): 383–387; Wood, *Negro in*

Chicago, 25; [Lancaster Citizens' Committee], *Report*, 52; Vice Commission of Philadelphia, *Report*, 62–63; Wisconsin Vice Committee, *Report*, 55; [Newark Citizens' Committee], *Report*, 69–71; James Weldon Johnson, *The Autobiography of an Ex-Coloured Man* (1912; New York, 1960), 115; Foster, *Pops Foster*, 26–37.

72. Quote from Erenberg, *Steppin' Out*, 150. See also Vice Commission of Philadelphia, *Report*, 72; Bowen, *Public Dance Halls*, 4; Peiss, *Cheap Amusements*, 101–102.

73. [Citizens' Committee of Portland, ME], *First Report*, 12; Vice Commission of Philadelphia, *Report*, 72.

74. [Citizens' Committee of Portland, ME], *First Report*, 13. See also [Social Survey Commission of Toronto], *Report*, 50; Bridgeport Vice Commission, *Report*, 40.

75. Bridgeport Vice Commission, *Report*, 40; [Citizens' Committee of Portland, ME], *First Report*, 23; [Moral Survey Committee], *Social Evil in Syracuse*, 45.

76. Story #33, "128 Second Ave.," 6 Sept. 1912; Story #56, "155 Allen Street," 14 Sept. 1912; Story #81, "267 Grand Street," 2 Oct. 1912; Story #238, "First Inspection District Gambling List," 31 Dec. 1912; Story #241, "Harry Green—Pool Parlor—267 Rivington St.—Bad Hangout," 27 Dec. 1912; all Kehillah; McAdoo, *Guarding a Great City*, 193–226; Wood, *Negro in Chicago*, 27; [Little Rock Vice Commission], *Report*, 25; Foster, *Pops Foster*, 34.

77. [Lancaster Citizens' Committee], *Report*, 51–53. See also [Law and Order League of Charleston, SC], *Special Report*, 27, 60–61.

78. Quotation from Story #6, "76 Second Ave.," 26 Aug. 1912, Kehillah. See also "Report of J. Kreisworth," 2nd Av., 13 Mar. 1901, NYC15; Story #11, "Cigar Store and Stuss House," 26 Aug. 1912; Story #12, "Tony's Poolroom & Crap House," 28 and 29 Aug. 1912; Story #76, "Disorderly Furnished Room House," 29 Sept. 1912; all Kehillah; [Little Rock Vice Commission], *Report*, 25; [Portland, OR Vice Commission], *Report*, 127–129; Foster, *Pops Foster*, 34.

79. "Arthur E. Wilson States," 22 Pell Street, 1 Mar. 1901; Quan Yick Nam to George W. Morgan, 12 Apr. 1901; both NYC15; Story #449, "Hop & Cocaine Storehouse—Chinese Gambling Joint—12 Pell Street," 18 Mar. 1913, Kehillah; Rose Hum Lee, "The Growth and Decline of Chinese Communities in the Rocky Mountain Region," PhD diss., University of Chicago, 1947, 184–188; David Te-Chao Cheng, *Acculturation of the Chinese in the United States: A Philadelphia Study* (Philadelphia, 1948), 93, 131, 205–207.

80. "Arthur E. Wilson States"; Quan Yick Nam; both NYC15; Story #449, Kehillah; [Lancaster Citizens' Committee], *Report*, 52; [Executive Committee], *Vice Conditions in Elmira*, 36.

81. [Newark Citizens' Committee], *Report*, 62. See also "Report of J. Kreisworth," NYC15; Story #11; Story #12; both Kehillah; [Little Rock Vice Commission], *Report*, 25; [Portland, OR Vice Commission], *Report*, 127–129; Foster, *Pops Foster*, 34.

82. [Vice Commission of Minneapolis], *Report*, 110.

83. Harry B. Smith and John Stromberg, "The Queen of Bohemia" (New York, 1890), sheet music, item 099, box 143, LSLC. On Russell, see Russell Lynes, *The Lonely Audience: A Social History of the Visual and Performing Arts in America, 1890–1950* (New York, 1985), 134.

84. "Hoyt's 'A Stranger in New York': A woman is always as old as she looks, but a man is as old as he feels" (Cincinnati, 1897), poster, card #var1994000929/PP, TPC; [Moral Survey Committee], *Social Evil in Syracuse*, 19, 34.

85. [Moral Survey Committee], *Social Evil in Syracuse*, 47; [Portland, OR Vice Commission], *Report*, 28; "Scarlet World," *Sunday Sun*, 31 Jan. 1904, 4; Rose, *Storyville*, 137, 139–140. See also Arceneaux, "Guidebooks to Sin," 397–405.

86. Clarke, "Report for Jacksonville, Fla.," 2; Bridgeport Vice Commission, *Report*, 45; Frost, *Gentlemen's Club*, 134–137.

87. Edgar Selden and Herbert Ingraham, "You Needn't Go to College if You've Been to College Inn" (New York, 1911), sheet music, item 186, box 154a, LSLC. See also Percy Gaunt and Charles H. Hoyt, "The Bowery," *I Wants to Be a Actor Lady*, liner notes, 13.

88. [Massachusetts Commission], *Report*, 16, 20; Lois W. Banner, *American Beauty* (New York, 1983); Valerie Steele, *Fashion and Eroticism: Ideals of Feminine Beauty from the Victorian Era to the Jazz Age* (New York, 1985); Kathy Peiss, "Making Faces: The Cosmetics Industry and the Cultural Construction of Gender, 1890–1930," *Genders* 7 (Spring 1990): 143–169.

89. [Portland, OR Vice Commission], *Report*, 27. See also Vice Commission of Philadelphia, *Report*, 75; [Newark Citizens' Committee], *Report*, 42; Bowen, "Dance Halls," 385; Rosen, *Lost Sisterhood*, 106–107; Frost, *Gentlemen's Club*, 100; Chauncey, *Gay New York*, 61.

90. Story #113, "Rosie Hertz," 14 Oct. 1912, Kehillah; [Portland, OR Vice Commission], *Report*, 25, 35; Kneeland, *Commercialized Prostitution*, 81; Johnson, *Autobiography*; Asbury, *Barbary Coast*, 225; Foster, *Pops Foster*, 33; Rose, *Storyville*, 40–42; Rosen, *Lost Sisterhood*, 87–88.

91. "Miss Lulu White," Blue Book facsimile page, reprinted in Rose, *Storyville*, 138.

92. [Lexington Vice Commission], *Report*, 16. See also Wood, *Negro in Chicago*, 25; [Newark Citizens' Committee], *Report*, 62–63; [Lancaster Citizens' Committee], *Report*, 19; Kneeland, *Commercialized Prostitution*, 108–111; McGovern, "'Sporting Life on the Line,'" 135–137; Gilfoyle, *City of Eros*, 236–237.

93. [Portland, OR Vice Commission], *Report*, 37, 43–44. See also [Citizens' Committee of Portland, ME], *First Report*, 28; Winthrop D. Lane, "Under Cover of Respectability: Some Disclosures of Immorality among Unsuspected Men and Women," *Survey* (25 Mar. 1916), 746; [Lancaster Citizens' Committee], *Report*, 19.

94. "Autobiography," typescript, 29, Alfred Decker Collection, Chicago Historical Society; "A Man About Town," in Rose, *Storyville*, 153–155; Natalie Sonnichsen, "The Mandarin Club. Doyer Street," 25 May 1912, box 1, C14; D'Emilio and Friedman, *Intimate Matters*, 182.

95. Kneeland, *Commercialized Prostitution*, 110–111; Vice Commission of Chicago, *Social Evil*, 115; [Shreveport Vice Commission], *Brief and Recommendations by Shreveport Vice Commission in Support of Suppression versus Regulation of Vice* (Shreveport, LA, 1915), 8; Asbury, *Barbary Coast*, 237–238; Czitrom, "Underworlds and Underdogs," 542.

96. T. H. Young diary, 13 July 1892, Alfred Decker Collection.

97. "Visitor's Celebration Was Quite Costly," 10 Feb. 1910, 2; "Says He Was Robbed by Detectives," 27 Nov. 1909, 2; "Tried to Rob Drunken Guest," 13 Feb. 1910, 3; "Robbed of Shoes in Drunken Stupor," 26 June 1908, 9; all *New Orleans Item*; J. Cheever Goodwin and Maurice Levi, "When Reuben Comes to Town" (New York, 1900), sheet music, item 035, box 150a, LSLC. See also Harry B. Smith and Maurice Levi, " 'The Wedding of the Reuben and the Maid' or 'They Were On Their Honeymoon' " (New York, 1901), sheet music, item 008, box 150a; Harry B. Smith and Maurice Levi, "My Little Bunco Queen" (New York, 1901), sheet music, item 135, box 148; Richard Carle and Maurice Levi, "An Innocent Young Maid" (New York, 1899), sheet music, item 101, box 141; all LSLC.

98. Vice Commission of Chicago, *Social Evil*, 115; "Conditions in San Francisco and at the Exposition," box 21, C14; "Seventy Thousand Visitors Here for the 1910 Carnival," 9 Feb. 1910, 2; "Homeward Bound Shriners Praise City's Hospitality: More Than 32,000 Visitors Registered During Week," 15 Apr. 1910, 6; both *New Orleans Item*; [Hartford Vice Commission], *Report*, 59; MacPhail, "When the Red Lights Went Out in San Diego," 27.

99. [Vice Commission of Minneapolis], *Report*, 84–85, 92; [Hartford Vice Commission], *Report*, 36; Shoenfeld interview, 186, William E. Wiener Oral History Library; Paul S. Boyer, *Urban Masses and Moral Order in America, 1820–1920* (Cambridge, MA, 1978), 214–215.

100. [Lancaster Citizens' Committee], *Report*, 33; Bridgeport Vice Commission, *Report*, 38; [Newark Citizens' Committee], *Report*, 111; [Hartford Vice Commission], *Report*, 49, 74; Vice Commission of Philadelphia, *Report*, 63. In a survey of Philadelphia prostitutes, a number of them said that they "entered the life" because they liked going to dance halls, movies, and the theater. See Vice Commission of Philadelphia, *Report*, 92–96.

101. [Newark Citizens' Committee], *Report*, 12, 76–86; Rosen, *Lost Sisterhood*, 102; Peiss, *Cheap Amusements*, 110–111.

102. [Newark Citizens' Committee], *Report*, 77.

103. [Massachusetts Commission], *Report*, 43–44; [Social Survey Commission of Toronto], *Report*, 13; Kathy Peiss, " 'Charity Girls' and City Pleasures: Historical Notes on Working-Class Sexuality, 1880–1920," in *Passion and Power: Sexuality in History*, ed. Kathy Peiss and Christina Simmons (Philadelphia, 1989), 57–69.

104. Bridgeport Vice Commission, *Report*, 23. See also [Hartford Vice Commission], *Report*, 54; [Citizens' Committee of Portland, ME], *First Report*, 8; Vice Commission of Philadelphia, *Report*, 59–60; Vice Commission of Chicago, *Social Evil*, 92.

105. [Public Welfare Commission of Grand Rapids], *Report of the Public Welfare Commission of Grand Rapids, Michigan: Presented to the Common Council, November 10, 1913* ([Grand Rapids], [1913]), 27; [Executive Committee], *Vice Conditions in Elmira*, 61.

106. [Hartford Vice Commission], *Report*, 57, 61; Bridgeport Vice Commission, *Report*, 59–60; "Investigation Report, D.O.," Newark. N.J., 30 Oct. 1918, 9–10, file: "New Jersey," box 24, C14; Joanne J. Meyerowitz, *Women Adrift: Independent Wage Earners in Chicago, 1880–1930* (Chicago, 1988), 115.

107. "Phil Sheridan's New City Sports Company: Two Sports" (Cincinnati, 1899), poster, card #var1993000379/PP, TPC; "The Club's Baby by Lawrence Sterner and Edw. G. Knoblaugh: The Girls Visit the Club" (Cincinnati, 1899), poster, card #var1994001091/PP, TPC.

108. "Investigation of Sandy," 1 Mar. 1913, 5, file: "1913, Apr–May," box 28, C14; "Ogden, "Investigation Report: 216 W. 46th St.," 19 Jan. 1917, box 31, C14; "May Irwin in *The Widow Jones* Supported by John C. Rice" (Cincinnati, 1895), poster, card #var1995002116/PP, TPC; Napoleon Sarony, "Black Crook Company" (1893), photograph, card #2004678706, PPLC; Meyerowitz, *Women Adrift*, 113–114; Lillian Faderman, *Odd Girls and Twilight Lovers: A History of Lesbian Life in Twentieth Century America* (New York, 1991), 59.

109. Thomas Nast, "All the Difference in the World," *Harper's Weekly* (26 Sept. 1868): 30.

110. [Hartford Vice Commission], *Report*, 27–31; [Newark Citizens' Committee], *Report*, 11, 70–71; [Vice Commission of Louisville], *Report*, 24; Chauncey, *Gay New York*, 81–83.

111. Bridgeport Vice Commission, *Report*, 27.

112. "Statement of Arthur E. Wilson," NYC15; "Investigation Report, 128th Street and 2nd Avenue," 21 Jan. 1912, file: "1912," box 1; "Investigative Report, 300 Seventh Avenue," 21 Jan. 1912, file: "1912," box 1; both C14. See also Vice Commission of Philadelphia, *Report*, 73; Bridgeport Vice Commission, *Report*, 34; [Newark Citizens' Committee], *Report*, 62.

113. "Deposition of Lawrence J. Beine," C14. See also Story #4, "Tillie Taub," 29 Aug. 1912, Kehillah.

114. Vice Commission of Philadelphia, *Report*, 18; [Public Welfare Commission of Grand Rapids], *Report*, 16–23.

115. [Public Welfare Commission of Grand Rapids], *Report*, 20; [Newark Citizens' Committee], *Report*, 47; Selcer, "Fort Worth," 58.

116. Vice Commission of Philadelphia, *Report*, 16; Vice Commission of Chicago, *Social Evil*, 97; [Executive Committee], *Vice Conditions in Elmira*, 20.

117. [Hartford Vice Commission], *Report*, 24; Vice Commission of Philadelphia, *Report*, 53; [Moral Survey Committee], *Social Evil in Syracuse*, 20.

118. [Newark Citizens' Committee], *Report*, 61; [Social Survey Commission of Toronto], *Report*, 9; Bascom Johnson and Paul M. Kinsie, "Prostitution in the United States," *Journal of Social Hygiene* 19 (Dec. 1933): 477.

119. Vice Commission of Chicago, *Social Evil*, 73; Bowen, "Dance Halls," 385.

120. Bingham Dai, *Opium Addiction in Chicago* (1937; Montclair, NJ, 1970), 140–141; [Portland, OR Vice Commission], *Report*, 6; Vice Commission of Philadelphia, *Report*, 12, 79–83; Vice Commission of Chicago, *Social Evil*, 36.

121. Jacqueline Jones, *Labor of Love, Labor of Sorrow: Black Women, Work, and the Family from Slavery to the Present* (New York, 1985); Joel Williamson, *A Rage for Order: Black/White Relations in the American South since Emancipation* (New York, 1986), 145. See also Arnold Genthe, *Genthe's Photographs of San Francisco's Old Chinatown*, ed. John Kuo Wei Tchen (New York, 1984), 61–62; Rosen, *Lost Sisterhood*, 150.

122. Quintard Taylor, *The Forging of a Black Community: Seattle's Central District from 1870 through the Civil Rights Era* (Seattle, 1994), 30. See also Story #19, "Abie Treibtz alias The Chink," 1 Sept. 1912, Kehillah; Wood, *Negro in Chicago*, 31; Vice Commission of Chicago, *Social Evil*, 38–39; Mark H. Haller, "Organized Crime in Urban Society: Chicago in the Twentieth Century," *Journal of Social History* 5 (Winter 1971–72): 220–221; Rosen, *Lost Sisterhood*, 75, 80–81; Kenney, *Chicago Jazz*, 11.

123. Wisconsin Vice Committee, *Report*, 39.

124. Vice Commission of Chicago, *Social Evil*, 70–71.

125. Story #276, "Saloon Hangout—31 Third Street—Owned By Poshkoff," 15 Jan. 1913; Story #495, "Koeller's Saloon & Pool Parlor—257 E. 10th St.," 31 Mar. 1913; "Desperate Little Yuddle—Strike Breaker," 26 Sept. 1913; all Kehillah; [Hartford Vice Commission], *Report*, 58. On the saloon as employment agency, see Kingsdale, "'Poor Man's Club,'" 482; Duis, *Saloon*, 180–181.

126. Story #19; Story #21, "Hairdressing Parlor," 3 Sept. 1912; Story #123, "Louis Webber alias Bridgie Webber," 21 Oct. 1912; all Kehillah. See also Story #242, "Saloon & Gambling Joint Owned by Louis Syrop—144 Allen St.," 16 Apr. 1913; Story #666, "List of Lawyers, Bondsmen, Runners, Steerers, etc., Who Work in and around the Essex Market Court—Second Avenue & First," 17 June 1913 to 20 Apr. 1914; Story #668, "The Following Is a List of Lawyers, Bondsmen, Steerers, etc., Who Work in and around the Jefferson Market Court—10th St.," 18 June 1913; all Kehillah.

127. "Frank Smith deposition," 11 Jan. 1901, NYC15; Story #155, "325 Bowery," 2 and 5 July 1914; Story #192, "123 Allen Street—Hop Joint—Owned by Abe Goldberg," 16 Nov. 1912; Story #197, "92 Second Avenue—Abe Rabbell's—Hangout," 7 Sept. 1912 to 19 July 1914; Story #202, "Hop Joint. 503 E. 15th Street. Joe," 24 Nov. 1912; Story #208, "Jonsey—Gambling—Hop and Cocaine Seller. 329 East 14th Street," 2 Dec. 1912 to 24 Sept. 1914; Story #811, "Yiddle November's Saloon—680 8th Ave.," 3 Nov. 1913; all Kehillah. For a definition of "gun" and "gun-mol" (girl thief), see Story #83, "Sam Solomon and Meyer Solomon—alias Sam Boston and Meyer Boston. Brothers," 3 Oct. 1912, Kehillah.

128. Story #5, "University Café," [Aug. 1912]; Story #69, "Kid Raggs," 28 Sept. 1912; both Kehillah; McAdoo, *Guarding a Great City*, 93–94; [Hartford Vice Commission], *Report*, 37; [Newark Citizens' Committee], *Report*, 99.

129. "Natalie De Bogory Report," 6 May [1915], file: "Strand Cafeteria," box 28, C14; Story #237, Kehillah; Shoenfeld interview, 117; L. to Walter G. Hooke, "Haymarket," 6 Aug. 1913; P. F. Lich to Walter G. Hooke, 7 June 1915; both box 28, C14; Kneeland, *Commercialized Prostitution*, 90; Czitrom, "Underworlds and Underdogs," 550.

130. In turn-of-the-century medical literature, "invert" was the term for gay men who transgressed gender boundaries and were more like women than men. See D'Emilio and Freedman, *Intimate Matters*, 226; Chauncey, *Gay New York*, 48–49.

131. Story #100, "Hyman Waxman—Saloon—291 Broome Street," 7 Oct. 1912; Story #113; both Kehillah; [Massachusetts Commission], *Report*, 21; [Vice Commission of Louisville], *Report*, 20; Foster, *Pops Foster*, 33; Lubove, "Progressives and the Prostitute," 326; Rosen, *Lost Sisterhood*, 109.

132. Thorstein Veblen, *Theory of the Leisure Class* (1899; with an introduction by Robert Lekachman, New York, 1979), 80–82.

133. For a similar representation of a pimp, see "Rice and Barton's Big Gaiety Spectacular Extravaganza Co.: The Gaiety Dancers" (Buffalo, NY, 1899), poster, card #var1993000327/PP, TPC.

134. Story #13, "Sucker Candy Store," 30 Aug. 1912, Kehillah; [Hartford Vice Commission], *Report*, 59; Frost, *Gentlemen's Club*, 135–137, 141.

135. Story #4, Kehillah; [Moral Survey Committee], *Social Evil in Syracuse*, 24; Wisconsin Vice Committee, *Report*, 14; Asbury, *Gem of the Prairie*, 262.

136. Rose, *Storyville, New Orleans*, 42–44; Story #32, "218 East 9th St.," 6 Sept. 1912; Story #113, "Jake Hertz," 14 Oct. 1912; all Kehillah; Gilfoyle, *City of Eros*, 265–267; Clifford G. Roe, *The Great War on White Slavery, or Fighting for the Protection of Our Girls* (n.p., 1911), 109–153; Asbury, *Gem of the Prairie*, 263–265, 268.

CHAPTER 3. RACE, RIOTS, AND RED-LIGHT DISTRICTS, 1906–1910

1. Roberta Senechal, *The Sociogenesis of a Race Riot: Springfield, Illinois, in 1908* (Urbana, IL, 1990), 21; David Delaney, *Race, Place, and the Law, 1836–1948* (Austin, TX, 1998), 94.

2. H. W. Turner to Director, Section on Vice and Liquor Control, Commission on Training Camp Activities, 12 Dec. 1918, file: "Turner, H. W.," box 24, C14. See also Alzada P. Comstock, "Chicago Housing Conditions, VI: The Problem of the Negro," *American Journal of Sociology* 18 (Sept. 1912), 241–257.

3. Margaret Washington commenting on the ballot, *National Notes*, 1914, 5, cited in Jacqueline Anne Rouse, "Out of the Shadow of Tuskegee: Margaret Murray Washington, Social Activism, and Race Vindication," *Journal of Negro History* 81 (Winter–Autumn 1996): 43.

4. "Reputational segregation" was not a term from the period. Even after the passage of residential segregation ordinances in the 1910s, urban Progressives rarely modified the word "segregation," usually assuming that the term predominantly applied to vice. For example, at the height of Wilson's segregation of the federal government, congressmen discussing a red-light abatement act never modified the term segregation. See [House] Judiciary Subcommittee of the Committee on the District of Columbia, *Abatement of Houses of Ill Fame: Hearing on Kenyon Act (S. 234)*, 1914, 8–11.

5. [Vice Commission of Minneapolis], *Report of the Vice Commission of Minneapolis to His Honor, James C. Haynes, Mayor* (Minneapolis, 1911), reprinted in *The Prostitute and the Social Reformer: Commercial Vice in the Progressive Era*, ed. Charles Rosenberg and Carroll Smith-Rosenberg (New York, 1974), 85–88; "Bishop Charles E. Cheney," in American Vigilance Association, *Testimony and Addresses on Segregation and Commercialized Vice*, Pamphlet No. 2 (Nov. 1912), 20, file 14, box L2, ASHA; Junius Boyd Wood, *The Negro in Chicago: How He and His Race Kindred Came to Dwell in Great Numbers in a Northern City; How He Lives and Works; His Successes and Failures; His Political Outlook* (Chicago, 1916), 6, 19, 25–29; Arthur A. Goren, *New*

York Jews and the Quest for Community: The Kehillah Experiment, 1908–1922 (New York, 1970), 137–139; Ivan Light, "The Ethnic Vice Industry, 1880–1944," *American Sociological Review* 42 (June 1977): 469; Kenneth L. Kusmer, *A Ghetto Takes Shape: Black Cleveland, 1870–1930* (Urbana, IL, 1976), 48–49; Quintard Taylor, *The Forging of a Black Community: Seattle's Central District from 1870 through the Civil Rights Era* (Seattle, 1994), 34; Vern Bullough and Bonnie Bullough, *The History of Prostitution* (Hyde Park, NY, 1964), 195.

6. Sophonisba P. Breckinridge, "The Color Line in the Housing Problem," *Survey* 29 (1 Feb. 1913): 575.

7. "Stirring Up the Fires of Race Antipathy," *South Atlantic Quarterly* 2 (Oct. 1903): 301; Thomas N. Page, *The Negro: The Southerner's Problem* (New York, 1904), 11–114; William M. Brown, *The Crucial Race Question, or Where and How Shall the Color Line Be Drawn* (Little Rock, AR, 1907), 138; William H. Jones, *Recreation and Amusement among Negroes in Washington, D.C.* (1927; Westport, CT, 1970), 162; Ivan Light, "From Vice District to Tourist Attraction: The Moral Career of American Chinatowns, 1880–1940," *Pacific Historical Review* 43 (Aug. 1974): 368–369, 381; Kusmer, *Ghetto Takes Shape*, 48; Richard F. Selcer, "Fort Worth and the Fraternity of Strange Women," *Southwestern Historical Quarterly* 96 (July 1992): 74–75; Glenda Elizabeth Gilmore, *Gender and Jim Crow: Women and the Politics of White Supremacy in North Carolina, 1896–1920* (Chapel Hill, NC, 1996), 72, 101.

8. [Law and Order League of Charleston, SC], *Special Report of the Law and Order League of Charleston, SC* ([Charleston], 1913), 13–14; Harold N. Rabinowitz, *Race, Ethnicity, and Urbanization: Selected Essays* (Columbia, MO, 1994), 144, 149–150.

9. *Plessy v. Ferguson*, 163 U.S. 537 (1896); Allan H. Spear, *Black Chicago: The Making of a Negro Ghetto, 1890–1920* (Chicago, 1967), 11, 17; Kusmer, *Ghetto Takes Shape*, 12, 35; Taylor, *Forging of a Black Community*, 5; Neil Larry Shumsky, "Tacit Acceptance: Respectable Americans and Segregated Prostitution, 1870–1910," *Journal of Social History* 19 (Summer 1986): 665; Barbara Meil Hobson, *Uneasy Virtue: The Politics of Prostitution and the American Reform Tradition* (1987; with a new preface, Chicago, 1990), 147. Most racial separation laws postdated the 1890s. See C. Vann Woodward, *The Strange Career of Jim Crow*, 3rd rev. ed. (New York, 1974), 33–34, 97–100; Joel Williamson, *A Rage for Order: Black/White Relations in the American South since Emancipation* (New York, 1986), 171, 175–178; David Delaney, *Race, Place, and the Law, 1836–1948* (Austin, TX, 1998), 98–99. See also Germaine A. Reed, "Race Legislation in Louisiana, 1864–1920," *Louisiana History* 6 (Fall 1965): 383–384.

10. Light, "From Vice District to Tourist Attraction," 370; Taylor, *Forging of a Black Community*, 28; Rosen, *Lost Sisterhood*, 80–81. Even in New Orleans, Asian prostitutes were present. See "Japanese Colony Enters Protest," *New Orleans Item*, 25 Sept. 1908, 4.

11. Vice Commission of Chicago, *The Social Evil in Chicago: A Study of Existing Conditions, with Recommendations* (Chicago, 1911), 38–39; Johnny Lala, tape recording, reel 4, 24 Sept. 1958, William Ransom Hogan Jazz Archive, Tulane University, New Orleans; Rose, *Storyville*, 67; Selcer, "Fort Worth," 73; Taylor, *Forging of a Black Community*, 28.

12. Wood, *Negro in Chicago*, 25; "Refused Admittance, Smashed Door Glass," *New Orleans Item*, 28 Apr. 1910; Herbert Asbury, *The French Quarter: An Informal History of the New Orleans Underworld* (New York, 1938), 388; Carl V. Harris, "Reforms in Government Control of Negroes in Birmingham, Alabama, 1890–1920," *Journal of Southern History* 38 (Nov. 1972): 572.

13. Frank Uriah Quillin, *The Color Line in Ohio* (Ann Arbor, MI, 1913), 132; Tomás Almaguer, *Racial Fault Lines: The Historical Origins of White Supremacy in California* (Berkeley, CA, 1994), 209; Kusmer, *Ghetto Takes Shape*, 48; Rosen, *Lost Sisterhood*, 80–81.

14. "Irate Husband Uses Black Jacks," 29 June 1908, 3; "Jesse James, Bad Negro, Murdered," 2 Sept. 1908, 2; "Fought Over Nickle; Riley Now in Jail," 2 Aug. 1908, 10; "Tom Turney Killed by John Finley," 28 Aug. 1910, 1; all *New Orleans Item*. See also "Negroes Arrested on Assault Charge," *New Orleans Item*, 11 Aug. 1908, 10.

15. Phillips and his friends had been drinking and walking out on their bills all over the district for the entire evening, but when they went to Antoine's restaurant, Antoine demanded that they pay up-front before he served them. Phillips used this refusal as the pretext for shooting Antoine. See "Wanted to 'Kill Nigger' and Phillips Landed in Jail: Hoodlums Attempted to Kill Restaurant Keeper in Restricted District," *New Orleans Item*, 24 Aug. 1908, 1.

16. John Dittmer, *Black Georgia in the Progressive Era, 1900–1920* (Urbana, IL, 1977), 32; Robert L. Zangrando, *The NAACP Crusade Against Lynching, 1909–1950* (Philadelphia, 1980), 9–11.

17. "Will Seek to Clean Up Basin Street," 1 Feb. 1910, 4; "Era Club and Ministers to Take Up Basin St. Matter," 2 Feb. 1910, 3; "Will Continue War on Basin Street," 22 Mar. 1910, 1; all *New Orleans Item*.

18. "Woman Says She Was Beaten by Man," 17 Sept. 1908, 1; "First Charge under White Slave Law," 9 Aug. 1910, 1; "Young Woman Says Messina Robbed Her," 17 Aug. 1910, 1; all *New Orleans Item*.

19. "Gauthreaux Reversed by Criminal Court," 18 Feb. 1910, 6; "Mary Hanley Again Up for Being Drunk," 28 July 1908, 2; " 'Spook Dancing' Jails Forgarty," 28 Oct. 1909, 2; "Three Italians in Saloon Fight," 19 Sept. 1908, 3; "McComb City Man Says He Was Robbed," 13 Oct. 1909, 10; "Loses Diamond in the Tenderloin," 24 Oct. 1909, 5; all *New Orleans Item*. See also Committee on the District of Columbia, U.S. Senate, *Regulation of Sale of Intoxicating Liquors in the District of Columbia: Hearings on the Bill (S. 6264)*, 1908, 22–23, 54; Edward J. Escobar, *Race, Police and the Making of a Political Identity: Mexican Americans and the Los Angeles Police Department, 1900–1945* (Berkeley, CA, 1999), 11–12.

20. In 1910, New Orleans's total population was 339,075, of which 89,262, or 26.3 percent of the residents, were black. See William S. Rossiter, *Increase of Population in the United States, 1910–1920: A Study of Changes in the Population of Divisions, States, Counties, and Rural and Urban Areas, in Sex, Color, and Nativity, at the Fourteenth Census* (Washington, DC, 1922), 79, 128. In 1910, the police arrested 10,052 "colored persons" and 15,035 white persons, totaling 25,087 arrests. See *Annual Report of Board of Commissioners of the Police Department and the Inspector of Police Force of the City*

of New Orleans for the Year of 1910 (New Orleans, 1911), 17, New Orleans Public Library. See also Monroe N. Work, "Crime among the Negroes of Chicago: A Social Study," *American Journal of Sociology* 6 (Sept. 1900): 209–211; Homer Hawkins and Richard Thomas, "White Policing of Black Populations: A History of Race and Social Control in America," in *Out of Order? Policing Black People*, ed. Ellis Cashmore and Eugene McLaughlin (London, 1991), 73.

21. "Race Hate Unphilosophic but Easy to Start," *New Orleans Item*, 10 Sept. 1908, 6.

22. "Letters from the People," *New Orleans Item*, 15 Sept. 1910, 8. The first raid was on South Rampart Street between Girod and Gravier streets; the next set of raids was in the greater Dryades and Felicity streets area. See "82 Negroes Jailed in Raid, Merely 'Standing Around,'" 11 Sept. 1910, 1; "Hard on the Negroes," 15 Sept. 1910, 8; "Dryades St. Merchants Protest," 18 Sept. 1910, 1, 9; "Another Negro Raid," 19 Sept. 1910, 16; "Letters from the People," 21 Sept. 1910, 6; all *New Orleans Item*. See also Senate Committee, *Intoxicating Liquors in the District of Columbia*, 84–87.

23. On vagrancy laws, see Harris, "Government Control of Negroes," 578–582; Amy Dru Stanley, "Beggars Can't Be Choosers: Compulsion and Contract in Postbellum America," *Journal of American History* 78 (Mar. 1992): 1265–1293; Lawrence Friedman, *Crime and Punishment in American History* (New York, 1993), 94, 100. On dangerous-and-suspicious ordinances, see Eugene J. Watts, "The Police in Atlanta, 1890–1905," *Journal of Southern History* 39 (May 1973): 171–172; Rabinowitz, *Race, Ethnicity, and Urbanization*, 172–173.

24. "Believe Prisoner May Be Burglar," 30 Aug. 1908, 10; "Kelley Given Limit by Second Recorder," 25 Oct. 1909; both *New Orleans Item*. See also Taylor, *Forging of a Black Community*, 41.

25. George Foster, *Pops Foster: The Autobiography of a New Orleans Jazzman*, as told to Tom Stoddard (Berkeley, CA, 1971), 33.

26. "Navarro Discharged," 7 Sept. 1908, 7; "Charles Navarro Is Acquitted," 26 Oct. 1909, 6; "Navarra [sic] Wants Another Chance," 29 Oct. 1909, 2; all *New Orleans Item*. See also "Fednandez [sic] and Danahay Sentenced," 3 Dec. 1909, 2; "Beating Story Play for Sympathy, Says Detective," 4 Mar. 1910, 1; both *New Orleans Item*.

27. [House] Judiciary Subcommittee, *Abatement of Houses of Ill Fame*, 26; Charles Crowe, "Racial Violence and Social Reform: Origins of the Atlanta Riot of 1906," *Journal of Negro History* 53 (July 1968): 246–247; Friedman, *Crime and Punishment*, 103–104, 385; Tera W. Hunter, *To 'Joy My Freedom: Southern Black Women's Lives and Labors after the Civil War* (Cambridge, MA, 1997), 125.

28. Crowe, "Racial Violence and Social Reform," 247–248; Marion Louise Scott, "The Atlanta Riot of 1906 and Press Coverage of Race-Related Crimes: A Comparative Analysis of News Stories and Editorials in the *Atlanta News*, *Georgian*, *Constitution* and *Journal*," MA thesis, University of Georgia, 1979, 4; Hunter, *To 'Joy My Freedom*, 125. On the Old Fourth Ward, see Thomas Mashburn Deaton, "Atlanta During the Progressive Era," PhD diss., University of Georgia, 1970, 165–166, 174–175; Dittmer, *Black Georgia*, 13.

29. On the crusade against disorderly houses, see the coverage in the *New Orleans*

Item from 28 Nov. 1902 to 25 Jan. 1903. For an articulation of the stance of the *Item's* editor, see "Encouragement of Immorality," 13 Dec. 1902, 4; "Blind, Weak, or Shameless?" 20 Dec. 1902, 4; "The Public's Verdict," 23 Dec. 1902, 4; all *New Orleans Item*. For representative coverage, see "Objectionable House," 28 Nov. 1902, 1; "Fight Opens on Immoral Houses," 10 Dec. 1902, 1; "'Something Doing' with the Police," 15 Dec. 1902, 1; "Would Not Be Surprised at Accepting Bribes," 31 Dec. 1902, 1; "Crush Out the Immoral Houses Outside of Storeyville [sic]," 1 Jan. 1903, 1; "Police of New Orleans Sit as Judge and Jury," 11 Jan. 1903, 1; all *New Orleans Item*.

30. "Several 'Bums' Fined: Officers Determined to Rid City of Them," 5 Dec. 1902, 2; "Tries One Hundred and Fifty Cases," 26 Dec. 1902, 1; "A Splendid Opportunity," 27 Dec. 1902, 4; all *New Orleans Item*.

31. "Opium Joint Raided," 10 Jan. 1903, 5; "Opium Smoking," 14 Jan. 1903, 3; "Opium Joint," 15 Jan. 1903, 1; all *New Orleans Item*. There were twenty-six people arrested over all, six of whom were women; however, the race of the arrestees is less well defined. At least six were Asian, one African-American, and two European-American, but the race of the other seventeen is not clear. Although people are usually categorized as white when no race is given, the content of the articles suggests that such an assumption cannot be made. The difficulty in determining the race of all the opium smokers is another sign that reputability was still more important than race when discussing vice during this period.

32. Mary Roberts Coolidge, *Chinese Immigration* (New York, 1909), 420. See also Charles J. McClain, *In Search of Equality: The Chinese Struggle Against Discrimination in Nineteenth-Century America* (Berkeley, CA, 1994), 306n53; Taylor, *Forging of a Black Community*, 30.

33. "Police Ask for Three More Vacate Notices," 2 Jan. 1903, 1; "Three Women Before Court," 14 Jan. 1903, 2; "Gamble Madly to Evade the Blame," 17 Jan. 1903, 1; "Spurgeon Closes Up," 18 Jan. 1903, 8; "Broke Story Law," 22 Jan. 1903, 2; "Story Conviction," 22 Jan. 1903, 2; "Mrs. Morgan Free," 29 Jan. 1903, 1; "Viola Clifford Fined," 6 Feb. 1903, 1; all *New Orleans Item*.

34. Charles Crowe, "Racial Massacre in Atlanta: September 22, 1906," *Journal of Negro History* 54 (Apr. 1969): 154–155; Dittmer, *Black Georgia*, 124–126; Senechal, *Sociogenesis*, 1.

35. David S. Cecelski and Timothy B. Tyson, eds., *Democracy Betrayed: The Wilmington Race Riot of 1898 and Its Legacy* (Chapel Hill, NC, 1998); William Ivy Hair, *Carnival of Fury: Robert Charles and the New Orleans Race Riot of 1900* (Baton Rouge, LA, 1976); Williamson, *Rage for Order*, 127–141; Michael J. Klarman, *From Jim Crow to Civil Rights: The Supreme Court and the Struggle for Racial Equality* (New York, 2004), 58.

36. Thomas Gibson, "Anti-Negro Riots in Atlanta," *Harper's Weekly* 50 (1906): 1457–1459; Ray Stannard Baker, *Following the Color Line: American Citizenship in the Progressive Era* (1908; with an introduction by Dewey W. Grantham Jr., New York, 1964), 3–25; Crowe, "Racial Massacre in Atlanta," 150–173; Williamson, *Rage for Order*, 141–151; Herbert Shapiro, *White Violence and Black Response: From Reconstruction to Montgomery* (Amherst, MA, 1988), 97–103, 129–130; Edward L. Ayers,

Southern Crossing: A History of the American South, 1877–1906 (New York, 1995), 267–269; Hunter, *To 'Joy My Freedom*, 124–129.

37. Dominic J. Capeci Jr. and Jack C. Knight, "Reckoning with Violence: W. E. B. Du Bois and the 1906 Atlanta Race Riot," *Journal of Southern History* 62 (Nov. 1996): 742. See also Mark Bauerlein, *Negrophobia: A Race Riot in Atlanta, 1906* (San Francisco, 2001), 206–209, 223–224. On Proctor, see Ralph E. Luker, "Missions, Institutional Churches, and Settlement Houses: The Black Experience, 1885–1910," *Journal of Negro History* 69 (Summer 1984): 106–107.

38. Capeci and Knight, "Reckoning with Violence," 741; Bauerlein, *Negrophobia*, 236–238, 253, 257–258.

39. Capeci and Knight, "Reckoning with Violence," 743; Bauerlein, *Negrophobia*, 271. On the Niagara Movement, see W. E. B. Du Bois, "The Niagara Movement," *Voice of the Negro* (Sept. 1905), in *W. E. B. Du Bois Speaks: Speeches and Addresses, 1890–1919*, ed. Philip S. Foner (New York, 1970), 619–622; Dittmer, *Black Georgia*, 140; Joanna Schneider Zangrando and Robert I. Zangrando, "Black Protest: A Rejection of the American Dream," *Journal of Black Studies* 1 (Dec. 1970): 145; Charles V. Hamilton, "Social Policy and the Welfare of Black Americans: From Rights to Resources," *Political Science Quarterly* 101 (1986): 242.

40. Capeci and Knight, "Reckoning with Violence," 746–749; Bauerlein, *Negrophobia*, 193, 255.

41. W. E. B. Du Bois, "Politics and Industry," *Proceedings of the National Negro Conference, 1909* (1909; New York, 1969), 79–86; W. E. B. Du Bois, "The Negro Problem," [1911], in *Du Bois Speaks*, 218–225; Carolyn Wedin, *Inheritors of the Spirit: Mary White Ovington and the Founding of the NAACP* (New York, 1998), 77–78.

42. Quotation from "Mob Law Scored [*sic*] by Washington," *Chicago Daily Tribune*, 20 Aug. 1908, 4. See also Jacqueline A. Rouse, "The Legacy of Community Organizing: Lugenia Burns Hope and the Neighborhood Union," *Journal of Negro History* 69 (Summer and Autumn 1984): 114–133; Anne Firor Scott, "Most Invisible of All: Black Women's Voluntary Associations," *Journal of Southern History* 56 (Feb. 1990): 14.

43. Dittmer, *Black Georgia*, 64. See also Rouse, "Legacy of Community Organizing," 118, 120, 130; Deaton, "Atlanta During the Progressive Era," 213–214; Hunter, *To 'Joy My Freedom*, 139–139. For parallel efforts by middle-class African-Americans, see Arvarh E. Strickland, *History of the Chicago Urban League* (Urbana, IL, 1966), 16; Dewey W. Grantham, *Southern Progressivism: The Reconciliation of Progress and Tradition* (Knoxville, TN, 1983), 176; Senechal, *Sociogenesis*, 178–179; William A. Link, *The Paradox of Southern Progressivism, 1880–1930* (Chapel Hill, NC, 1992), 121.

44. Dewey W. Grantham Jr., "Hoke Smith: Progressive Governor of Georgia, 1907–1909," *Journal of Southern History* 15 (Nov. 1949): 433.

45. "Troops Fire on Mob, 1 Lynched in State Capital," 15 Aug. 1908, 1; "Capital Mob Slays Again," 16 Aug. 1908, 1; "2 Regiments Go; One Other Ready," 16 Aug. 1908, 1; "Mob Will Feel Weight of Law," 17 Aug. 1908, 1; "Ruin Wrought by Mob in the Negro District of Springfield," 17 Aug. 1908, 2; "Night of Unrest in Springfield," 18 Aug. 1908, 1–2; all *Chicago Daily Tribune*. See also James L. Crouthamel, "The Springfield

Race Riot of 1908," *Journal of Negro History* 45 (July 1960): 164–181; Senechal, *Sociogenesis*, 15–49; Shapiro, *White Violence and Black Response*, 103–104.

46. Mary White Ovington, "The National Association for the Advancement of Colored People," *Journal of Negro History* 9 (Apr. 1924): 107–116; Charles Flint Kellogg, *NAACP: A History of the National Association for the Advancement of Colored People* (Baltimore, 1973), 9–11; James M. McPherson, "Introduction," *Proceedings of the National Negro Conference, 1909*.

47. William English Walling, "The Race War in the North," *Independent* 65 (Sept. 1908): 554.

48. Mary White Ovington, "How the National Association for the Advancement of Colored People Began," *Crisis* (Aug. 1914): 184. On Vardaman and Tillman, see Edward L. Ayers, *The Promise of the New South: Life after Reconstruction* (New York, 1993), 225–228, 412–413; Williamson, *Rage for Order*, 96–98; C. Vann Woodward, *Origins of the New South, 1877–1913* (Baton Rouge, LA, 1951), 350–352.

49. "Blacks Organize to Wipe Out Vice," *Chicago Daily Tribune*, 19 Aug. 1908, 4. See also "Negroes Hope in Iron Laws," 16 Aug. 1908, 3; "Blacks Will Band to Wipe Out Vice," 17 Aug. 1908, 2; both *Chicago Daily Tribune*; "Mayors Will Form Law and Order League," *New Orleans Item*, 17 Aug. 1908, 1; "Stamp Out Vice Aim of Negroes," 18 Aug. 1908, 2; "National Fight on Crime Favored," 24 Aug. 1908, 4; both *Chicago Daily Tribune*; "Negroes to Form National Law and Order Assanation [*sic*]," *New Orleans Item*, 29 Aug. 1908, 1.

50. "Bishop Lampton Tells Negroes to Keep Their Place," *New Orleans Item*, 21 Jan. 1910, 5. See also "Makes Plea for Higher Morality among Negroes," *New Orleans Item*, 23 Jan. 1910, 12. For an earlier expression of this view by an AME minister, see "Undesirables of Both Colors Blamed," *New Orleans Item*, 16 Aug. 1908, 9.

51. For general histories of the two organizations, see Kellogg, *NAACP*; Nancy J. Weiss, *The National Urban League, 1910–1940* (New York, 1974).

52. Walling, "Race War," 529–534; L. Hollingsworth Wood, "The Urban League Movement," *Journal of Negro History* 9 (Apr. 1924): 117–126; Strickland, *Chicago Urban League*, 16; Louis R. Harlan, "The Secret Life of Booker T. Washington," *Journal of Southern History* 37 (Aug. 1971): 412; Weiss, *National Urban League*, 10, 60–61, 66; James M. McPherson, *The Abolitionist Legacy: From Reconstruction to the NAACP* (Princeton, NJ, 1975), 387; Wedin, *Inheritors of the Spirit*, 134.

53. McPherson, *Abolitionist Legacy*, 390; Zangrando and Zangrando, "Black Protest," 145–146. The NAACP also fought on the local and state levels, but its leaders put most of their hopes in the efficacy of national laws and federal court decisions. On the juridical emphasis in race reform, see Hamilton, "Social Policy," 243–245.

54. Wood, "Urban League Movement," 118; Weiss, *National Urban League*, 29; David Levering Lewis, "Parallels and Divergences: Assimilationist Strategies of Afro-American and Jewish Elite from 1910 to the Early 1930s," *Journal of American History* 71 (Dec. 1984): 551–552; Walter T. Howard and Virginia M. Howard, "Family, Religion, and Education: A Profile of African-American Life in Tampa Florida, 1900–1930," *Journal of Negro History* 79 (Winter 1994): 8–9.

55. Strickland, *Chicago Urban League*, 16; Gilbert Osofsky, "Progressivism and the

Negro: New York, 1900–1915," *American Quarterly* 16 (Summer 1964): 168; Weiss, *National Urban League*, 117–119. This inward orientation widened with World War I when Urban Leaguers stepped up their efforts to coordinate black employment in previously all-white workplaces, a much more racial concern. Nevertheless, the organization's ongoing commitment to "health, housing, and recreation," as well as their continued concern about the conduct of migrants, showed the Urban League's origins in reputational reform. Quotation from Wood, "Urban League Movement," 123. See also Wood, *Negro in Chicago*, 31; Wood, "Urban League Movement," 117–126; Strickland, *Chicago Urban League*, 11–13; Weiss, *National Urban League*, 110; William M. Tuttle Jr., *Race Riot: Chicago in the Red Summer of 1919* (New York, 1970), 99–100; Lewis, "Parallels and Divergences," 552; Howard and Howard, "Family, Religion, and Education," 9.

56. "Graham Taylor Reviews the Situation," in American Vigilance Association, *Testimony and Addresses*, Pamphlet No. 2: 22, ASHA; Rosen, *Lost Sisterhood*, 75; Robert M. Fogelson, *Big-City Police* (Cambridge, MA, 1977), 32, 41; Kusmer, *Ghetto Takes Shape*, 50.

57. Gibson, "Anti-Negro Riots in Atlanta," 1458; "Arson and Murder," *Chicago Daily Tribune*, 16 Aug. 1908, 4.

58. Roger L. Rice, "Residential Segregation by Law," *Journal of Southern History* 34 (May 1968): 181–182; Woodward, *Origins*, 555.

59. *State v. Gurry*, 121 Md. 534, 88 A. 546 (1913); *Carey v. City of Atlanta*, 143 Ga. 192, 84 So. 456 (1915).

60. The dry states were Georgia, Oklahoma, Alabama, Mississippi, North Carolina, and Tennessee. See Leonard Stott Blackey, *The Sale of Liquor in the South: The History of the Development of a Normal Social Restraint in Southern Commonwealths*, Studies in History, Economics, and Public Law 51 (New York, 1912), 3; Woodward, *Origins*, 389; Link, *Paradox*, 96.

61. Crowe, "Racial Violence and Social Reform," 235. Indeed, drys in Alabama declared 22 Sept. 1907 a day for prohibition advocacy. See James Benson Sellers, *The Prohibition Movement in Alabama, 1702 to 1943*, James Sprunt Studies in History and Political Science 26, no. 1 (Chapel Hill, NC, 1943), 115. See also Baker, *Following the Color Line*, 25; Capeci and Knight, "Reckoning with Violence," 741.

62. Blackey, *Sale of Liquor*; Morton Keller, *Regulating a New Society: Public Policy and Social Change in America, 1900–1933* (Cambridge, MA, 1994), 132.

63. Baker, *Following the Color Line*, 36; Sellers, *Prohibition Movement in Alabama*, 164–167; Woodward, *Origins*, 389; Harris, "Government Control of Negroes," 577–578; Dewey W. Grantham, *Southern Progressivism: The Reconciliation of Progress and Tradition* (Knoxville, TN, 1983), 165–172; Link, *Paradox*, 108.

64. "Seven Ask Council for Saloons," *New Orleans Item*, 29 Mar. 1910, 1.

65. "Stamp Out Vice Aim of Negroes," *Chicago Tribune*, 18 Aug. 1908, 2; Crouthamel, "Springfield Race Riot," 164–181; Senechal, *Sociogenesis*, 31.

66. Blackey, *Sale of Liquor*; Keller, *Regulating a New Society*, 132.

67. "New High-License Bills," 243; Frederic H. Wines and John Koren, *The Liquor Problem in Its Legislative Aspects: An Investigation Made under the Direction of*

Charles W. Eliot, Seth Low and James C. Carter, Sub-Committee of the Committee of Fifty to Investigate the Liquor Problem (Boston, 1897), 199; Barker, *Saloon Problem and Social Reform*, 135; Thomas J. Noel, *The City and the Saloon: Denver, 1858–1916* (1982; with a new introduction, Niwot, CO, 1996), 35; Roy Rosenzweig, *Eight Hours for What We Will: Workers and Leisure in an Industrial City, 1870–1920* (Cambridge, MA, 1983), 184–185.

68. John E. George, "The Saloon Question in Chicago," *Economic Studies* 2 (Apr. 1897): 92–94; "Prohibitionists Like the Shattuck Regulation Bill," 10 June 1908, 2; "New Saloon Law Is Explained in Detail," 16 July 1908, 2; "Slow in Separating Whites and Blacks in City Saloons," 19 July 1908, 3; all *New Orleans Item*; John Koren, *Alcohol and Society* (New York, 1916), 74–76; Harris, "Government Control of Negroes," 578.

69. John Koren, *Economic Aspects of the Liquor Problem: An Investigation Made for the Committee of Fifty under the Direction of Henry W. Farnum* (Boston, 1899), 171; "The Brewers at Chicago," *Survey* 27 (11 Nov. 1911): 1175–1176; D. E. Tobias to Walker [*sic*] H. [*sic*] Hooke, 13 Sept. 1910, file: "Tobias, David Elliot," box 15, C14; Jon M. Kingsdale, "The 'Poor Man's Club': Social Functions of the Urban Working-Class Saloon," *American Quarterly* 25 (Oct. 1973): 487; Rosenzweig, *Eight Hours*, 43–44; Perry R. Duis, *The Saloon: Public Drinking in Chicago and Boston, 1880–1920* (Urbana, IL, 1983), 159. For examples of racialization, see William McAdoo, *Guarding a Great City* (New York, 1906), 147–148; Rosenzweig, *Eight Hours*, 27–28. In the early twentieth century, there were fewer vituperative, and racialized, condemnations of the Irish than in the mid-nineteenth century, perhaps because, like German saloon-keepers, they were ubiquitous and familiar. See Duis, *Saloon*, 152–157.

70. D. E. Tobias to Walker [*sic*] H. [*sic*] Hooke, 13 Sept. 1910, C14; Harris, "Government Control of Negroes," 572–573; Rosenzweig, *Eight Hours*, 47–48.

71. Bulletin #54, 14 Aug. 1911, file: "Putnam, G. H.," box 13; Gilchrist Stewart to F. H. Whiting [*sic*], 18 Sept. 1912, file: "St.-Sz.," box 14; E. A. Warren, Treasurer of *Amsterdam News*, to Mr. Hooke, 5 Oct. 1912, box 2; all C14. See also McAdoo, *Guarding a Great City*, 95–97, 100–101.

72. William Banks to the Committee of Fourteen, 25 Sept. 1914, file: "West 4th to 40th Sts."; Fritz Laelzer to the Committee of Fourteen, 28 Sept. 1916, file: "Lenox Ave–Lexington Ave"; both box 17, C14.

73. D. E. Tobias to Walter G. Hooke, 22 Sept. 1915, file: "Mr. Moore," box 11; D. E. Tobias to Fred R. Moore, 24 Sept. 1913, and D. E. Tobias to Walter G. Hooke, 10 Sept. 1913, file: "Tobias, David Elliot," box 15; all C14.

74. William Banks to the Committee of Fourteen, 23 Sept. 1912, file: "West 4th to 40th Sts." See also Leroy Wilkins to the Committee of Fourteen, 16 Sept. 1913, file: "Eldridge St.–5th Ave."; R. H. Richardson to the Committee of Fourteen, 19 Sept. 1913, file: "West 41st–81st"; all box 17, C14.

75. James Reese Europe to the Committee of Fourteen, 25 Sept. 1911, box 1; W. E. B. Du Bois to William S. Bennett [*sic*], 23 Sept. 1911, file: "Du Bois, W. E. B.," box 11; Edward A. Warren to Mr. Hooke, 5 Oct. 1912, box 2; all C14; Kathy Ogren, *The Jazz Revolution: Twenties America and the Meaning of Jazz* (New York, 1989), 39. The Hotel Marshall was at 127–129 West 53rd Street. See James Marshall to Messrs Hook

[*sic*] and Whitin, 11 Oct. 1912, box 2, C14. For more on Marshall's club, see James Weldon Johnson, *Black Manhattan* (1930; New York, 1968), 118–120; David Levering Lewis, *When Harlem Was In Vogue* (New York, 1979), 29.

76. Ogren, *Jazz Revolution*, 38; James Reese Europe to the Committee of Fourteen, 25 Sept. 1911, C14.

77. W. E. B. Du Bois to Frederick H. Whitin, 14 Oct. 1912; F. H. Whitin to William E. B. Du Bois, 15 Oct. 1912; W. E. B. Du Bois to Frederick H. Whitin, 18 Oct. 1912; W. E. B. Du Bois to Frederick H. Whitin, 29 Oct. 1912; all file: "Du Bois, W. E. B.," box 11, C14.

78. D. E. Tobias to Hon. Fred R. Moore, 24 Sept. 1913, file: "Tobias, David Elliot," box 15, C14. On Fred Moore, see August Meier, *Negro Thought in America, 1880–1915: Racial Ideologies in the Age of Booker T. Washington; With a New Introduction* (Ann Arbor, MI, 1988), 228–229.

79. David F. Musto, *The American Disease: Origins of Narcotic Control*, expanded ed. (New York, 1987), 5–8; H. Wayne Morgan, *Drugs in America: A Social History, 1800–1980* (Syracuse, NY, 1981), 92–94; Joseph F. Spillane, *Cocaine: From Medical Marvel to Modern Menace in the United States, 1884–1920* (Baltimore, 2000), 121.

80. For the opening salvo of the scare, see "Urges Police to Get After Cocaine Sellers," *New Orleans Item*, 10 Aug. 1910, 5.

81. "Will Form League to Have Law Enforced," 22 Aug. 1910, 1; "Going After Mayor, Council, and Police," 26 August 1910; both *New Orleans Item*. Lawrence was the minister of the First Baptist Church of New Orleans.

82. "Anderson Liquor License Called For to Prove Ownership," 10 Aug. 1910, 1; "The Anderson Case," 13 Aug. 1910, 4; "Saloon Man Found Guilty on Evidence Given by Minister," 22 Aug. 1910, 1; "Anderson Case Is Being Watched by All Saloonists," 1 Oct. 1910, 1; all *New Orleans Item*. On Anderson, see Rose, *Storyville*, 42–47.

83. "Unpunished Crime," 15 Aug. 1910, 6; "Give Us Action," 22 Aug. 1910, 6; "Dr. J. B. Lawrence's Work Commended," 22 Aug. 1910, 10; "The Anderson Case," 13 Sept. 1910, 6; "Gives Promise to Enforce Law," 16 Sept. 1910, 1; all *New Orleans Item*. On the specifics of the Anderson case, see "He Shows Anderson's License but Aucoin Says 'Manana'" 11 Aug. 1910, 1; "Tom Anderson Let Go," 12 Aug. 1910, 1; "Anderson Case Postponed," 20 Aug. 1910, 5; "Tom Anderson Admits His Guilt," 12 Sept. 1910, 1; "A Just Decision," 24 Sept. 1910, 4; "Anderson Loses in Supreme Court," 17 Oct. 1910, 1; all *New Orleans Item*.

84. "Unpunished Crime," 15 Aug. 1910, 6; "The Gay-Shattuck League," 23 Aug. 1910, 6; "Going After Mayor, Council, and Police"; "The Law and the Barroom," 27 Aug. 1910, 4; "Says City Should Be Governed by Law," 12 Sept. 1910, 12; "Barroom Regulation," 17 Sept. 1910; "Mayor Behrman's Reasons," 14 Oct. 1910, 10; all *New Orleans Item*.

85. "Saloon Man Bonded," 29 Aug. 1910, 5; "Bannano Under Arrest," 4 Sept. 1910, 13; "After Liquor Men on License Law," 17 Sept. 1910, 8; "82 Negroes Jailed in Raid; Merely 'Standing Around,'" 11 Sept. 1910, 1; "Hard on the Negroes," 15 Sept. 1910, 8; "Dryades St. Merchants Protest," 18 Sept. 1910, 1; all *New Orleans Item*. On the anticocaine campaign, see "Want Sale of Cocaine Stopped," 24 Sept. 1910, 2; "Cocaine

Seller Heavily Fined," 17 Sept. 1910, 1; "Cocaine Victims Hard to Handle," 17 Sept. 1910, 10; "Wage War on Sellers of Cocaine," 3 Oct. 1910, 1; "Sale of Cocaine Must Be Stopped, Declares Inspector," 19 Oct. 1910, 2; " 'Cocaine Day' in the City Courts," 11 Nov. 1910, 4; all *New Orleans Item*. On police support during the cocaine scares, see Spillane, *Cocaine*, 119.

86. "Aaron Martin Sold 470 Ounces of Cocaine in Nine Months," *New Orleans Item*, 11 Oct. 1910, 5; Musto, *American Disease*, 8, 98, 101; Spillane, *Cocaine*, 119–122.

87. Baker, *Following the Color Line*, 46–47; *Opium Problem: Message from the President of the United States*, 61st Cong., 2d sess., 1910, S. Doc. 377, 50; "Grand Jury Makes Report on Cocaine," 8 Oct. 1910, *New Orleans Item*, 3; Musto, *American Disease*, 6–7; Williamson, *Rage for Order*, 142. Spillane, *Cocaine*, 94–95, 119–120.

88. Edward Hunting Williams, "The Drug Menace in the South," *Medical Record* 85 (7 Feb. 1914): 247, cited in Spillane, *Cocaine*, 119.

89. *Opium Problem*, 48–50; Hair, *Carnival of Fury*, 77; Musto, *American Disease*, 43–44. On simplifying the causality of crime to cocaine, see Spillane, *Cocaine*, 118–119.

90. J. W. Garner, University of Illinois, in W. F. Willcox, ed., "Discussion of the Paper by Alfred H. Stone, 'Is Race Friction between Blacks and Whites in the United States Growing and Inevitable?' " *American Journal of Sociology* 13 (May 1908): 828–831; Baker, *Following the Color Line*, 104; Williamson, *Rage for Order*, 142; Spillane, *Cocaine*, 93–99, 120.

91. "Sold Cocaine," 2 Oct. 1910, 2; "Aucoin the Tender," 5 Oct. 1910, 8; "More Arrests in Cocaine Cases," 6 Oct. 1910, 1; "Aaron Martin Sold 470 Ounces"; "Two Charged with Selling Cocaine," 23 Oct. 1910, 1; "Dr. Sayre B. Knapp Pleads Not Guilty," 25 Oct. 1910, 1; "Denials and More Denials in Case of Claude Simon," 19 Nov. 1910, 10; "Two Sentenced for Selling Cocaine," 7 Dec. 1910, 2; "Important Catch in Cocaine Case," 8 Dec. 1910, 5; " . . . Guilty of Selling Cocaine," 23 Dec. 1910, 1; "Mr. Huberwald Discharged," 23 Dec. 1910, 16; "Fourcault Appeals the Cocaine Case," 6 Jan. 1911; all *New Orleans Item*. The pharmacist was Aaron Martin and the district proprietor was George Fourcault, whose last name was also spelled as Fourcald, Foucalt, and Foucault. On the role of drugstores in the "shadow market" for cocaine, see Spillane, *Cocaine*, 154–157.

92. "Grand Jury Makes Report on Cocaine," 8 Oct. 1910, 3; "Will Regulate Wholesale of Deadly Cocaine," 22 Oct. 1910, 1, 2; "Wholesalers in Favor of Board's Cocaine Laws," 27 Oct. 1910, 1, 2; "Pair Guilty of Selling Cocaine," 5 Nov. 1910, 10; " 'Cocaine Day' "; "Four Sentenced for Selling Cocaine," 14 Nov. 1910, 3; "Drug Ordinance to Be Introduced Tuesday," 19 Nov. 1910, 10; "Cocaine Ordinance Favorably Reported," 5 Dec. 1910, 11; "Violation of New Drug Act Charged," 10 Dec. 1910, 1; "State Board to Fight Cocaine," 19 Dec. 1910, 3; all *New Orleans Item*.

93. "Grand Jury Makes Report"; "Aaron Martin Sold 470 Ounces"; both *New Orleans Item*; Musto, *American Disease*, 7, 43–44; Spillane, *Cocaine*, 116.

94. "Saloon Regulation Impossible—Lawrence," 12 Nov. 1910, 1; "Law Enforcement League Chartered," 14 Dec. 1910, 6; "Law Enforcement League Demands," 15 Feb. 11, 6; all *New Orleans Item*.

95. "Gay-Shattuck Law May Affect Balls," 21 Dec. 1910, 10; "After the Ball," 6 Jan. 1911, 10; "(First) 'Dry' Ball Chases Dancers to Saloon Near Odd Fellows' Hall," 8 Jan. 1911, 2; "Brewers' Officers Fined $50 Each for Violating Law," 27 Jan. 1911, 1; "Must Get Regular Saloon Licenses," 8 Feb. 1911, 6; all *New Orleans Item*. The New Year's balls were a test for the Mardi Gras balls.

96. "Will Read Drug Paper at Meet," 18 Oct. 1910, 5; "Cocaine Crusade Attracts Attention," 24 Oct. 1910, 1; "Government to Limit Cocaine Traffic," 13 Nov. 1910, 8; "Drug Ordinance to Be Introduced"; "Cocaine Ordinance Favorably Reported," 5 Dec. 1910, 11; all *New Orleans Item*.

97. "Police Dragnet Out for 'Cokes,'" 8 Oct. 1910, 2; "To Stop Abuse of Cocaine," 29 Oct. 1910, 4; both *New Orleans Item*. The arrest of George Fourcault, a well-known district proprietor, was particularly significant. See "Important Catch in Cocaine Case," 8 Dec. 1910, 5; "Patrolman Under Serious Charges," 9 Dec. 1910, 4; " . . . Guilty of Selling Cocaine"; "Fourcault Appeals the Cocaine Case"; all *New Orleans Item*.

98. Taylor, *Forging of a Black Community*, 41.

99. Crowe, "Racial Violence and Social Reform," 245; Arthur S. Link and Richard L. McCormick, *Progressivism* (Arlington Heights, IL, 1983), 96–99; Hunter, *To 'Joy My Freedom*, 125.

CHAPTER 4. THE VICE TRUST

1. Clifford Geertz, "Local Knowledge: Fact and Law in Comparative Perspective," in *Local Knowledge: Further Essays in Interpretive Anthropology* (New York, 1983), 175, 215–234. For an overview of the international white slavery scare, see Edward J. Bristow, *Prostitution and Prejudice: The Jewish Fight Against White Slavery, 1870–1939* (New York, 1982). For the European variations of the general white slavery narrative, see Judith R. Walkowitz, *City of Dreadful Delight: Narratives of Sexual Danger in Late Victorian London* (Chicago, 1992), 81–120; Alain Corbin, *Women for Hire: Prostitution and Sexuality in France after 1850*, trans. Alan Sheridan (Paris, 1978; English trans. Cambridge, MA, 1990), 275–298; Laurie Bernstein, *Sonia's Daughters: Prostitutes and Their Regulation in Imperial Russia* (Berkeley, 1995), 146–166. In colonial and quasi-colonial settings, analyzing "local" discourse is more difficult. People from the metropole deployed anti-prostitution rhetoric to different purposes, and with different emphases, than local elites. See Donna J. Guy, *Sex and Danger in Buenos Aires: Prostitution, Family, and Nation in Argentina* (Lincoln, NE, 1991), 108–129; Elizabeth B. Van Heyningen, "The Social Evil in the Cape Colony, 1868–1902: Prostitution and the Contagious Diseases Acts," *Journal of Southern African Studies* 10 (Apr. 1984): 170–197; Antoinette Burton, *Burdens of History: British Feminists, Indian Women, and Imperial Culture, 1865–1915* (Chapel Hill, NC, 1994), 127–169; Gail Hershatter, *Dangerous Pleasures: Prostitution and Modernity in Twentieth-Century Shanghai* (Berkeley, CA, 1997), 181–192, 199–204, 220–229, 235–291.

2. Robert H. Wiebe, *The Search for Order, 1877–1920* (New York, 1967), 52–53, 164 (for quotation). See also Richard Hofstadter, *The Paranoid Style in American Politics and Other Essays* (New York, 1965), 29, 31–32; Samuel Eliot Morison, *The Oxford*

History of the American People (New York, 1965), 732; Morton Keller, *Regulating a New Society: Public Policy and Social Change in America, 1900–1933* (Cambridge, MA, 1994), 118.

3. George David Smith and Richard Sylla, "The Transformation of Financial Capitalism: An Essay on the History of American Capital Markets," *Financial Markets, Institutions and Instruments* 2 (May 1993): 1–5; Samuel P. Hays, *The Response to Industrialism, 1885–1914* (Chicago, 1957), 48–52.

4. Most historians of Progressive-era prostitution have either left the Vice Trust metaphor unanalyzed or dismissed it as muckraking exaggeration. See Mark Thomas Connelly, *The Response to Prostitution in the Progressive Era* (Chapel Hill, NC, 1980), 102; Bristow, *Prostitution and Prejudice*, 171–172, 210–211, 309; Ruth Rosen, *The Lost Sisterhood: Prostitution in America, 1900–1918* (Baltimore, 1982), 134–135; Barbara Meil Hobson, *Uneasy Virtue: The Politics of Prostitution and the American Reform Tradition* (New York, 1987; with a new preface, Chicago, 1990), 142, 145; Timothy J. Gilfoyle, *City of Eros: New York City, Prostitution, and the Commercialization of Sex, 1790–1920* (New York, 1992), 264–265.

5. Robert E. Riegel, "Changing American Attitudes toward Prostitution," *Journal of the History of Ideas* 29 (July–Sept. 1968): 437–452. On the evangelical roots of purity reform and rescue work, see Carroll Smith-Rosenberg, "Beauty, the Beast, and the Militant Woman: A Case Study in Sex Roles and Social Stress in Jacksonian America," in *Disorderly Conduct: Visions of Gender in Victorian America* (New York, 1985), 109–128; David Pivar, *Purity Crusade: Sexual Morality and Social Control, 1868–1900* (Westport, CT, 1973); Peggy Pascoe, *Relations of Rescue: The Search for Female Moral Authority in the American West, 1874–1939* (New York, 1990).

6. Bristow, *Prostitution and Prejudice*, 36; David R. Roediger, *The Wages of Whiteness: Race and the Making of the American Working Class* (London, 1991), 65–67, 74.

7. Roediger, *Wages of Whiteness*, 65–66; Sean Wilentz, *Chants Democratic: New York City and the Rise of the American Working Class, 1788–1850* (New York, 1984), 61–103.

8. Thomas M. Norwood, *Plutocracy; or, American White Slavery; A Politico-Social Novel* (New York, 1888), 32–38; Helen L. Sumner, *The White Slave; or, "The Cross of Gold"* (Chicago, 1896); Francis A. Adams, *Who Rules America? Truths About Trusts* (New York, 1899), 9; Charles Edward Russell, *Business: The Heart of the Nation* (New York, 1911), 24. On the antebellum antecedents of the slaveholder/trust comparison, see David Brion Davis, "Images of Conspiracy in the Slavery Controversy: Conceptual Problems and Theoretical Framework," in *The Slave Power Conspiracy and the Paranoid Style* (Baton Rouge, LA, 1969), 3–31.

9. W. J. Ghent, *Our Benevolent Feudalism* (New York, 1902), 184; Robert Fleming, *Depraved Finance* (New York, 1904), 54; George Creel, "The Feudal Towns of Texas," *Harper's Weekly* 60 (23 Jan. 1915): 76.

10. John S. Garner, ed., *The Company Town: Architecture and Society in the Early Industrial Age* (New York, 1992), 5; Bruce Palmer, *"Man Over Money": The Southern Populist Critique of American Capitalism* (Chapel Hill, NC, 1980), 114; Matthew Josephson, *The Robber Barons: The Great American Capitalists, 1861–1901* (1934; New York, 1962), v–vi.

178   NOTES TO PAGES 71–72

11. Russell, *Business*, 89; U.S. Commission on Industrial Relations, *Industrial Relations: Final Report and Testimony*, vol. 1, 64th Cong., 1st sess., 1916, S. Doc. 415, 34–35; Richard Hofstadter, "What Happened to the Antitrust Movement? Notes on the Evolution of an American Creed," in *The Business Establishment*, ed. Earl F. Cheit (New York, 1964), 114–136. On the republican strains in anti-monopolism, see Gretchen Ritter, *Goldbugs and Greenbacks: The Antimonopoly Tradition and the Politics of Finance in America, 1865–1896* (Cambridge, 1997), 3–7.

12. Ronald G. Walters, "The Erotic South: Civilization and Sexuality in American Abolitionism," *American Quarterly* 25 (May 1973): 180. The sexual themes are particularly strong in abolition's own white slavery literature. See *White Slavery in America*, Anti-Slavery Tracts 2 (New York, [ca. 1855–1856]); Richard Hildreth, *The White Slave; or, Memoirs of a Fugitive* (Boston, 1852).

13. Bristow, *Prostitution and Prejudice*, 36–37; the Hugo quotation that Bristow cited is from Josephine Butler, *Personal Reminiscences of a Great Crusade*, new ed. (London, 1911), 13. On state-regulated prostitution in Britain, see Judith R. Walkowitz, *Prostitution and Victorian Society: Women, Class, and the State* (Cambridge, 1980).

14. Alfred S. Dyer, *The European Slave Trade in English Girls* (London, 1880); Kathleen Barry, *Female Sexual Slavery* (1979; New York, 1984), 21–24; Corbin, *Women for Hire*, 275–280.

15. *White Slavery In Chicago: A White Slave's Own Story*, pamphlet, [1907], box 1, C14; *White Slave Traffic*, 61st Cong., 2d sess., 1909, H. Rep. 47, 12–13, 30; Egal Feldman, "Prostitution, the Alien Woman, and the Progressive Imagination, 1910–1915," *American Quarterly* 19 (Summer 1967): 192–206; Rosen, *Lost Sisterhood*, 44, 119.

16. George Kibbe Turner, "Daughters of the Poor: A Plain Story of the Development of New York City as Leading Center of the White Slave Trade of the World, under Tammany Hall," *McClure's Magazine* 34 (Nov. 1909): 45–47. See also Jane Addams, *A New Conscience and an Ancient Evil* (New York, 1912), 108; Clifford G. Roe, *The Great War on White Slavery; or, Fighting for the Protection of Our Girls* (n.p., 1911), 97–100.

17. *Opium Problem: Message from the President of the United States*, 61st Cong., 2d sess., 1910, S. Doc. 377, 49–50; Paula Giddings, *When and Where I Enter: The Impact of Black Women on Race and Sex in America* (New York, 1984), 26–31; Jacquelyn Dowd Hall, "'The Mind That Burns in Each Body': Women, Rape, and Racial Violence," in *Powers of Desire: The Politics of Sexuality*, ed. Ann Snitow, Christine Stansell, and Sharon Thompson (New York, 1983), 328–349.

18. Progressive-era reformers almost always argued that "white slavery" was a misnomer. See Roe, *Great War on White Slavery*, 97; Theodore A. Bingham, *The Girl that Disappears: The Real Facts about the White Slave Traffic* (Boston, 1911), 15–17; Addams, *New Conscience*, 18, 26–30, 160–163; O. Edward Janney, *White Slave Traffic*, (New York, 1911), 13; Vice Commission of Chicago, *The Social Evil in Chicago: A Study of Existing Conditions, with Recommendations* (Chicago, 1911), 41.

19. Kauffman, *House of Bondage*, 2–3, 18–20, 51–52; U.S. Immigration Commission, *Importing Women for Immoral Purposes*, 61st Cong., 2d sess., 1909, S. Doc. 196, 17–18; Janney, *White Slave Traffic*, 41–43; Turner, "Daughters of the Poor," 45–48.

20. Turner, "Daughters of the Poor," 54.

21. Addams, *New Conscience*, 169–170. See also Jacqueline Jones, *Labor of Love, Labor of Sorrow: Black Women, Work, and the Family from Slavery to the Present* (New York, 1985), 155–156.

22. Arthur A. Goren, *New York Jews and the Quest for Community: The Kehillah Experiment, 1908–1922* (New York, 1970), 135–144.

23. On the anti-ring ends of anti-vice reformers, see Goren, *New York Jews*, 135–144; Eric Anderson, "Prostitution and Social Justice: Chicago, 1910–1915," *Social Service Review* 48 (June 1974): 203–228; Jeremy P. Felt, "Vice Reform as a Political Technique: The Committee of Fifteen in New York, 1900–1901," *New York History* 54 (1973): 24–51; Elizabeth C. MacPhail, "When the Red Lights Went Out in San Diego," *Journal of San Diego History* 20 (Spring 1974): 2–28; James R. McGovern, "'Sporting Life on the Line': Prostitution in Progressive Era Pensacola," *Florida Historical Quarterly* 54 (Oct. 1975): 131–144; Paul H. Hass, "Sin in Wisconsin: The Teasdale Vice Committees of 1913," *Wisconsin Magazine of History* 49 (Winter 1965–66): 138–151; Timothy J. Gilfoyle, *City of Eros: New York City, Prostitution, and the Commercialization of Sex, 1790–1920* (New York, 1992), 299–302.

24. Neil Larry Shumsky, "Vice Responds to Reform: San Francisco, 1910–1914," *Journal of Urban History* 7 (Nov. 1980): 42; H. Gordon Frost, *The Gentlemen's Club: The Story of Prostitution in El Paso* (El Paso, TX, 1983), 145–150, 154; James B. Jones Jr., "Municipal Vice: The Management of Prostitution in Tennessee's Urban Experience, Part I: The Experience of Nashville and Memphis, 1854–1917," *Tennessee Historical Quarterly* 50 (Spring 1991): 36–38.

25. American Vigilance Association, *Testimony and Addresses on Segregation and Commercialized Vice*, Pamphlet No. 2 (Nov. 1912), file 14, box L2, ASHA; George M. Reynolds, *Machine Politics in New Orleans, 1897–1926* (New York, 1936), 157–158; Frost, *Gentlemen's Club*, 150–151, 174–181, 187–192.

26. Franklin Hichborn, "California's Campaign Against Entrenched Vice," *Survey* 32 (25 July 1914): 430; Edward Alsworth Ross, *Sin and Society: An Analysis of Latter-Day Iniquity* (Boston, 1907), 165–166; Charles A. Beard, *American City Government: A Survey of Newer Tendencies* (New York, 1912), 191–195. See also Paul S. Boyer, *Urban Masses and Moral Order in America, 1820–1920* (Cambridge, MA, 1978), 169–170; Ernest S. Griffith, *A History of American City Government: The Conspicuous Failure, 1870–1900* (New York, 1974), 78–80. For a definition of "natural monopolies," see Richard T. Ely, *Monopolies and Trusts* (New York, 1906), 42–43, 59–61; Jeremiah W. Jenks, *The Trust Problem* (New York, 1900), 57.

27. Twenty-eight cities and four states (Illinois, Maryland, Massachusetts, and Wisconsin) conducted vice investigations between 1910 and 1917. See Joseph Mayer, *The Regulation of Commercialized Vice: An Analysis of the Transition from Segregation to Repression in the United States* (New York, 1922), 11, 52–54. On the anti-vice associations, see Roland Wagner, "Virtue Against Vice: A Study of Moral Reformers and Prostitutes in the Progressive Era," PhD diss., University of Wisconsin, 1971; Anderson, "Prostitution and Social Justice," 208, 214–218; Allan M. Brandt, *No Magic Bullet: A Social History of Venereal Disease in the United States since 1880, with a New Chapter on AIDS* (New York, 1987), 38–53.

28. "'The White Slave,'" *Survey* 30 (12 July 1913): 507–510; Connelly, *Response to Prostitution*, 114–115; Rosen, *Lost Sisterhood*, 15–16; Harold S. Wilson, *McClure's Magazine and the Muckrakers* (Princeton, NJ, 1970), 221–222. Even John D. Rockefeller Jr. used the white slavery scare strategically. Rockefeller sent copies of Reginald Wright Kauffman's melodramatic novel, *The House of Bondage*, to dozens of his acquaintances to garner support for anti-vice reform. For their responses, see files 85–87, box 10, series: "Boards," RG 2-OMR, RFA.

29. Quotation from Roe, *Girls Who Disappeared*, 22. See also [Frederick H. Whitin] to Ethel V. Fraser, 17 Dec. 1909, box 1; Wirt W. Hallam to Fred H. Whitin, 15 May 1912, box 2; both C14.

30. Compare, for example, Robert O. Harland, *The Vice Bondage of a Great City; or, The Wickedest City in the World* (Chicago, 1912) and John P. Peters, "Suppression of the 'Raines Law Hotels,'" *Annals of the American Academy of Political and Social Science* 32 (Nov. 1908): 556–566.

31. Pimps were the narrative and juridical target in both the Rockefeller Grand Jury Presentment and Roe's Chicago pandering cases. See *Rockefeller Grand Jury Presentment*, reprinted in Kauffman, *House of Bondage*, 478–479; for examples of cases Roe tried, see vol. 25, MS 1028, Chicago Committee of Fifteen, Department of Special Collections, Regenstein Library, University of Chicago. See also Hobson, *Uneasy Virtue*, 144–45; David J. Langum, *Crossing Over the Line: Legislating Morality and the Mann Act* (Chicago, 1994), 261–264.

32. On Rockefeller's attitude toward white slavery sensationalism, see John D. Rockefeller Jr., "Introduction," in George J. Kneeland, *Commercialized Prostitution in New York City*, rev. ed. (New York, 1917), vii–x. On Roe's view of publicity, see Roe, *Great War on White Slavery*, 372–373. On Roe's deliberate distortions, see Walter C. Reckless, *Vice in Chicago* (Chicago, 1933), 36–39. The differences between Roe and Rockefeller did not, however, keep Rockefeller from hiring Roe to prepare a preliminary survey of prostitution in New York City when Rockefeller established the Bureau of Social Hygiene in 1911. See John D. Rockefeller Jr. to Clifford G. Roe, 26 Jan. 1911, file 42, box 7, series: "Boards," RG 2-OMR, RFA. For Roe's report, see Clifford G. Roe, "The Committee of Three," 3 Apr. 1912, file 42, box 7, series: "Boards," RG 2-OMR, RFA.

33. Wirt W. Hallam to Frances Keller [*sic*], 4 Dec. 1911; Frederick H. Whitin to Wirt Hallam, 9 Dec. 1911; Wirt W. Hallam to Frederick H. Whitin, 12 Dec. 1911; all box 1, C14. Wirt Hallam was a member of the Chicago Vice Commission and the Illinois Vigilance Association. Whitin and Hallam's debate over strategy continue in box 2, C14.

34. Wirt W. Hallam to Fred H. Whitin, 15 May 1912, box 2; Wirt W. Hallam to Frederick H. Whitin, 26 July 1912, box 2; Frederick H. Whitin to J. Frank Chase, 15 Feb. 1918, box 4; [Chairman William Adams Brown] to Hon. John F. Hylan, Mayor, 15 June 1918, box 4; "The Committee of Fourteen," typescript, 1921, 5–6, file: "Fesler, Mayo 1921," box 83; all C14.

35. Abraham Flexner explained the Bureau of Social Hygiene's tolerance of the more rhetorically flamboyant to Starr Murphy, another Rockefeller associate, by argu-

ing that white slavery agitation "has everywhere been a precursor to a larger interest in the problem of prostitution." See Abraham Flexner to Starr J. Murphy, 21 July 1913, file: 197, box 9, subseries 2, series 3, Bureau of Social Hygiene, RFA.

36. On established reformers purposefully restraining their rhetoric, see Frederick H. Whitin to Wirt Hallam, 16 July 1912, box 1; Frederick H. Whitin to the Massachusetts Anti-Saloon League, 26 June 1913, box 2; Frederick H. Whitin to John P. Peters, 18 Nov. 1916, file: "Peters, John. P., 1915–1916," box 12; all C14. On Rosenwald, Carnegie, and Schiff, see Julius Rosenwald to Hon. James R. Mann, 12 Mar. 1912, file 8, box 11, Julius Rosenwald Papers, Department of Special Collections, Regenstein Library, University of Chicago; Samuel P. Thrasher to John D. Rockefeller Jr., 13 Mar. 1915, file 39, box 6, series: "Boards," RG 2-OMR, RFA; "American Social Hygiene Association: Minutes of a Special Meeting of the Executive Committee," 27 May 1915, file 3, box 5, ASHA; New York Committee of Fifteen to John D. Rockefeller Jr., "Confidential," 14 Mar. 1901, file 40, box 6; "Com. 14 Guarantors [sic]," [1914], file 41, box 6; both series: "Boards," RG 2-OMR, RFA. On individuals and short-term organizations taking a less-conciliatory stance toward wealthy elites, see Graham Taylor to William R. Taylor, 28 May 1913, file: "Letters. 1913," box: "Outgoing to 1919," GTP; Boyer, *Public Masses and Moral Order*, 215–216.

37. Chicago reformers took the lead in the national campaign against vice by founding the American Vigilance Association in 1912. At that time, Chicago served as the AVA's central office, while New York only housed the library and an editorial department. See Clifford G. Roe, "The American Vigilance Association," *Journal of Criminal Law and Criminology* 3 (Jan. 1913): 806–809. A year later, in 1913, Rockefeller brokered a merger of the AVA with the American Federation for Sex Hygiene to form the American Social Hygiene Association, which had its headquarters in New York City. The merger alienated the Chicagoans, causing most to resign. See American Social Hygiene Association, *First Annual Report, 1913–1914*, 13, file 1, box 170; "Minutes of the First Annual Meeting of the American Vigilance Association," 17 Feb. 1913, file 6, box 2; both ASHA; Burnham, "The Progressive Era Revolution in American Attitudes Toward Sex," *Journal of American History* 59 (Mar. 1973): 897–898. Wirt Hallam, never one to mince words, felt that the New York reformers, particularly those associated with ASHA, had "really been the enemies of our Chicago work." See Wirt Hallam to Frederick H. Whitin, 15 Feb. 1916, box 3, C14.

38. Representative discussions of white slavery narratives include Feldman, "Prostitution," 192–206; Connelly, *Response to Prostitution*, 115–125; Rosen, *Lost Sisterhood*, 114, 123–130, 133; Mary de Young, "Help, I'm Being Held Captive! The White Slave Fairy Tale of the Progressive Era," *Journal of American Culture* 6 (1983): 96–99; Frederick K. Grittner, *White Slavery: Myth, Ideology, and American Law* (New York, 1990), 66–72.

39. For contemporary definitions of "debt peonage," see *Clyatt v. United States*, 197 U.S. 207 (1905); "Peonage," *Reports of the Immigration Commission*, vol. 2, 61st. Cong., 3d sess., 1910, S. Doc. 747, 444. See also Pete Daniel, *The Shadow of Slavery: Peonage in the South, 1901–1969* (Urbana, IL, 1972), 9–18.

40. Subcommittee of House Committee on Appropriations, *Sundry Civil Appro-*

priation Bill for 1914: Hearings, 62nd Cong., 3rd Sess., 1913, 884; Rosen, *Lost Sister-hood*, 30–31; Roy Lubove, "The Progressives and the Prostitute," *Historian* 24 (May 1962): 308–330. On rescue work, see Smith-Rosenberg, "Beauty, the Beast, and the Militant Woman," 109–128; Pascoe, *Relations of Rescue*.

41. U.S. Immigration Commission, *Importing Women*, 23–25; Addams, *New Conscience*, 20–22; "Sketch I: Edwin W. Simms [*sic*], United States District Attorney, Chicago, from His Article in the 'Woman's World,' Published by Geo. H. Currier," in Mrs. C. I. Harris, *Modern Herodians; Or, Slaughterers of Innocents* (Portland, OR, 1909), 8–11.

42. U.S. Immigration Commission, *Importing Women*, 22; Roe, *Great War on White Slavery*, 172; Janney, *White Slave Traffic*, 36; [Lancaster Citizens' Commission], *A Report on Vice Conditions in the City of Lancaster, Pa.* ([Lancaster], 1913), 63; Maude E. Miner, *Slavery of Prostitution: A Plea for Emancipation* (New York, 1916), 105.

43. Clifford G. Roe, *Panders and Their White Slaves* (New York, 1910); for Mona M.'s story, see 37–43; for Stella's story, see 27–29; and for Adelaide McD.'s, see 47–49. See also Kauffman, *House of Bondage*, 40–70. One of the first initiatives of the Bureau of Investigation was to post copies of peonage laws in brothels so that prostitutes would know that even if they were in debt to their madam, they did not have to stay in the brothel. See Subcommittee of House Committee on Appropriations, *Sundry Civil Appropriation Bill*, 881, 884; Langum, *Crossing Over the Line*, 56, 60.

44. U.S. Immigration Commission, *Importing Women*, 23. See also Mrs. T. P. Curtis, *The Traffic in Women* (Boston, n.d.), 8; Addams, *New Conscience*, 20–22. On neurasthenia and moral degeneration, see George M. Beard, *American Nervousness, Its Causes and Consequences* (New York, 1881); John S. Haller Jr. and Robin M. Haller, *The Physician and Sexuality in Victorian America* (1974; reprint, Carbondale, IL, 1995), 5–43, 102–105.

45. George Kibbe Turner, "The City of Chicago: A Study of the Great Immoralities," *McClure's Magazine* 28 (Apr. 1907): 581; Melvin L. Severy, *Gillette's Social Redemption* (Boston, 1907), 367–369, 372–398; Rosen, *Lost Sisterhood*, 130. On company stores, see Charles B. Fowler, Daniel Bloomfield, and Henry P. Dutton, *Report of the Committee of the Economic and Social Implications of the Company Store and the Scrip System*, ([Washington, DC], Mar. 1936), 18–20, pamphlet collection, Hagley Museum and Library, Wilmington, Delaware; Jacquelyn Dowd Hall, James Leloudis, Robert Korstad, Mary Murphy, Lu Ann Jones, and Christopher B. Daly, *Like a Family: The Making of a Southern Cotton Mill World* (Chapel Hill, NC, 1987), 129–131.

46. Economic historians Ransom and Sutch describe this type of relationship as a monopoly because of the "absence of alternative sources of credit, and . . . the magnitude of the credit prices charged." See Roger Ransom and Richard Sutch, "Credit Merchandising in the Post-Emancipation South: Structure, Conduct, and Performance," *Explorations in Economic History* 16 (1979): 76. On debt peonage and monopoly stores more generally, see Roger Ransom and Richard Sutch, *One Kind of Freedom: The Economic Consequences of Emancipation* (Cambridge, 1977), 126–170.

47. James B. Allen, *The Company Town in the American West* (Norman, OK,

1966), 129; Margaret Von Staden, "My Life: The History of a Prostitute's Life in San Francisco," typescript, n.d., 103–104, 117–118, 149, files 107–109, HLP; Harland, *Vice Bondage*, 40.

48. I calculated the price inflation for company towns using the cash value of scrip cited in John A. Fitch, "The Human Side of Large Outputs: Steel and Steel Workers in Six American States," *Survey* 27 (Jan. 1912): 1530. For the district comparison, see Turner, "City of Chicago," 581.

49. On scrip and the infrequent settling of accounts in company towns, see U.S. Commissioner of Labor, *Report on Conditions of Employment in the Iron and Steel Industry*, vol. 3, 62d Cong., 1st sess., 1913, S. Doc. 110, 387–394. For an excerpt of a madam's ledger book, see [Moral Survey Committee of Syracuse], *The Social Evil in Syracuse: Being the Report of an Investigation of the Moral Condition of the City Conducted by a Committee of Eighteen Citizens* (Syracuse, NY, 1913), 95–101, reprinted in *Prostitution in America: Three Investigations, 1902–1914* (New York, 1976).

50. U.S. Immigration Commission, *Importing Women*, 7; James Bronson Reynolds, "Procuring and Prostitution in New York," in Roe, *Great War on White Slavery*, 213–215; Vice Commission of Chicago, *Social Evil*, 285; *Annual Report of the [Chicago] Committee of Fifteen for the Year Ending April 30, 1915*, file: "2, Committee of Fifteen," GTP; Lubove, "Progressives and the Prostitute," 317; Burnham, "Progressive Era Revolution," 888.

51. Point 2d of the "Memorandum re. New Jersey Injunction and Abatement Law" [10 May 1916], file 1, box L3, ASHA, is that *"every* house of prostitution is in itself a miniature segregated district" (emphasis in original). See also Kneeland, *Commercialized Prostitution*, 99; Hichborn, "California's Campaign," 430; Harriet B. Laidlaw, "Notes," typescript, n.d., file 77, HLP.

52. Frederick H. Whitin to Mrs. Austin, 23 June 1914, file: "1914, June," box 3, C14. See also *Annual Report, 1914–1915*, file: "2, Committee of Fifteen," GTP; Frederick H. Whitin to John P. Peters, 18 Nov. 1916, C14.

53. Janney, *White Slave Traffic*, 150; Rev. R. P. Shuler, "The Houses in Our Midst," *Pastor's Bulletin No. 9, Anti-Vice Bulletins* (Austin, TX, [1914]), 26, Center for American History, University of Texas, Austin; American Social Hygiene Association, *The Segregation of Prostitution and the Injunction and Abatement Law Against Houses of Prostitution*, Publication 73 (1917), file 1, box L3, ASHA; Howard B. Woolston, *Prostitution in the United States*, vol. 1, *Prior to the Entrance of the United States into the World War* (New York, 1921), 120.

54. John P. Peters to the editor of the [*New York*] *Evening Post*, 3 Jan. 1913, file: "1912, Proposed Morals Commission," box 83, C14; [Vice Commission of Minneapolis], *Report of the Vice Commission of Minneapolis to His Honor, James C. Haynes, Mayor* (Minneapolis, 1911), reprinted in *The Prostitute and the Social Reformer: Commercial Vice in the Progressive Era*, ed. Charles Rosenberg and Carroll Smith-Rosenberg (New York, 1974), 93–95; *People v. Fegelli*, 148 N.Y.S. 979 (N.Y. 1914); Lubove, "Progressives and the Prostitute," 309–311, 319–320.

55. "Rabbi Hirsch's Address," in American Vigilance Association, *Testimony and Addresses*, Pamphlet No. 2: 13, ASHA; Shuler, "Houses in Our Midst," 26; [Lancaster

Citizens' Committee], *Report*, 67; American Social Hygiene Association, *Segregation of Prostitution*, pamphlet, n.d., file 2, box 170, ASHA.

56. Turner, "City of Chicago," 584; Addams, *New Conscience*, 36–37; [Portland, OR Vice Commission], *Report of the Portland Vice Commission to the Mayor and City Council of the City of Portland, Oregon* (Portland, 1913), 212; Al Rose, *Storyville, New Orleans: Being an Authentic, Illustrated Account of the Notorious Red-Light District* (Tuscaloosa, AL, 1974), 44, 46; Frost, *Gentlemen's Club*, 100–103; Griffith, *Conspicuous Failure*, 78–80.

57. Hichborn, "California's Campaign," 430; Carl Hovey, "The Police Question: Chicago Struggling to Solve It; Philadelphia Blinded and Bound," *Metropolitan* ([1910]), 50, file: "Chicago. Police. Pamphlets Concerning," GTP; [Lancaster Citizens' Committee], *Report*, 73; Mayer, *Regulation of Commercialized Vice*, 15; Melvin G. Holli, "Urban Reform in the Progressive Era," in *The Progressive Era*, ed. Lewis L. Gould (Syracuse, NY, 1974), 137.

58. Abe Shoenfeld, interview by Arthur Goren, 6 Feb. 1965, typescript, 117–119, William E. Wiener Oral History Library of the American Jewish Committee, Jewish Division, New York Public Library; Dun and Bradstreet credit reports, 1913, file 24, box 4, Chicago Municipal Court, Chicago Historical Society; Beard, *American City Government*, 162; James Bryce, *The American Commonwealth*, new ed. (New York, 1911), vol. 2, 399–401.

59. Beard, *American City Government*, 192–193. Customers who regularly used a significant amount of electricity late at night received "liberal rebates." See John R. Commons, "Municipal Electricity Lighting," in *Municipal Monopolies*, ed. Edward W. Bemis (New York, 1899), 79–88. Late-night users received better rates, in part, because they helped balance out the load factor, meaning that they needed electricity when other customers did not, thus evening out the demand for electrical power. See Thomas P. Hughes, *Networks of Power: Electrification in Western Society, 1880–1930* (Baltimore, 1983), 217–226.

60. Graham Taylor testimony, "Proceedings of the City Vice Commission," 18 Jan. 1913, 20–21, file 3, box 23, Chicago Commons Collection, Chicago Historical Society; Bridgeport Vice Commission, *The Report and Recommendations of the Bridgeport Vice Commission* (Bridgeport, CT, 1916), 23; "Scarlet Sisters Everleigh: How Vice Grew Up in Chicago," *Chicago Sunday Tribune*, 26 Jan. 1936, part 7, 7; Joy J. Jackson, *New Orleans in the Gilded Age: Politics and Urban Progress, 1880–1896* (Baton Rouge, LA, 1969), 254; Rosen, *Lost Sisterhood*, 82; Gilfoyle, *City of Eros*, 247–248.

61. "Why Policemen of Atlanta Do Not, and Will Not, Protect Vice," Men and Religion Bulletin No. 41, *Atlanta Constitution*, 15 Jan. 1913, 7; *Annual Report for the [Chicago] Committee of Fifteen for the Year Ending April 30, 1914*, file: "2, Committee of Fifteen," GTP; Kneeland, *Commercialized Prostitution*, 3–51. On the use of industrial imagery, see John B. Hammond, "The Iowa 'Red Light' Injunction Law and its Success," in Roe, *Great War on White Slavery*, 358–361; William E. Chandler, "The 'Necessary Evil,'" Chandler's Bulletin No. 11, Chicago Law and Order League, file: "1912, June," box 2, C14.

62. Katharine Houghton Hepburn, *Woman Suffrage and the Social Evil* (New

York, n.d.), 5–6, file 104, HLP; B. S. Steadwell, "Introduction," in Roe, *Great War on White Slavery*, 16–17; Edwin W. Sims, cited in Harriet B. Laidlaw, "The White Slave Traffic or Commercialized Vice," typescript, n.d., 2, file 110, HLP; "Why Policemen of Atlanta," 7; Graham Taylor, "The Police and Vice in Chicago," *Survey* 23 (6 Nov. 1909): 163.

63. Turner, "City of Chicago," 582. See also Edwin W. Sims, cited in Laidlaw, "White Slave Traffic," 2, HLP; Roe, *Great War on White Slavery*, 186–188; Ernest A. Bell, *War on the White Slave Trade* ([Chicago], 1911), 257; Jean Turner Zimmerman, *America's Black Traffic in White Girls*, 8th ed. (Chicago, 1912). In addition to the cattle metaphor, Harriet Laidlaw also compared prostitutes to grain and red-light districts to mills. See Laidlaw, "The A.B.C. of the Question," typescript, [1912], 1, 3, file 77, HLP. The fact that the Progressive era predates Henry Ford's assembly lines means that Swift's or Armour's meat-packing "disassembly" lines were the likely industrial referents. See Chandler, *Visible Hand*, 293–302.

64. Oliver E. Williamson, "Transaction-Cost Economics: The Governance of Contractual Relations," in *Industrial Organization*, ed. Oliver E. Williamson (Brookfield, VT, 1990), 234–235; *The New Palgrave: A Dictionary of Economics*, s.v. "capital good" and "economic organization and transaction costs."

65. Graham Taylor, "The Story of the Chicago Vice Commission," *Survey* 26 (6 May 1911): 242; John P. Peters to the editor of the [*New York*] *Evening Post*, C14; Harland, *Vice Bondage*, 18; Ellen M. Henrotin, "The Part Women Are Taking," in Roe, *Great War on White Slavery*, 94; *Fegelli* 148 N.Y.S. 979.

66. Taylor, "Story of the Chicago Vice Commission," 242; Curtis, *Traffic in Women*, 9–12; Vice Commission of Philadelphia, *Report*, 38; [Lancaster Citizens' Committee], *Report*, 77–78; Miner, *Slavery of Prostitution*, 160–161; Woolston, *Prostitution in the United States*, 122. See also Thomas C. Mackey, *Red Lights Out: A Legal History of Prostitution, Disorderly Houses and Vice Districts, 1870–1917* (New York, 1987), 123–124.

67. U.S. Immigration Commission, *Importing Women*, 32; Vice Commission of Philadelphia, *Report*, 20; Rev. R. P. Shuler, "Facts and Figures that Do Not Lie," *Pastor's Bulletin No. 24, Anti-Vice Bulletins* (Austin, TX, [1914]), 56; Woolston, *Prostitution in the United States*, 118–119; Rosen, *Lost Sisterhood*, 41–42. Progressives thought "wasteful extravagances" such as ready-made clothes, trips to amusement parks, and summer vacations caused inflation. See Daniel Horowitz, *The Morality of Spending: Attitudes toward the Consumer Society in America, 1875–1940* (1985; paperback, Chicago, 1992), 74–75.

68. *The Penguin Dictionary of Economics*, new ed., s.v. "multiplier"; John Maynard Keynes, *The General Theory of Employment, Interest, and Money* (1936; Amherst, NY, 1997), 85, 113–131; "Vice, Police, and Law Enforcement and a Morals Commission," typescript, [1912], 3–6, file: "1912, Proposed Morals Commission," box 83, C14; Harland, *Vice Bondage*, 107; Ellen M. Henrotin, "The Social Evil," manuscript, n.d., 19, file 19, box 2, Ellen Martin Henrotin Papers, Schlesinger Library, Radcliffe Institute for Advanced Study, Harvard University; [Lancaster Citizens' Committee], *Report*, 65–67; Samuel P. Thrasher to the President and Directors, [19 May 1914], file: "2—Committee of Fifteen," GTP.

69. Beard, *American City Government*, 220. See also Lincoln Steffens, *The Shame of the Cities* (1904; New York, 1948), 294–295; Harland, *Vice Bondage*, 3; [Lancaster Citizens' Committee], *Report*, 65–67; George J. Kneeland, "Commercialized Prostitution and the Use of Property," *Social Hygiene* 2 (Oct. 1916): 564.

70. Vice Commission of Philadelphia, *Report*, 13–16; Harland, *Vice Bondage*, 107; Laidlaw, "White Slave Traffic," 7, HLP; [Moral Survey Committee], *Social Evil in Syracuse*, 11; "Prospectus," typescript, [1918], file: "3—Committee of Fifteen," GTP.

71. On the arguments of district supporters, see [Vice Commission of Minneapolis], *Report*, 84–85; J. L. Hamery, *Can Vice Be Abolished? A Startling Story of Police Graft and Failure of Segregation in Des Moines, Iowa*, pamphlet, [1912], box 2, C14; Chicago Hotel-Keepers Protective Association, "Paid Reformers: A Menace," poster, [1916], file: "2—Committee of Fifteen," GTP.

72. The Chicago Vice Commissioners made the often-cited estimate that district proprietors and their business relations made $15,000,000 in profits. See Vice Commission of Chicago, *Social Evil*, 32, 95–116. See also Marcus Braun to John D. Rockefeller Jr., 2 Apr. 1910, file 38, box 6, series: "Boards," RG 2-OMR, RFA; U.S. Immigration Commission, *Importing Women*, 28; Shuler, "Facts and Figures," 56; Delos F. Wilcox, *Great Cities in America: Their Problems and Their Government* (New York, 1910), 144.

73. Judge Dike, cited in Roe, *Great War on White Slavery*, 176. See also "Rabbi Hirsch's Address," 13; Vice Commission of Philadelphia, *Report*, 44–45; [Morals Efficiency Commission, Pittsburgh], *Report and Recommendations of the Morals Efficiency Commission, Pittsburgh, Pa.* (Pittsburgh, 1913), 12–13.

74. Edward A. Ross, *Changing America: Studies in Contemporary Society* (New York, 1912), 97–98; [Frederick H. Whitin] to Prince A. Morrow, 28 Nov. 1907, box 1, C14; Mayer, *Regulation of Commercialized Vice*, 11; Rosen, *Lost Sisterhood*, 42; Alfred D. Chandler Jr., *Strategy and Structure: Chapters in the History of the American Industrial Enterprise* (Cambridge, MA, 1962), 37–38; Hays, *Response to Industrialism*, 9–13.

75. Ellen M. Henrotin, "The Ravages of Prostitution," manuscript, n.d., 2–3, file 17, Ellen Martin Henrotin Papers. See also Robert A. Woods, "Banners of a New Army," *Survey* 29 (8 Mar. 1913): 813; Vice Commission of Philadelphia, *Report*, 20; [Lancaster Citizens' Committee], *Report*, 62–67.

76. Vice Commission of Chicago, *Social Evil*, 32–35; Harland, *Vice Bondage*, 10; Jane Addams, cited in Laidlaw, "White Slave Traffic," 3, HLP; Bingham, *Girls that Disappear*, 37; Robert McMurdy, "The Use of the Injunction to Destroy Commercialized Prostitution," *Journal of Criminal Law and Criminology* 19 (Feb. 1929): 513; Lubove, "Progressives and the Prostitutes," 310–311; Rosen, *Lost Sisterhood*, 70–71.

77. Turner, "Daughters of the Poor," 59; Jane Addams, "A Challenge to the Contemporary Church," *Survey* reprint, 5, file 104, HLP; "Men Responsible for Social Evil," *Atlanta Constitution*, 28 Jan. 1913, 3.

78. Vice Commission of Chicago, *Social Evil*, 32–33, 47; "Rockefeller Bureau of Social Hygiene," *Survey* 29 (8 Mar. 1913): 802; Kneeland, *Commercialized Prostitution*, 77; Lubove, "Progressives and the Prostitute," 310–311.

79. "Miss Kate Adam's Address," in American Vigilance Association, *Testimony*

and Addresses, Pamphlet No. 1: 7, ASHA; Kehillah reports, 8 Aug. 1913, 6 Aug. 1913, 5 Aug. 1913, and 2 Aug. 1913, box 2, C14; [Portland, OR Vice Commission], *Report,* 68–70. On Max Hochstim, see Bristow, *Prostitution and Prejudice,* 170; Gilfoyle, *City of Eros,* 261–264.

80. Graham Taylor, "Recent Advances Against the Social Evil in New York," *Survey* 24 (17 Sept. 1910): 858–865; Peters, "Suppression of the 'Raines Law Hotels,'" 562–563; [Vice Commission of Minneapolis], *Report,* 39; Ross, "Sinning by Syndicate," in *Sin and Society,* 105–131; Hays, *Response to Industrialism,* 50, 84–85; Mark J. Roe, *Strong Managers, Weak Owners: The Political Roots of American Corporate Finance* (Princeton, NJ, 1994), 3–7.

81. George Kibbe Turner, "The Strange Woman," *McClure's Magazine,* 41 (May 1913): 30. See also Vice Commission of Chicago, *Social Evil,* 87, 89, 105, 231; Beard, *American City Government,* 186; Marcus Braun to John D. Rockefeller Jr., 2 Apr. 1910, file 38, box 6, series: "Boards," RG 2-OMR, RFA. On real estate owners and agents, see "Name Plate Ordinances," box 4, C14; Hammond, "Iowa 'Red Light' Injunction Law," 363, 367–368; Rosen, *Lost Sisterhood,* 28–29, 77.

82. "Jenkin Lloyd Jones' Address," in American Vigilance Association, *Testimony and Addresses,* Pamphlet No. 2: 15, ASHA. See also Vice Commission of Chicago, *Social Evil,* 33; [Portland, OR Vice Commission], *Report,* 71–73; Bascom Johnson, "The Injunction and Abatement Law," *Social Hygiene* 1 (Mar. 1915): 231–232.

83. Frederick H. Whitin to Tribune Printing Co., 12 Feb. 1914, file T, box 15, C14; *American Film Institute Catalog of Motion Pictures: Feature Films, 1911–1920; Film Entries,* ed. Patricia King Hanson and Alan Gevinson (Berkeley, CA, 1988), 944, 457, 852. See also Leslie Fishbein, "Harlot or Heroine? Changing Views of Prostitution, 1870–1920," *Historian* 43 (Nov. 1980): 27–28; Kevin Brownlow, *Behind the Mask of Innocence: Sex, Violence, Prejudice, Crime; Films of Social Conscience in the Silent Era* (Berkeley, CA, 1990), 74–81.

84. *Traffic in Souls,* dir. George Loane Tucker (1913). Although none of the titles in the movie use the phrase "Vice Trust," Universal used it in the advertising campaign for the movie. See Brownlow, *Behind the Mask,* 77.

85. Tucker also reinforced his message visually, for, as a *Variety* critic observed, "there's a laugh on the Rockefeller investigators" because one of the white slavers was a dead ringer for "John D." See *Variety* (28 Nov. 1913): 12, cited in Brownlow, *Behind the Mask,* 75. Even so, moviemakers did not want to alienate reformers—especially if they could provide a positive quotation. Universal sent complimentary tickets to the Committee of Fourteen and asked for their reaction. See J. W. Grey to the Committee of Fourteen, 24 Dec. 1913, file: "1913, Dec.," box 3, C14. Unfortunately for Universal, Whitin's conclusion was that the movie was "not . . . objectionable." See Frederick H. Whitin to Tribune Printing Co., C14.

86. Lester F. Scott to Frederick H. Whitin, 22 Oct. 1913, file: "People's Institute," box 12; John Collier to Frederick Whitin, 23 Oct. 1913, file: "1913, October," box 3; W. D. McGuire Jr. to Frederick Whitin, 12 Nov. 1913, file: "1913, Nov.," box 3; Frederick H. Whitin to W. D. McGuire Jr., 15 Nov. 1913, file: "1913, Nov.," box 3; all C14; Brownlow, *Behind the Mask,* 74–75.

87. "Statement for Publicity by the Chairman," [1907], vol. 1, box 86; "Coopera-
tion between the Committee of Fourteen and the Surety Companies," [1916], file:
"Surety Companies," box 20; "Necrographer" to Fred Whitin, 4 Sept. 1909, box 1; all
C14.

88. "Investigative Report," 26 Aug. 1915, box 29; Investigative reports from 9 Jan.
1916, 27 Jan. 1916, and 13 Apr. 1916, box 30; all C14. See also "Sex O'Clock in America,"
Current Opinion 55 (1913): 113.

89. "Keepers of Disorderly Houses Turn on the Police" and "The 'Vice Trust' in
New York City," *Current Opinion* 54 (1913): 5–6; Kneeland, *Commercialized Prostitu-
tion*, 157, 171–172; "Organized Vice as a Vested Interest," *Current Literature* 52 (1912):
292. On "bigness," see Louis D. Brandeis, "A Curse of Bigness," in *Other People's
Money, and How the Bankers Use It* (New York, 1914), 162–188; Thomas K. McCraw,
Prophets of Regulation (Cambridge, MA, 1984), 108–109.

90. Peters, "Suppression of 'Raines Law Hotels,'" 565–566; [Hartford Vice Com-
mission], *Report of the Hartford Vice Commission: Hartford, Connecticut* (Hartford
[1913]), 11; "The Wreak of Commercialized Vice," *Survey* 35 (5 Feb. 1916): 532–533;
Frederick H. Whitin, "Obstacles to Vice Repression," *Social Hygiene* 2 (Apr. 1916):
150–152; Miner, *Slavery of Prostitution*, 125.

91. The use of case precedent is inherently analogical, but occasionally jurists
made their comparisons explicit. See *Congressional Record*, 61st Cong., 2d sess., 1910,
45, pt. 2: 810–812, 816–821, 1035–1039; *Hoke v. United States*, 227 U.S. 308 (1913); *State
v. Gilbert*, 147 N.W. 953, (Minn. 1914). See also Cass R. Sunstein, "On Analogical
Reasoning," *Harvard Law Review* 106 (Jan. 1993): 741–791; Dennis R. Klinck, "Metaphor," in *The Word of the Law: Approaches to Legal Discourse* (Ottawa, 1992), 335–370.
Since the passage of the Sherman Anti-Trust Act, jurists have successfully argued that
regulation includes prohibition. See *Champion v. Ames*, 188 U.S. 321 (1903); Robert
Eugene Cushman, "The National Police Power under the Commerce Clause of the
Constitution," section 2, *Minnesota Law Journal* 3 (May 1919): 382–392; Grittner,
White Slavery, 49–50.

92. Senator Philander C. Knox, "Development of the Federal Power to Regulate
Commerce," *Yale Law Journal* 17 (Jan. 1908): 144–148; Cushman, "National Police
Power," 382–392; John Edgar Hoover, "Organized Protection Against Organized Pred-
atory Crimes," *Journal of Criminal Law and Criminology* 24 (1933): 473–482; Lan Cao,
"Illegal Traffic in Women: A Civil RICO Proposal," *Yale Law Journal* 96 (May 1987):
1297–1322; Jay A. Rosenberg, "Constitutional Rights and Civil Forfeiture Actions,"
Columbia Law Review 88 (Mar. 1988): 390–406; B. A. Glesner, "Landlords as Cops:
Torts, Nuisance and Forfeiture Standards Imposing Liability on Landlords for Crime
on the Premises," *Case Western Reserve Law Review* 42 (1992): 679–791; Lynn N.
Hughes, "Don't Make a Federal Case Out of It: The Constitution and the Nationaliza-
tion of Crime," *American Journal of Criminal Law* 25 (Fall 1997): 151–163.

93. "National Merger to Fight White Slavery," *Survey* 27 (30 Mar. 1912): 1991–1992;
Mayer, *Regulation of Commercialized Vice*, 30; Aldoph F. Niemoeller, *Sexual Slavery
in America* (New York, 1935), 193–197, 203–205; Grittner, *White Slavery*, 74–75, 86–88;
Langum, *Crossing Over the Line*, 27–30, 38–41.

94. Graham Taylor, "Morals Commission and Police Morals," *Survey* 30 (12 Apr. 1913): 63–64; American Social Hygiene Association, *Segregation of Prostitution and the Injunction and Abatement Law*, ASHA; Rosen, *Lost Sisterhood*, 125; Langum, *Crossing Over the Line*, 59–60. Prosecutors were sometimes able to indict the financial backers who received a portion of the brothel's proceeds, but the evidence had to be incontrovertible. See *Fegelli* 148 N.Y.S. 979, judgment affirmed 108 N.E. 1103 (N.Y 1915). In contrast, see *State v. Topham*, 123 P. 888 (Utah 1912).

95. "National Merger," 1991–1992; American Social Hygiene Association, *First Annual Report*, 15, ASHA; Johnson, "Injunction and Abatement Law," 231–256; "Relation of the American Social Hygiene Association to Community Welfare: Department of Legal Measures," typescript, 25 Oct. 1923, file 1, box 1, ASHA; Mackey, *Red Lights Out*, 122–125.

96. Roe, "American Vigilance Association," 806–807; "The Injunction and Abatement Law," *American Social Hygiene Association Bulletin* 3 (Apr. 1916): 2–3; Woolston, *Prostitution in the United States*, 174–175.

97. Roe, "American Vigilance Association," 807–808; American Social Hygiene Association, *First Annual Report*, 13–15, 118; ASHA; "Minutes of the Meeting of the Executive Committee," 5 May 1914, file 2, box 5, ASHA; American Social Hygiene Association, *Second Annual Report, 1914–1915*, 17–22, file 1, box 170, ASHA; Mayer, *Regulation of Commercialized Vice*, 23, 26; Mackey, *Red Lights Out*, 125–126.

98. *White Slave Traffic*, 12; *Congressional Record*, 820, 1035–1038; *Hoke* 227 U.S. 308; *United States v. Westman*, 182 F. 1017 (U.S.D.C. Or. 1910); Berkeley Davids, "Construction of the 'Mann Act,'" *Law Notes* 17 (Mar. 1914): 225–226; Connelly, *Response to Prostitution*, 58–59; Langum, *Crossing Over the Line*, 40–44.

99. *White Slave Traffic Act of June 25, 1910*, 36 Stat. 825; *White Slave Traffic*, 9–11; Berkeley Davids, "Application of Mann Act to Noncommercial Vice," *Law Notes* 20 (Nov. 1916): 144–146; Cushman, "National Police Power," 390; Henry F. May, *The End of American Innocence: A Study of the First Years of Our Own Time, 1912–1917* (New York, 1959), 343; Brandt, *No Magic Bullet*, 33–34. That anti-trust regulation was intrinsic to the construction of the Mann Act is apparent in the brief Edwin W. Sims prepared for Mann. See "Self-Crimination under the White-Slave Law," *Congressional Record*, 806–808. On Sims's role in the construction of the Mann Act, see Langum, *Crossing Over the Line*, 38–40.

100. Connelly, *Response to Prostitution*, 58–59; Grittner, *White Slavery*, 86–87; Langum, *Crossing Over the Line*, 38–41. On the Pure Food and Drug Act, see James Harvey Young, *Pure Food: Securing the Pure Food and Drugs Act of 1906* (Princeton, NJ, 1989). On the Mann-Elkins Act, see Herbert Hovenkamp, *Enterprise and American Law, 1836–1937* (Cambridge, MA, 1991), 145, 165. On the Interstate Commerce Commission, see McCraw, *Prophets of Regulation*, 61–63.

101. "Commercialized Vice a National Problem," *Survey* 29 (8 Mar. 1913): 800; Graham Taylor, "The War on Vice," *Survey* 29 (8 Mar. 1913): 811–812; Davids, "Application of Mann Act," 145; Daniel J. Leab, "Women and the Mann Act," *Amerikastudien / American Studies* 21 (1976): 55–65.

102. "Clash of New Conscience with Our Court Decisions," *Survey* 29 (8 Mar.

1913): 800–801; *Caminetti v. United States*, 242 U.S. 470 (1917); Arthur B. Spingarn, *Laws Relating to Sex Morality in New York City*, rev. ed. (New York, 1926), 48; Berto Rogers, "The Mann Act and Noncommercial Vice," *Law Notes* 37 (July 1933): 107–108; Langum, *Crossing Over the Line*, 43, 48–58, 65–71. Nevertheless, the commerce clause, and its dissociation from business, set crucial precedents for the expansion of federal regulation. See Cushman, "National Police Power," 289–319, 381–412, 452–483; Hughes, "Don't Make a Federal Case," 151–163.

103. "Commercialized Vice a National Problem," 800; Harvey D. Jacob, "White Slavery," *Case and Comment* 23 (June 1916): 20–22; Woolston, *Prostitution in the United States*, 175; Leab, "Women and the Mann Act," 57.

104. Pandering statutes, like contract labor laws, turned on the making of illegal employment contracts. See *State v. Stone*, 120 P. 76 (Wash. 1912); *Smith v. State*, 164 S.W. 825 (Tex. Cr. App. 1914); *People v. De Martini*, 142 P. 898 (Cal. App. 1914); *Ex parte Hollman*, 60 S.E. 19 (S.C. 1908); *Ex parte George*, 180 F. 785 (U.S.D.C. 1910); *Darnborough v. Joseph Benn and Sons*, 187 F. 580 (U.S.C.C.A. 1911). See also Roscoe Pound, "Liberty of Contract," *Yale Law Journal* 18 (May 1909): 484. For a model pandering law, see Janney, *White Slave Traffic*, 178–181. On contract labor regulations, see Sec. 4 and Sec. 5 of the *Alien Immigration Act of March 3*, 1903, c. 1012, 32 Stat. 1213; "Contract Labor and Induced and Assisted Immigration," *Reports of the Immigration Commission*, vol. 2, 61st. Cong., 3d sess., 1910, S. Doc. 747, 376–380.

105. On jurisdictional disputes, see *Hewitt v. State*, 167 S.W. 40 (Tex. Cr. App. 1914); *State v. Harper*, 138 P. 495 (Mont. 1914); "State Statutes," *American Social Hygiene Association Bulletin* (Jan. 1916): 6.

106. On the Mann Act, see "Construction of White Slave Act," *Law Notes* 17 (Nov. 1913): 141; Davids, "Construction of the 'Mann Act,'" 225; Grittner, *White Slavery*, 45–47. On disorderly house laws, see *Nelson v. Territory*, 49 P. 920 (Okl. 1897); *Jones v. State*, 133 P. 1134 (Okl. Cr. App. 1913). On pandering, see *People v. Van Bever*, 93 N.E. 725 (Ill. 1911); Woolston, *Prostitution in the United States*, 175.

107. *State v. Columbus*, 133 P. 455 (Wash. 1913); *Boyle v. State*, 161 S.W. 1049 (Ark. 1913); *Jones v. State*, 162 S.W. 1142 (Tex. Cr. App. 1914); Lubove, "Progressives and the Prostitute," 326. On contract labor, see *Alien Contract Labor*, 51st. Cong., 1st sess., 1890, H. Rep. 2997, 2–3; *Lees v. United States*, 150 U.S. 476 (1893); *Hepner v. United States*, 213 U.S. 103 (1909); "Contract Labor and Induced and Assisted Immigration," 381–386.

108. Jurists were not alone in comparing white slavery with the *padrone* system. See Louis Lichtenstein to Mr. Whiting [*sic*], 26 Jan. 1909, box 22, C14; Gunther Peck, "Reinventing Free Labor: Immigrant *Padrones* and Contract Laborers in North America, 1885–1925," *Journal of American History* 83 (Dec. 1996): 848–871.

109. Mayer, *Regulation of Commercialized Vice*, 30–32.

110. For a copy of the law, see "Iowa Injunction and Abatement Law" in [Moral Survey Committee], *Social Evil in Syracuse*, 119–121. In 1909, Iowa passed the first red-light abatement act, which served as a legislative model for other states. See Edwin R. A. Seligman, ed., *The Social Evil: With Special Reference to Conditions in the City of New York*, rev. ed. (New York, 1912), 241–242; "Injunction and Abatement Laws of

Iowa and Nebraska," typescript, [1914], 2, file 1, box L3, ASHA; Rosen, *Lost Sisterhood*, 28–29.

111. *People v. Barbiere*, 166 P. 812 (Cal. App. 1917); *People v. Casa Co.*, 169 P. 454 (Cal. App. 1917); *People v. Clark*, 108 N.E. 994 (Ill. 1915); Wisconsin Vice Committee, *Report and Recommendations of the Wisconsin Legislative Committee to Investigate the White Slave Traffic and Kindred Subjects* ([Madison], 1914), 95; Charles S. Ascher and James M. Wolf, " 'Red Light' Injunction and Abatement Acts," *Columbia Law Review* 20 (May 1920): 605–608.

112. Kneeland, "Commercialized Prostitution and the Use of Property," 571; [Vice Commission of Minneapolis], *Report*, 23–24; [Little Rock Vice Commission], *Report of the Little Rock Vice Commission* ([Little Rock], 1913), 10; [Portland, OR Vice Commission], *Report*, 100–104. One the maxims of equity, which guides civil adjudication, is to "look at the intent, not the form." See James Brown Scott, *Cases on Equity Jurisdiction* (New York, 1906), vol. 1, x, 300; Roscoe Pound, "The Progress of the Law, 1918–1919: Equity, Part 2," *Harvard Law Review* 33 (Apr. 1920): 815.

113. *Lismore v. State*, 126 S.W. 853 (Ark. 1910); *Cooper v. State*, 150 N.W. 207 (Neb. 1914); [Portland, OR Vice Commission], *Report*, 103–104; Rosen, *Lost Sisterhood*, 74. Disorderly house fines were an important source of revenue. See [Vice Commission of Minneapolis], *Report*, 24; Frederick H. Whitin, "The Social Evil in Kansas City," *Survey* 27 (27 Jan. 1912): 1644; George Creel, "Where Is the Vice Fight," *Harper's Weekly* 59 (10 Oct. 1914): 342.

114. The court of chancery, which hears equity cases, was specifically created to deal with problems that the criminal courts were unable to address. See Joseph Story, *Commentaries on Equity Jurisprudence, as Administered in England and America*, 4th ed. (Boston, 1846), vol. 1, 17–32; William F. Walsh, *A Treatise on Equity* (Chicago, 1930), 12–29.

115. *Gilbert* 147 N.W. 953; *Cooper* 150 N.W. 207; Hammond, "Iowa 'Red Light' Injunction Law," 359, 363, esp. 367; Vice Commission of Philadelphia, *Report*, 38–39. Partnership was the dominant form of corporate governance through the nineteenth century. See Thomas R. Navin and Marian V. Sears, "The Rise of a Market for Industrial Securities, 1887–1902," *Business History Review* 29 (June 1955): 105–138; Naomi R. Lamoreaux, "Partnership, Corporations, and the Theory of the Firm," *American Economic Review* 88 (May 1998): 66–71.

116. The courts ruled that equity was an appropriate jurisdiction to abate public nuisances, even if the maintenance of the nuisance was also a crime. See *State v. Rabinowitz*, 118 P. 1040 (Kan. 1911); *Weiss v. Superior Court of San Diego County*, 159 P. 464 (Cal. App. 1916). See also Walsh, *Treatise on Equity*, 204–205; Mackey, *Red Lights Out*, 183–184. By 1920, thirty-nine states, Alaska, and the District of Columbia had red-light abatement laws. See Mayer, *Regulation of Commercialized Vice*, 31; George E. Worthington, "Injunction and Abatement Law Against Houses of Prostitution," *United League News* 3 (Apr. 1923): 1, file 14, box L2, ASHA.

117. *Mugler v. Kansas*, 123 U.S. 623 (1887); *Gilbert* 147 N.W. 953; *State v. Lane*, 147 N.W. 951 (Minn. 1914); *Clark* 108 N.E. 994. See also Zechariah Chafee Jr., "The Progress of the Law, 1919–1920: Equitable Relief Against Torts," *Harvard Law Review*

34 (Feb. 1921): 398; Archibald H. Throckmorton, *Illustrative Cases on Equity Jurispru-dence*, 2nd ed. (St. Paul, MN, 1923), 16–22.

118. *State v. Nichols*, 145 P. 986 (Wash. 1915); *Barbiere* 166 P. 812; *State v. Clark*, 178 N.W. 419 (Ia. 1920). In contrast, owners were rarely proven culpable under disorderly house laws. See *Hazelwood v. Commonwealth*, 132 S.W. 567 (Ky. 1910); "Disorderly House," *Second Decennial Digest* 9; "Injunction and Abatement Laws of Iowa and Nebraska," 2, ASHA.

119. *State v. Fanning*, 47 N.W. 215 (Neb. 1914); *State v. Jerome*, 141 P. 753 (Wash. 1914); *State v. Schropfer*, 142 P. 119 (Wash. 1914); *People v. Dillman*, 174 P. 951 (Cal. App. 1918); G. H. Gobar, "Constitutional Law: Validity of 'Red Light Law' Taxation," *California Law Review* 2 (Sept. 1914): 498; Worthington, "Injunction and Abatement Law," 1; Rosen, *Lost Sisterhood*, 29.

120. *Jerome* 141 P. 753; *Casa Co.* 169 P. 454; *Chase v. Proprietors of Revere House*, 122 N.E. 162 (Mass. 1919). See also Wirt W. Hallam, "The Reduction of Vice in Certain Western Cities through Law-Enforcement" *Social Diseases* (Apr. 1912), reprinted in [Moral Survey Committee], *Social Evil in Syracuse*, 113; McMurdy, "Use of the Injunction," 516.

121. One of the most important innovations of the red-light abatement laws was that private citizens could bring suit without having to show specific damages. See *Fanning* 47 N.W. 215; *Edison v. Ramsey*, 92 S.E. 513 (Ga. 1917); Johnson, "Injunction and Abatement Law," 231–232; Mackey, *Red Lights Outs*, 126–128. Thus empowered, private anti-vice associations could start injunction and abatement proceedings. See *People ex rel. Thrasher v. Smith*, 114 N.E. 31 (Ill. 1916); *Chase* 122 N.E. 162. Samuel P. Thrasher was the superintendent of the Chicago Committee of Fifteen, while J. Frank Chase was the secretary of the New England Watch and Ward Society.

122. *Gilbert* 147 N.W. 953; *Nichols* 145 P. 986. On reformers' antipathy toward juries, see Kneeland, "Commercialized Prostitution and the Use of Property," 569–570; [Lexington Vice Commission], *Report of the Vice Commission of Lexington, Ky.*, 2nd ed. (Lexington, 1915), 57–59; Ascher and Wolf, "'Red Light' Injunction and Abatement Acts," 606; Lawrence M. Friedman, *Crime and Punishment in American History* (New York, 1993), 247–250.

123. *Lane* 147 N.W. 951; *Barbiere* 166 P. 812; *Chase* 122 N.E. 162; Mayer, *Regulation of Commercialized Vice*, 16; Rosen, *Lost Sisterhood*, 29; Mackey, *Red Lights Out*, 130.

124. Johnson, "Injunction and Abatement Law," 256. See also Kneeland, "Commercialized Prostitution and the Use of Property," 568; Wisconsin Vice Committee, *Report*, 96. Often, just publishing the names of landlords was sufficient to get them to change their rental practices. See "'15 Committee' Names Vice Property Owners," *Record Herald*, 9 July 1913, file: "Committee of 15, 1913," box 2, Clifford W. Barnes Papers, Chicago Historical Society; "Using the Mails to War in San Francisco," *Survey* 35 (8 Jan. 1916): 418.

125. Hammond, "Iowa 'Red Light' Injunction Law," 358–370; Johnson, "Injunction and Abatement Law," 252–254; American Social Hygiene Association, *Segregation of Prostitution and the Injunction and Abatement Law*, ASHA; Rosen, *Lost Sisterhood*,

28–29; John D'Emilio and Estelle B. Freedman, *Intimate Matters: A History of Sexuality in America* (New York, 1988), 211.

126. [Portland, OR Vice Commission], *Report*, 92; Wisconsin Vice Committee, *Report*, 96; Johnson, "Injunction and Abatement Law," 256; Franklin Hichborn, "Time, Dr. Rosenstirn, and the Abatement Act," publicity slip, [California] State Law Enforcement League, [1920], file 2, box L3, ASHA; Mackey, *Red Lights Out*, 8–9; Langum, *Crossing Over the Line*, 59.

127. "Buffalo's Waning Red Lights," *Survey* 36 (27 May 1916): 218; "Vice Conditions," *Social Hygiene Bulletin* 4 (Jan. 1917): 2; American Social Hygiene Association, *Segregation of Prostitution and the Injunction and Abatement Law*, ASHA; Johnson, "Injunction and Abatement Law," 254; Creel, "Where Is the Vice Fight," 34; Rosen, *Lost Sisterhood*, 30; Mackey, *Red Lights Out*, 131. For a timetable of district closures, see Mayer, *Regulation of Commercialized Vice*, 11.

128. *State v. Fanning*, 149 N.W. 413 (Neb. 1914); Wisconsin Vice Committee, *Report*, 27, 94–95; American Social Hygiene Association, *Segregation of Prostitution and the Injunction and Abatement Law*, ASHA; "Indianapolis, Ind.," *American Social Hygiene Association Bulletin* 4 (Jan. 1917): 2; Woolston, *Prostitution in the United States*, 240.

129. Timothy Egan, "Soldiers of the Drug War Remain on Duty," *New York Times*, 1 Mar. 1999, sec. A, 1, 16; Rosenberg, "Constitutional Rights," 391–392; Max Lowenthal, *The Federal Bureau of Investigation* (New York, 1950), 13–21; Don Whitehead, *The FBI Story: A Report to the People* (New York, 1956), 21–25.

130. Rosen, *Lost Sisterhood*, xiii, 19.

CHAPTER 5. THE WAR ON VICE, 1910–1919

1. Graham Taylor, "The Police and Vice in Chicago," *Survey* 23 (6 Nov. 1910): 165; "Disciplining Chicago's Police" and "Vice Investigation Demanded by Churches," *Survey* 23 (12 Feb. 1910): 695–696; "Vice Commission to Clean Chicago," *Survey* 23 (26 Mar. 1910): 96–962; "Report of the Chicago Vice Commission," *Survey* 26 (15 Apr. 1911): 99; Graham Taylor, "The Story of the Chicago Vice Commission," *Survey* 26 (6 May 1911): 239–247; Eric Anderson, "Prostitution and Social Justice: Chicago, 1910–1915," *Social Service Review* 48 (June 1974): 203–228. On Sumner, see Graham Taylor, "Dean Sumner—Chicago's Citizen Clergyman," *Survey* 33 (2 Jan. 1915): 348.

2. "Report of the Vice Commission of Chicago: Editorial Comments," file 2, box 41, Julius Rosenwald Papers, Department of Special Collections, Regenstein Library, University of Chicago.

3. "Report of the Vice Commission of Chicago: Letters," file 2, box 41, Julius Rosenwald Papers; Walter Lippmann, "Well Meaning but Unmeaning: The Chicago Vice Report," in *Preface to Politics* (New York, 1913), 122–158.

4. Maude E. Miner, "The Chicago Vice Commission," *Survey* 26 (6 May 1911): 217. See also Frederick H. Whitin to Clinton Rogers Woodruff, 4 Sept. 1914, file: "1911–14," box 21, C14.

5. Graham Romneyn Taylor, "Chicago Vice Report Barred from Mails," *Survey* 27

(7 Oct. 1911): 923; [Law and Order League of Charleston, SC], *Special Report of the Law and Order League of Charleston, S.C.* ([Charleston], 1913), 11; Paul S. Boyer, *Urban Masses and Moral Order in America, 1820–1920* (Cambridge, MA, 1978), 198–199; Mark Thomas Connelly, *The Response to Prostitution in the Progressive Era* (Chapel Hill, NC, 1980), 98.

6. Taylor, "Police and Vice In Chicago," 165; Wisconsin Vice Committee, *Report and Recommendations of the Wisconsin Legislative Committee to Investigate the White Slave Traffic and Kindred Subjects* ([Madison], 1914), 27; "Some Early Stages of the Chicago Fight Against Prostitution: Walter T. Sumner," *Social Hygiene* 6 (Apr. 1920): 281–282.

7. "National Merger to Fight White Slavery," *Survey* 27 (30 Mar. 1912): 1991–1992; John C. Burnham, "The Progressive Era Revolution in American Attitudes toward Sex," *Journal of American History* 59 (Mar. 1973): 897; Anderson, "Prostitution and Social Justice," 206.

8. "National Merger to Fight White Slavery," 1991; James Bronson Reynolds to E. L. Keyes, file 30, box 6, series: "Boards," RG 2-OMR, RFA; [Moral Survey Committee], *The Social Evil in Syracuse: Being the Report of an Investigation of the Moral Condition of the City Conducted by a Committee of Eighteen Citizens* (Syracuse, NY, 1913), 10–11, reprinted in *Prostitution in America: Three Investigations, 1902–1914* (New York, 1976).

9. "The American Social Hygiene Association," *Social Hygiene* 1 (Dec. 1914): 2–3; William F. Snow, "Progress, 1900–1915," *Social Hygiene* 2 (Jan. 1916): 337–338; "A History and a Forecast," *Social Hygiene* 5 (Oct. 1919): 555; Anderson, "Prostitution and Social Justice," 207.

10. "Minutes of the Meeting of the Executive Committee of the American Social Hygiene Association," 13 Feb. 1914, file 2, box 5, ASHA; "Law Notes," *American Social Hygiene Association Bulletin* 2 (May 1915): 3–4 (hereafter *ASHA Bulletin*); "Publications of the American Social Hygiene Association," *ASHA Bulletin* 4 (Apr. 1917), 4; "History and a Forecast," 562–564.

11. File 1: "Curfews," legal box 2; file 3: "Dance Halls," legal box 2; file 1: "Injunction and Abatement, State and Local Laws, 1913–31," legal box 3; file 2: "Injunction and Abatement, Court Cases, 1912–1917," legal box 3; file 6: "Prostitution, 1912–1929," legal box 4; file 3: Rooming Houses, 1907–49," legal box 7; all ASHA. See also Martha P. Falconer, "Report of the Committee on Social Hygiene of the National Conference of Charities and Correction," *Social Hygiene* 1 (Sept. 1915), 520–521; Bascom Johnson, *Injunction and Abatement Laws Against Houses of Lewdness, Assignation, and Prostitution*, pamphlet, 1915; American Social Hygiene Association, *The Segregation of Prostitution and the Injunction and Abatement Law Against Houses of Prostitution*, Publication No. 75, pamphlet, 1917; both file 1, legal box 3, ASHA; "History and a Forecast," 559.

12. "New Methods of Grappling with the Social Evil," *Current Opinion* 54 (1913): 308–310; "The Social Evil: Vice Reports and Investigations," *National Municipal Review* 5 (Oct. 1916): 698; Joseph Mayer, "The Passing of the Red Light District—Vice Investigation Results," *Social Hygiene* 4 (Apr. 1918): 199. Roy Lubove, "The Progressives and the Prostitute," *Historian* 24 (May 1962): 318–319.

13. "National Merger to Fight White Slavery," 1991. See also Frederick H. Whitin to Donald A. Adams, 13 Feb. 1913, file: "1913, Feb.," box 2, C14.

14. "Relation of the American Social Hygiene Association to Community Welfare: Department of Legal Measures," 25 Oct. 1923, file 1, box 1, ASHA; Lubove, "Progressives and the Prostitute," 319; Connelly, *Response to Prostitution*, 92. See also Graham Taylor, "The War on Vice," *Survey* 29 (8 Mar. 1913): 811–813.

15. On isomorphism, see Paul J. Dimaggio and Walter J. Powell, "The Iron Cage Revisited: Institutional Isomorphism and Collection Rationality in Organizational Fields," in *The New Institutionalism in Organizational Analysis*, ed. Walter J. Powell and Paul J. Dimaggio (Chicago, 1991).

16. "Minutes of the Meeting of the Executive Committee," 5 May 1914 and 10 Dec. 1914, file 2, box 5, ASHA; "History and a Forecast," 558; Frederick W. Betts, "History of the Moral Survey Committee of Syracuse," *Social Hygiene* 1 (May 1915): 187–188. On Kneeland and his role in the Chicago Vice Commission, see Taylor, "Story of the Chicago Vice Commission," 241.

17. [Lancaster Citizens' Committee], *A Report on Vice Conditions in the City of Lancaster, Pa.* ([Lancaster], 1913), 5; [Moral Survey Committee], *Social Evil in Syracuse*, 2, 10–11; "Laws and Their Enforcement," *ASHA Bulletin* 1 (Sept. 1914): 5; Betts, "History of the Moral Survey Committee," 187–188; Bridgeport Vice Commission, *The Report and Recommendations of the Bridgeport Vice Commission* (Bridgeport, CT, 1916), 13; [Executive Committee, Womens' League for Good Government], *Vice Conditions in Elmira: Being a Report of an Investigation of the Moral Condition of the City, Conducted by the Executive Committee of the Womens' League for Good Government* (Elmira, NY, 1913), 3; [Newark Vice Commission], *Report on the Social Evil Conditions of Newark, New Jersey to the People of Newark* ([Newark], [1914]), 30; Vice Commission of Philadelphia, *A Report on Existing Conditions with Recommendations to the Honorable Rudolph Blankenburg, Mayor of Philadelphia* ([Philadelphia], 1913), 2; [Lexington Vice Commission], *Report of the Vice Commission of Lexington, Kentucky*, 2nd ed. (Lexington, 1915), 9–10; Winthrop D. Lane, "Under Cover of Respectability: Some Disclosures of Immorality among Unsuspected Men and Women," *Survey* (25 Mar. 1916), 747; Connelly, *Response to Prostitution*, 197n14. The cities were Baltimore, Maryland; Boston, Massachusetts; Bridgeport, Connecticut; Chicago, Illinois; Elmira, New York; Lancaster, Pennsylvania; Lexington, Kentucky; Newark, New Jersey; New York, New York; Paducah, Kentucky; Philadelphia, Pennsylvania; Richmond, Virginia; and Syracuse, New York.

18. "Minutes of the Meeting of the Executive Committee," 14 Oct. 1915, file 3 box 5, ASHA.

19. Marion M. Jackson, "The Atlanta Campaign Against Commercialized Vice," *Social Hygiene* 3 (Apr. 1917): 179; "Pioneer Experiences: John J. Eagan, Atlanta," *Social Hygiene* (Oct. 1919): 585–587. For an example of these bulletins, see "The Houses in Our Midst," Men and Religion Bulletin No. 21, *Atlanta Constitution*, 25 Sept. 1912, 3.

20. "Music and Dance Will Be Barred," *Atlanta Constitution*, 7 Sept. 1912, 1–2; "Vice Commission Will Make Report Oct. 7," *Atlanta Constitution*, 19 Sept. 1912, 3.

21. "Chief Beavers Planning Fight on Cheap Hotels," *Atlanta Constitution*, 25 Sept. 1912, 1–2.

22. "Women and Ministers Visit District Today to Help Unfortunates," *Atlanta Constitution*, 26 Sept. 1912, 1; "Women Cannot Live in Houses," *Atlanta Constitution*, 28 Sept. 1912, 1; "Beavers Must Not Go Too Far," *Atlanta Constitution*, 29 Sept. 1912, 2.

23. [Atlanta Vice Commission], *Report of the Vice Commission to the Mayor and Council of the City of Atlanta, Ga.* ([Atlanta], 1912), 24–25. See also "Vice Commission Strikes a Snag," *Atlanta Constitution*, 27 Sept. 1912, 1; "Vice Commission Has Gone Completely Out of Business," *Atlanta Constitution*, 11 Jan. 1913, 3.

24. Franklin Hichborn, *Story of the Session of the California Legislature of 1913* (San Francisco, 1913), 323; Bridgeport Vice Commission, *Report*, 12; Joseph Mayer, *The Regulation of Commercialized Vice: An Analysis of the Transition from Segregation to Repression in the United States* (New York, 1922), 10; Frederick H. Whitin, "Obstacles to Vice Repression," *Social Hygiene* 2 (Apr. 1916): 145.

25. [Vice Commission of Minneapolis], *Report of the Vice Commission of Minneapolis to His Honor, James C. Haynes, Mayor* (Minneapolis, 1911), 11, reprinted in *The Prostitute and the Social Reformer: Commercial Vice in the Progressive Era*, ed. Charles Rosenberg and Carroll Smith-Rosenberg (New York, 1974); [Hartford Vice Commission], *Report of the Hartford Vice Commission: Hartford, Connecticut* (Hartford, [1913]), 10. Bridgeport closed its district during the investigation. See Bridgeport Vice Commission, *Report*, 15–16.

26. "St. Louis, Missouri, Courts and Prostitution," *ASHA Bulletin* 3 (May 1916): 2; "Moral Progress in Kansas City," *Social Hygiene* 2 (July 1916): 466–469; J.S., "Lexington, Ky.," 3 Oct. 1917, file: "Kentucky, Louisville 1 of 4," box 8, CTCA.

27. "Police Board Says Beavers Proved He Was Insubordinate," *Atlanta Journal*, 27 July 1915, 1; "Suspension for Chief," *Atlanta Journal*, 3 Aug. 1915, 1, 5; Jackson, "Atlanta Campaign," 181–184.

28. Betts, "History of the Moral Survey Committee," 192–193. See also Frederick H. Whitin to T. A. Clarkson, 20 May 1915, file: "1915—May–Dec," box 21, C14; Abraham Flexner, "Next Steps in Dealing with Prostitution," *Social Hygiene* 1 (Sept. 1915): 535; [Vice Commission of Louisville], *Report of the Vice Commission, Louisville, Kentucky: Survey of Existing Conditions with Recommendations to the Hon. John H. Buschemeyer, Mayor* (Louisville, 1915), 37.

29. Alaska and Washington, DC, also had injunction and abatement acts. See Mayer, *Regulation of Commercialized Vice*, 45.

30. Franklin Hichborn, "The Organization that Backed the California Red Light Abatement Bill," *Social Hygiene* 1 (Mar. 1915): 199; Thomas D. Eliot, "Social Hygiene at the Panama–Pacific International Exposition," *Social Hygiene* 1 (June 1915): 409. The Barbary Coast and the "District" were adjacent to each other, with the main "lines" being Kearny and Pacific streets, respectively. The downtown Tenderloin was near the hotel and theater district, roughly contained within Geary, Powell, Market, and Levenworth streets. See Bascom Johnson, "Moral Conditions in San Francisco at the Panama–Pacific Exposition," *Social Hygiene* 1 (Sept. 1915): 601–605; Bascom

Johnson, "Preliminary Report on Moral Conditions in California, June 24th to July 21st 1917," map, file: "California, San Diego 1 of 2," box 5, CTCA.

31. "California Women and the Vice Situation," *Survey* 30 (3 May 1913): 162–163; Neil Larry Shumsky, "Vice Responds to Reform," *Journal of Urban History* 7 (Nov. 1980): 31–47.

32. Hichborn, *Story of the Session of the California Legislature of 1911* (San Francisco, 1911), 175–176; Hichborn, *Story of the Session of the California Legislature of 1913*, 340–343; Hichborn, "Organization that Backed," 194.

33. "California Women," 162; Franklin Hichborn, "California's Campaign Against Entrenched Vice," *Survey* 32 (25 July 1914): 430; "California Red-Light Abatement Law Still in Doubt," *Survey* 33 (14 Nov. 1914): 167; Franklin Hichborn, "California's Fight for a Red Light Abatement Law," *Social Hygiene* 1 (Dec. 1914): 6–8.

34. Quotation from Hichborn, "California's Fight," 8. See also Hichborn, "Organization that Backed," 196; "Nation-Wide Social Hygiene Activities," *Social Hygiene* 2 (Apr. 1916): 296.

35. Hichborn, "Organization that Backed," 203.

36. Hichborn, "Organization that Backed," 204. For a national airing of this dispute, see "The Redlight Vote," *Survey* 33 (2 Jan. 1915): 344.

37. Hichborn, "Organization that Backed," 194n1.

38. *Annual Report of the Committee of Fifteen for the Year Ending April 30, 1914*, Committee of Fifteen, file 2: "1914–1916," GTP. See also *Annual Report, Committee of Fifteen*, [1911], file 39, box 6, series: "Boards," RG 2-OMR, RFA; Clifford W. Barnes, "The Story of the Committee of Fifteen of Chicago," *Social Hygiene* 4 (Jan. 1918): 146–147; Anderson, "Prostitution and Social Justice," 214.

39. *Annual Report of the Committee of Fifteen . . . 1914*; *Annual Report of the Committee of Fifteen for the Year Ending April 30, 1916*, Committee of Fifteen, file 2: "1914–1916"; both GTP; "Committee of Fifteen of Chicago," *Social Hygiene* 2 (July 1916): 464.

40. *Annual Report of the Committee of Fifteen . . . 1916*; GTP.

41. "Vice Conditions and Reform in New Orleans," *Social Hygiene* 3 (July 1917): 403–404; George Bellamy to H. S. Braucher, 11 June 1917, file: "Alabama 1.4," box 1, CTCA; Johnson, "Moral Conditions in San Francisco," 609. For a list of cities that closed their districts between 1906 and 1919, see *Standard Statistics of Prostitution, Gonorrhoea, Syphilis*, 1919, pamphlet, file 1, box 170, ASHA.

42. [Vice Commission of Minneapolis], *Report*, 74; "Present Vice Conditions in Lexington and Louisville, Kentucky," *ASHA Bulletin* 3 (May 1916): 3; "Campaign Against Vice in Buffalo, New York," *Social Hygiene* 2 (July 1916): 466.

43. "Resort Keeper Takes Her Life," *Atlanta Constitution*, 26 Sept. 1912, 9; "Women and Ministers Visit District Today," 2.

44. Betts, "History of the Moral Survey Committee," 191. See also Whitin, "Obstacles to Vice Repression," 148–149.

45. "Investigation," 1 Mar. 1913, file: "1913a—Apr.–May," box 28; [D.O.], "Forester's Hunters Hall," 9 Jan. 1916, box 30; [D.O.], "Forester's Hunters Hall," 27 Jan. 1916, box 30; H.K., "Investigation Report: 1370 Avenue A," 22 June 1917, box 31; all C14. See also

[Hartford Vice Commission], *Report*, 12; George J. Kneeland, "Commercialized Prostitution and the Liquor Traffic," *Social Hygiene* 2 (Jan. 1916): 81; "The Latest from Terre Haute," *Social Hygiene* 2 (Jan. 1916): 136.

46. "Passing of Vice District as Women Occupants See It," *Atlanta Constitution*, 28 Sept. 1912, 3.

47. Wirt W. Hallam, "The Reduction of Vice in Certain Western Cities through Law Enforcement," *Social Diseases* (Apr. 1912), reprinted in [Moral Survey Committee], *Social Evil in Syracuse*, 113–114; Dr. Edward Beecher Hooker, "The Abatement of Prostitution," *New England Medical Gazette* (Feb. 1915), cited in "Note and Comment," *Social Hygiene* 2 (Jan. 1916): 132; [House] Judiciary Subcommittee of the Committee on the District of Columbia, *Abatement of Houses of Ill Fame: Hearing on Kenyon Act (S. 234)*, 1914, 9–11.

48. [Vice Commission of Minneapolis], *Report*, 72; Clifford Gray Twombly, "The City [Lancaster, PA] that Followed Up Its Report on Vice Conditions," *Social Hygiene* 1 (June 1915): 391; Bridgeport Vice Commission, *Report*, 19, 34; Kneeland, "Commercialized Prostitution and the Liquor Traffic," 77.

49. Samuel M. Auerbach to Frederick H. Whitin, 22 Aug. 1915, file: "Inv. Brooklyn and Queens (1914–1915)," box 29; D.O., "Chadwick Novelty Café," 21 Nov. 1915, box 30; both C14; P.K., "Macon, Ga.," 11 Oct. 1917, file: "Atlanta, Ga. 2 of 3," box 6, CTCA; Vice Commission of Philadelphia, *Report*, 36; [Vice Commission of Louisville], *Report*, 35; Twombly, "City that Followed Up," 390; Whitin, "Obstacles to Vice Repression," 150.

50. "Jos. Mehling," 26 Apr. 1916, box 30, C14; David Lawrence, "Washington—The Cleanest Capital in the World," *Social Hygiene* 3 (July 1917): 316–317; [Newark Citizens' Committee], *Report*, 39; Bascom Johnson, "Preliminary Survey of Moral Conditions near Fort Logan H. Roots, Pulaski County, Arkansas," 23 May 1917, 7, file: "Arkansas 1917," box 4; Joseph R. Mayer to Raymond B. Fosdick, 10 July 1917, 4, file: "Arizona 17," box 3; both CTCA.

51. Bridgeport Vice Commission, *Report*, 50.

52. Johnson, "Preliminary Survey . . . Pulaski County, Arkansas," 6, CTCA. See also "Report," 30 Jan. 1914, file: "1913–1914," box 28, C14. Robert A. Woods, "Prohibition and Social Hygiene," *Social Hygiene* 5 (Apr. 1919): 139.

53. Twombly, "City that Followed Up," 390; [Hartford Vice Commission], *Report*, 11; Whitin, "Obstacles to Vice Repression," 152; "The New Vice Crusade in Atlanta," *Social Hygiene* 2 (Jan. 1916): 137.

54. D.O., "55 Ralph Ave. Cor. Monroe," 10 Dec. 1915, Box 30, C14; P.K., "Macon, Ga.," 2; J.S., "Key West, Fla.," 26 July 1917, 2, file: "West Florida," box 6; both CTCA; [Vice Commission of Minneapolis], *Report*, 64; [Hartford Vice Commission], *Report*, 14.

55. "In re: Avenel," 29 July 1913, file: "1913," box 28; D.O., "Anna M. Kerrigan," 31 May 1916, box 30; J.A.S., "Tokio-Wallicks-Pre Catalan-Jacks," 19 Jan. 1917, box 31; all C14; "Commercialized Prostitution in New York City in 1916," *Social Hygiene* 3 (Apr. 1917): 282; [Hartford Vice Commission], *Report*, 13; Hallam, "Reduction of Vice," 117.

56. Kneeland, "Commercialized Prostitution and the Liquor Traffic," 72; [Newark Citizens' Committee], *Report*, 37–39.

57. [Hartford Vice Commission], *Report*, 35–36; [Executive Committee], *Vice Conditions in Elmira*, 7; [Newark Citizens' Committee], *Report*, 64; Whitin, "Obstacles to Vice Repression," 149; Twombly, "City that Followed Up," 391.

58. [Hartford Vice Commission], *Report*, 36. See also "Moral Progress in Kansas City," 468.

59. "The Menace of Paid Reformers," typescript; Chicago Hotel Keepers Protective Association, "Paid Reformers: A Menace," poster, ca. 1915; Samuel P. Thrasher, "Report to the Board of Directors," 8 Feb. 1916, 4; all Committee of Fifteen, file 2: "1914–1916," GTP. See also "Hotel Men in the Fight Against Vice," *Survey* 35 (29 Jan. 1916): 504.

60. "Hotel Men in the Fight," 504; "Hotels and Vice Control," *ASHA Bulletin* 2 (Feb. 1916): 2.

61. *Annual Report of the Committee of Fifteen for the Year Ending April 30, 1915*, Committee of Fifteen, file 2: 1914–1916, GTP.

62. Kneeland, "Commercialized Prostitution and the Liquor Traffic," 86–88; Lawrence, "Washington," 316–317; Barnes, "Committee of Fifteen of Chicago," 152; John P. Peters, "Story of the Committee of Fourteen of New York," *Social Hygiene* 4 (July 1918): 363–368.

63. On transaction costs, outsourcing, and the disaggregation of services, see Ronald H. Coase, "The Nature of the Firm," *Economica* 4 (1937): 386–405; Ronald H. Coase, "The Nature of the Firm: Origins, Meaning, Influences," *Journal of Law, Economics, and Organization* 4 (1988): 3–47.

64. Kneeland, "Commercialized Prostitution and the Liquor Traffic," 71; [Vice Commission of Minneapolis], *Report*, 65; Bridgeport Vice Commission, *Report*, 34–35, 54; [Newark Citizens' Committee], *Report*, 40–44; "Prostitution and the Liquor Traffic in Boston, Mass.," *Social Hygiene* 2 (Oct. 1916): 616–617.

65. Chas. S. Briggs, "Report," 30 Jan. 1914, file: "1913–1914," box 28; D.O., "Perry's Inn," 14 June 1916, box 30; both C14; [Newark Citizens' Committee], *Report*, 64; Bridgeport Vice Commission, *Report*, 26; Kneeland, "Commercialized Prostitution and the Liquor Traffic," 74–75; "Prostitution and the Liquor Traffic in Boston, Mass.," 617.

66. "Resumé of Reports on Cabarets," Winter 1916–17, 7–8, file: "Inv. Rep. Cabarets," box 31, C14; [Massachusetts Commission for the Investigation of White Slave Traffic], *Report of the Commission for the Investigation of the White Slave Traffic, So Called* (reprinted from [Massachusetts] House [Document] No. 2881, Feb. 1914), 15, reprinted in *Prostitution in America: Three Investigations, 1902–1914* (New York, 1976); [Newark Citizens' Committee], *Report*, 71; Kneeland, "Commercialized Prostitution and the Liquor Traffic," 75; "Report of Boston Vice Conditions," July 1917, file: "Alabama 37," box 3, CTCA.

67. Bridgeport Vice Commission, *Report*, 19; [Newark Citizens' Committee], *Report*, 43; Whitin, "Obstacles to Vice Repression," 156–158; Frederick H. Whitin to Raymond B. Fosdick, 18 Dec. 1917, file: "Arkansas, Little Rock," box 4, CTCA.

68. Bridgeport Vice Commission, *Report*, 19–22; [Newark Citizens' Committee], *Report*, 57–59.

69. C. D. Benson, "Trenton, N.J.," 1 Dec. 1917, file: "Arkansas, Little Rock," box 4, CTCA; Flexner, "Next Steps in Dealing with Prostitution," 534–535.

70. [Hartford Vice Commission], *Report*, 11.

71. "Investigation Report," 28 Mar. 1913, file: "1913," box 28; D.O., "Bushwick Café," 13 Apr. 1916, box 30; both C14; Bridgeport Vice Commission, *Report*, 28; [Newark Citizens' Committee], *Report*, 60–61, 63.

72. Bridgeport Vice Commission, *Report*, 26; "The Master's Voice," *Chicago Tribune*, 13 Jan. 1914, file: "Committee of Fifteen, Newspaper Clippings, 1914," box 2, Clifford Barnes Collection, Chicago Historical Society.

73. "7," [1914], file: "1914," box 28, C14; Bridgeport Vice Commission, *Report*, 20, 25, 28–29; [Newark Citizens' Committee], *Report*, 60.

74. Vice Commission of Philadelphia, *Report*, 79; see also p. 82.

75. David F. Musto, *The American Disease: Origins of Narcotic Control*, expanded ed. (New York, 1987), 122; David T. Courtwright, *Dark Paradise: Opiate Addiction in America before 1940* (Cambridge, MA, 1982), 1–2; Joseph F. Spillane, *Cocaine: From Medical Marvel to Modern Menace in the United States, 1884–1920* (Baltimore, 2000), 105–106, 141.

76. [Vice Commission of Minneapolis], *Report*, 64; Twombly, "City that Followed Up," 390–391; Falconer, "Report of the Committee on Social Hygiene," 517; "San Antonio, Texas, Closes Its Segregated District," *Social Hygiene* 1 (Sept. 1915): 630; "Campaign Against Vice in Buffalo, New York," 466.

77. Of the 102 prostitutes interviewed in Newark, 24 came from the city (36.4%), 56 from the state (60.6%), 93 from the United States (89.4%), and 9 from abroad (8.8%). See [Newark Citizens' Committee], *Report*, 158. By comparison, in Hartford 63.6 percent came from outside the city; in New York, 55.1 percent; in Philadelphia, 42.6 percent; and in Syracuse, 68 percent. See [Hartford Vice Commission], *Report*, 45; George J. Kneeland, *Commercialized Prostitution in New York City*, rev. ed. (New York, 1917), 208–209; Vice Commission of Philadelphia, *Report*, 84; [Moral Survey Committee], *Social Evil in Syracuse*, 103. See also Bridgeport Vice Commission, *Report*, 17.

78. [Hartford Vice Commission], *Report*, 12. See also D.O., "J. Ph. Mohr," 9 Aug. 1916, box 30, C14.

79. [Portland, OR Vice Commission], *Report of the Portland Vice Commission to the Mayor and City Council of the City of Portland, Oregon* (Portland, 1913), 26.

80. [Portland, OR Vice Commission], *Report*, 27, 43, 51–52.

81. "Charity Workers Visit Women of Tenderloin," *Atlanta Constitution*, 27 Sept. 1912, 1–2. See also Bridgeport Vice Commission, *Report*, 48–50; [Lexington Vice Commission], *Report*, 25.

82. "Atlanta Women Not Expected," *Atlanta Constitution*, 29 Sept. 1912, 2.

83. "Ministers Name Vice Commission," *Atlanta Constitution*, 7 Jan. 1913, 3; "Vice Crusade Hits Dawson," *Atlanta Constitution*, 19 Jan. 1913, 3F.

84. [Lexington Vice Commission], *Report*, 25; Bridgeport Vice Commission, *Report*, 12–13; [Vice Commission of Louisville], *Report*, 59; "The Vice Problem in Philadelphia," *Survey* 30 (24 May 1913): 259.

85. "The Injunction and Abatement Law in Indianapolis," *Social Hygiene* 3 (Jan.

1917): 137–139; New England Watch and Ward Society, *Annual Report*, 8–10, box 1, Special Collections, Harvard Law School Library.

86. E. J. Glenny to Joseph E. Ransdell, 4 Dec. 1917, file: "4 of 4 New Orleans, La.," box 8; J.S., "Key West, Fla.," 28 July 1917, file: "West Fla.," box 6; both CTCA; Twombly, "City that Followed Up," 390.

87. "Old Red-Light District Like Earthquake City," clipping, file: "Committee of Fifteen, Newspaper Clippings, 1915–1936," box 2, Clifford W. Barnes Collection; Bascom Johnson, "Preliminary Report on Moral Conditions in California"; Edward H. Griffith, "Preliminary Report: Conditions Surrounding Camp Zachary Taylor, Louisville, Kentucky," 7 Oct. 1917, file: "Kentucky, Louisville 1 of 4," box 8; both CTCA.

88. "Manuel Da Silva," 27 May 1916, file: "1916," box 31, C14; Joseph R. Mayer to Raymond B. Fosdick, 29 Sept. 1917, file: "Arizona 17," box 3, CTCA; Bridgeport Vice Commission, *Report*, 34.

89. "Re: saloons, etc.," 6 June 1913, file: "1913 June–July"; "Re. saloons in Manhattan and Bronx," 5 Apr. 1913, file: "1913"; "Report," 30 Jan. 1914, file: "1913–1914"; all box 28, C14; "The Pittsburgh, Pa., Bureau of Public Morals," *Social Hygiene* 1 (June 1915): 499; Bridgeport Vice Commission, *Report*, 28–29.

90. Betts, "History of the Moral Survey Committee," 191.

91. "Re: saloons, etc."; "Special Report: Club Inspection," 15 Apr. 1915, file: "1914–1915," box 28; "Resumé of Reports on Cabarets," 1; all C14; [Hartford Vice Commission], *Report*, 27.

92. "Resumé of Reports on Cabarets," 11, C14; Lawrence, "Washington," 320; Bridgeport Vice Commission, *Report*, 29; [Newark Citizens' Committee], *Report*, 60–61; Twombly, "City that Followed Up," 393–395; "The Pittsburgh, Pa., Bureau of Public Morals," 498–499; Johnson, "Moral Conditions in San Francisco," 598.

93. Raymond B. Fosdick, *Chronicle of a Generation: An Autobiography* (New York, 1958), 90, 128, 135–136, 251; Allan M. Brandt, *No Magic Bullet: A Social History of Venereal Disease in the United States since 1880, with a New Chapter on AIDS* (New York, 1987), 53; *The Encyclopedia of New York*, s.v. "Rockefeller Foundation."

94. Fosdick, *Chronicle of a Generation*, 137–138; M. J. Exner, "Prostitution in Its Relation to the Army on the Mexican Border," *Social Hygiene* 3 (Apr. 1917): 205; Brandt, *No Magic Bullet*, 53–54.

95. Fosdick, *Chronicle of a Generation*, 138.

96. William F. Snow, "Social Hygiene and the War," *Social Hygiene* 3 (July 1917): 441–442; Raymond B. Fosdick, "Fit for Fighting—and After," 416, file 131, box 2, ASHA; Nancy K. Bristow, *Making Men Moral: Social Engineering During the Great War* (New York, 1996), 6–8.

97. "Selective Conscription Law, Sections 12, 13, and 14," reprinted in Snow, "Social Hygiene and the War," 431–432.

98. Newton D. Baker to the mayors of the cities and the sheriffs of the counties in the neighborhood of all military training camps, 10 Aug. 1917, reprinted in Franklin Martin, "Social Hygiene and the War," *Social Hygiene* 3 (Oct. 1917): 620–621; *Documents Regarding Alcoholic Liquors and Prostitution in the Neighborhood of Military Camps and Naval Stations*, ca. 1918, pamphlet, 8, file 8, box 131, ASHA.

99. *United States v. Casey*, 247 F. 362 (1918); *Pappens v. United States*, 252 F. 5 (1918); *United States v. Hicks*, 256 F. 7 (1919); *McKinley v. United States*, 249 U.S. 397 (1919); *Grancourt v. United States*, 258 F. 25 (1919); *De Four v. United States*, 260 F. 596 (1919).

100. Snow, "Social Hygiene and the War," 442. On the Commission itself, see Raymond B. Fosdick, "The War and Navy Departments Commissions on Training Camp Activities," *Annals of the American Academy of Political and Social Science* 79 (Sept. 1918): 130–142; Brandt, *No Magic Bullet*, 52–95.

101. Samuel P. Thrasher to Graham Taylor, 15 July 1918, file: "Committee of Fifteen to Graham Taylor," GTP; Raymond B. Fosdick to Starr J. Murphy, 22 May 1917, file: "Arizona 18," box 3, CTCA; Snow, "Social Hygiene and the War," 421, 437–438; George J. Anderson, "Making the Camps Safe for the Army," *Annals of the American Academy of Political and Social Science* 79 (Sept. 1918): 144–145.

102. J. H. Foster to Raymond B. Fosdick, 10 May 1917, file: "Arkansas 13," box 4, CTCA; "A History and a Forecast," *Social Hygiene* 5 (Oct. 1919): 556; Franklin Martin, "Social Hygiene and the War," 607; Fosdick, *Chronicle of a Generation*, 145, 151; Brandt, *No Magic Bullet*, 73–74.

103. Rockefeller Foundation, letter, 11 Oct. 1917, file 592, box 60, RG-1; Raymond B. Fosdick to George E. Vincent, 17 Nov. 1917, file 739, box 79, series 100, RG-1; both Rockefeller Foundation, Rockefeller Archive Center, Pocantico Hills, NY; "Minutes of the Executive Committee," 13 Sept. 1917, file 6, box 5, ASHA; Martin, "Social Hygiene and the War," 607. For a breakdown of the CTCA's budget, see Raymond B. Fosdick to George E. Vincent, 18 Jan. 1918, file 740, box 79, RG-1, Rockefeller Foundation.

104. Walter Clarke, "Report for Macon, Ga.," 14 Sept. 1917, file: "Atlanta, Ga. 2 of 3," box 6; M. J. Exner to Raymond B. Fosdick, 6 July 1917, file: "Alabama 6," box 1; both CTCA.

105. "City Council Proceedings," 12 Oct. 1917, Library Archives Department, Noel Memorial Library, Louisiana State University in Shreveport; "Shreveport's Vice District Doomed by Vote of 1,376 to 734 for Its Elimination," *Shreveport Times*, 16 Nov. 1917, 1. For other cities' efforts to attract camps to their vicinity, see Bristow, *Making Men Moral*, 60; Garna L. Christian, "Newton Baker's War on El Paso Vice," *Red River Valley Historical Review* 5 (Spring 1980): 55–67.

106. Clarke, "Report for Macon, Ga.," CTCA. See also "Minutes of Meeting of July 26, 1917," file: "Ca. 1.1," box 5; Griffith, "Preliminary Report"; both CTCA.

107. Raymond B. Fosdick to William L. Martin, 7 July 1917, file: "Alabama 1.3," box 1; Raymond B. Fosdick to Glenn Toole, 31 Oct. 1917, file: "Atlanta, Ga. 2 of 3," box 6; both CTCA; Snow, "Social Hygiene and the War," 433–435; Fosdick, *Chronicle of a Generation*, 146; Brandt, *No Magic Bullet*, 75–76.

108. H. S. Braucher to George A. Bellamy, 11 June 1917, file: "Alabama 1.4," box 1, CTCA; Bristow, *Making Men Moral*, 103–105. These averages are based on the camp-by-camp tallies by Bristow, *Making Men Moral*, 230–239.

109. Willard B. Thorp, Edwin F. Hallenbeck, W. E. Crabtree, and H. N. Goff to Newton Baker, 11 June 1917, file: "California, San Diego 1 of 2," box 5, CTCA.

110. *Standard Statistics of Prostitution, Gonorrhoea, Syphilis*, ASHA; Mayer, *Regulation of Commercialized Vice*, 9; Fosdick, *Chronicle of a Generation*, 147. See also Raymond B. Fosdick to Joe Mitchell Chapple, 27 June 1917, file: "Alabama 1.3," box 1; Walter Clarke, "Report for Pensacola, Fla.," 18 Sept. 1917, file: "Florida Pensacola," box 6; Walter Clarke, "Report for Augusta, Ga.," 12 Sept. 1917, file: "Atlanta, Ga. 2 of 3," box 6; all CTCA; Mayer, *Regulation of Commercialized Vice*, 9n1; Brandt, *No Magic Bullet*, 72–77.

111. *Next Steps: One, Two, Three*, pamphlet, file 2, box 131, ASHA. See also Ruth Rosen, *The Lost Sisterhood: Prostitution in America, 1900–1918* (Baltimore, 1982), 36; Bristow, *Making Men Moral*, 112.

112. "Beware!" poster, file 3, box 131, ASHA. See also Jane Deeter Rippin, "Social Hygiene and the War: Work with Women and Girls," *Social Hygiene* 5 (Jan. 1919): 126; Hilton Howell Railey, "A Survey of Moral Conditions near Fort Logan H. Roots," 20 Aug. 1917, file: "Arkansas Little Rock," box 4, CTCA; Bascom Johnson, "Law Enforcement Against Prostitution from the Point of View of the Public Official," *National Municipal Review* 9 (July 1920): 428.

113. Rippin, "Social Hygiene and the War," 126; Bascom Johnson, "Preliminary Survey of Moral Conditions Surrounding Fort Riley, Near Junction City and Manhattan, Kansas," 31 May–4 June 1917, file: "Kansas," box 7, CTCA; [Albert E. Webster], "Conference and Observations at Grant Park," 8 Sept. 1917, file 380, box 24; B. B. Howell and M. Abbey, "Record of Investigation at Rockford, Ill.," 22–24 Sept. 1917, file 380, box 24; both ESDP; Joseph R. Mayer to Raymond B. Fosdick, 29 Sept. 1917, 7–8, file: "Arizona 17," box 3, CTCA.

114. H. L. Mencken, "'Reformers' Oppose Sanitary Measures Against Disease," *Evening Mail*, 18 Sept. 1917; Frederick H. Whitin to Raymond B. Fosdick, 24 Sept. 1917; Raymond B. Fosdick to Frederick H. Whitin, 26 Sept. 1917; all file: "Alabama 37, 2 of 2," box 3, CTCA.

115. Brandt, *No Magic Bullet*, 87; Hobson, *Uneasy Virtue*, 183; John D'Emilio and Estelle B. Freedman, *Intimate Matters: A History of Sexuality in America* (New York, 1988), 212. This chronology is different from the one offered by Foucault, who argued that medical discourse about sexuality became preeminent during the nineteenth century. See Michel Foucault, *The History of Sexuality*, vol. 1, *An Introduction*, trans. Robert Hurley (Paris 1976; English trans. New York, 1978).

116. *Hello, Soldier Sport, Want to Have a Good Time?* pamphlet, file 6, box 131, ASHA. See also "Venereal Diseases: Facts for Every Man," 10, file 6, box 170, ASHA.

117. Maude E. Miner, "Report of the Committee on Protective Work for Girls: October 1, 1917 to April 1, 1918," 15 Apr. 1918, file 381, box 24, ESDP.

118. Raymond B. Fosdick to Ethel Sturges Dummer, 20 Sept. 1917, file 377, box 24, ESDP.

119. Ethel Sturges Dummer to Mrs. Gregory, 8 Nov. 1917, file 377, box 24; *Committee on Protective Work for Girls*, pamphlet, file 377, box 24; both ESDP; Brandt, *No Magic Bullet*, 81–82.

120. "Miss Miner Discusses Plans of the Committee on Protective Work for Girls, Created by the C.T.C.A.," *ASHA Bulletin* 5 (Mar. 1918): 3–4. See also "Protection of

Girls in Wartime," typescript, ca. 1917, file 378, box 24; Miner, "Report of the Committee on Protective Work for Girls"; both ESDP; *The War and Navy Departments Commissions on Training Camp Activities*, ca. 1918, pamphlet, 19–20, file 8, box 131, ASHA; Bristow, *Making Men Moral*, 114–115.

121. "Committee on Protective Work for Girls," n.d., file 377; Maude E. Miner to Mrs. William F. Dummer, 17 Apr. 1918, file 378; both box 24, ESDP; Bristow, *Making Men Moral*, 125–127.

122. Jane Deeter Rippin, "Outline of Organization and Methods: Section on Women and Girls, Law Enforcement Division, War and Navy Department Commissions on Training Camp Activities," 1 July 1918, file 381, box 24, ESDP; Henrietta S. Additon, "Work among Delinquent Women and Girls," *Annals of the American Academy of Political and Social Science* 79 (Sept. 1918): 155.

123. Ethel Sturges Dummer to Paul Kellogg, 23 May 1919, 13, file 235, box 16, ESDP; Rosen, *Lost Sisterhood*, 35; Barbara Meil Hobson, *Uneasy Virtue: The Politics of Prostitution and the American Reform Tradition* (1987; with a new preface, Chicago, 1990), 165–168, 175–176.

124. Bascom Johnson, *Next Steps: A Program of Activities Against Prostitution and Venereal Disease for Communities Which Have Closed Their "Red Light" Districts*, American Social Hygiene Association Publication No. 126 (Washington, DC, 1918), 10–11, file 2, box 131, ASHA.

125. Miner, "Report on the Committee on Protective Work for Girls," 13–14, ESDP; Martha P. Falconer, "The Part of the Reformatory Institution in the Elimination of Prostitution," *Social Hygiene* 5 (Jan. 1919): 2–3; Brandt, *No Magic Bullet*, 88–89.

126. Mary Macey Dietzler, *Detention Houses and Reformatories as Protective Social Agencies in the Campaign of the United States Government Against Venereal Diseases* (Washington, DC, 1922), 48, 89, 109–110, 113, 132–134, 149–150; Falconer, "Part of the Reformatory Institution," 4.

127. Jane Deeter Rippin to Mrs. William Dummer, 29 Oct. 1918, file 379, box 24, ESDP; *Circular from the Attorney General of the United States*, 3 Apr. 1918 cited in [Howard L. Kern], *Special Report of the Attorney General of Porto Rico to the Governor of Porto Rico Concerning the Suppression of Vice and Prostitution in Connection with the Mobilization of the National Army at Camp Las Casas* (San Juan, 1917), 7; David Pivar, "Cleansing the Nation: The War on Prostitution, 1917–1921," *Prologue: Journal of the National Archives* 12 (Spring 1980): 32–33; Bristow, *Making Men Moral*, 124–125.

128. Dietzler, *Detention Houses and Reformatories*, 5–6.

129. [Kern], *Special Report of the Attorney General of Porto Rico*, 8–9, 14.

130. Before the war, vice investigators found it much easier to read the sexual signifiers and determine whether a woman was a prostitute, promiscuous, or prim. See "Investigation Report," 30 Jan. 1914, Gilligan's Café, file: "1913–1914," box 28, C14. For typical categorizing phrases, see "Investigation Report," 19 Jan. 1917, 216 West 46th Street, box 31; "Investigation Report, D.O.," 4 June 1918, Paterson, N.J., 14, file "Paterson, N.J.," box 24; "Grand Central Palace," 4 May 1918, file: "1918," box 4; all C14.

131. "General Conditions and Conversations," 31 Aug. 1917, Trenton, N.J., 2, file:

"Trenton, N.J.," box 24; "12 Feb. 1917, 2137/2139 Boston Road," box 32; "Investigation Report, D.O.," 16 Nov. to 20 Nov. 1918, Providence, R.I., 8, file: "Special New Eng. Towns," box 24; "Investigation Report," 16 Apr. 1918, Philadelphia, Pa., 12, file: "Philadelphia," box 24; "Investigation Report," 19 Jan. 1917, 216 West 46th Street, box 31; "Investigation Report," 8 Mar. 1917, 153/155 West 47th Street, box 31; all C14.

132. "Investigation Report, D.O.," 21 Nov. to 23 Nov. [1918], Fall River, Mass., 9, file: "Special New Eng. Towns," box 24, C14. See also "Investigation Report," 4 June 1917, Old Homestead, box 32, C14.

133. In addition to being called "bleeders," these women were also known as "cock-teasers" and "leg pullers." See "Central Casino," 8 July 1916, file: 1916, box 31; "Investigation Report, D.O.," 21 Nov. to 23 Nov. [1918], box 24; both C14. See also "Niagara Falls, N.Y.," 12 Aug. 1917, file: "Ft. Niagara," box 25, C14.

134. "Investigation Report," 19 Mar. 1917, 2926 Eighth Ave., box 32, C14. See also "Investigation Report, D.O.," 21 Nov. to 23 Nov. [1918], C14.

135. "Investigation Report," 17 Feb. 1917, 2926 Eighth Ave., box 32, C14. See also "Investigation Report," 19 Jan. 1917, 216 West 46th Street, box 31, C14.

136. "Investigation Report," 29 Mar. 1919, 57/67 Smith St. Brooklyn, file: "Bklyn.—Investig. Reports," box 32; "Report of D.O.," 28 Nov. to 5 Dec. 1919, New Haven, Conn., 7, 9, file: "Special New Eng. Towns," box 24; 16 Dec. 1916, 2137/2139 Boston Road, SW, box 32; "H.K., June 28th 1919," file: "Bklyn.—Investig. Reports," box 32; "Grand Central Palace," 4 May 1918, file: "1918," box 4; all C14. See also P.M.K., "Atlanta Georgia," 5–7 July 1919, file: "Atlanta, Ga. 1 of 3," box 6, CTCA.

137. Newton Baker, "Council of National Defense," 26 May 1917, file: "S.S. Act: Sec. 12 and 13," box 24; Frederick H. Whitin to John Purroy Mitchel, 15 Oct. 1917, file: "1917," box 4; "General Conditions and Conversations," 2 Sept. 1917, New Egypt, N.J., file: "New Jersey," box 24; all C14; B. B. Howell, "Summary," file 380, box 24, ESDP; Bristow, *Making Men Moral*, 117.

138. Brandt, *No Magic Bullet*, 69.

139. *V.D.: Putting It up to the Men*, pamphlet, 8, file 5, box 131, ASHA. See also *Standard Statistics of Prostitution, Gonorrhea, Syphilis*, 3, ASHA.

140. *Hello, Soldier Sport*, ASHA; John H. Stokes, *Today's World Problem in Disease Prevention* (Washington, DC, 1919), 105, cited in Brandt, *No Magic Bullet*, 72; *V.D.: Putting It up to the Men*, 8, ASHA.

141. H. L. Mencken, "'Reformers' Oppose Sanitary Measures"; *Next Steps: One, Two, Three*, ASHA; [Webster], "Conference and Observations," 8 Sept. 1917, file 380, box 24, ESDP; Rosen, *Lost Sisterhood*, 36; D'Emilio and Freedman, *Intimate Matters*, 212; Brandt, *No Magic Bullet*, 80–82, 87; Bristow, *Making Men Moral*, 112, 118, 126.

142. Maude E. Miner to Mrs. William F. Dummer, 17 Apr. 1918, file 378, box 24, ESDP; Pivar, "Cleansing the Nation," 33; Bristow, *Making Men Moral*, 126–127.

143. Jessie Binford to Mrs. William F. Dummer, 9 Oct. 1918; Jessie Binford to Mrs. William F. Dummer, 22 Oct. 1918; both file 402, box 25, ESDP.

144. Anna Garlin Spencer to Mrs. [Edith Houghton] Hooker, 18 Dec. 1920, file 403, box 25; Alice Blackwell to Jane Addams, [Dec. 1920], file 403, box 25; Edith Abbott to Jessie Binford, 10 Feb. 1921, file 453, box 25; all ESDP; Pivar, "Cleansing the

Nation," 34–36, 39. See also *The American Plan: For Concerted Action on the Part of the National and Allied Agencies to Stamp Out the Venereal Diseases*, pamphlet, file 10, box 171, ASHA.

145. Jane Deeter Rippin to Mrs. William Dummer, 29 Oct. 1918, file 379, box 24; Katherine C. Bushnell, "Compulsion for Women—License for Men," *Light* ([1920]): 17–20, file 403, box 25; Anna Garlin Spencer to Mrs. [Edith Houghton] Hooker, 18 Dec. 1920, file 403, box 25; Alice Stone Blackwell to Jane Addams, [Dec. 1920]; all EDSP; Minutes, 4 Apr. 1921, "Minute Book 1919–1921," Friends' Association for the Promotion of Social Purity, Friends' Library, London; Pivar, "Cleansing the Nation," 33–34. On Josephine Butler and the fight against the Contagious Diseases Acts, see Judith R. Walkowitz, *Prostitution and Victorian Society: Women, Class, and the State* (New York, 1980).

146. Anna Garlin Spencer to Mrs. [Edith Houghton] Hooker, 18 Dec. 1920, file 403, box 25, ESDP; Dietzler, *Detention Houses and Reformatories*, 154.

CHAPTER 6. THE SYNDICATE

1. Henry W. Zorbaugh, *The Gold Coast and the Slum: A Sociological Study of Chicago's Near North Side* (Chicago, 1929), 116. See also Walter C. Reckless, *Vice in Chicago* (Chicago, 1933), 69; Martha Bensley Bruère, *Does Prohibition Work? A Study of the Operation of the Eighteenth Amendment Made by the National Federation of Settlements Assisted by Social Workers in Different Parts of the United States* (New York, 1927), 12, 83; Clare V. McKanna, "Hold Back the Tide: Vice Control in San Diego, 1870–1930," *Pacific Historian* 28 (1984): 54–64; David E. Ruth, *Inventing the Public Enemy: The Gangster in American Culture* (Chicago, 1996), 28.

2. Lawrence M. Friedman, *Crime and Punishment in American History* (New York, 1993), 265.

3. William F. Snow, "Social Hygiene and the War," *Social Hygiene* 3 (July 1917): 417–450. See also Norman H. Clark, *Deliver Us from Evil: An Interpretation of American Prohibition* (New York, 1976), 128–129; Allan M. Brandt, *No Magic Bullet: A Social History of Venereal Disease in the United States since 1880, with a New Chapter on AIDS* (New York, 1987), 70–77.

4. Herbert Asbury, *The Great Illusion: An Informal History of Prohibition* (Garden City, NY, 1950), 255, 309; David E. Kyvig, *Repealing National Prohibition* (Chicago, 1979), 10–19; Sean Dennis Cashman, *Prohibition: The Lie of the Land* (New York, 1981), 120–121; Ruth, *Inventing the Public Enemy*, 43–45; Dennis Jay Kenney, *Organized Crime in America* (Belmont, CA, 1995), 5–6, 155; Friedman, *Crime and Punishment*, 262.

5. Association Against the Prohibition Amendment, *Scandals of Prohibition Enforcement* (Washington, DC, 1929), reprinted in National Commission on Law Observance and Enforcement, *Enforcement of the Prohibition Laws*, 71st Cong., 3d sess., 1931, S. Doc. 307 (hereafter *Wickersham Report*), vol. 5, 204–205; Reckless, *Vice in Chicago*, 97–98; Virgil W. Peterson, *The Mob: 200 Years of Organized Crime in New*

York (Ottowa, IL, 1983), 125, 131–135; Mary M. Stolberg, *Fighting Organized Crime: Politics, Justice, and the Legacy of Thomas E. Dewey* (Boston, 1995), 8–10; Kyvig, *Repealing National Prohibition*, 27.

6. *Guzik v. United States*, 54 F.2d. 618 (CCA 7th, 1931); V. O. Key Jr., "Police Graft," *American Journal of Sociology* 40 (Mar. 1935): 625–626; "Scarlet Sisters Everleigh: How Vice Grew Up in Chicago," *Chicago Sunday Tribune*, 26 Jan. 1936, part 7, 7; Herbert Asbury, *Gem of the Prairie: An Informal History of the Chicago Underworld* (1940; with an introduction by Perry R. Duis, DeKalb, IL, 1986), 261–262; Asbury, *Great Illusion*, 293; Al Rose, *Storyville, New Orleans: Being an Authentic, Illustrated Account of the Notorious Red-Light District* (Tuscaloosa, AL, 1974), 47; Jesse George Murray, *The Legacy of Al Capone: Portraits and Annals of Chicago's Public Enemies* (New York, 1975), 19; Paula Petrik, "Capitalists with Rooms: Prostitutes in Helena, Montana, 1865–1900," in *Prostitution, Drugs, Gambling, and Organized Crime*, ed. Eric H. Monkkonen (Munich, 1992), 605–617.

7. "Scarlet Sisters Everleigh," *Chicago Sunday Tribune*, 26 Jan. 1936, part 7, 7. This information is for "Johnnie Turio," but the similarity of the names is too striking not to believe that Turio and Torrio were the same person. See *Vigilance* (Jan. 1913), cited in [Lancaster Citizens' Commission], *A Report on Vice Conditions in the City of Lancaster, Pa.* ([Lancaster], 1913), 66. For the relative profitability of urban vice, see James R. McGovern, "'Sporting Life on the Line': Prostitution in Progressive Era Pensacola," *Florida Historical Quarterly* 54 (Oct. 1975): 144; Robert F. Selcer, "Fort Worth and the Fraternity of Strange Women," *Southwestern Historical Quarterly* 96 (July 1992): 67; Elizabeth C. MacPhail, "When the Red Lights Went Out in San Diego," *Journal of San Diego History* 20 (Spring 1974): 11; Laurence Bergreen, *Capone: The Man and the Era* (London, 1995), 134.

8. [Portland, OR Vice Commission], *Report of the Portland Vice Commission to the Mayor and City Council of the City of Portland, Oregon* (Portland, 1913), 19, 28, 40.

9. *Steinberg v. United States*, 14 F.2d. 564 (CCA 2nd, 1926); Asbury, *Great Illusion*, 298; Asbury, *Gem of the Prairie*, 338.

10. *The Penguin Dictionary of Economics*, s.v. "cartel"; Jeffrey A. Miron and Jeffrey Zwiebel, "The Economic Case Against Drug Prohibition," *Journal of Economic Perspectives* 9 (Autumn 1995): 175–192.

11. *Capriola v. United States*, 61 F.2d. 5 (CCA 7th, 1932); *Meyer v. United States*, 67 F.2d. 223 (CCA 9th, 1933).

12. John Kobler, *Ardent Spirits: The Rise and Fall of Prohibition* (New York, 1973), 178.

13. *Weinstein v. United States*, 11 F.2d. 505 (CCA 1st, 1926); *Wickersham Report*, vol. 4, 303–311; *United States v. Wills*, 36 F.2d. 855 (CCA 3rd, 1929); *Capriola* 61 F.2d. 5; Frederick Lewis Allen, *Only Yesterday: An Informal History of the 1920s* (1931; New York, 1964), 204–224; Asbury, *Great Illusion*, 291–292.

14. James O'Donnell Bennett, *Chicago Gangland: The True Story of Chicago Crime* (Chicago, 1929), reprinted in *Wickersham Report*, vol. 4, 375–376; Humbert S. Nelli, "Italians and Crime in Chicago: The Formative Years, 1890–1920," *American*

Journal of Sociology 74 (Jan. 1969): 373–391; Asbury, *Gem of the Prairie*, 247–254, 264, 276–280; Cashman, *Prohibition*, 61–62; Bergreen, *Capone*, 30–33; Kobler, *Capone*, 21–22, 32, 46–48.

15. Bennett, *Chicago Gangland*, in *Wickersham Report*, vol. 4, 376; "Scarlet Sisters Everleigh," *Chicago Sunday Tribune*, 19 Jan. 1936, part 7, 1, 8, 26 Jan. 1936, part 7, 7, and 2 Feb. 1936, part 7, 7; Asbury, *Gem of the Prairie*, 259–260, 264–269, 298–303; Kobler, *Capone*, 48–50.

16. *Wickersham Report*, vol. 4, 298; Bennett, *Chicago Gangland*, in *Wickersham Report*, vol. 4, 375–379; Asbury, *Gem of the Prairie*, 322–323; Asbury, *Great Illusion*, 294–301; Nelli, "Italians and Crime," 386; Mark H. Haller, "Organized Crime in Urban Society: Chicago in the Twentieth Century," *Journal of Social History* 5 (Winter 1971–72): 213; Kobler, *Capone*, 51–55, 71; Cashman, *Prohibition*, 62, 69; Kenney, *Organized Crime in America*, 124–125.

17. Bennett, *Chicago Gangland*, in *Wickersham Report*, vol. 4, 372–373; Allen, *Only Yesterday*, 205–207, 215; Asbury, *Great Illusion*, 295–298; Nelli, "Italians and Crime," 390; Haller, "Organized Crime in Urban Society," 219–220; Murray, *Legacy of Al Capone*, 17–18; Kobler, *Capone*, 62–67; Cashman, *Prohibition*, 63.

18. Bennett, *Chicago Gangland*, in *Wickersham Report*, vol. 4, 373; Allen, *Only Yesterday*, 215; Asbury, *Great Illusion*, 200–203; Kyvig, *Repealing National Prohibition*, 27; Cashman, *Prohibition*, 112–116.

19. Allen, *Only Yesterday*, 216–224; Key, "Police Graft," 624–636; Asbury, *Great Illusion*, 295–303; Kobler, *Capone*, 61; Bergreen, *Capone*, 96–97.

20. Asbury, *Great Illusion*, 204; Haller, "Organized Crime in Urban Society," 220; Murray, *Legacy of Al Capone*, 15–16; Peterson, *Mob*, 137–139; Ruth, *Inventing the Public Enemy*, 70; Bergreen, *Capone*, 45–48, 101–104; Stolberg, *Fighting Organized Crime*, 9–11.

21. "561 Seventh Ave., Manhattan," 19 Aug. 191, file: "1919"; "105/107 Eldridge St., Manhattan," file: "1919"; "Greenwich Village Heath," file: "1920"; all box 34, C14. See also Rose Keefe, *The Man Who Got Away: The Bugs Moran Story; A Biography* (Nashville, 2005), 193.

22. Ivan Light, "The Ethnic Vice Industry, 1880–1944," *American Sociological Review* 42 (June 1977): 471; Kenney, *Organized Crime in America*, 129; Ruth, *Inventing the Public Enemy*, 37; Friedman, *Crime and Punishment*, 272–273. On the changing meaning of "gun moll," see H. L. Mencken, *The American Language: An Inquiry into the Development of English in the United States*, 3rd ed. (New York, 1931), 670.

23. Michael Woodiwiss, *Organized Crime and American Power: A History* (Toronto, 2001), 228; John Dickie, *Cosa Nostra: A History of the Sicilian Mafia* (London, 2004), 214.

24. Bennett, *Chicago Gangland*, in *Wickersham Report*, vol. 4, 357; Dickie, *Cosa Nostra*, 1, 221–222.

25. Bennett, *Chicago Gangland*, in *Wickersham Report*, vol. 4, 372–382; Haller, "Organized Crime in Urban Society," 221; Dickie, *Cosa Nostra*, 220–222.

26. Bennett, *Chicago Gangland*, in *Wickersham Report*, vol. 4, 398–399; Keefe, *Man Who Got Away*, 8–12.

27. A. Guckenheimer & Bros. Co. v. United States, 3 F.2d 786 (CCA 3rd, 1925); Weinstein 11 F.2d 505; O'Shaughnessy v. United States 17 F.2d 225 (CCA 5th, 1927); Wyatt v. United States 23 F.2d 791 (CCA 3rd, 1928).

28. Ruth, Inventing the Public Enemy, 73–74; Woodiwiss, Organized Crime and American Power, 228–229.

29. "Talk of the Town: Men's Shop," New Yorker (22 Sept. 1928): 15; Bennett, Chicago Gangland, in Wickersham Report, vol. 4, 392–393, 415; Asbury, Great Illusion, 204–205; Bergreen, Capone, 45–47; Ruth, Inventing the Public Enemy, 63–69.

30. Allen, Only Yesterday, 204; William J. Helmer, The Gun that Made the Twenties Roar (London, 1969); Kobler, Capone, 91; Bergreen, Capone, 167–169.

31. Miron and Zwiebel, "Economic Case Against Drug Prohibition," 175–192. See also Allen, Only Yesterday, 219–220; H. C. Brearley, Homicide in the United States (Chapel Hill, NC, 1932), 64–65; Key, "Police Graft," 624–636; Light, "Ethnic Vice Industry," 471; Kyvig, Repealing National Prohibition, 27; Morton Keller, Regulating a New Society: Public Policy and Social Change in America, 1900–1933 (Cambridge, MA, 1994), 157.

32. Allen, Only Yesterday, 215–216; Peterson, Mob, 116–118; Robert M. Fogelson, Big-City Police (Cambridge, MA, 1977), 72–73; Rose, Storyville, 67–68, 213–215.

33. Allen v. United States, 47 F.2d 688 (CCA 7th, 1924); United States v. Wexler, 79 F.2d 526 (CCA 2nd, 1935); Joy Jackson, "Prohibition in New Orleans: The Unlikeliest Crusade," Louisiana History 19 (Sept. 1978): 273, 281; Kenneth D. Rose, American Women and the Repeal of Prohibition (New York, 1996), 47–48; Woodiwiss, Organized Crime and American Power, 189; James Morone, Hellfire Nation: The Politics of Sin in American History (New Haven, CT, 2003), 326–327.

34. Allen 47 F.2d 688.

35. Wexler 79 F.2d 526. On Wexler, see also Stanley Walker, The Night Club Era (New York, 1933; paperback Baltimore, 1999), 61–62; "End of Wexler," Time (11 Dec. 1933); "Milestones," Time (7 July 1952).

36. Fogelson, Big-City Police, 117; Allen, Only Yesterday, 215–216; Cashman, Prohibition, 80, 98; Peterson, Mob, 125; Bergreen, Capone, 150; Stolberg, Fighting Organized Crime, 7–14.

37. Key, "Police Graft," 629; Asbury, Great Illusion, 299–301; Cashman, Prohibition, 69–70; Bergreen, Capone, 149–150.

38. Bennett, Chicago Gangland, in Wickersham Report, vol. 4, 394–395; Asbury, Gem of the Prairie, 340–354; Kobler, Capone, 119–123, 128–132; Bergreen, Capone, 151–163; Murray, Legacy of Al Capone, 50–67.

39. Bennett, Chicago Gangland, in Wickersham Report, vol. 4, 378; Association Against the Prohibition Amendment, Scandals, in Wickersham Report, vol. 5, 208–209; Allen, Only Yesterday, 217–219; Asbury, Great Illusion, 292–306; Haller, "Organized Crime in Urban Society," 220; Kenney, Organized Crime in America, 126; Cashman, Prohibition, 79, 100; Kobler, Capone, 134–135; Bergreen, Capone, 170–175. For a discussion of the instability of cartels, see D. K. Osborne, "Cartel Problems," American Economic Review 66 (Dec. 1976): 835–844; David E. Mills and Kenneth G. Elzinga, "Cartel Problems: Comment," American Economic Review 68 (Dec. 1978): 938–941;

Andrew Postlewaite and John Roberts, "A Note of the Stability of Large Cartels," *Econometrica* 45 (Nov. 1977): 1877–1878.

40. "It Is the Law," *Time* (28 May 1923); "State Rights," *Time* (11 June 1923); Allen, *Only Yesterday*, 209; Daniel J. Whitener, *Prohibition in North Carolina*, James Sprunt Studies in History and Political Science 27 (Chapel Hill, NC, 1945): 184; Jimmie Lewis Franklin, *Born Sober: Prohibition in Oklahoma, 1907–1959* (Norman, 1971), 78–80; Richard F. Hamm, *Shaping the Eighteenth Amendment: Temperance Reform, Legal Culture, and the Polity, 1880–1920* (Chapel Hill, NC, 1995), 266–267; Thomas R. Pegram, *Battling Demon Rum: The Struggle for a Dry America, 1850–1933* (Chicago, 1998), 159–160.

41. *Annual Report of the Secretary of the Treasury on the State of the Finances for the Fiscal Year Ended June 30, 1926* (Washington DC, 1927), 141; Roy A. Haynes, *Prohibition Inside Out* (New York, 1923), 102–114; Clark, *Deliver Us from Evil*, 160.

42. Walker, *Night Club Era*, 213. See also Kobler, *Ardent Spirits*, 227; Paul Chevigny, *Gigs: Jazz and the Cabaret Laws in New York City* (New York, 1991), 42, 54–55.

43. *Marcante v. United States*, 49 F.2d 156 (CCA 10th, 1931). See also Jackson, "Prohibition in New Orleans," 274–175.

44. *Booth v. United States*, 57 F.2d 192 (CCA 10th, 1932). On the Earlsboro, Pottawatomie Country, OK scandal, see Franklin, *Born Sober*, 92.

45. *Rossi v. United States*, 49 F.2d 1 (CCA 9th, 1931). See also *Weniger v. United States*, 47 F.2d 692 (CCA 9th, 1931).

46. Walker, *Night Club Era*, 52, 75–76; Kobler, *Ardent Spirits*, 229.

47. Walker, *Night Club Era*, 159–160; Whitener, *Prohibition in North Carolina*, 186; Hamm, *Shaping the Eighteenth Amendment*, 267.

48. Walker, *Night Club Era*, 218–220. See also Kobler, *Ardent Spirits*, 234. In a "gyp joint," hostesses urged men to spend huge amounts of money, but the management did not play the check-writing game at the end of the evening, See "Olga," [1927], file: "1927–1928," box 35, C14.

49. Perry R. Duis, *The Saloon: Public Drinking in Chicago and Boston, 1880–1920* (Urbana, IL, 1983), 233–234; Roy Rosenzweig, *Eight Hours for What We Will: Workers and Leisure in an Industrial City, 1870–1920* (Cambridge, MA, 1983), 117–122.

50. Kobler, *Ardent Spirits*, 236; Clark, *Deliver Us from Evil*, 163–164; Pegram, *Battling Demon Rum*, 160.

51. Morris Markey, "Reporter at Large," *New Yorker* (1 May 1926): 24. See also F. H. Whitin to Royal Scott, 1 Aug. 1924, file: "1924," box 6, C14; Allen, *Only Yesterday*, 210; "Milestones," *Time* (24 Mar. 1941); Kobler, *Ardent Spirits*, 223.

52. *United States v. All Buildings*, 28 F.2d 774 (D. C., D. Kans., 2nd Division, 1928); *United States v. Cunningham*, 37 F.2d 349 (D. C., D. Neb., Chadron Division, 1929); Clark, *Deliver Us from Evil*, 140–141; Cashman, *Prohibition*, 48; Pegram, *Battling Demon Rum*, 151.

53. *Wickersham Report*, vol. 4, 339–346; Association Against the Prohibition Amendment, *Scandals*, in *Wickersham Report*, vol. 5, 204–205; Charles Merz, *The Dry Decade* (Garden City, NY, 1932), 60, 148–152; Reckless, *Vice in Chicago*, 198–199; Key,

"Police Graft," 624–636; Asbury, *Great Illusion*, 338; Clark, *Deliver Us from Evil*, 160–165; John C. Burnham, "New Perspectives on the Prohibition 'Experiment' of the 1920s," *Journal of Social History* 2 (Fall 1968): 51–68; Cashman, *Prohibition*, 48–49; Stephen Fox, *Blood and Power: Organized Crime in Twentieth-Century America* (New York, 1989), 50.

54. "Talk of the Town: Victims," *New Yorker* (11 July 1925): 2. See also Haynes, *Prohibition Inside Out*, 271–272; *Wickersham Report*, vol. 4, 342; Jackson, "Prohibition in New Orleans," 268; Lewis A. Erenberg, *Steppin' Out: New York Nightlife and the Transformation of American Culture, 1890–1930* (Westport, CT, 1981), 238.

55. This lack of regulation partially explains the statistics showing more speakeasies during Prohibition than before it. See Cashman, *Prohibition*, 44; Kobler, *Ardent Spirits*, 223–224, 354.

56. "Entertainers Café," 21 Dec. 1923, JPA. *United States v. Budar*, 9 F.2d 162 (D. C., E.D. Wis., 1925); *Rossi v. United States*, 16 F.2d 712 (CCA 8th, 1926); *United States v. General Amusement Co. of Arizona*, 19 F.2d 630 (D. C., D. Ariz., 1927); *United States v. Kelly*, 24 F.2d 133 (D. C., D. Idaho, S.D., 1927); *United States v. Butler Hotel Co.*, 32 F.2d 324 (D. C., W.D. Wash., N.D., 1929); Allen, *Only Yesterday*, 91; Walker, *Night Club Era*, 99; Reckless, *Vice in Chicago*, 123–124.

57. *Notary v. United States*, 16 F.2d 434 (CCA 8th, 1926); *Briggs v. United States*, 45 F.2d 479 (CCA 6th, 1930).

58. "Talk of the Town: Market Note," *New Yorker* (18 July 1925): 5. See also Walker, *Night Club Era*, 88; Kobler, *Ardent Spirits*, 224.

59. This figure is the daily wage for unskilled plant workers in 1925. See Paul A. David and Peter Solar, "A Bicentenary Contribution to the History of the Cost of Living in America," *Research in American History* (Greenwich, CT, 1977), vol. 2, 1–80. See also Irving Fisher, *The "Noble Experiment"* (New York, 1930), cited in Clark, *Deliver Us from Evil*, 147–148.

60. "Talk of the Town: Within the Law," *New Yorker* (10 May 1930), 19.

61. *Budar* 9 F.2d 162; *Notary* 16 F.2d 434; *Rossi* 16 F.2d 712; *Briggs* 45 F.2d 479.

62. *Notary* 16 F.2d 434.

63. "Talk of the Town: Victims," 2.

64. *Butler Hotel Co.* 32 F.2d 324.

65. "Talk of the Town: Victims," 2.

66. Bennett, *Chicago Gangland*, in *Wickersham Report*, vol. 4, 373, 396; Reckless, *Vice in Chicago*, 118, 127; Cashman, *Prohibition*, 44.

67. *Wyatt* 23 F.2d 791; *Matteis v. United States*, 57 F.2d 999 (CCA 7th, 1932).

68. Walker, *Night Club Era*, 71. See also Erenberg, *Steppin' Out*, 238–242; Kobler, *Ardent Spirits*, 228.

69. *United States v. Slater*, 278 F. 266 (D. C., E.D. Pa., 1922); *Norris v. United States*, 34 F.2d 839 (CCA 3rd, 1929); *Flynn v. United States*, 57 F.2d 1044 (CCA 8th, 1932); *Tremont v. United States*, 65 F.2d 949 (CCA 8th, 1933); Paul Aaron and David Musto, "Temperance and Prohibition in America: A Historical Overview," in *Alcohol and Public Policy: Beyond the Shadow of Prohibition; Panel on Alternative Policies*

Affecting the Prevention of Alcohol Abuse and Alcoholism, ed. Mark H. Moore and Dean R. Gerstein (Washington, DC, 1981), 158. For the background of the Norris case, see "In Philadelphia," *Time* (24 Sept. 1928).

70. *United States v. Dowling*, 278 F. 630 (D. C., S.D. Fla., 1922); Pegram, *Battling Demon Rum*, 152; Morone, *Hellfire Nation*, 319.

71. Anita Loos, *Gentlemen Prefer Blondes* (1925; London, 1982), 140–142; Clark, *Deliver Us from Evil*, 172–174; Richard Griffith and Arthur Mayer, with the assistance of Eileen Bowser, *The Movies*, rev. ed. (New York, 1970), 191–199; Kathy Ogren, *The Jazz Revolution: Twenties America and the Meaning of Jazz* (New York, 1989), 82–84.

72. F. Scott Fitzgerald, *The Great Gatsby* (1926; London, 1994), 53.

73. Fitzgerald, *Great Gatsby*, 45–62.

74. "Investigations of Vice Conditions During National Democratic Convention," June 1924, file: "1924, Democratic National Convention"; "Report of Investigation of Vice Conditions in Harlem," [June 1924], file: "1924, Democratic National Convention"; both box 35, C14; "Talk of the Town: Prominent," *New Yorker* (1 Aug. 1925): 4; "Silver Tradition," *Time* (12 Aug. 1929); Walker, *Night Club Era*, 60, 289; Reckless, *Vice in Chicago*, 134–135; Kobler, *Ardent Spirits*, 228; Cashman, *Prohibition*, 43–45.

75. Ellin Mackay, "Why We Go to Cabarets: A Post-Debutante Explains," *New Yorker* (28 Nov. 1925): 7–8. See also Fitzgerald, *Great Gatsby*, 56; Erenberg, *Steppin' Out*, 236–237.

76. "Law Enforcement and Police," 3 Dec. 1922, JPA; *Rossi* 16 F.2d 712; *Booth* 57 F.2d 192.

77. *Notary* 16 F.2d 434; *Rossi* 16 F.2d 712; *Matteis* 57 F.2d 999.

78. "Investigations of Vice Conditions During National Democratic Convention"; "Report of Investigation of Vice Conditions in Harlem"; both C14; Reckless, *Vice in Chicago*, 146–149.

79. Asbury, *French Quarter*, 455. See also Reckless, *Vice in Chicago*, 201.

80. "Speedway Inn, Burnham Ill.," 9 Dec. 1923, JPA; "Cabaret: Cicero, Illinois," 4 Dec. 1923, JPA; "Olga"; "Continental Hotel, B'way & 41st," 12 Jan. 1928, file: "1927–1928," box 35; both C14; Reckless, *Vice in Chicago*, 123–125, 145, 200, 231–233; Willoughby Cyrus Waterman, *Prostitution and Its Repression in New York City, 1900–1931* (New York, 1932), 147–148.

81. "Law Enforcement and Police," 29 Nov. 1922, JPA. See also "Jesse Binford Deposition," Jan. 1923, JPA; Reckless, *Vice in Chicago*, 147.

82. *Annual Report of the Secretary of the Treasury on the State of the Finances for the Fiscal Year Ended June 30, 1920, with Appendices* (Washington, DC, 1921), 1504, 1512–1517; *Annual Report of the Secretary of the Treasury on the State of the Finances for the Fiscal Year Ended June 30, 1921, with Appendices* (Washington, DC. 1922), 996–999; *Annual Report of the Secretary of the Treasury on the State of the Finances for the Fiscal Year Ended June 30, 1923, with Appendices* (Washington, DC, 1924), 789–790; *Annual Report of the Secretary of the Treasury . . . 1926*, 140–141; *Annual Report of the Secretary of the Treasury on the State of the Finances for the Fiscal Year Ended June 30, 1927, with Appendices* (Washington, DC, 1928), 118; Haynes, *Prohibition Inside Out*, 12, 117, 129.

83. K. Austin Kerr, *Organized for Prohibition: A New History of the Anti-Saloon League* (New Haven, CT, 1985), 223; Hamm, *Shaping the Eighteenth Amendment*, 253; Pegram, *Battling Demon Rum*, 153–154.

84. *Annual Report of the Secretary of the Treasury on the State of the Finances for the Fiscal Year Ended June 30, 1917, with Appendices* (Washington, DC, 1918), 190–191.

85. David F. Musto, *The American Disease: Origins of Narcotic Control*, expanded ed. (New York, 1987), 122; David T. Courtwright, *Dark Paradise: Opiate Addiction in America before 1940* (Cambridge, MA, 1982), 1–2; Joseph F. Spillane, *Cocaine: From Medical Marvel to Modern Menace in the United States, 1884–1920* (Baltimore, 2000), 105–106, 141.

86. *United States v. Jin Fuey Moy*, 241 U.S. 392 (1915). The court reaffirmed this decision in *United States v. Doremus*, 249 U.S. 86 (1919) and applied it to the Volstead Act in *United States v. Yuginovich*, 256 U.S. 450 (1921). See also Musto, *American Disease*, 122.

87. *Webb v. United States*, 249 U.S. 94 (1919); *Annual Report of the Secretary of the Treasury . . . 1920*, 1506, 1545–1548; Musto, *American Disease*, 132; David Courtwright, Herman Joseph, and Don Des Jarlais, *Addicts Who Survived: An Oral History of Narcotic Use in America, 1923–1965* (Knoxville, 1989), 8–9; Friedman, *Crime and Punishment*, 355.

88. *Annual Report of the Secretary of the Treasury . . . 1920*, 1505–1506; *Annual Report of the Secretary of the Treasury . . . 1921*, 1022–1023; Courtwright et al., *Addicts Who Survived*, 8–9; Friedman, *Crime and Punishment*, 355; Jill Jonnes, *Hep-Cats, Narcs, and Pipe Dreams: A History of America's Romance with Illegal Drugs* (New York, 1996), 50–52.

89. *Annual Report of the Secretary of the Treasury . . . 1920*, 1506; *Annual Report of the Secretary of the Treasury . . . 1921*, 989; Musto, *American Disease*, 151; 175–178; Jonnes, *Hep-Cats*, 53–56. On the New Haven Clinic, see David F. Musto and Manuel R. Ramos, "A Follow-Up Study of the New Haven Morphine Maintenance Clinic of 1920," *New England Journal of Medicine* 304 (30 Apr. 1981): 1071–1077.

90. On the Shreveport Clinic, see Musto, *American Disease*, 167–175. For Butler's 1978 oral account of his experiences, see Courtwright et al., *Addicts Who Survived*, 281–289.

91. Courtwright et al., *Addicts Who Survived*, 8–9, 26, 319–320.

92. *Sullivan v. United States*, 15 F.2d 809 (CCA 4th, 1926).

93. *Sullivan* 15 F.2d 809; *United States v. Sullivan*, 274 U.S. 259 (1927). See also *Steinberg v. United States*, 14 F.2d 564 (CCA 2nd, 1926); *Levenstein v. Commissioner of Internal Revenue*, 19 BTA 99 (1930).

94. *Sullivan* 274 U.S. 259.

95. "Talk of the Town," *New Yorker* (27 Mar. 1926): 7.

96. *Capone v. United States*, 51 F.2d 609 (1931); *United States v. Wexler*, 79 F.2d 526 (CCA 2nd, 1935); *Benetti v. United States*, 97 F.2d 263 (CCA 9th, 1938).

97. *Guzik* 54 F.2d 618.

98. *Green v. Commissioner of Internal Revenue*, 11 BTA 185 (1928); *Capone* 51 F.2d 609; *Wexler* 79 F.2d 526; "End of Wexler."

99. *Annual Report of the Secretary of the Treasury on the State of the Finances for the Fiscal Year Ended June 30, 1924* (Washington, DC, 1925) 789–790; *Annual Report of the Secretary of the Treasury on the State of the Finances for the Fiscal Year Ended June 30, 1925* (Washington, DC, 1926), 384, 857.

100. Cashman, *Prohibition*, 46. See also Merz, *Dry Decade*, 98; Kobler, *Ardent Spirits*, 98.

101. The Prohibition Unit took in money from a range of sources, including the legitimate sale of liquor, wine, and cordials. It also gained money from tax penalties, civil settlements, property seizures, and fines from cases, including conspiracy cases. Unfortunately, the Treasury Department's annual reports reported these figures inconsistently and aggregated them differently from year to year.

102. *Annual Report of the Secretary of the Treasury . . . 1926*, 868; *Annual Report of the Secretary of the Treasury on the State of the Finances for the Fiscal Year Ended June 30, 1928* (Washington, DC, 1929), 186; *Annual Report of the Secretary of the Treasury on the State of the Finances for the Fiscal Year Ended June 30, 1929* (Washington, DC, 1930), 84. No figures exist for 1927.

103. *Annual Report of the Secretary of the Treasury . . . 1924*, 57; *Annual Report of the Secretary of the Treasury . . . 1925*, 383; *Annual Report of the Secretary of the Treasury . . . 1926*, 869. See also Haynes, *Prohibition Inside Out*, 275.

104. Kobler, *Ardent Spirits*, 260–262.

105. *Annual Report of the Secretary of the Treasury . . . 1923*, 905. By 1925, "organized dens" had turned into "organized gangs of liquor-law violators." See *Annual Report of the Secretary of the Treasury . . . 1925*, 383.

106. *Annual Report of the Secretary of the Treasury . . . 1927*, 118.

107. *Allen* 4 F.2d 688; *Wills* 36 F.2d 855; *Biemer v. United States*, 5 F.2d 1045 (CCA 7th, 1932); *Rossi* 49 F.2d 1.

108. *Slater* 278 F. 266; *Belvin v. United States*, 12 F.2d 548 (CCA 4th, 1926); *Rubio v. United States*, 22 F.2d 766 (CCA 9th, 1927); *Scaffidi v. United States*, 37 F.2d 203 (CCA 1st, 1930). See also Haynes, *Prohibition Inside Out*, 273–274; *Annual Report of the Secretary of the Treasury . . . 1923*, 905.

109. On conspiracy in American culture, see Richard Hofstadter, "The Paranoid Style in American Culture," *Harper's Magazine* (Nov. 1964): 77–86; Gordon S. Wood, "Conspiracy and the Paranoid Style: Causality and Deceit in the Eighteenth Century," *William and Mary Quarterly*, Ser. 3, 39 (July 1982): 401–441; David Brion Davis, "Some Themes of Counter-Subversion: An Analysis of Anti-Masonic, Anti-Catholic, and Anti-Mormon Literature," *Mississippi Valley Historical Review* 47 (Sept. 1960): 205–224; David Brion Davis, "Some Ideological Functions of Prejudice in Ante-Bellum America," *American Quarterly* 15 (Summer 1963): 115–125.

110. *United States v. Dennee*, 25 F. 818 (C. C., D. La., 1877); *Becher v. United States*, 5 F.2d 45 (CCA 2nd, 1924); *United States v. Frank*, 12 F.2d 796 (D. C., D. R. I., 1926); *Burkhardt v. United States*, 13 F.2d 841 (CCA 6th, 1926); *Rossi* 49 F.2d 1.

111. *Dowling* 278 F. 630.

112. *United States v. Kissel*, 218 U.S. 601 (1910); *United States v. American Tobacco Co.*, 221 U.S. 106 (1911).

113. *Allen* 4 F.2d 688; *Becher* 5 F.2d 45; A. *Guckenheimer* 3 F.2d 786; *Biemer* 54 F.2d 1045.

114. As elucidated by Oliver Wendell Holmes in *Kissel*, this definition became canonical. See *Kissel* 218 U.S. 601; *Booth* 57 F.2d 192.

115. *Slater* 278 F. 266.

116. *Dowling* 278 F. 630.

117. *National Prohibition Act*, reprinted in Merz, *Dry Decade*, Appendix E, 318.

118. *Weinstein* 11 F.2d 505. See also *Belvin* 12 F.2d 548; *Wills* 36 F.2d. 855; *Capriola* 61 F.2d. 5.

119. Other authors debunk the image of highly organized criminal conspiracies. See Merz, *Dry Decade*, 63–64; Daniel Bell, "The Myth of the Cosa Nostra," *New Leader* 45 (Dec. 1963): 12–15; Alan A. Block, "History and the Study of Organized Crime," *Urban Life* 6 (Jan. 1978).

120. Allen, *Only Yesterday*, 91; Morone, *Hellfire Nation*, 333.

121. Allen, *Only Yesterday*, 212; Merz, *Dry Decade*, 158–182; Clark, *Deliver Us from Evil*, 140–180; Burnham, "New Perspectives on the Prohibition 'Experiment,'" 51–68.

122. Bruère, *Does Prohibition Work?*; Keller, *Regulating a New Society*, 140. On Bruère's study, see Clark, *Deliver Us from Evil*, 148; Kyvig, *Repealing National Prohibition*, 24–25.

123. Clark Warburton, *The Economic Results of Prohibition* (New York, 1932), 108, 260. Testing this assertion, Miron and Zwiebel show that alcohol-related illnesses declined significantly during the 1920s. See Jeffrey A. Miron and Jeffrey Zwiebel, "Alcohol Consumption During Prohibition," *American Economic Review* 81 (May 1991): 242–247. See also Joseph R. Gusfield, *Symbolic Crusade: Status Politics and the American Temperance Movement*, 2nd ed. (Urbana, IL, 1983), 118–119; Clark, *Deliver Us from Evil*, 146–147; Kyvig, *Repealing National Prohibition*, 23–25.

124. Haynes, *Prohibition Inside Out*, 228–237; Bruère, *Does Prohibition Work?* 58, 61; Clark, *Deliver Us from Evil*, 148, 168; Paula S. Fass, *The Damned and the Beautiful: American Youth in the 1920s* (New York, 1977), 315–324; Kyvig, *Repealing National Prohibition*, 25–35.

125. John D. Rockefeller Jr., "Foreword," in *Toward Liquor Control*, Raymond B. Fosdick and Albert L. Scott (New York 1933), vii–xi; Asbury, *Great Illusion*, 328–330; Gusfield, *Symbolic Crusade*, 128–129; Clark, *Deliver Us from Evil*, 168–169, 200; Kyvig, *Repealing National Prohibition*, 178–182.

CONCLUSION. PROGRESSIVISM, PROHIBITION, AND POLICY OPTIONS

1. Frederick J. Hoffman, "Philistine and Puritan in the 1920s," *American Quarterly* 1 (Autumn 1949): 247–263; Richard Hofstadter, *The Age of Reform: From Bryan to F.D.R.* (New York, 1955), 287–291.

2. *Buchanan v. Warley*, 245 U.S. 60 (1917); Elliott M. Rudwick, *Race Riot! 1917: At East St. Louis, July 2, 1917* (Cleveland, 1964).

3. William M. Tuttle Jr., *Race Riot: Chicago in the Red Summer of 1919* (New York, 1970).

Essay on Sources

This project started out as a history of drug use, but I quickly discovered two things. First, excellent work already existed on drug use. And second, people at the turn of the century, both reformers and users, saw connections between nonmedical drug use and other aspects of urban culture. While historians now see dancing, drinking, gambling, sex, and drug-taking as issues more separate than connected, contemporaries subsumed them under the single heading of "vice." As a result, I broadened the scope of this book from drugs to vice. In so doing, I sought to synthesize various strands of historiography.

DRUGS

David Musto and David Courtwright set the gold standard for studying the history of drugs in America. Musto, in his landmark book *The American Disease: Origins of Narcotic Control*, expanded ed. (New York: Oxford University Press, 1987), emphasized the interplay between changing medical practices and the politics of regulation. In contrast, Courtwright, in *Dark Paradise: Opiate Addiction in America before 1940* (Cambridge, MA: Harvard University Press, 1982), detailed how the demographic shift among opiate users from middle-class female medical addicts to young working-class men using drugs recreationally affected popular attitudes toward drugs and their legality. Although very different in focus, together Musto's and Courtwright's books complement each other and provide the best introduction to the field. Joseph Spillane's *Cocaine: From Medical Marvel to Modern Menace in the United States, 1884–1920* (Baltimore: Johns Hopkins University Press, 2000), similarly well-written and thoroughly researched, offers a superb scholarly discussion of the marketing, medical application, and recreational use of cocaine.

Charles Terry and Mildred Pellens's *The Opium Problem* (New York: Committee on Drug Addictions, in Collaboration with the Bureau of Social Hygiene, 1928) serves as the essential source for primary material. With stunning breadth and depth, it covers a wide range of topics published between 1867 and 1927. For those unwilling to wade through the two massive tomes comprising *The Opium Problem*, H. Wayne Morgan's *Yesterday's Addicts: American Society and Drug Abuse, 1865–1920* (Norman: University of Oklahoma Press, 1974) is a good starting point for printed primary sources. Like Terry and Pellens, Morgan assembled a range of representative medical and reform sources.

For more personal accounts of drug use in the early twentieth century, Bingham Dai's *Opium Addiction in Chicago* (Montclair, NJ: Patterson Smith, [1937] 1970) contains oral histories of addicts living in Chicago in the 1930s. In *Addicts Who Survived: An Oral History of Narcotic Use in America, 1923–1965* (Knoxville: University of Tennessee Press, 1989), David Courtwright, Herman Joseph, and Don Des Jarlais collected interviews with methadone users living in New York City who were over sixty years old. Organized thematically, the book offers insight into different aspects of drug addicts' lives, including getting hooked, scoring, and attempts to get clean.

ALCOHOL

Since the regulation of vice focuses more on coercion than persuasion, I found the literature on the temperance movement less useful than the books that concentrated on altering the alcohol trade. The best of that literature includes Perry Duis, *The Saloon: Public Drinking in Chicago and Boston, 1880–1920* (Urbana: University of Illinois Press, 1983); K. Austin Kerr, *Organized for Prohibition: A New History of the Anti-Saloon League* (New Haven, CT: Yale University Press, 1985); and Richard Hamm, *Shaping the Eighteenth Amendment: Temperance Reform, Legal Culture, and the Polity, 1880–1920* (Chapel Hill: University of North Carolina Press, 1995). *The Saloon*, by offering a comparison between Boston and Chicago, demonstrates how different legislative and enforcement strategies shaped the working-class drinking culture of two major American cities. More of an organizational history than Duis's social history, Kerr described how middle-class antipathy toward the saloon united moderate wets with temperance advocates. This alliance, institutionalized in the Anti-Saloon League, oversaw the passage of National Prohibition. Taking a more juridical approach, Hamm analyzed the legal origins of Prohibition in *Shaping the Eighteenth Amendment*. Focused explicitly on the relationship between drinking and the law, this tour-de-force study explores the legislative assault on alcohol production, distribution, and use. But Hamm did not stop there; he went further, lucidly detailing the way alcohol producers, sellers, and drinkers dodged reformers' attempts to restrict their business and their pleasure.

Among contemporary sources, Frederic H. Wines and John Koren's *The Liquor Problem in Its Legislative Aspect* (Boston: Houghton Mifflin, 1897) serves as admirable introduction to moderate attitudes on late nineteenth-century alcohol reform. Funded by the Committee of Fifty, an academically oriented organization, *The Liquor Problem* describes both drinking habits and their regulation.

PROSTITUTION

The books on prostitution vary widely in terms of approach, intended audience, and quality of research. Without question, the best for the Progressive era include Ruth Rosen's *The Lost Sisterhood: Prostitution in America, 1900–1918* (Baltimore: Johns Hopkins University Press, 1982); Mark Thomas Connelly's *The Response to Prostitution in the Progressive Era* (Chapel Hill: University of North Carolina Press, 1980);

Timothy Gilfoyle's *City of Eros: New York City, Prostitution, and the Commercializa-tion of Sex, 1790–1920* (New York: W. W. Norton, 1992); and Roy Lubove's "The Progressives and the Prostitute," *Historian* 24 (May 1962): 308–330. Connelly and Lubove primarily focused on the anti-vice movement, while Rosen and Gilfoyle adopted a more expansive approach. Gilfoyle adeptly portrayed the integration of prostitution into Manhattan's neighborhoods. Rosen, on the other hand, excelled at analyzing the social relationships in which prostitutes found themselves enmeshed.

Among primary sources, vice commission reports provide the best printed material available. The groundbreaking *Social Evil in Chicago: A Study of Existing Conditions, with Recommendations* (Chicago: Gunthorp-Warren, 1911) stands as the exemplar, but all the published reports yield insight into the business of prostitution, the movement against the sporting world, and the particularities of vice in different cities. George Kneeland's *Commercialized Prostitution in New York City*, rev. ed. (New York: Cen-tury, 1917), an investigation sponsored by the Rockefeller-funded Bureau of Social Hygiene, is another excellent city-specific study.

SYNTHESIS

Although most scholarship concentrates on a single vice, two types of work adopt a more synthetic approach: those that focus on reform and those that center on neigh-borhood life. In the first category, Paul Boyer's *Urban Masses and Moral Order in America, 1820–1920* (Cambridge, MA: Harvard University Press, 1978) does an excel-lent job describing the cyclical patterns of moral reform in the nineteenth and early twentieth centuries. In *Regulating a New Society: Public Policy and Social Change in America, 1900–1933* (Cambridge, MA: Harvard University Press, 1994), Morton Keller bundled moral reform with other topics, including immigration and protective legisla-tion, to discuss Progressive-era attempts at social engineering.

If Boyer and Keller provide the best overviews, the city-centered books of Arthur Goren, Al Rose, and Herbert Asbury show the interconnected networks of labor, leisure, politics, and crime. One of the most beautifully written books I have ever read, Goren's *New York Jews and the Quest for Community: The Kehillah Experiment, 1908–1922* (New York: Columbia University Press, 1970) illuminates the cultural and class tensions in Jewish attempts to investigate and decrease crime on the Lower East Side.

Al Rose's *Storyville, New Orleans: Being an Authentic, Illustrated Account of the No-torious Red-Light District* (Tuscaloosa: University of Alabama Press, 1974) and Herbert Asbury's many popular city histories, from *Gem of the Prairie: An Informal History of the Chicago Underworld* (DeKalb: Northern Illinois University Press, [1940] 1986) to *The French Quarter: An Informal History of the New Orleans Underworld* (New York: A. A. Knopf, 1936) and *The Barbary Coast: An Informal History of the San Francisco Under-world* (New York: A. A. Knopf, 1933), take a significantly less-academic tone, but these books stand out because Rose and Asbury presented the sporting world within the larger context of urban life, including each city's popular recreation and popular politics.

Although he does not write about one city as such, Ivan Light, in "From Vice District to Tourist Attraction: The Moral Career of American Chinatowns, 1880–

1940," *Pacific Historical Review* 43 (1974): 367–394, explored the dynamics of vice and neighborhood development with analytical nuance, historical specificity, and great theoretical utility.

I found three published primary sources particularly helpful for thinking about vice in its urban context: Jacob Riis's *How the Other Half Lives: Studies among the Tenements of New York* (New York: Dover, [1890] 1971); Jane Addams's *The Spirit of Youth and the City Streets* (Urbana: University of Illinois Press, [1909] 1972); and Michael Gold's semiautobiographical novel, *Jews Without Money* (New York: H. Liveright, 1930). Although Riis famously exposed the horrors of tenement housing in *How the Other Half Lives*, he did so in part by describing the evils of intermixing residences with criminal haunts and low-down dives. Addams directly addressed the problem of commercialized prostitution in *A New Conscience and an Ancient Evil* (New York: Macmillan, 1912), but her less-famous *The Spirit of Youth and the City Streets* examines a wider range of influences that drew urban youths into less-reputable recreation. Finally, Michael Gold's *Jews Without Money* provides the perfect counterpart to Goren's *New York Jews and the Quest for Community*. Both bring the Lower East Side alive, and neither underplays the criminal culture that added to the neighborhood's distinctive character.

POPULAR CULTURE

Four exceptional books defined the historical study of American popular culture: Roy Rosenzweig's *Eight Hours for What We Will: Workers and Leisure in an Industrial City, 1870–1920* (Cambridge: Cambridge University Press, 1983); Lewis Erenberg's *Steppin' Out: New York Nightlife and the Transformation of American Culture, 1890–1930* (Westport, CT: Greenwood Press, 1981); John Kasson's *Amusing the Million: Coney Island at the Turn of the Century* (New York: Hill & Wang, 1978); and Kathy Peiss's *Cheap Amusements: Working Women and Leisure in Turn-of-the-Century New York* (Philadelphia: Temple University Press, 1986). Rosenzweig, Erenberg, Kasson, and Peiss looked at phenomena such as holiday picnics, the dance craze, amusement-park attendance, and going to the movies. In the process, they made working-class leisure a vibrant area of inquiry. I disagree with their representation of commercial vice as preceding reputable recreation, and I particularly dispute their contention that commercial popular culture is distinct from disreputable leisure, but I could not have written this book without the foundation they established.

The next generation of historians complicated existing categories by exploring additional facets of urban popular culture. Three works stand out: Kathy Ogren's *The Jazz Revolution: Twenties America and the Meaning of Jazz* (New York: Oxford University Press, 1989); George Chauncey's *Gay New York: Gender, Urban Culture, and the Makings of the Gay Male World, 1890–1940* (New York: Basic Books, 1994); and Elizabeth Clement's *Love for Sale: Courting, Treating, and Prostitution in New York City, 1900–1945* (Chapel Hill: University of North Carolina Press, 2006). Through both argument and anecdote, these books plumb the boundless excitement that the new popular culture seemed to promise its participants.

RACE

The question of race in red-light districts is particularly fraught, because segrega-tion by reputation shifts the practices of Jim Crow in complicated ways. Other than Kevin Mumford's *Interzones: Black/White Sex Districts in Chicago and New York in the Early Twentieth Century* (New York: Columbia University Press, 1997), few works address the issue in any sustained manner. Instead, the topic comes through in frag-ments in books devoted to other subjects, usually the history of black or Asian commu-nities in specific cities.

Race riots are the other area where historians talk about race in red-light districts. In the early twentieth century, a number of race riots occurred in and around vice districts. Charles Crowe's two articles, "Racial Violence and Social Reform: Origins of the Atlanta Riot of 1906," *Journal of Negro History* 53 (July 1968): 234–256, and "Racial Massacre in Atlanta: September 22, 1906," *Journal of Negro History* 54 (Apr. 1969): 150–173, offer the best discussion of the Atlanta riot. Roberta Senechal's *The Sociogenesis of a Race Riot: Springfield, Illinois, in 1908* (Urbana: University of Illinois Press, 1990) covers the Springfield riot with greater felicity than the title would suggest. And both Elliott M. Rudwick's *Race Riot at East St. Louis, July 2, 1917* (Carbondale: Southern Illinois University Press, 1964) and William M. Tuttle Jr.'s *Race Riot: Chicago in the Red Summer of 1919* (New York: Atheneum, 1970) deserve their status as classics in the field.

ECONOMIC AND LEGAL CHANGE

As a cultural historian, I first encountered the relationship between economic and social change in Richard Fox and Jackson Lears's collection *Culture of Consumption: Critical Essays in American History, 1880–1980* (New York: Pantheon Books, 1983). Whether discussing cultural hegemony or the adoption of an outer-directed ethos of therapeutic release, the essays in this collection brought an updated Marxism to the study of American culture that I never quite abandoned. On the other hand, except for Daniel Horowitz's *The Morality of Spending: Attitudes toward the Consumer Society in America, 1875–1940* (Baltimore: Johns Hopkins University Press, 1985), a close schol-arly analysis of the shifts Lears broadly outlined, the books that most influenced this study are much more old-fashioned. Samuel P. Hays's *The Response to Industrialism, 1885–1914* (Chicago: University of Chicago Press, 1957) and Thomas Cochran and William Miller's *The Age of Enterprise*, rev. ed. (New York: Macmillan, [1942] 1961) offer excellent overviews of social, economic, and industrial change in the late nine-teenth and early twentieth centuries.

The legal histories on which I relied for my conceptual framework share the clarity that comes with a strong thesis, good narrative structure, and a scrupulous evidentiary base. Over the years, I turned repeatedly to Morton Horwitz's *The Transformation of American Law, 1870–1960: The Crisis of Legal Orthodoxy* (New York: Oxford Univer-sity Press, 1992) and Herbert Hovenkamp's *Enterprise and American Law, 1836–1937* (Cambridge, MA: Harvard University Press, 1991). Although not directly on the topic of vice, these books contextualize the legal changes happening in urban reform.

CITY GOVERNMENT

Early in my research I decided that, during the Gilded Age, the most exciting political fights of the era took place not on Capitol Hill, but in the streets of city wards. This realization opened up whole new vistas for understanding the dynamism of late nineteenth-century reform. From the period, my favorite works include Charles Park-hurst's vituperative *Our Fight with Tammany* (New York: C. Scribner's Sons, 1895), George Washington Plunkitt's wickedly amusing opinion pieces, collected by journalist William L. Riordan in *Plunkitt of Tammany Hall* (New York: Signet Classic, [1905] 1996), and the more measured but still delightfully cynical *Guarding a Great City* (New York: Harper & Bros., 1906) by William McAdoo, a former police commissioner of New York City.

The best histories of Manhattan's urban machine also originate from the early twentieth century. Gustavus Myers first published *The History of Tammany Hall* (New York: Dover, 1971) in 1901, and he presented a revised and enlarged edition in 1917. Together with M. R. Werner's *Tammany Hall* (Garden City, NY: Doubleday, Doran, 1928), these books offer the most comprehensive portrayal of New York's ward politics in the late nineteenth century. A modern work, Daniel Czitrom's "Underworld and Underdogs: Big Tim Sullivan and Metropolitan Politics in New York, 1889–1913," *Journal of American History* 78 (Sept. 1991): 536–558, gives an in-depth analysis of the political career, economic networks, and social milieu of a single, important Tammany politician.

For a well-researched view into the machine politics of a city other than New York, I recommend George M. Reynolds's *Machine Politics in New Orleans, 1897–1926* (New York: Columbia University Press, 1936). James Bryce's *The American Commonwealth*, new ed. (New York: Macmillan, [1888] 1911), an exceptional survey of government in the United States, includes descriptions of the machines in several cities.

Martin Schiesl's *The Politics of Efficiency: Municipal Administration and Reform in America, 1880–1920* (Berkeley: University of California Press, 1977) presents an absolutely invaluable framework for understanding city government. No other book on the topic approaches its clarity and insight. Finally, although not addressing municipal politics per se, Richard L. McCormick's "The Party Period and Public Policy: An Exploratory Hypothesis," *Journal of American History* 66 (Sept. 1979): 279–298, makes a eye-opening argument about what happens when the government moves from primarily distributive practices to regulatory functions.

CITY SPACE

As I shifted my focus from drug use to the topic of vice more generally, I realized that my story would emphasize the history of red-light districts. Neil Larry Shumsky's "Tacit Acceptance: Respectable Americans and Segregated Prostitution, 1870–1910," *Journal of Social History* 19 (Summer 1986): 665–679; his "Vice Responds to Reform: San Francisco, 1910–1914," *Journal of Urban History* 7 (Nov. 1980): 31–47; and his

Index

Page numbers in *italics* indicate figures and illustrations.

restaurants, 35
roadhouses, 124, 125, 127–28
Rockefeller, John D., Jr., 74, 75, 82, 181n37
Rockefeller Foundation, 106
Roe, Clifford G.: on American Vigilance
  Association, 92; *The Great War on White
  Slavery*, 79; pandering laws and, 84; *Pan-
  ders and Their White Slaves*, 75–76; white
  slavery and, 74, 91, 118
Rogers, W. A., 14
Rosenwald, Julius, 21, 75
Rothstein, Arnold, 116, 120
Russell, Lillian, 39

saloonkeepers. *See* proprietors
saloons: closing of, and disaggregation of
  services, 124; cocaine scare and, 65–66;
  description of, 35; electric signs and, 25;
  geographic limits on, 5, 9, 11; mixing of
  races in, 53, 63; musical entertainment in,
  37–38; padlocking of, 86; pimps in, 47;
  Prohibition and, 63, 118, 119, 128, 135; prostitution in, 19, 29, 31, 45, 82, 104, 114; regulation of, 55–56, 63–64, 97–98; renaming of, 35; restaurants in, 16; to service
  soldiers, 105; in vice districts, 12, 24;
  women in, 30–31. *See also* proprietors
San Diego, California, 107
San Francisco, California, 7, 95–96, 97, 102
scatteration, 87, 98, 122
Section of Women and Girls, 108–9
segregation: definition of, 51; racial, 51–52,
  53, 56, 61–63, 138; reputational, 3, 5, 9–10,
  21–22, 50, 51–52, 107
Selective Service Act, Sections 12 and 13,
  105–6, 115
Sherman Anti-Trust Act, 133
Shreveport, Louisiana, 9, 10, 107, 130
Sims, Edwin W., 84
social control by law, 17, 55–56, 62–68, 94
The Social Evil in Chicago (report), 91
Social Evil Ordinance, St. Louis, Missouri,
  7–8
social-order policing, 55–56, 62–68
speakeasies, 122, 124–27
sporting class: aesthetics of, 25–28; charity
  girls and, 42–43; clothing of, 40–41; customers of, 31, 32, 33, 34–35, 41–42, 43, 47;

definition of, 24; ethos of, 4, 39–41, 43, 47–
  49; fracture of, 104, 113, 114–15; gender
  roles and, 39–40, 43, 44, 45–47, 48, 49;
  male employment in, 46–47; race and, 34,
  46, 50, 53–55, 56; as subculture, 39; values
  and interests of, 39–40. *See also* pimps;
  prostitutes
Springfield, Illinois, race riot, 52, 57, 59–61
Stead, W. T., 20
Stewart, H. E., 60–61
St. Louis, Missouri, Social Evil Ordinance,
  7–8
Storyville, New Orleans, 7, 9, 24, 25, 42, 53–
  54, 107
A Stranger in New York theater poster, 39
streetwalkers, 35, 43, 99, 100
Struve, Billy, 33
stuss houses, 38
St. Valentine's Day Massacre, 120–21
Sullivan, "Big Tim," 6
Sullivan, Manley, 130
Sumner, Walter T., 21, 90, 91
Syracuse, New York, 92, 95, 97–98, 103

tacit localization, 9–10, 11–12, 15–16, 20
Tacoma, Washington, 7
Tammany Hall: Committee of Five, 12, 13,
  14, 17; Parkhurst and, 11; Turner and, 72
Taylor, Graham, 90–91, 152n93
The Tenderfoot: sheet music, 26, 28; theater
  poster, 27, 28
theater posters: High Roller's Burlesque
  Company, *iv*, 36–37; for "The Ladies Ali-
  mony Club," 43, 44, 45; for *A Parlor
  Match (Enough Said!)*, 47, 48; for *A
  Stranger in New York*, 39; *The Tenderfoot*,
  27, 28; "The Tiger Lilies," 31, 32, 33
theaters, 28–29, 36
Thrasher, Samuel, 96–97
"The Tiger Lilies" lithograph, 31, 32, 33
Tillman, Benjamin, 60
Tilyou, George, 24
Tobias, David E., 64
toleration of vice: Capra and, 1–2; implicit
  legitimacy and, 4, 22; machine and, 77–
  78; mugwumps and, 7, 20; Progressives
  and, 3. *See also* red-light districts; reputational segregation

Torrio, Johnny, 116, 117–19, 121
Traffic in Souls (movie), 81
Treasury Department, 115, 122, 123–24, 128–32
Tucker, George Loane, 81
Turner, George Kibbe, 72–73
Tweed, "Boss" William, 6

United States v. Jin Fuey Moy, 129
unit taxes, 122–23
U.S. Supreme Court, 9, 129, 130–31, 138

vagrancy laws, 54, 55
Van Bever, Julia and Maurice, 49, 118
Van Wyck, Robert A., 13
Vardaman, James, 60
Veiller, Lawrence, 10
venereal disease, detention of women with, 108–10, 112–13
venues in vice districts, 30–39
vertical integration of crime, 121, 133
vice commissions: ASHA and, 84, 92–93; in Chicago, 20–21, 90–91; follow-up by, 95; national role of, 89
vice districts: city courts and, 10; constitutionality of, 9; creation of, 7–9, 20, 24–29, 52–53; geographic stability of, 23–24; origins of, 7; politics of, 11–15; violence in, 53–54. *See also* red-light districts; reputational segregation
Vice Trust, 80–83, 82, 85–87
violence: of crime cartels, 120–21; gang-related, 139; during Prohibition, 120–21, 135; in vice districts, 53–54. *See also* race riots
Volstead Act, 115, 130, 133

Walker, Stanley, 122
Wallace, Idaho, 123

Walling, William English, 60
war on drugs, 139–40
Washington, Booker T., 51, 58, 65
Washington, Margaret Murray, 51
Wayman, John, 118
Webb v. United States, 129, 130
Weinstein v. United States, 133
Werlain, Philip, 54
Wexler, Irving "Waxey Gordon," 119, 120
White, Lulu, 41
white-light districts, 4, 25–26, 28–29, 29, 98
white slavery scare: anti-vice reform and, 73–75; debt peonage and, 75–77; economic analysis of, 139–40; influence on law enforcement, 70, 83–87; narratives of, 69, 71–73, 75; prosecution of urban vice and, 87; terminology and origins of, 70–73
white slave traffic acts, 84–85. *See also* Mann Act
Whitin, Frederick: Committee of Fourteen and, 19, 64, 65; on rescue work, 77; views on women of, 107; white slavery narratives and, 74
Williams, Edward Huntington, 66
Willis-Campbell Act, 130
Wilmington, North Carolina, race riot, 57
women: in commercial venues, 35; as customers, 42–43, 44, 45; as madams, 31; in resorts, 42–43, 44, 45; as saloon proprietors, 151n78; in saloons, 30–31; sexually active, treatment of during WWI, 108–10, 112–13; sexual objectification of, 111; sporting, during Prohibition, 127. *See also* mixed-sex drinking; prostitutes
World War I, 105–12
Wright, Hamilton, 67

Ziegfeld, Florence, 29